Sor
Hunters

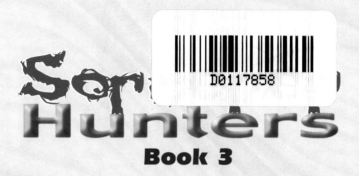

Book 3

Sorcerer Hunters

Book 3

by Satoru Akahori & Ray Omishi

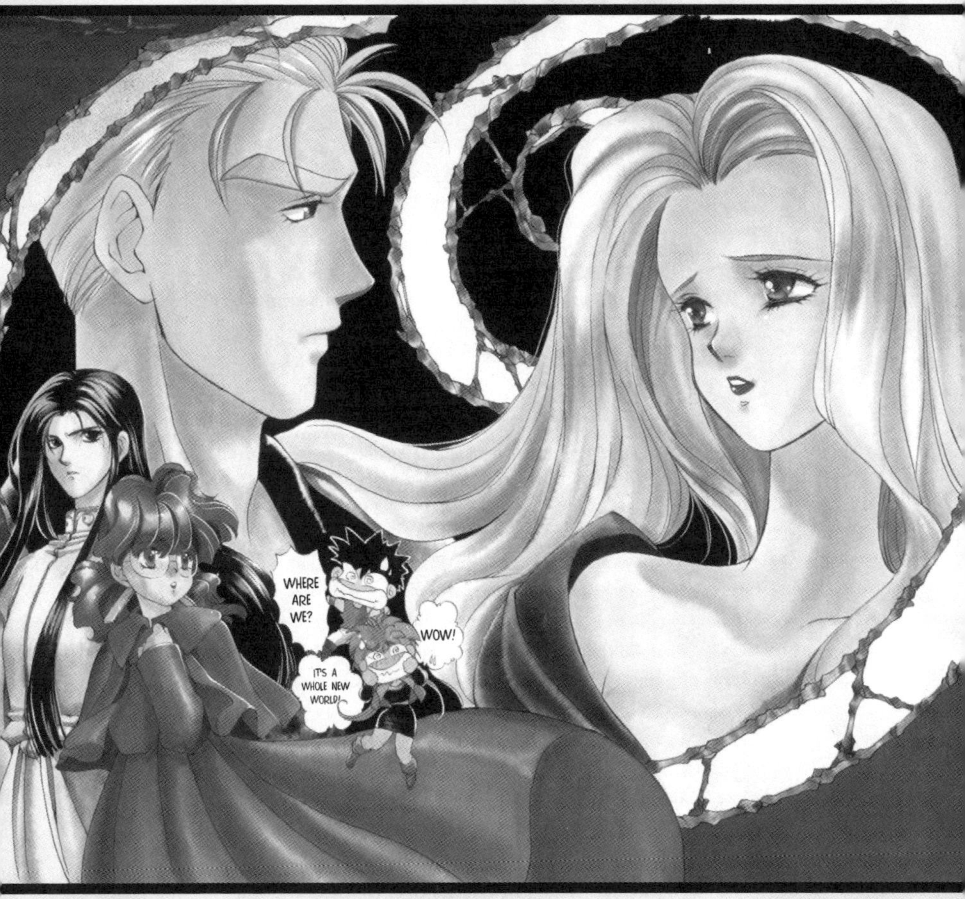
WHERE ARE WE?
WOW!
IT'S A WHOLE NEW WORLD!

TOKYOPOP Manga

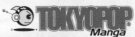

TOKYOPOP Presents
Sorcerer Hunters 3 by Satoru Akahori & Ray Omishi
TOKYOPOP is a registered trademark and
TOKYOPOP Manga is a trademark of Mixx Entertainment, Inc.
ISBN: 1-892213-55-9
First Printing April 2001

11	10	9	8	7	6	5	4	3	2

This volume contains the Sorcerer Hunters installments from
TOKYOPOP Magazine issues 4-2 through 4-7 in their entirety.

Translator - Anita Sengupta. Retouch Artist - Ryan Caraan.
Graphic Assistants - Steve Kindernay, Dao Sirivisal. Graphic Designer - Akemi Imafuku.
Associate Editors - Michael Schuster, Katherine Kim. Editor - Mary Coco. Senior Editor - Jake Forbes.
Production Manager - Fred Lui.
Email: editor@Press.TOKYOPOP.com
Come visit us at www.TOKYOPOP.com.

TOKYOPOP
Los Angeles - Tokyo

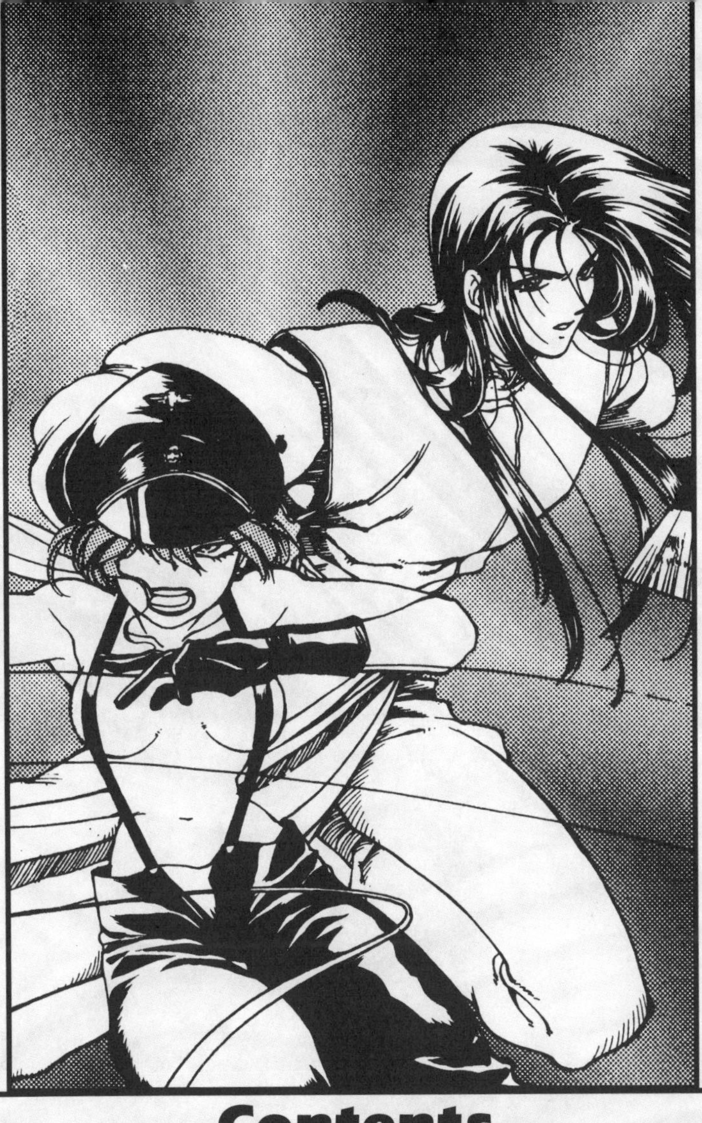

Contents

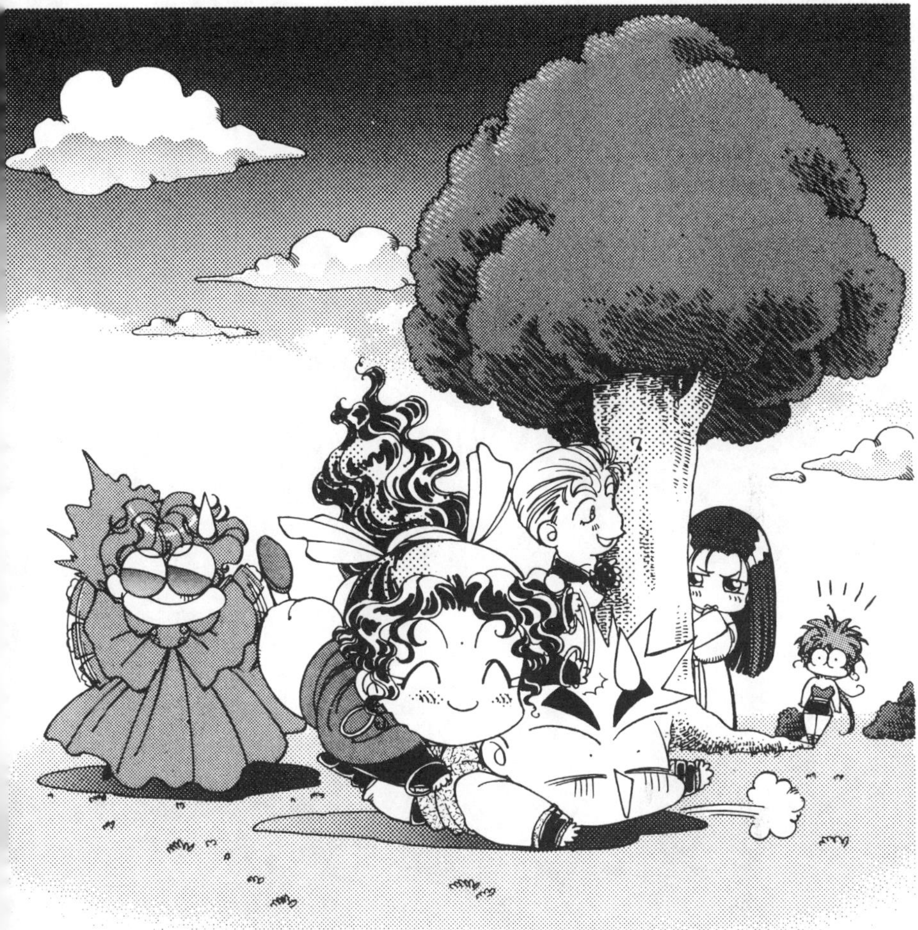

The Spellbook of the Necromancer, Part 3

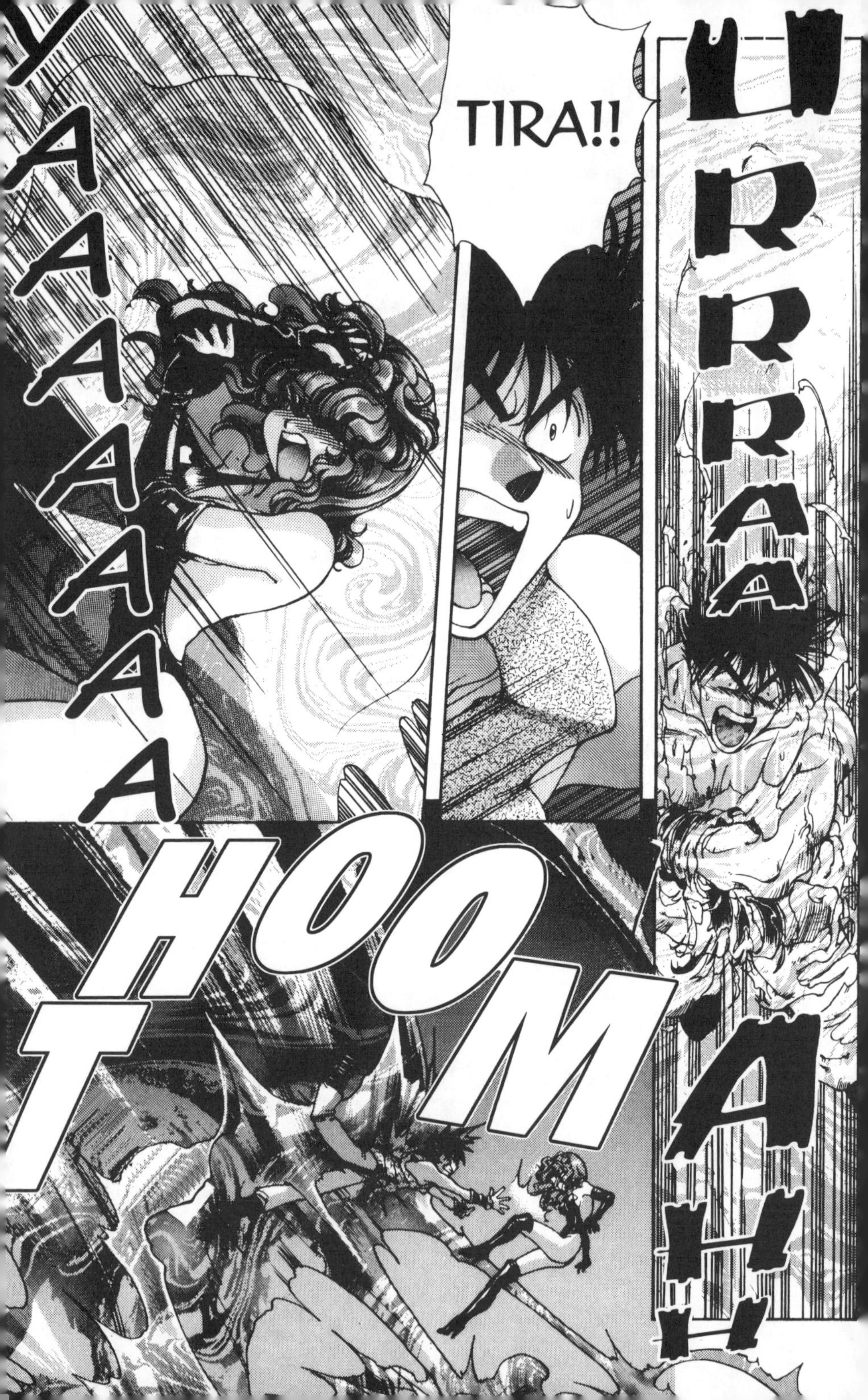
YAAAAAA
TIRA!!
URRRAAAH!!
THOOM

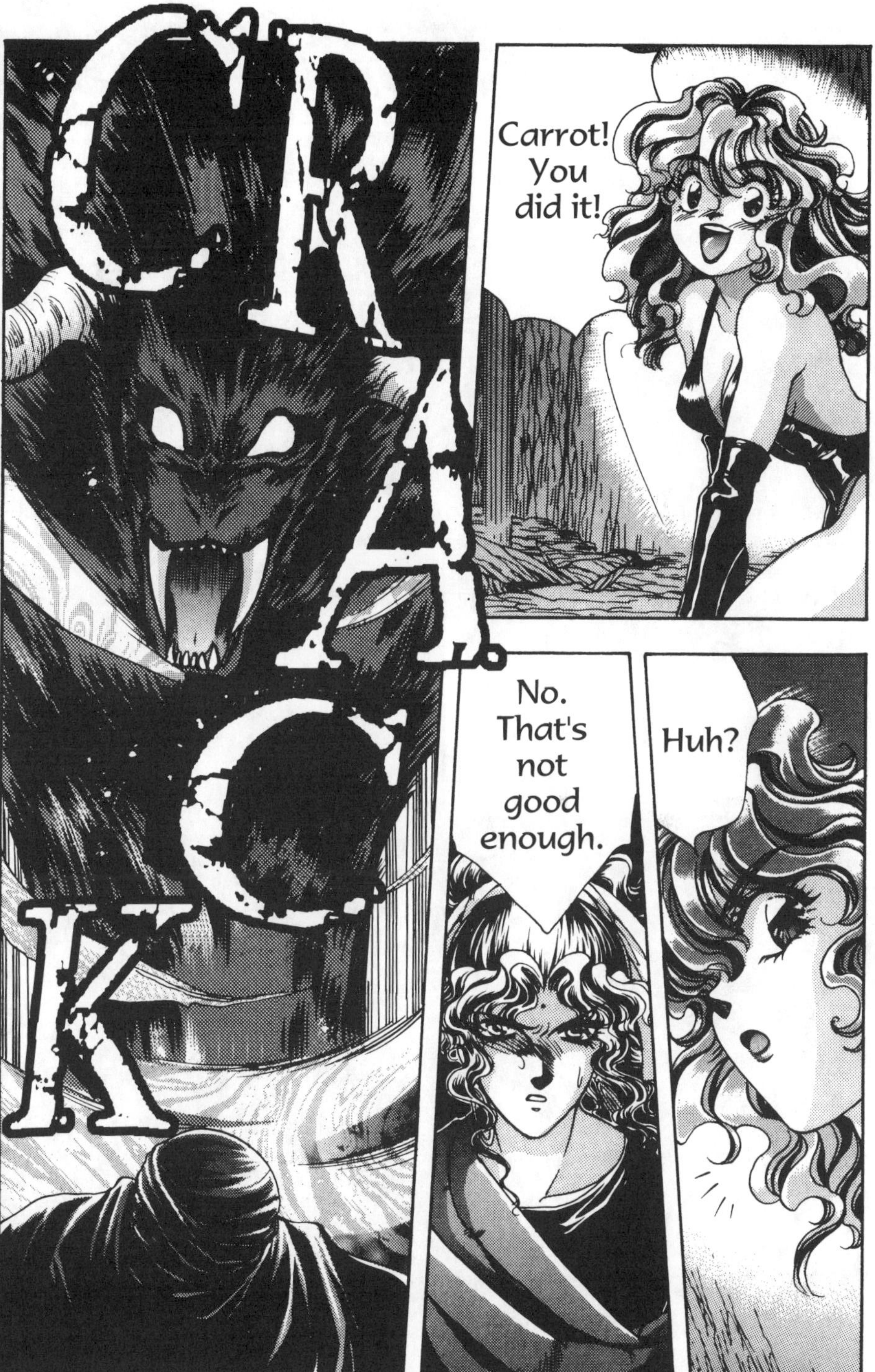
CRACK
Carrot! You did it!
No. That's not good enough.
Huh?

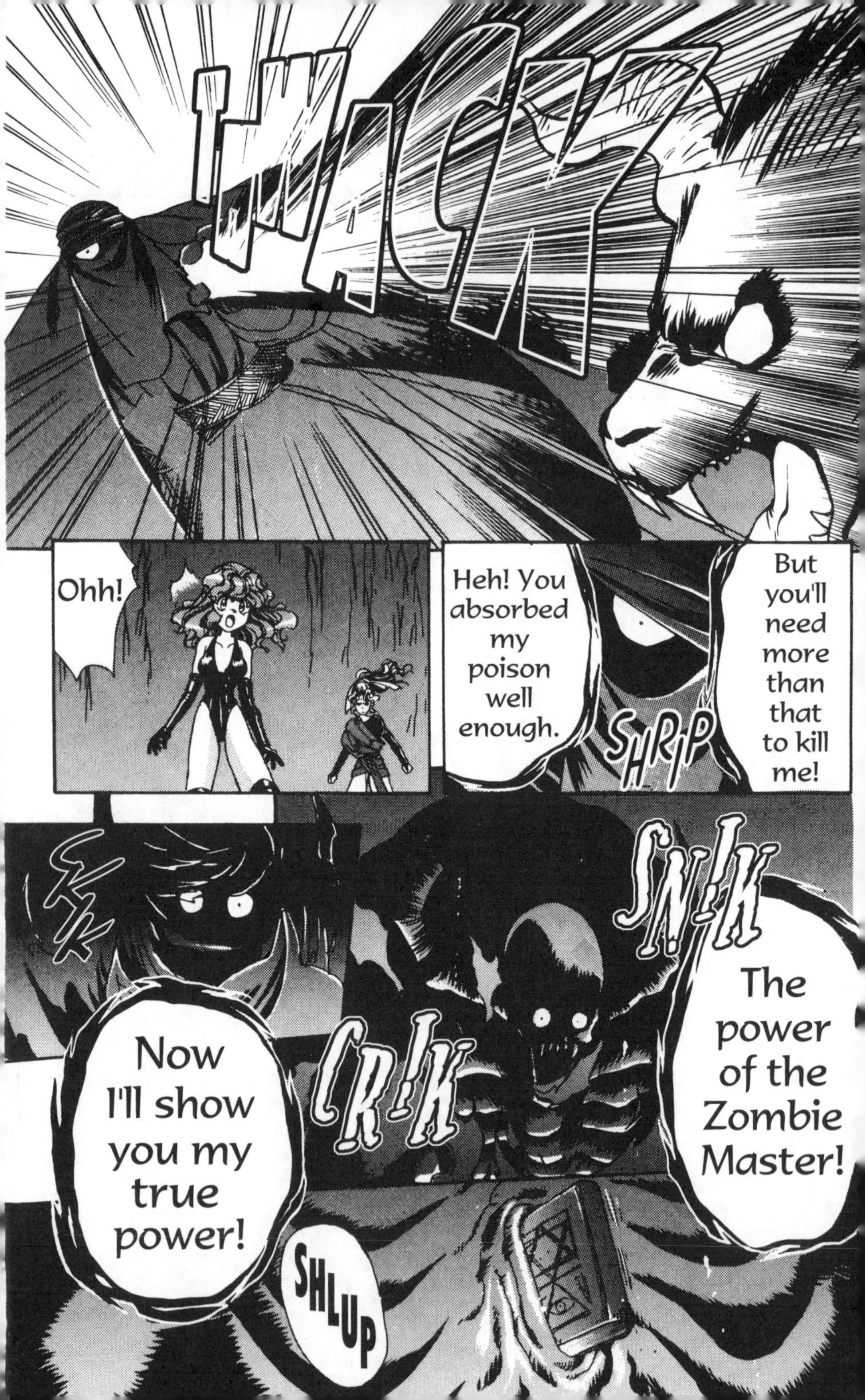
WHACK
Ohh!
Heh! You absorbed my poison well enough.
SHRIP
But you'll need more than that to kill me!
SNIK
CRIK
Now I'll show you my true power!
The power of the Zombie Master!
SHLUP

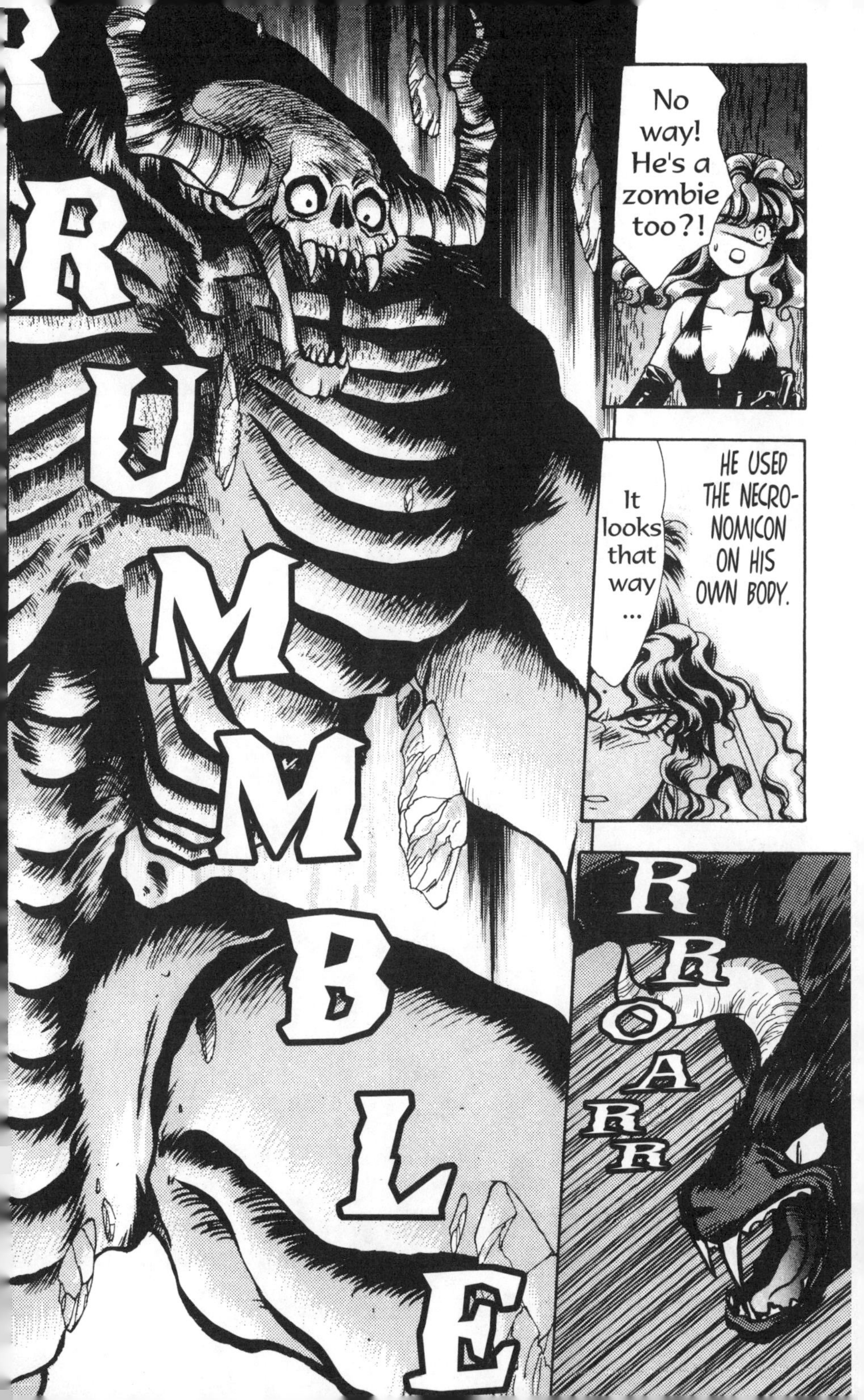
RUMMBLE
No way! He's a zombie too?!
It looks that way...
HE USED THE NECRO-NOMICON ON HIS OWN BODY.
RROARRR

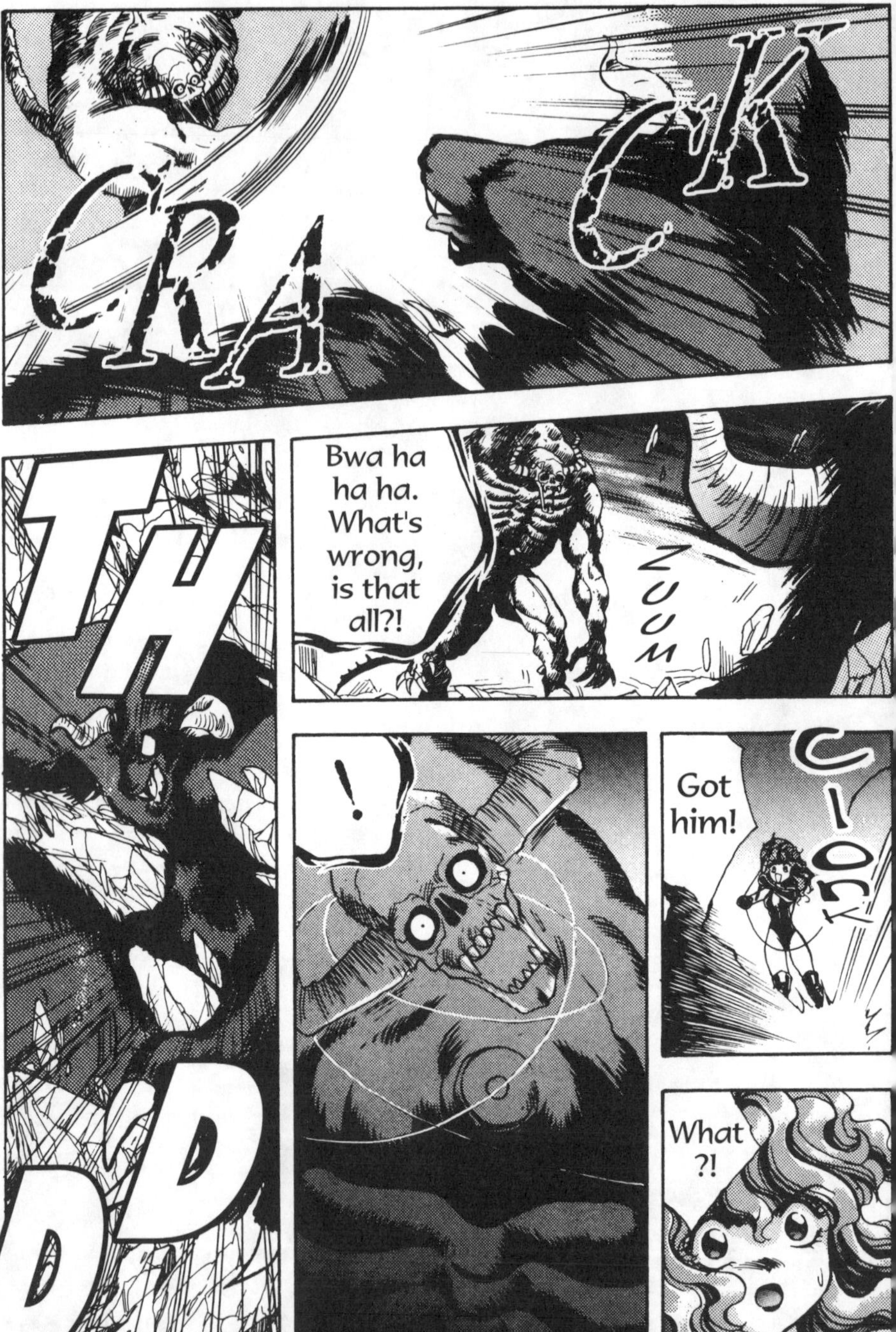
CRA
CK
THD
D
Bwa ha ha ha. What's wrong, is that all?!
ZUUUM
!
Got him!
What ?!

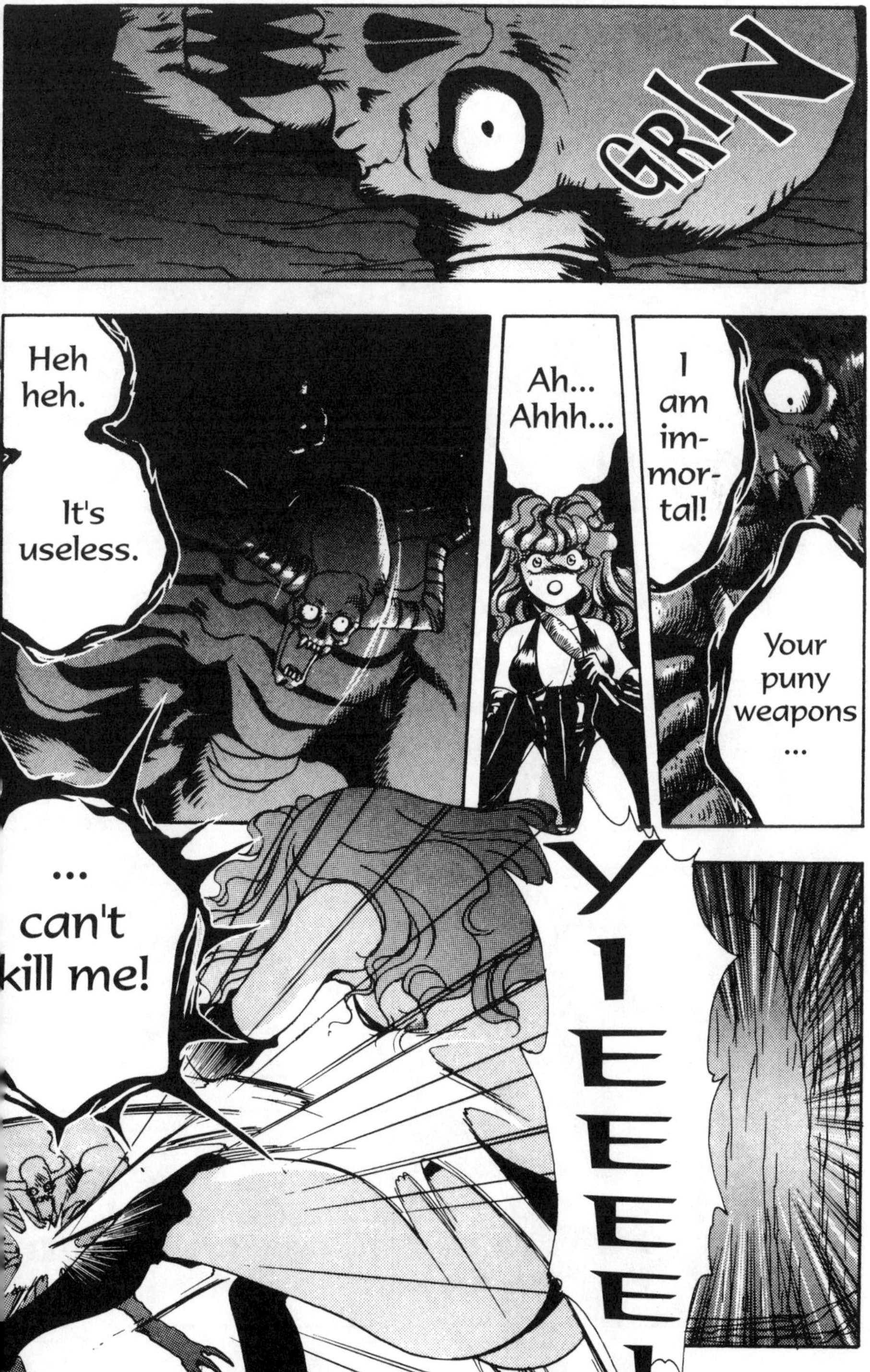
GRIN
Heh heh.
It's useless.
Ah... Ahhh...
I am im-mor-tal!
Your puny weapons ...
... can't kill me!
YIEEEEE!

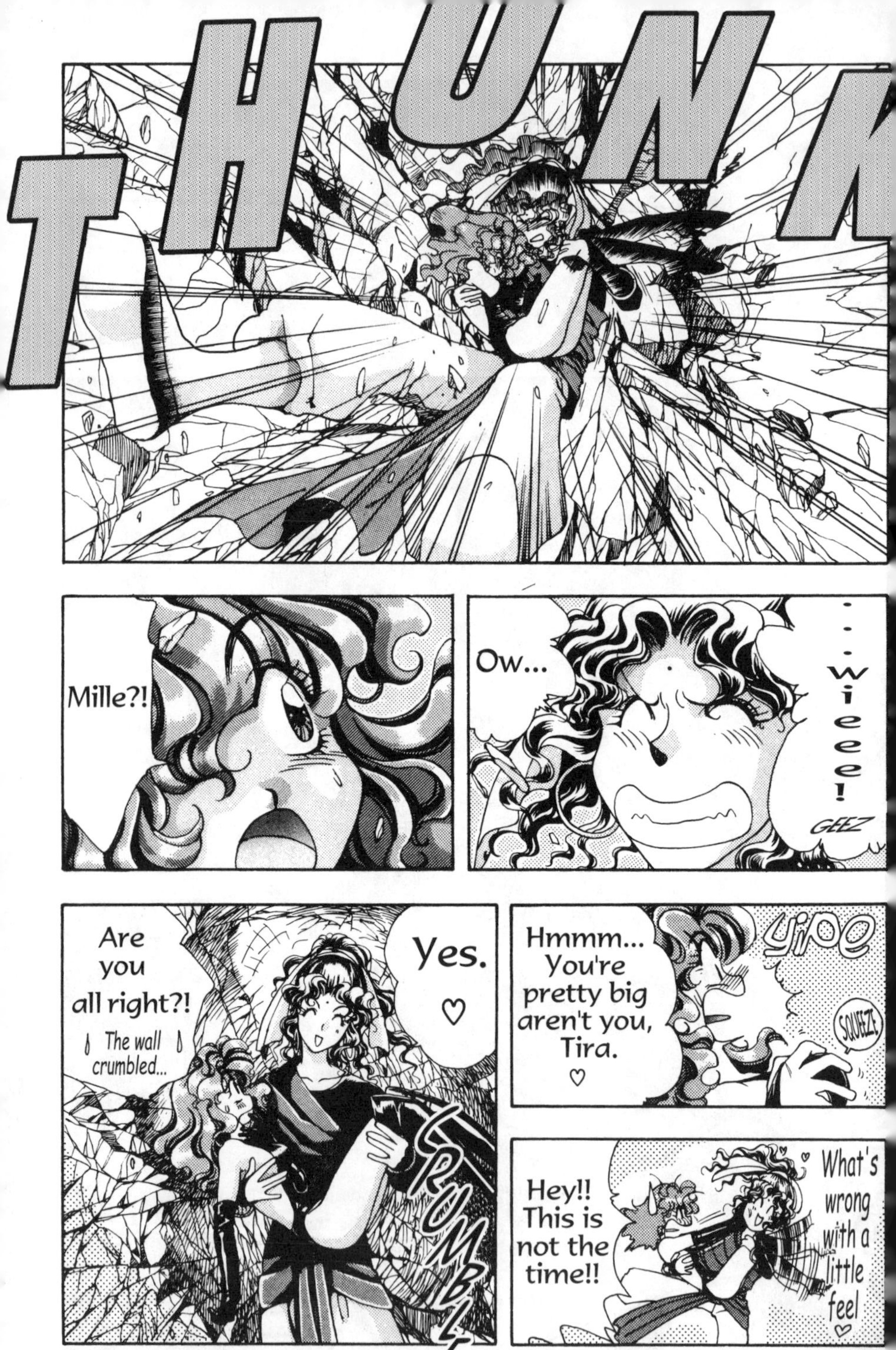
THUNK
Mille?!
Ow...
...wieeee!
GEEZ
Are you all right?!
The wall crumbled...
Yes. ♡
TRUMBLE
Hmmm... You're pretty big aren't you, Tira. ♡
yipe
SQUEEZE
Hey!! This is not the time!!
What's wrong with a little feel ♡

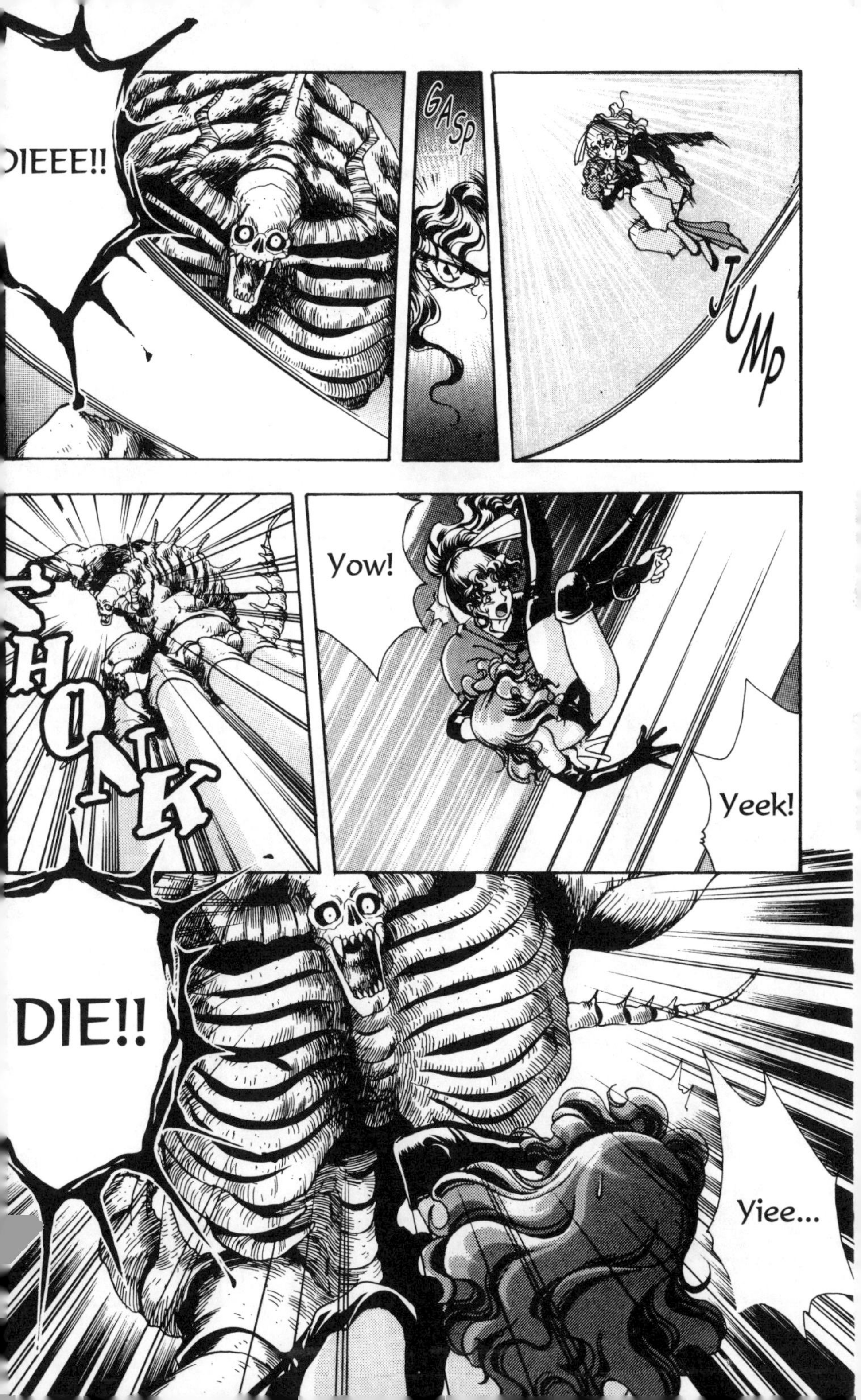
DIEEE!!
GASP
JUMP
Yow!
Yeek!
DIE!!
Yiee...

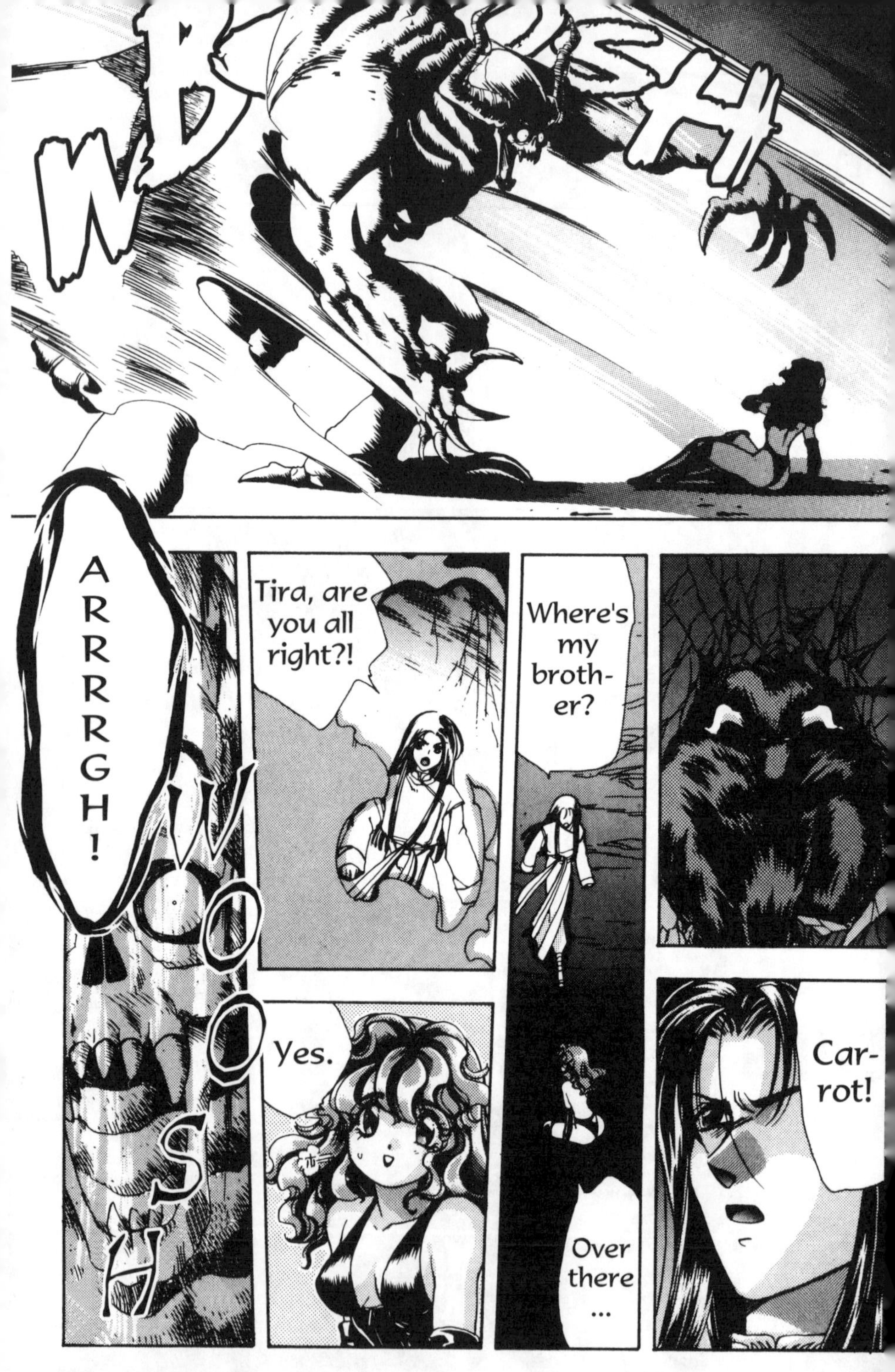
WBSH
ARRRRRGH!
WOOOSH
Tira, are you all right?!
Yes.
Where's my brother?
Over there...
Carrot!

Tira! Marron! Duck!

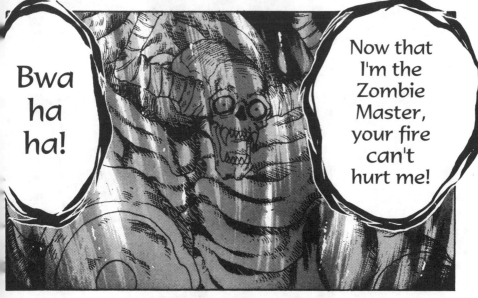

Bwa ha ha!

Now that I'm the Zombie Master, your fire can't hurt me!

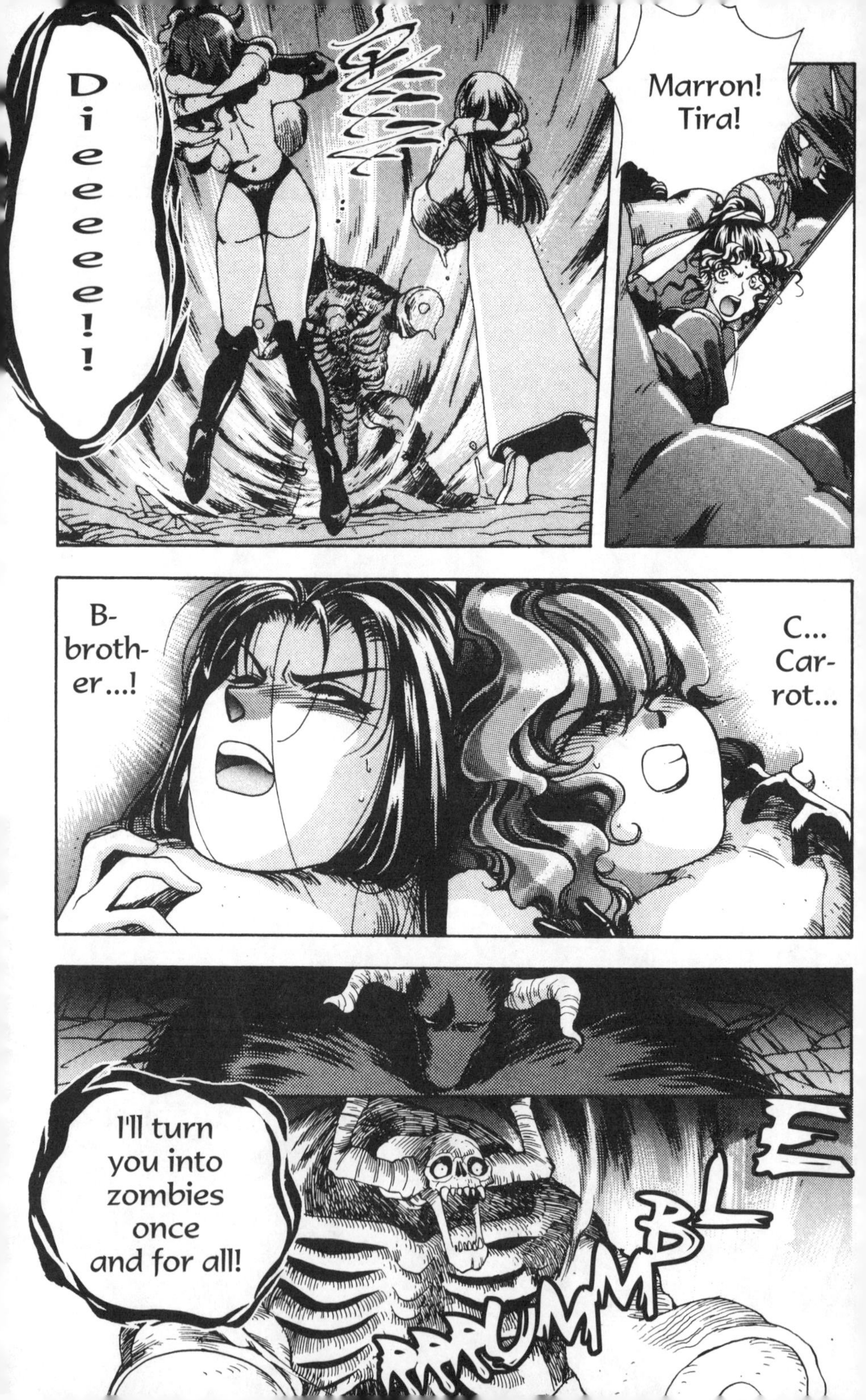
Dieeeeee!!
Marron! Tira!
B-broth-er...!
C... Car-rot...
I'll turn you into zombies once and for all!
RRRUMMBLE

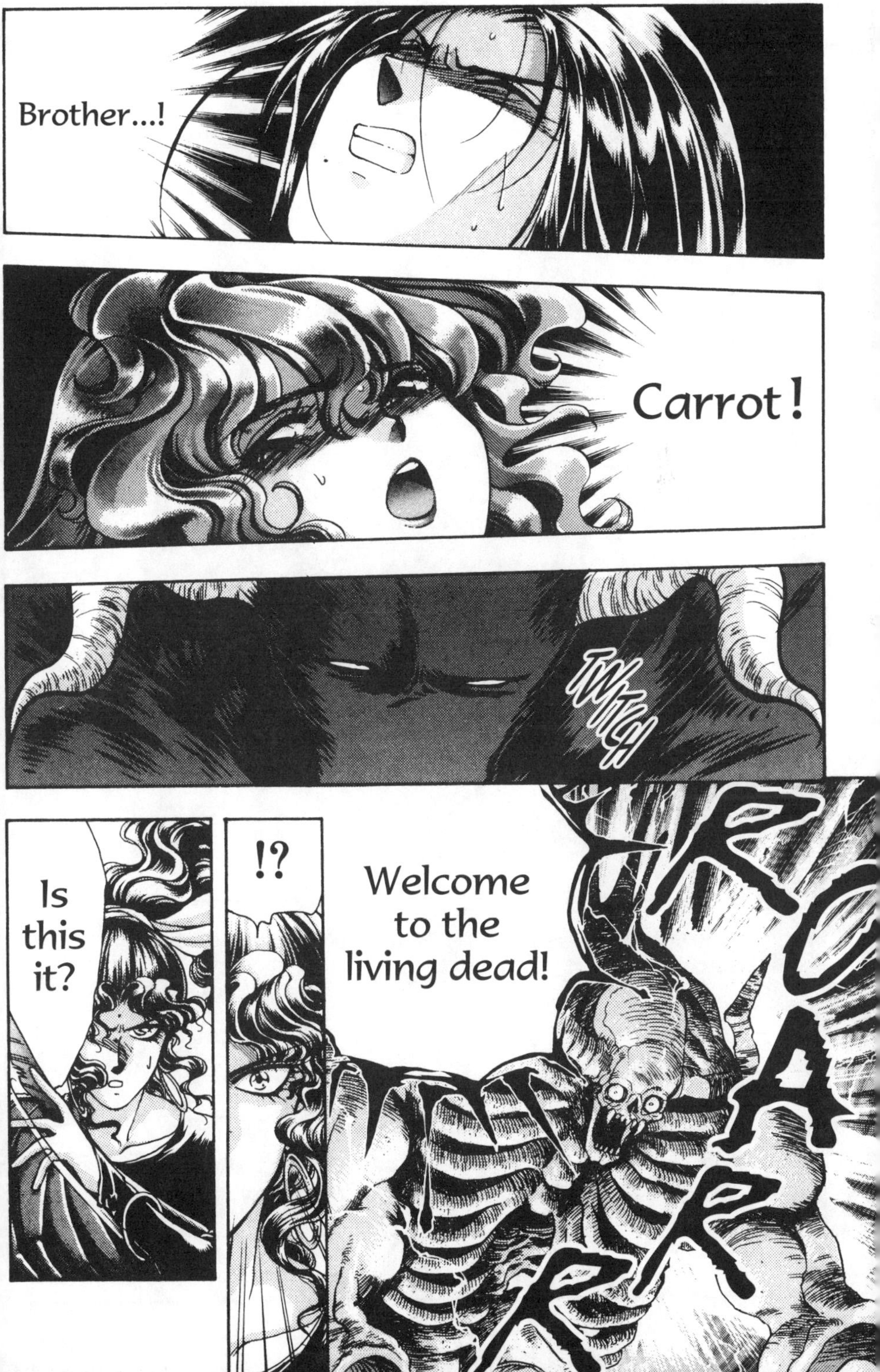
Brother...!
Carrot!
TWITCH
Is this it?
!?
Welcome to the living dead!

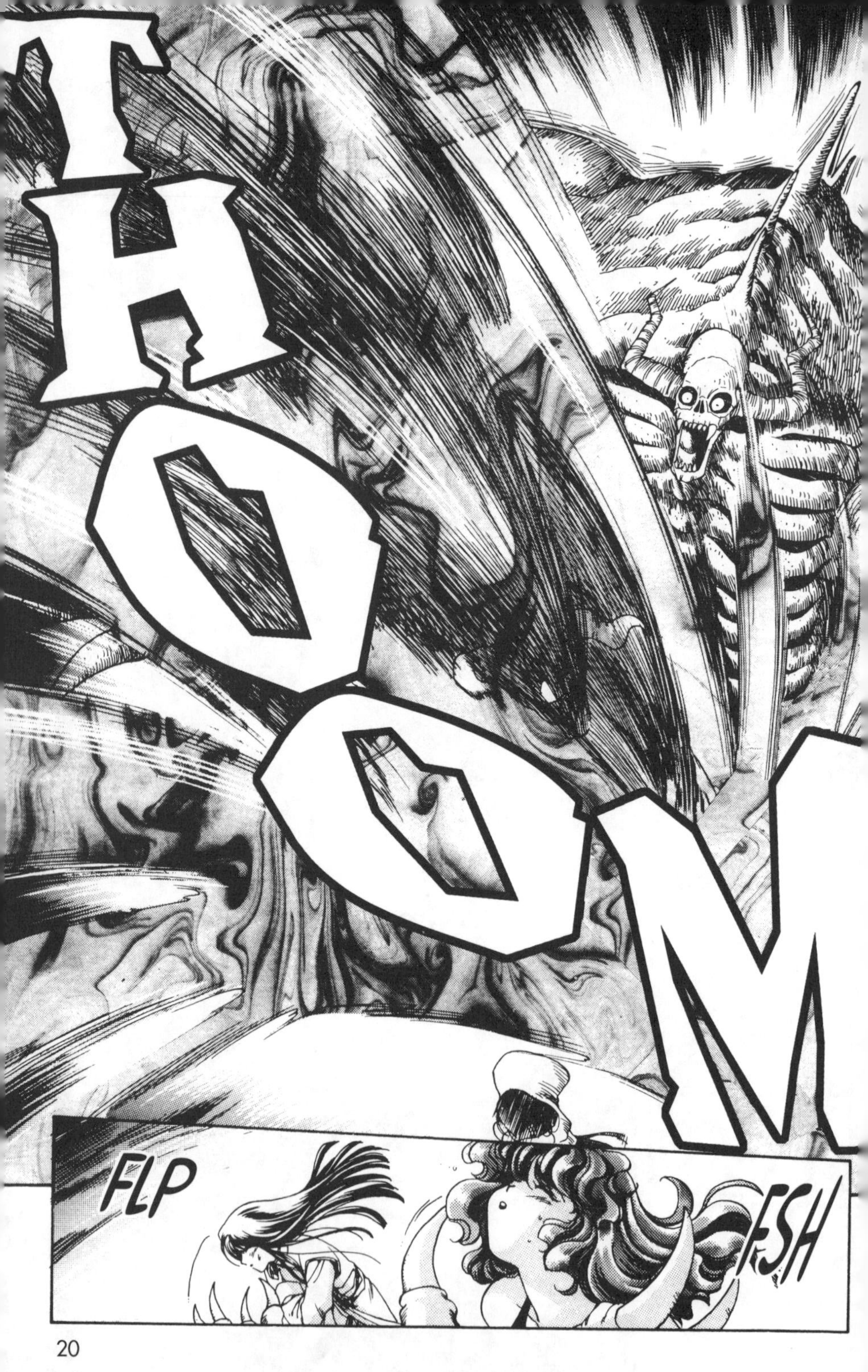
THOOM
FLP
FSH

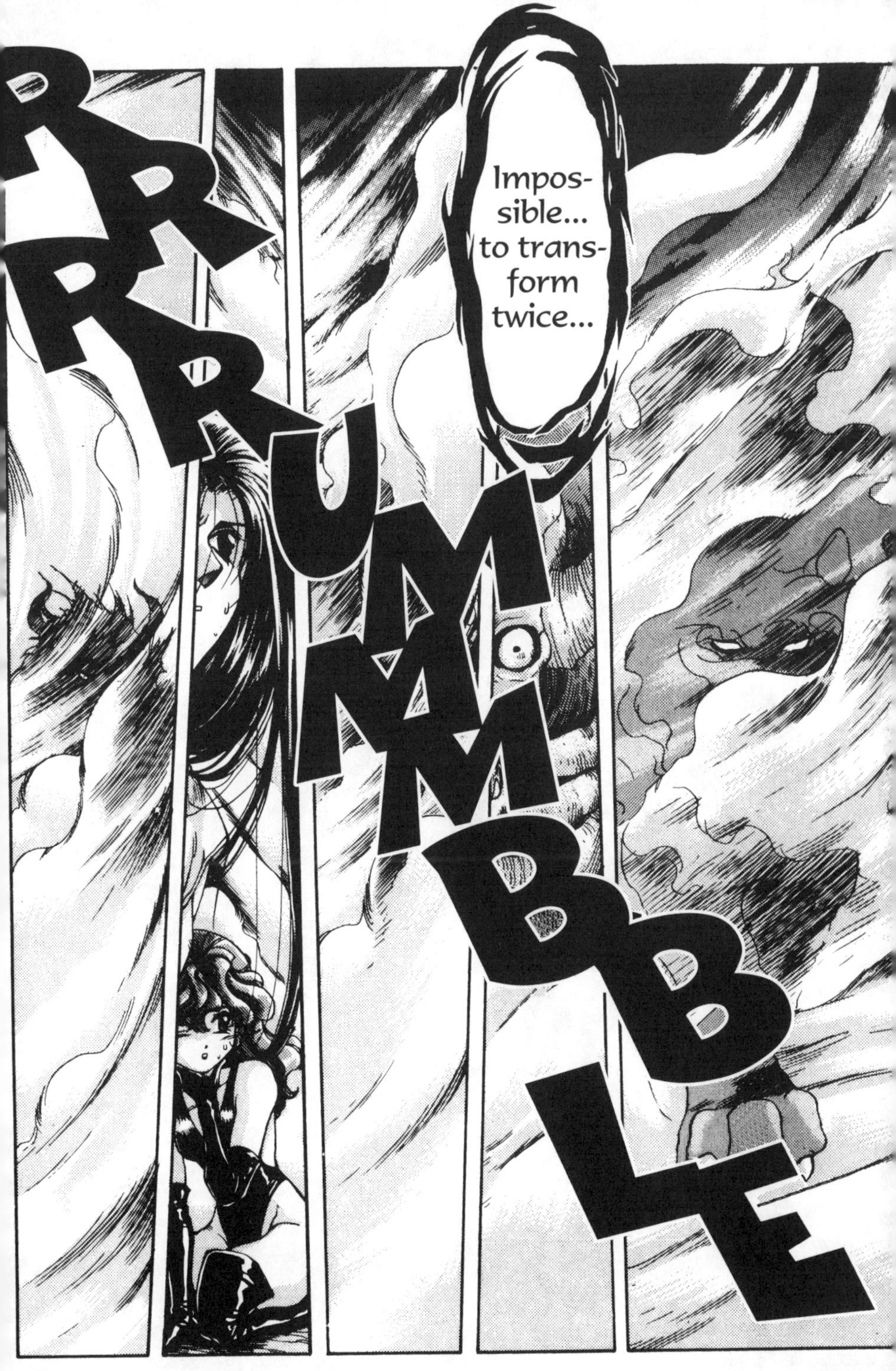

RRRUMMMBBLE
Impos-
sible...
to trans-
form
twice...

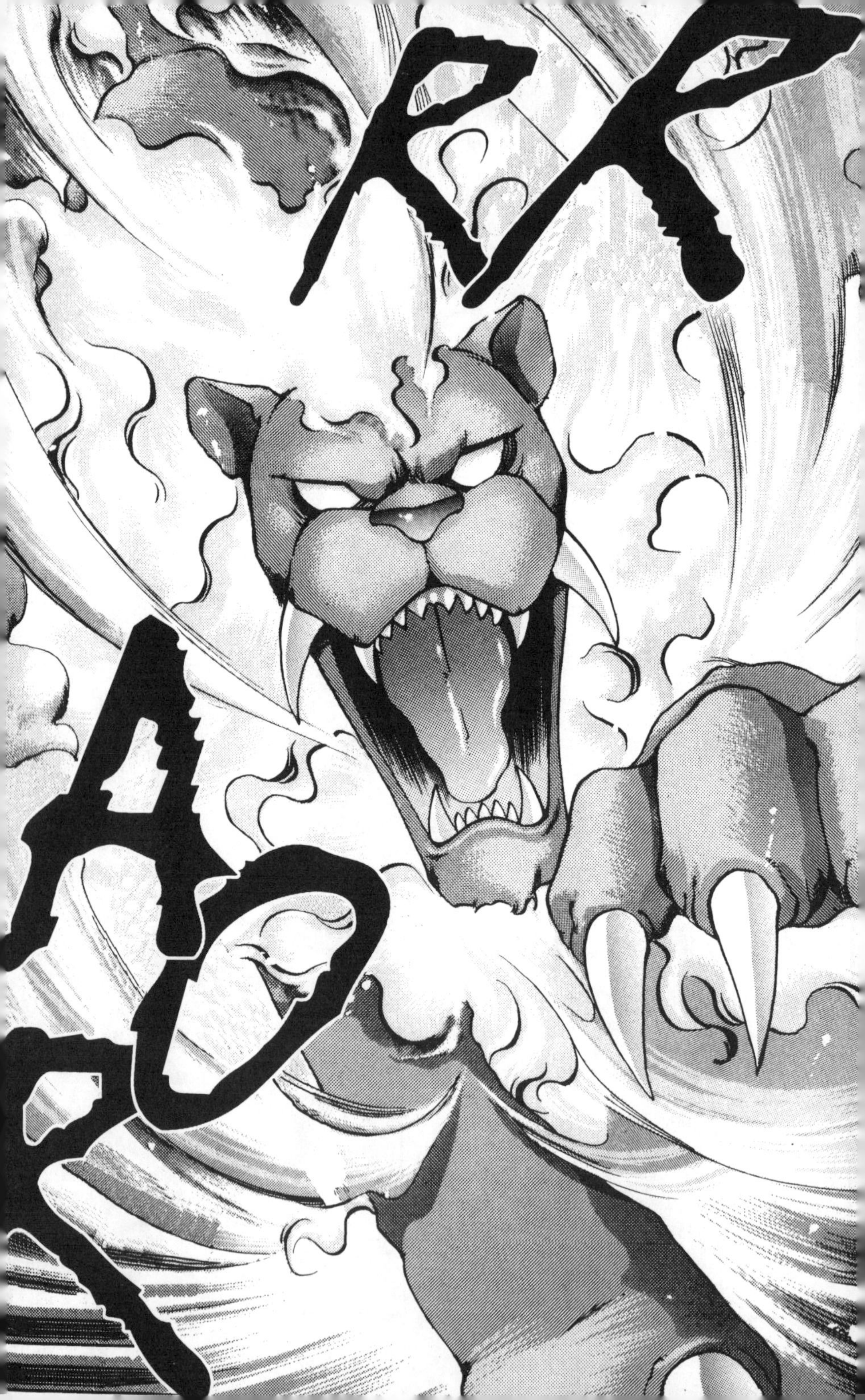

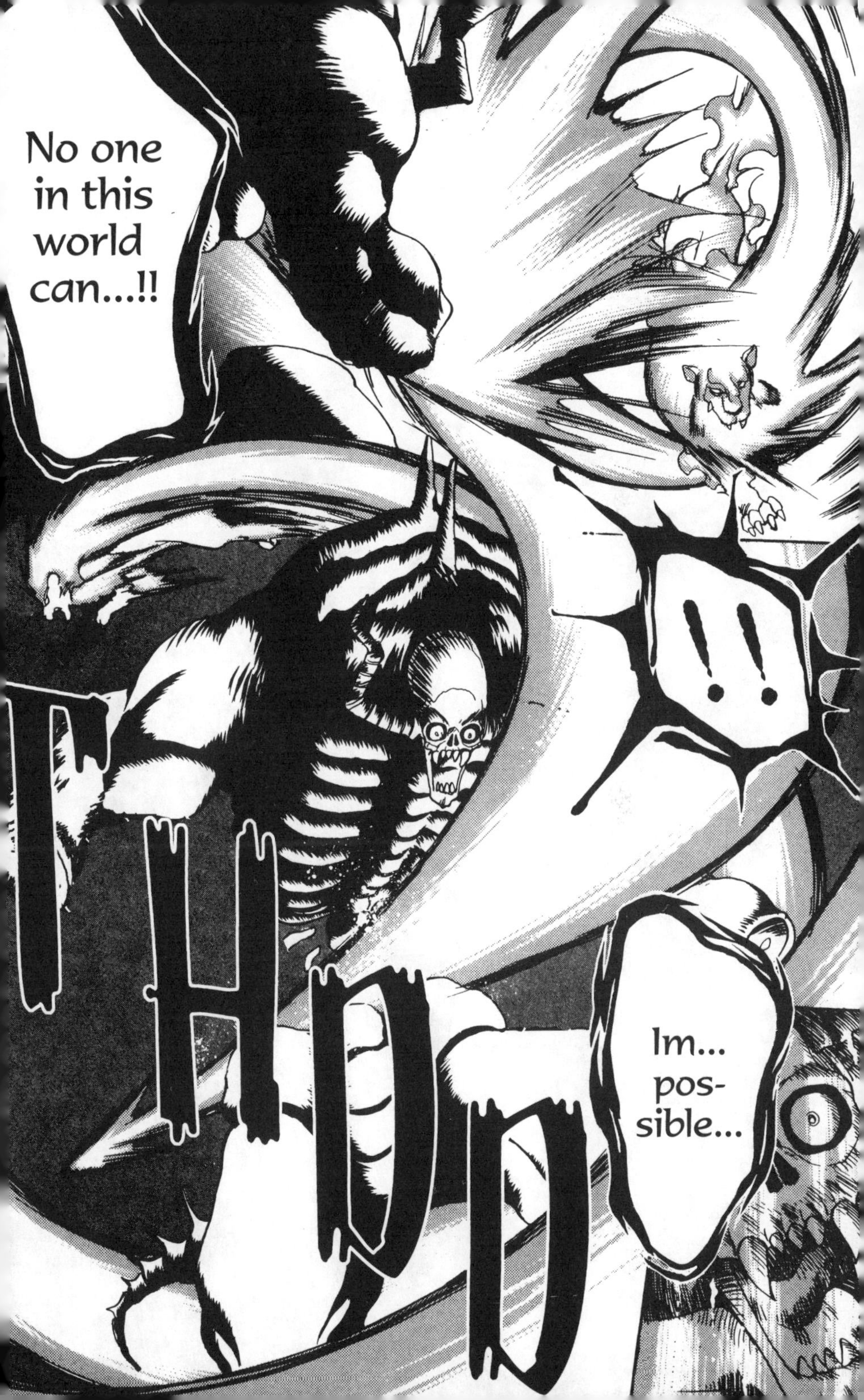
No one in this world can...!!
!!
THDD
Im... pos- sible...

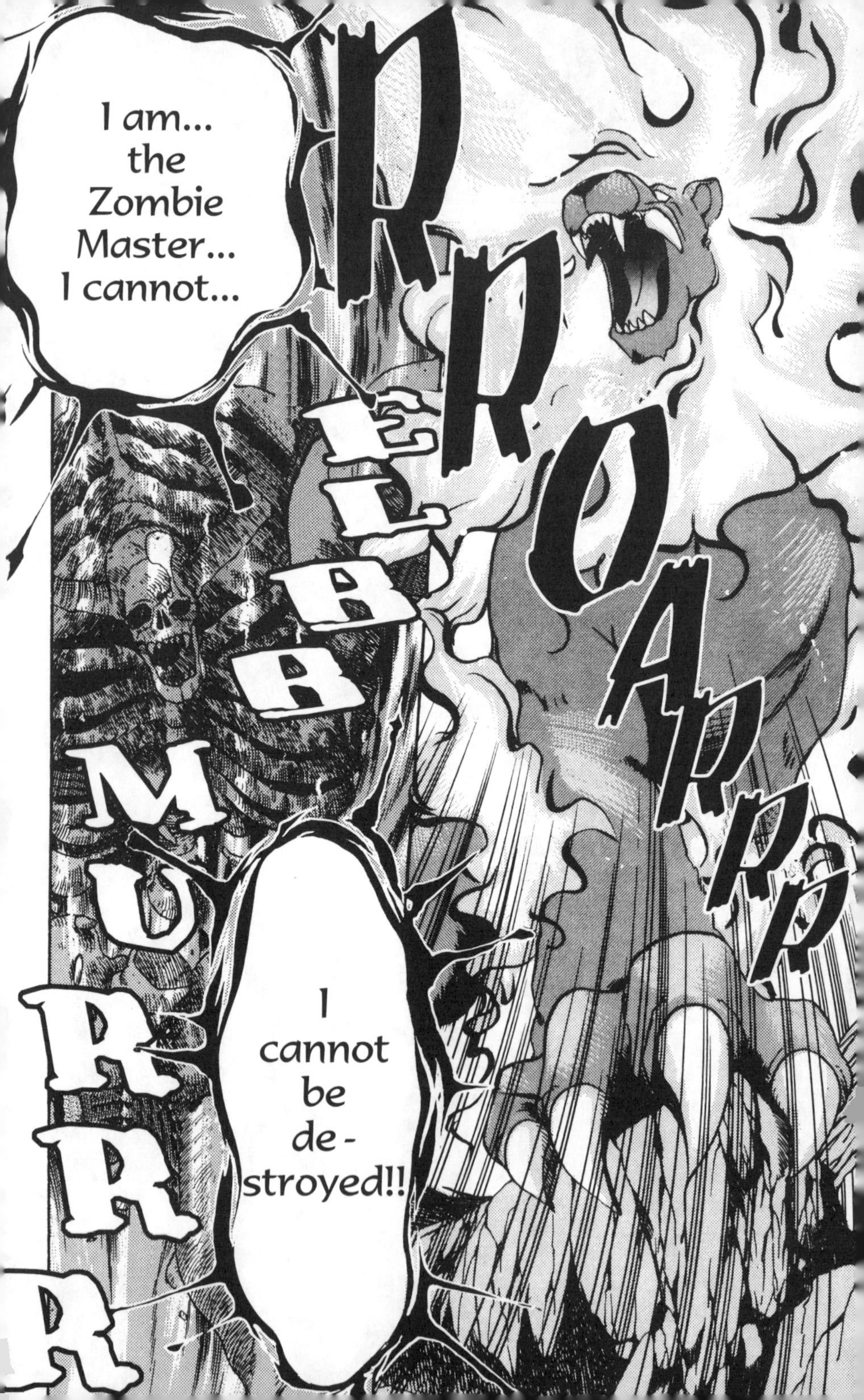
I am... the Zombie Master... I cannot...
I cannot be de - stroyed!!

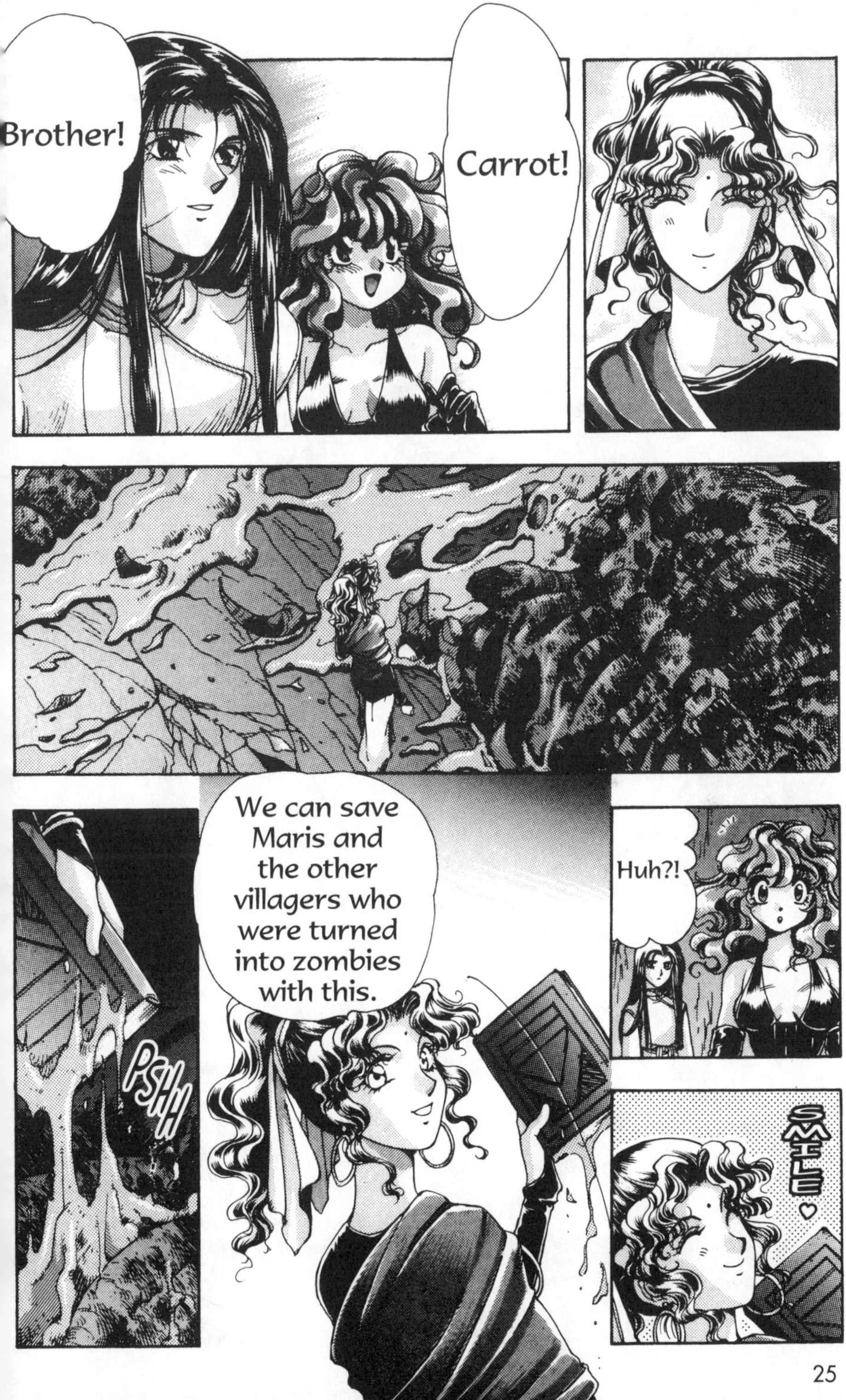
Brother!
Carrot!
We can save Maris and the other villagers who were turned into zombies with this.
PSHH
Huh?!
SMILE ♥

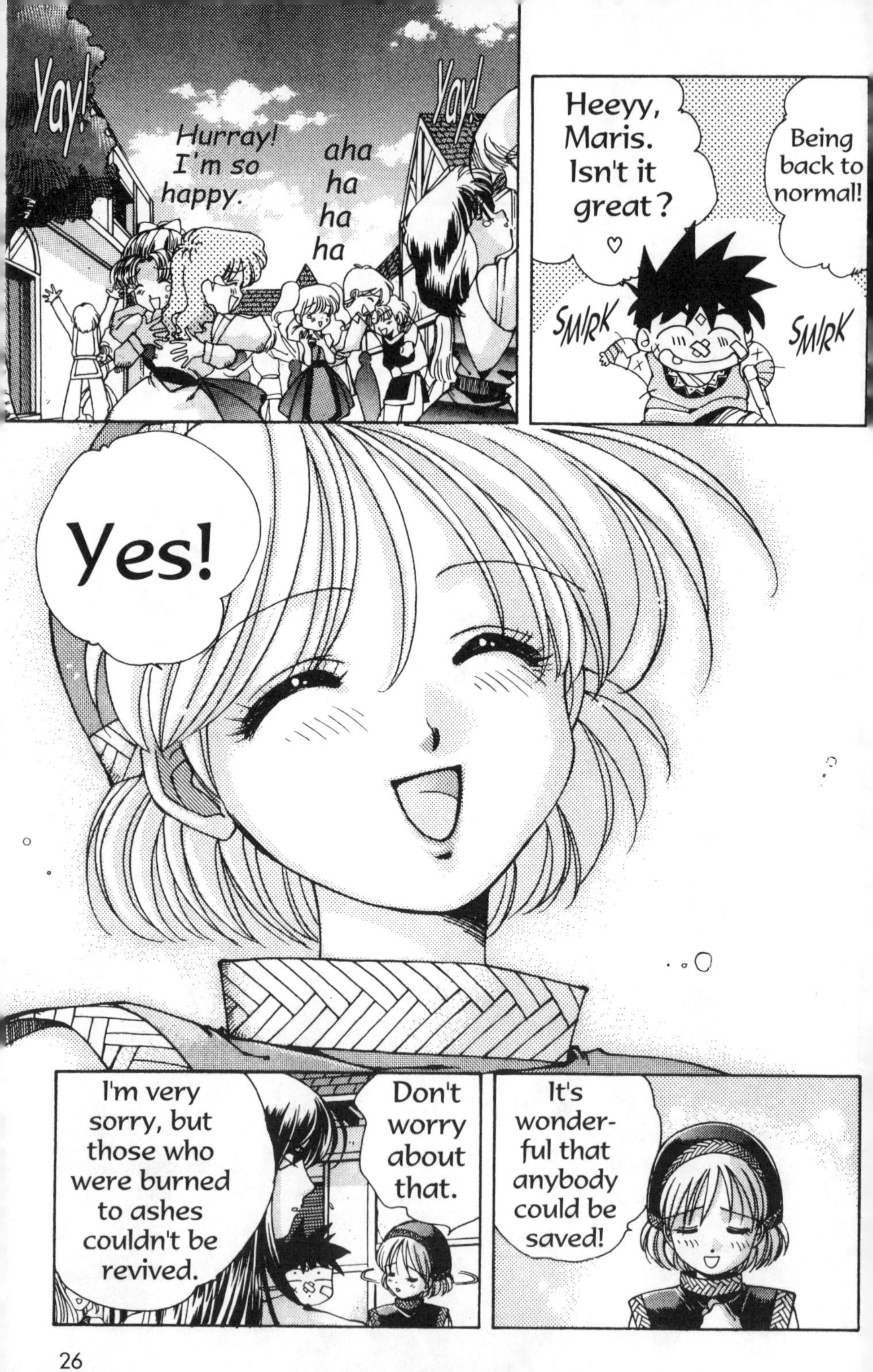
Yay!
Hurray! I'm so happy.
aha ha ha ha
Yay!
Heeyy, Maris. Isn't it great? ♡
SMIRK
Being back to normal!
SMIRK
Yes!
I'm very sorry, but those who were burned to ashes couldn't be revived.
Don't worry about that.
It's wonder-ful that anybody could be saved!

But anyway Maris... ♡

Now that you've returned to the living...

How about it?! Want to go on a date? ♡ *nyee* ♡ *hee* *hee*

Come to think of it, where is Mille Feuille?

Oh?

Now that you mention it...

What?! Where did he go?

. . . . . .

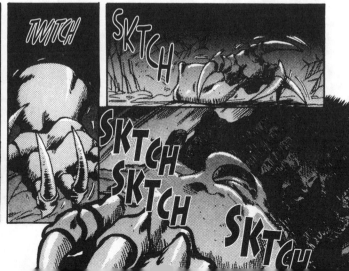

TWITCH

SKTCH!

SKTCH

SKTCH

SKTCH

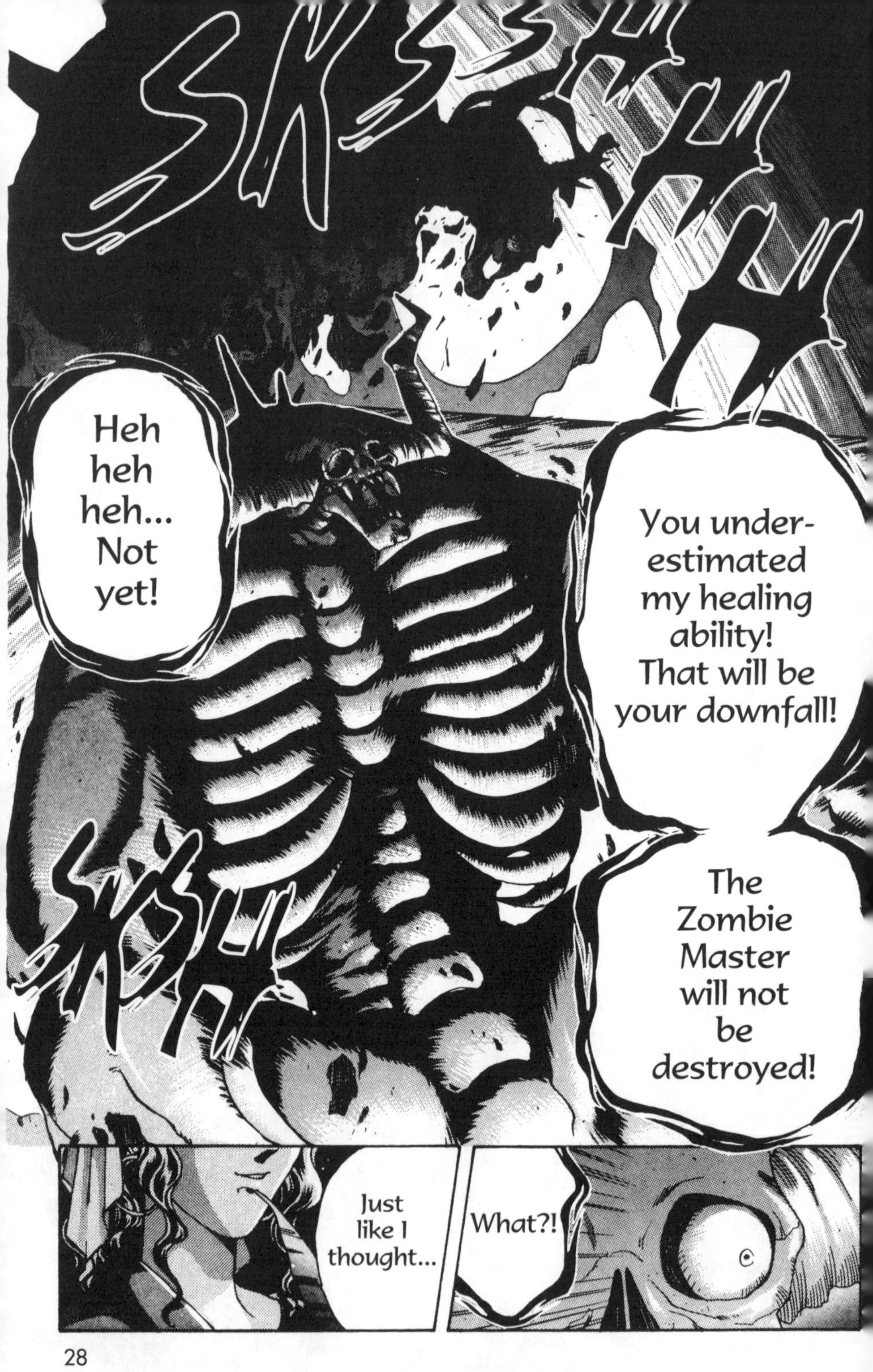
Heh heh heh... Not yet!
You under-estimated my healing ability! That will be your downfall!
The Zombie Master will not be destroyed!
Just like I thought...
What?!

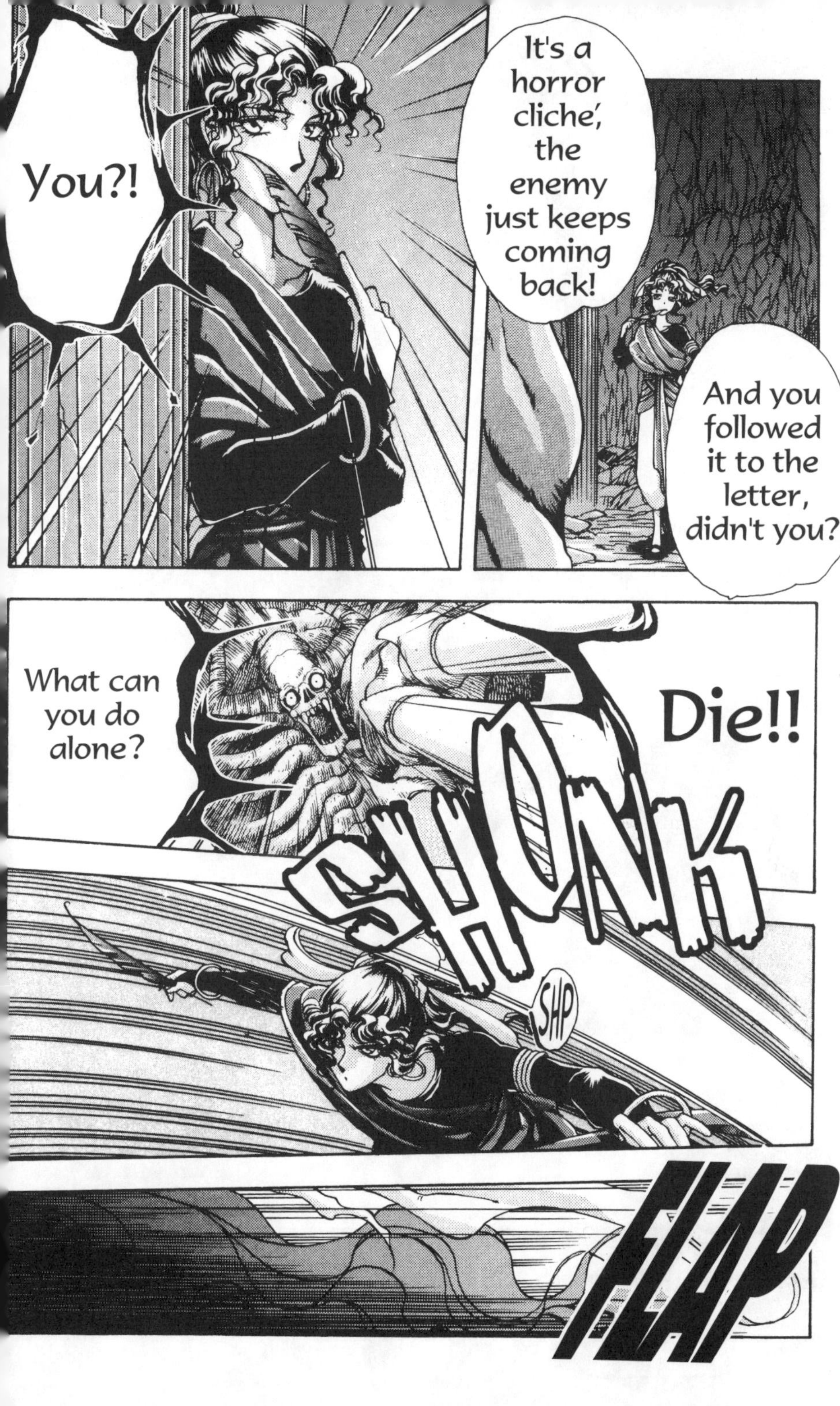
You?!
It's a horror cliche', the enemy just keeps coming back!
And you followed it to the letter, didn't you?
What can you do alone?
Die!!
SHONK
SHP
FLAP

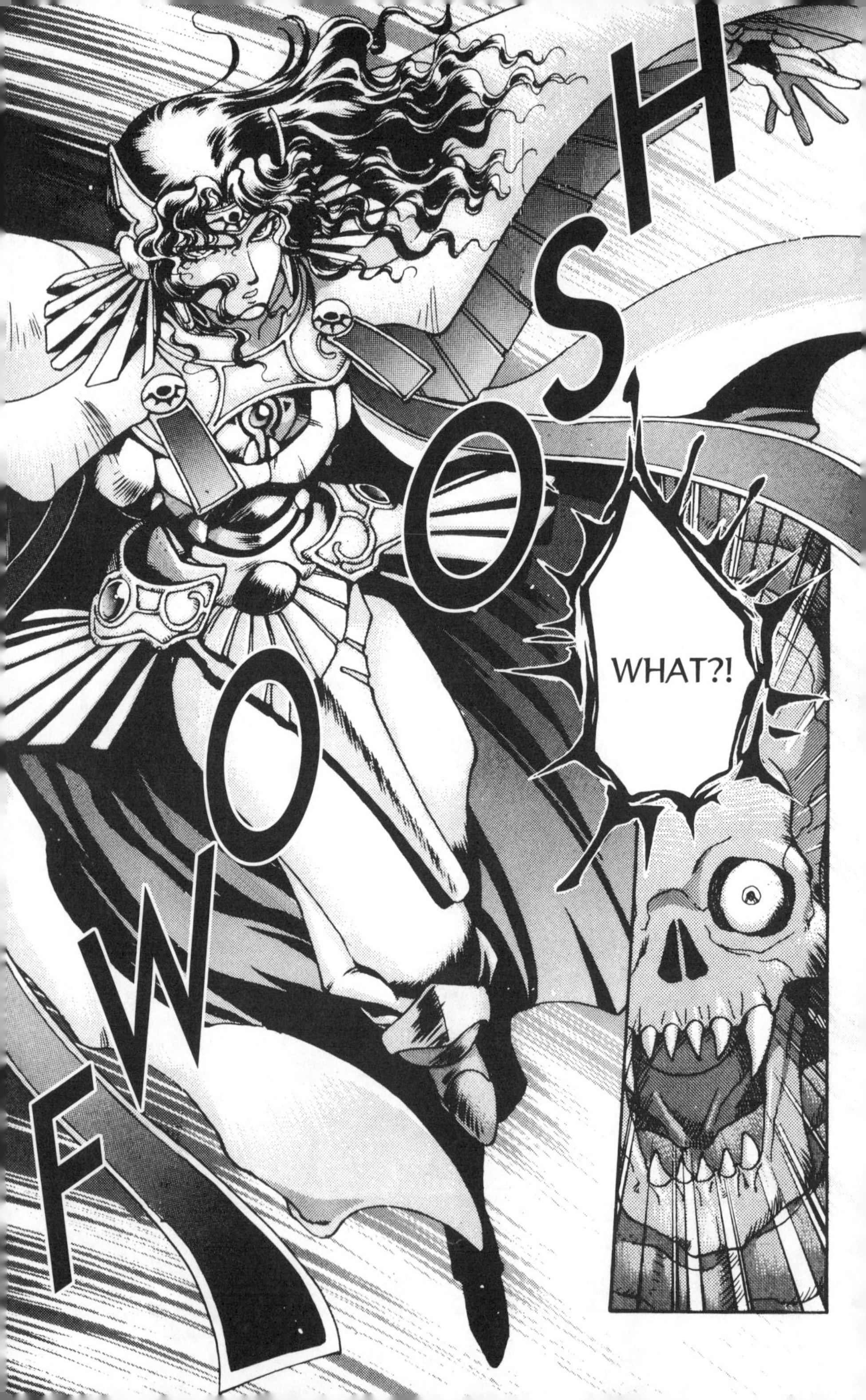
FWOOOSH
WHAT?!

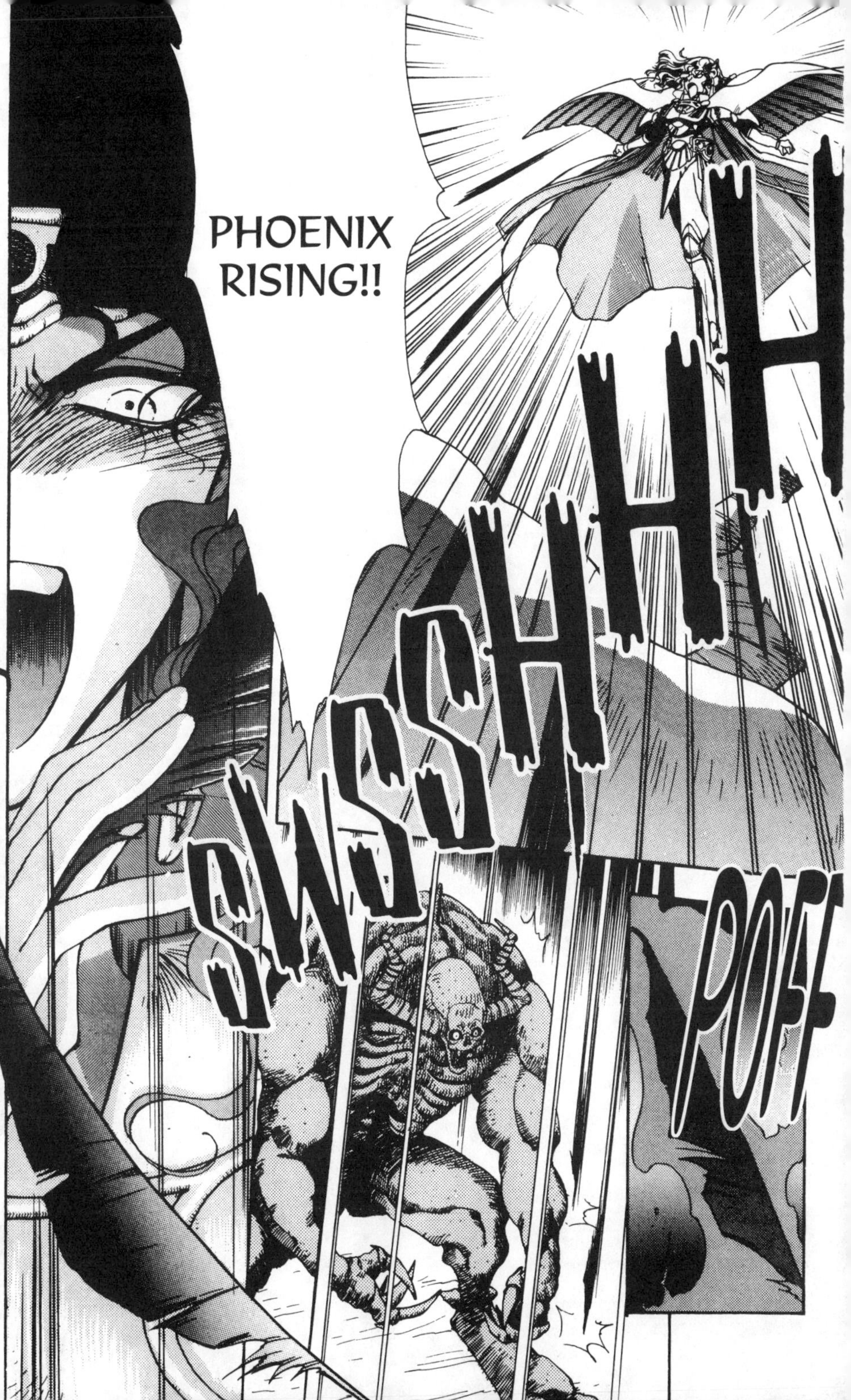
PHOENIX RISING!!
SWSSHHHH
POFF

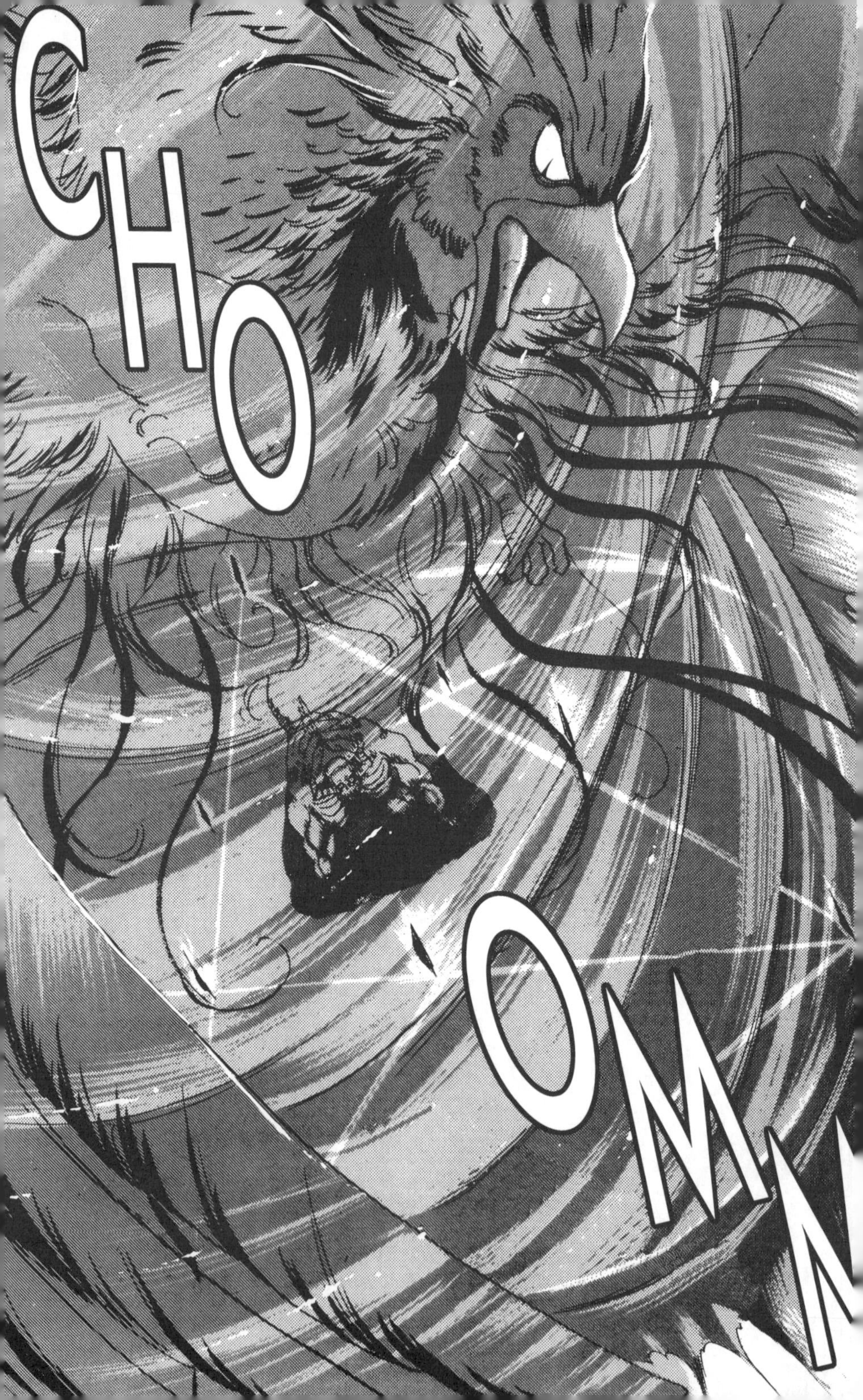
CHOOMM

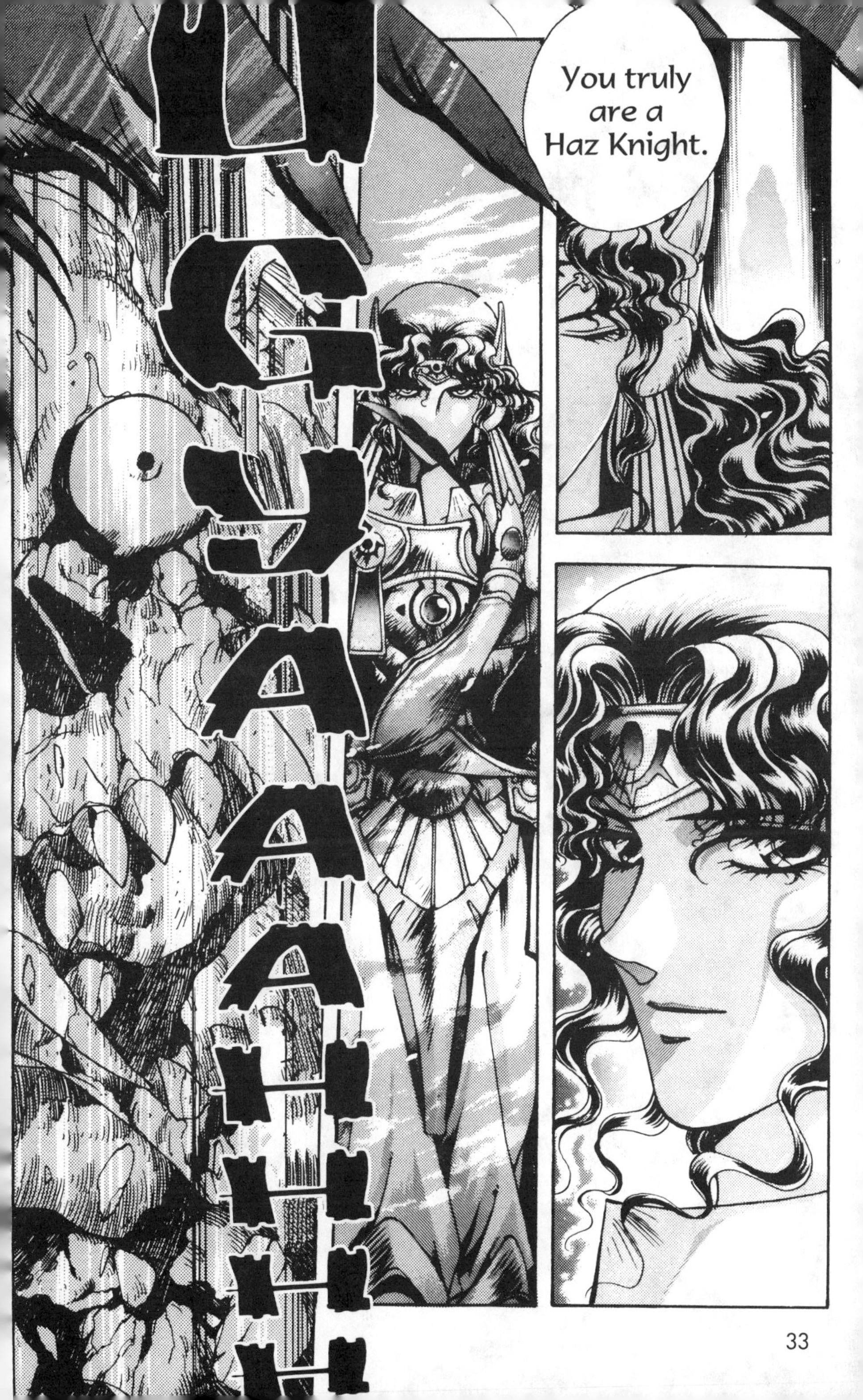
GYAAAHHHH
You truly are a Haz Knight.

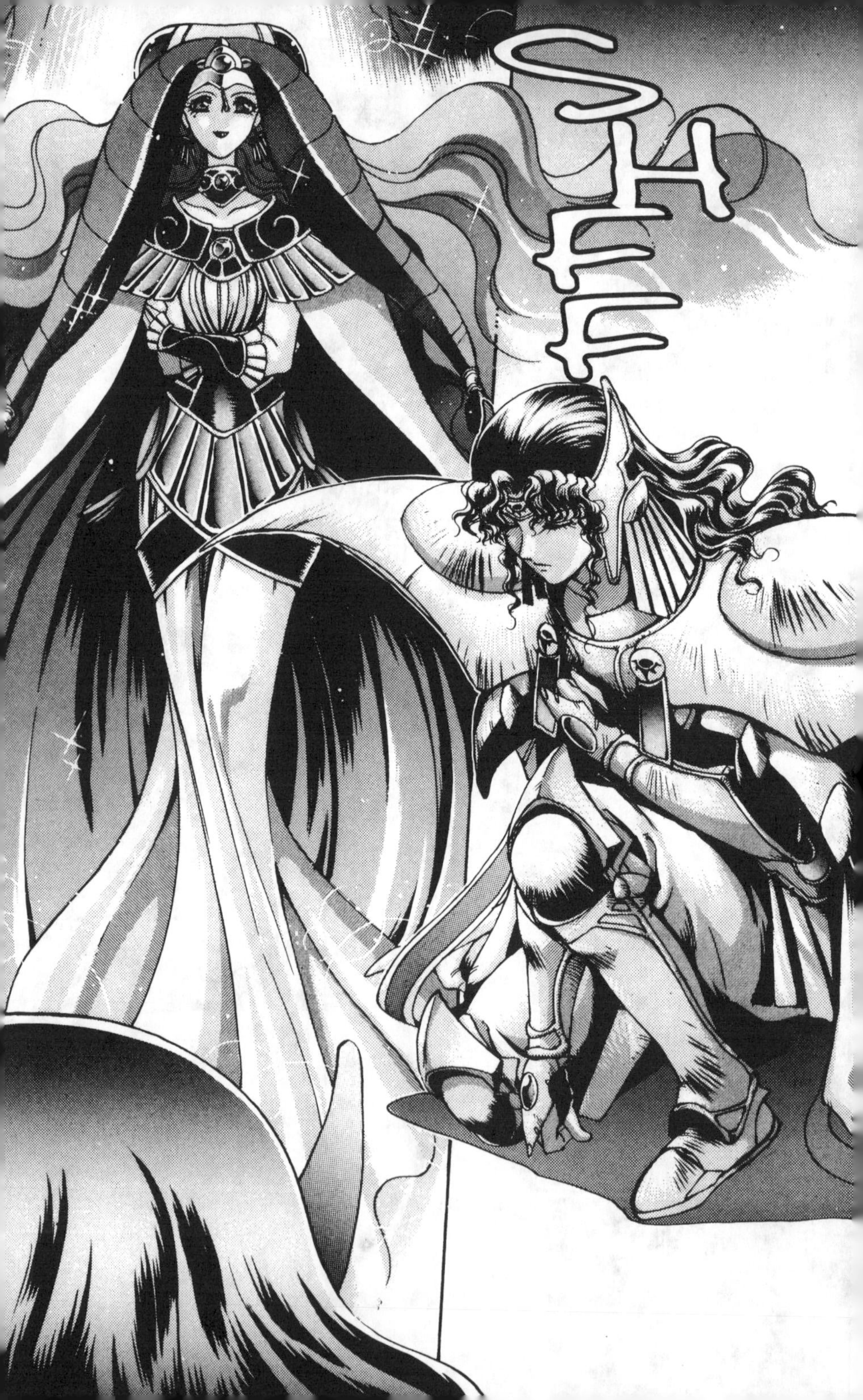
SHFF

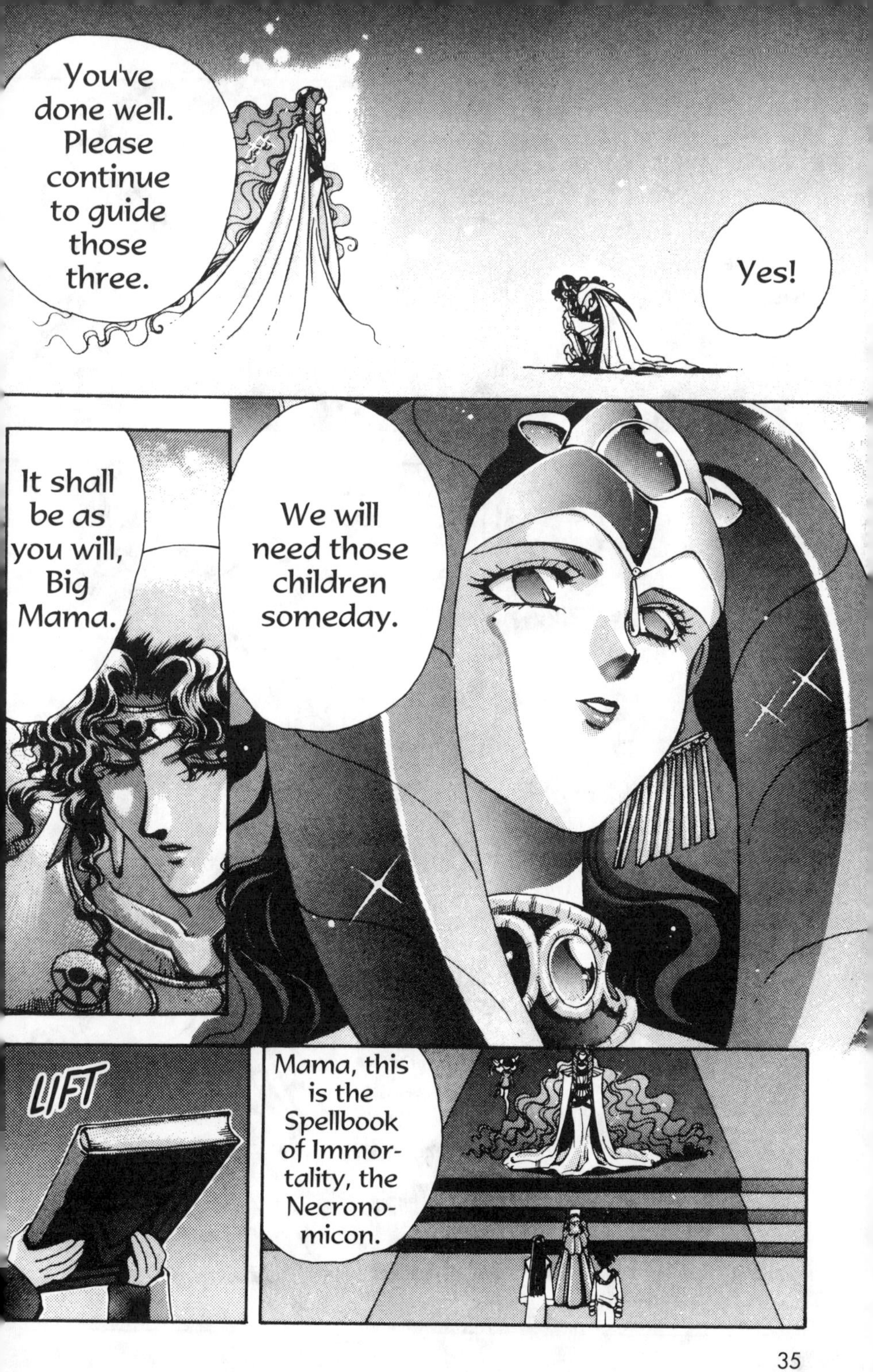
You've done well. Please continue to guide those three.
Yes!
It shall be as you will, Big Mama.
We will need those children someday.
LIFT
Mama, this is the Spellbook of Immortality, the Necronomicon.

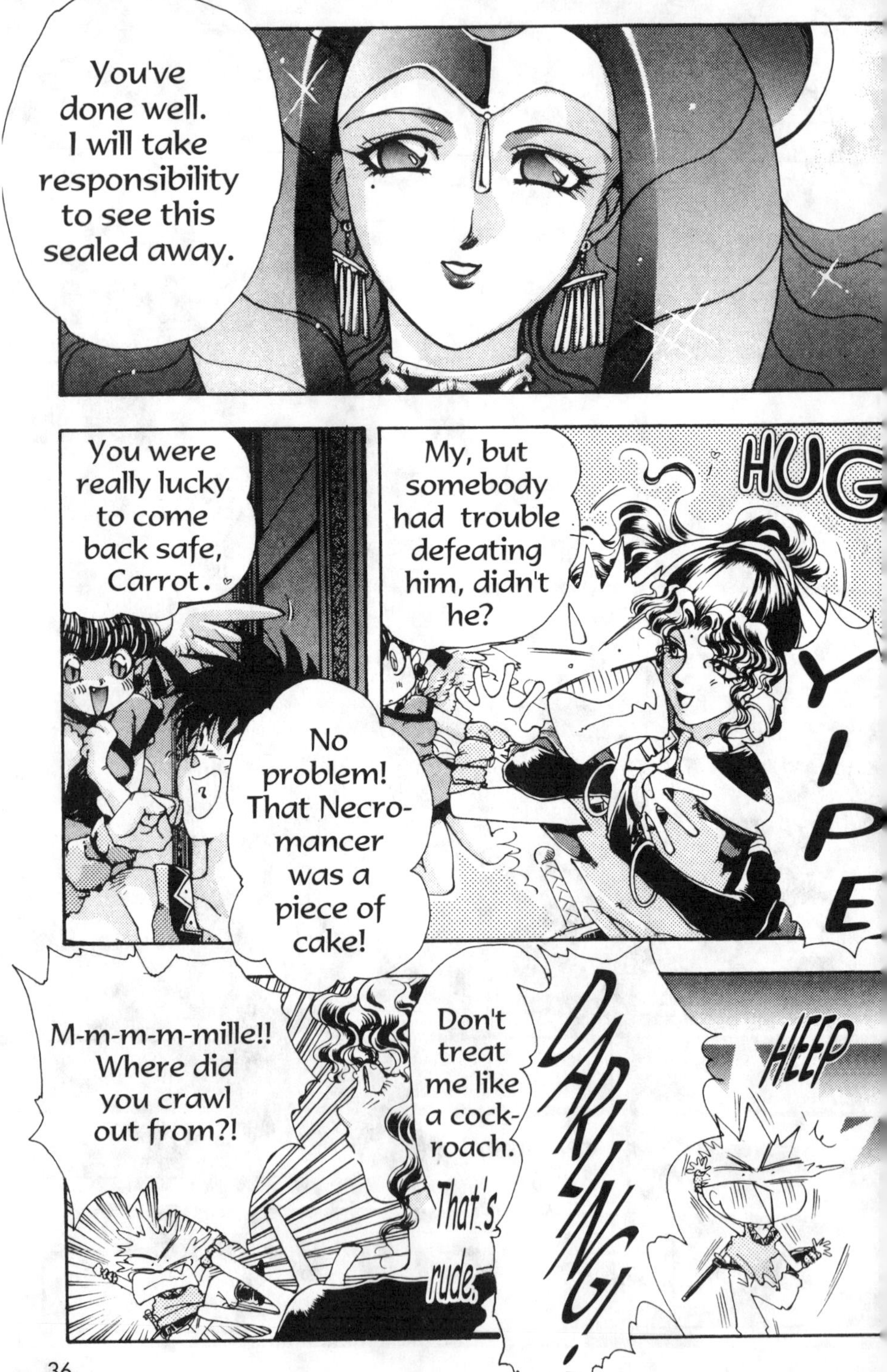
You've done well. I will take responsibility to see this sealed away.
You were really lucky to come back safe, Carrot.
No problem! That Necromancer was a piece of cake!
My, but somebody had trouble defeating him, didn't he?
HUG
YIPE
M-m-m-m-mille!! Where did you crawl out from?!
Don't treat me like a cockroach.
That's rude.
DARLING!
HEEP

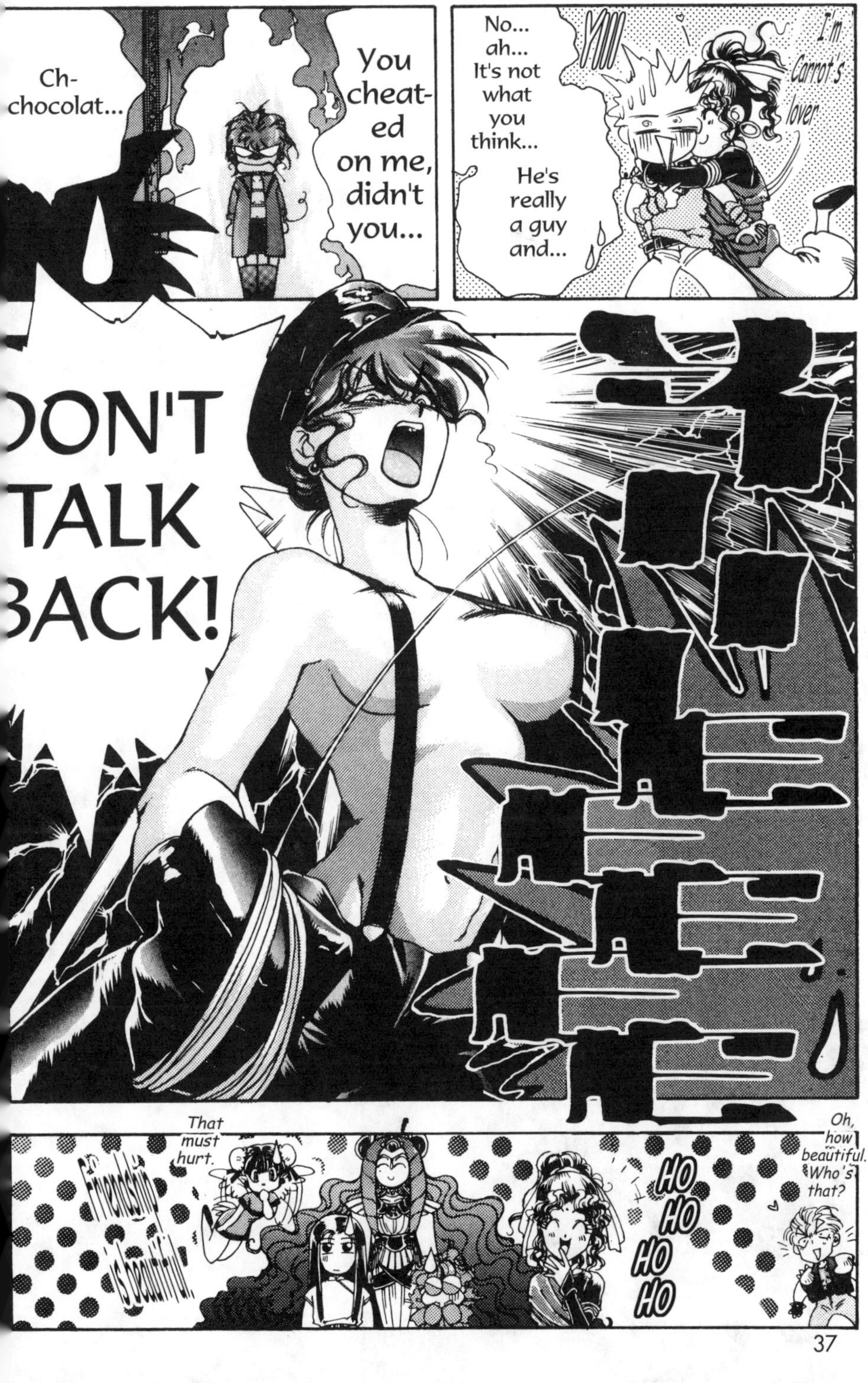

Ch-chocolat...
You cheat-ed on me, didn't you...
YANK
No... ah... It's not what you think...
He's really a guy and...
I'm Carrot's lover
DON'T TALK BACK!
That must hurt.
Friendship is beautiful.
HO HO HO HO
Oh, how beautiful. Who's that?

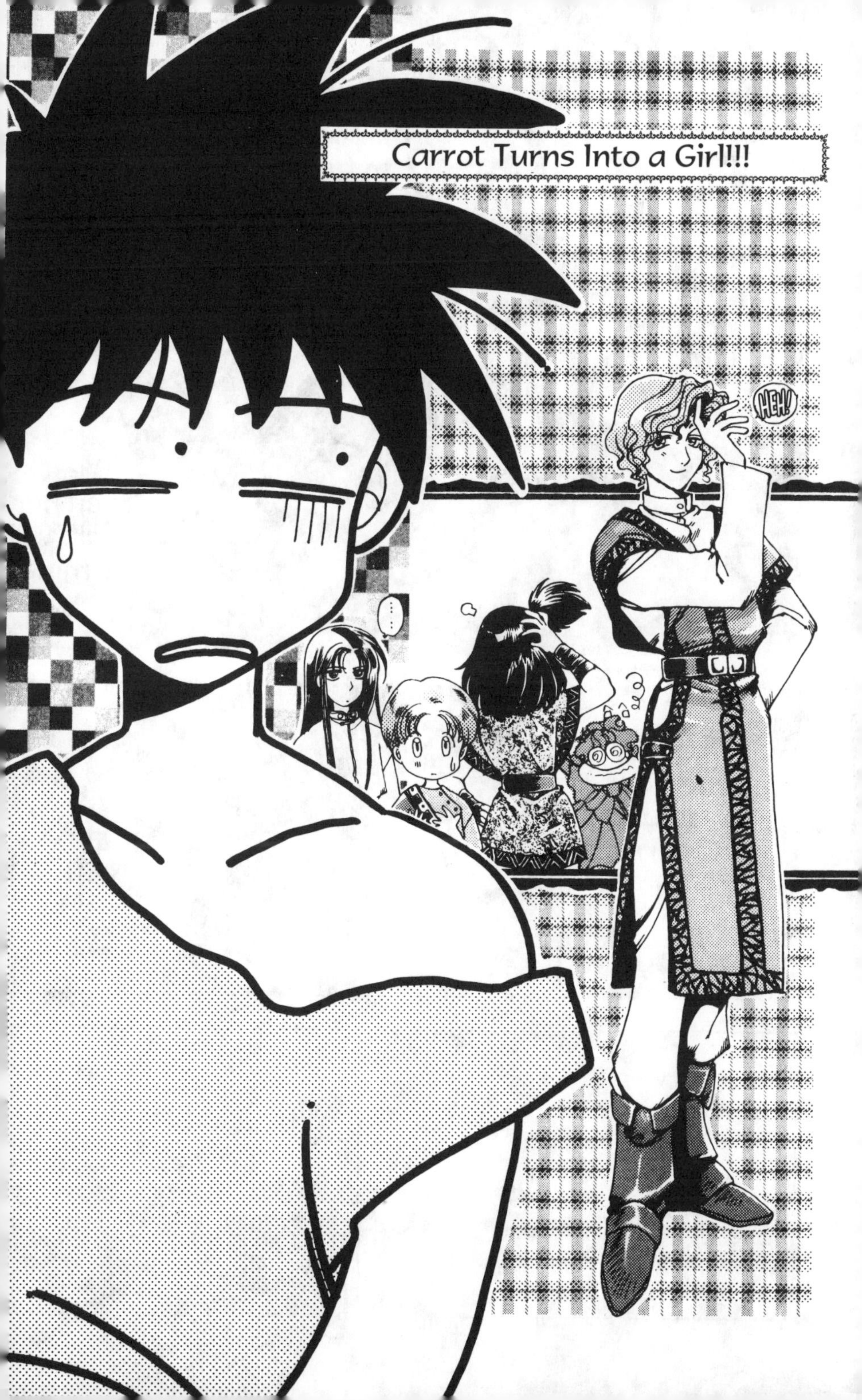
Carrot Turns Into a Girl!!!
HEH!
...

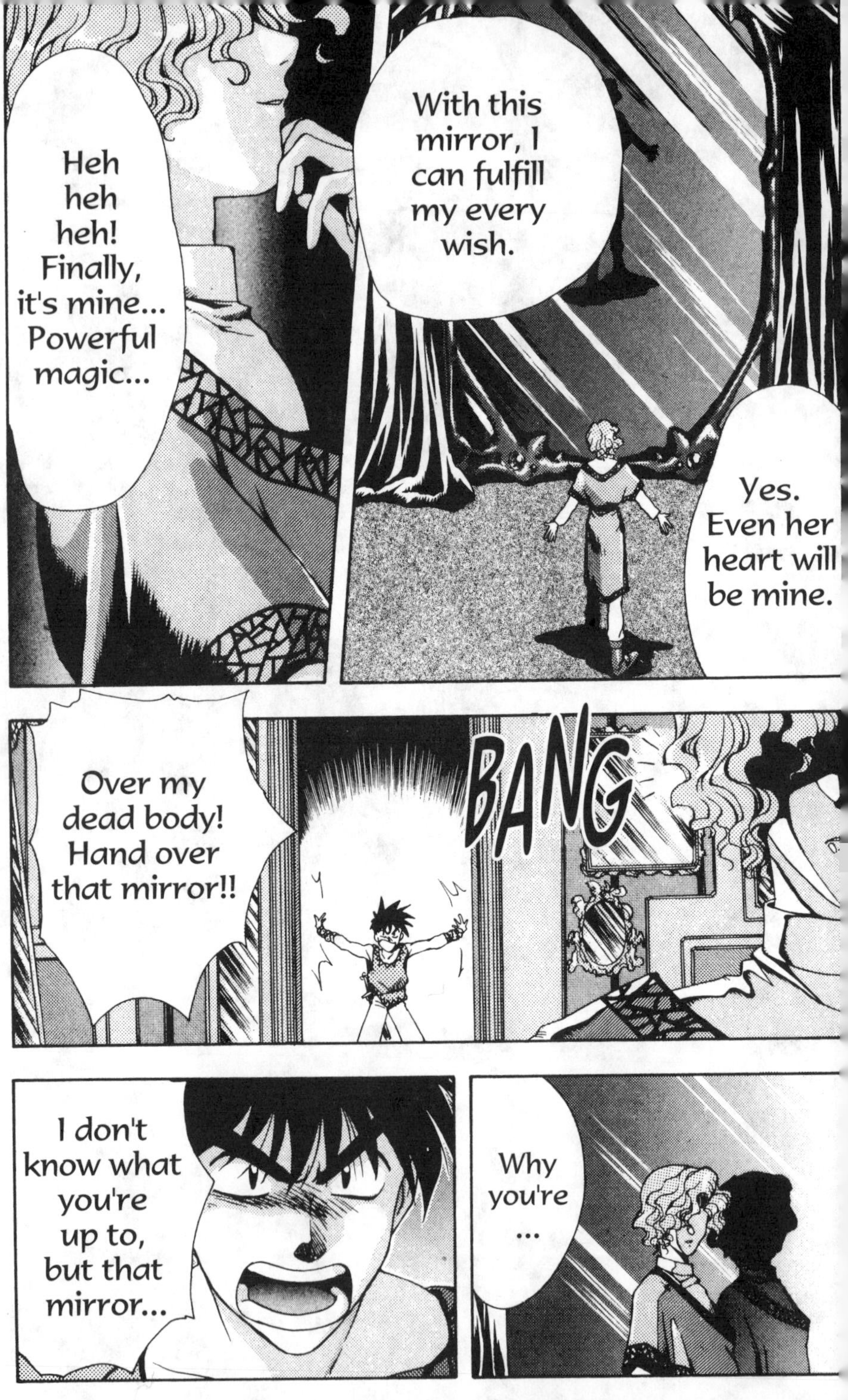

Heh heh heh! Finally, it's mine... Powerful magic...
With this mirror, I can fulfill my every wish.
Yes. Even her heart will be mine.
Over my dead body! Hand over that mirror!!
BANG
I don't know what you're up to, but that mirror...
Why you're ...

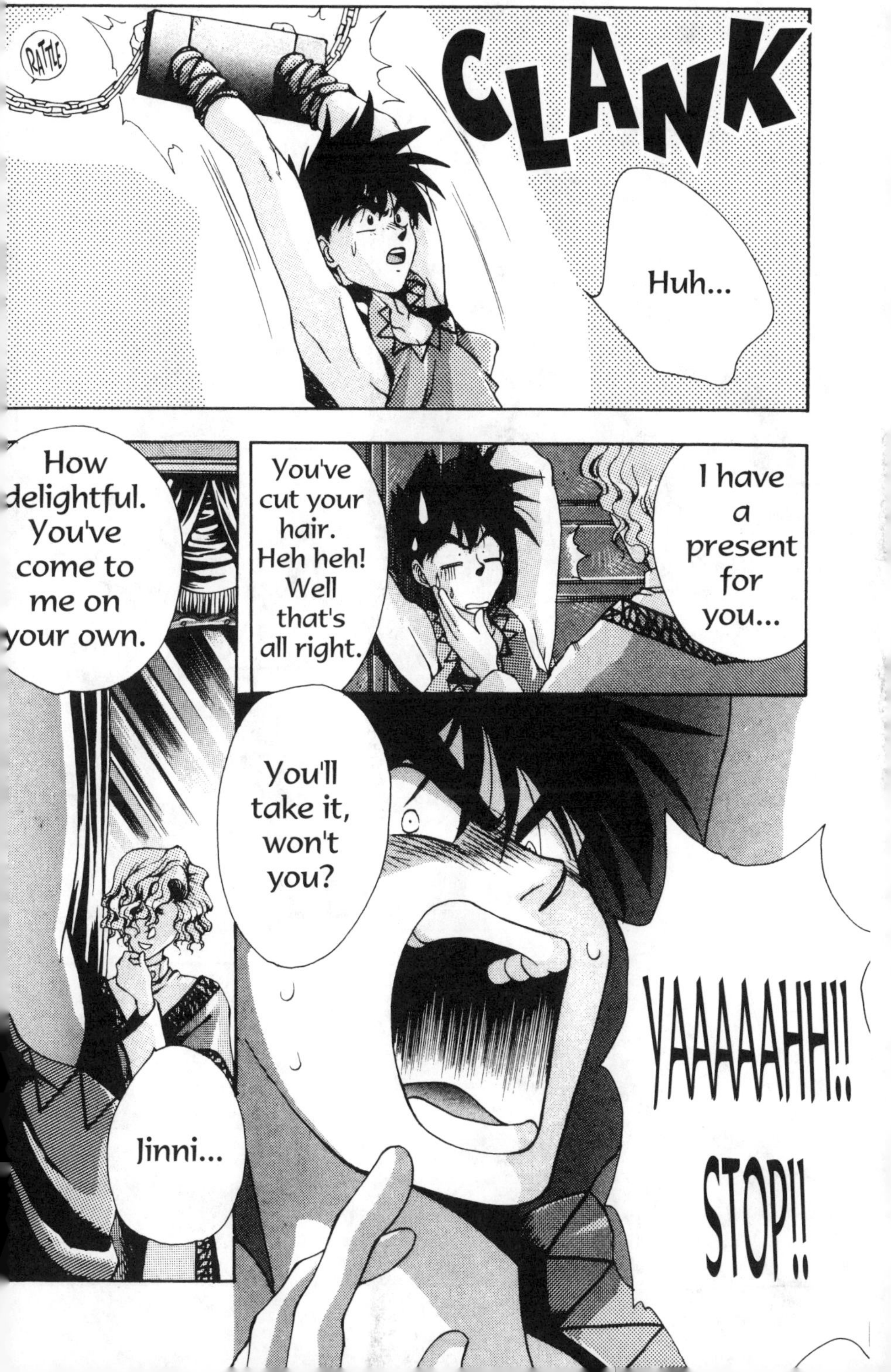
RATTLE
CLANK
Huh...
How delightful. You've come to me on your own.
You've cut your hair. Heh heh! Well that's all right.
I have a present for you...
You'll take it, won't you?
Jinni...
YAAAAHH!!!
STOP!!

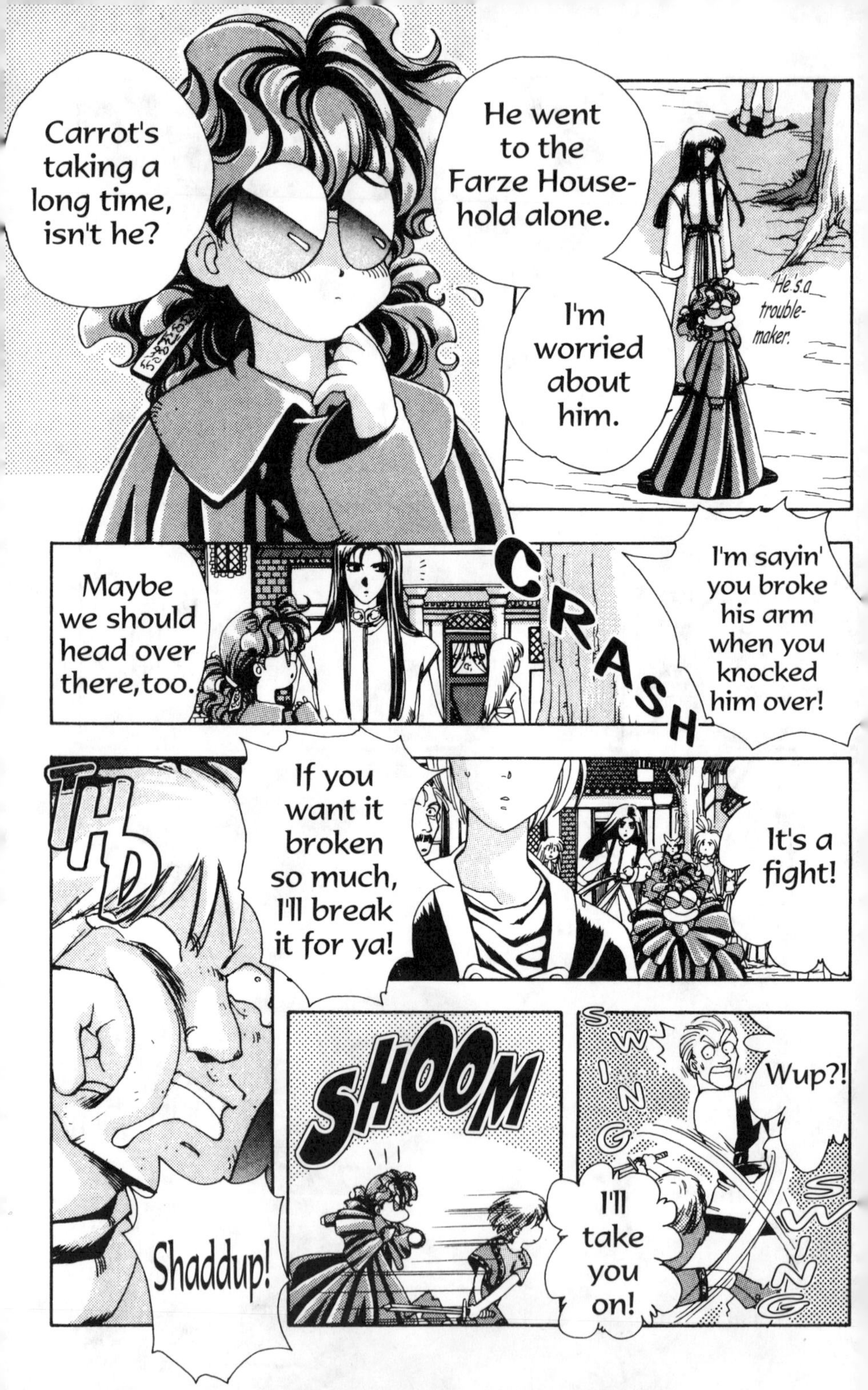
Carrot's taking a long time, isn't he?
He went to the Farze Household alone.
I'm worried about him.
He's a troublemaker.
Maybe we should head over there, too.
CRASH
I'm sayin' you broke his arm when you knocked him over!
THD
Shaddup!
If you want it broken so much, I'll break it for ya!
It's a fight!
SHOOM
SWING
Wup?!
I'll take you on!
SWING

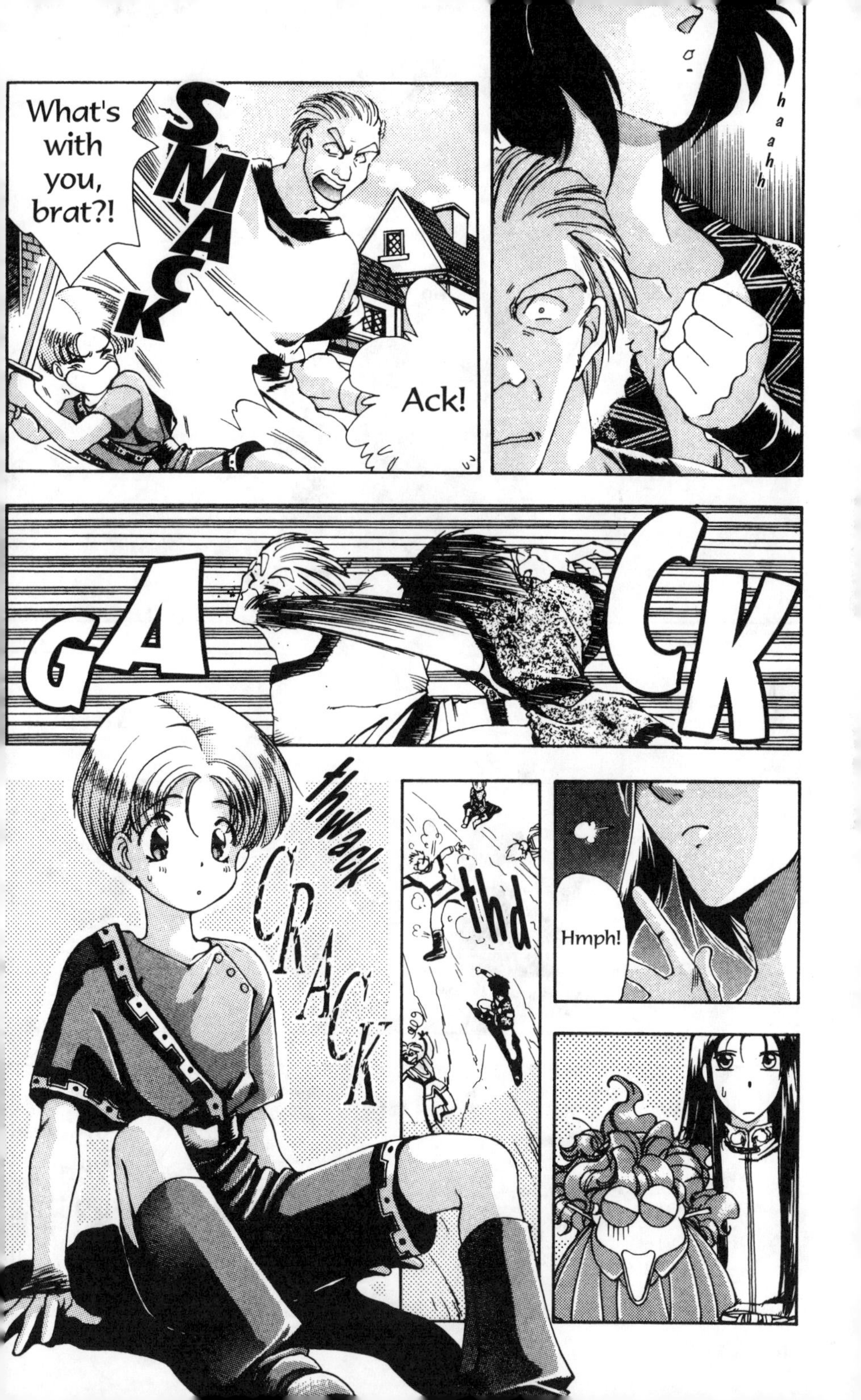

What's with you, brat?!
SMACK
Ack!
haahh
GACK
thwack
CRACK
thd
Hmph!

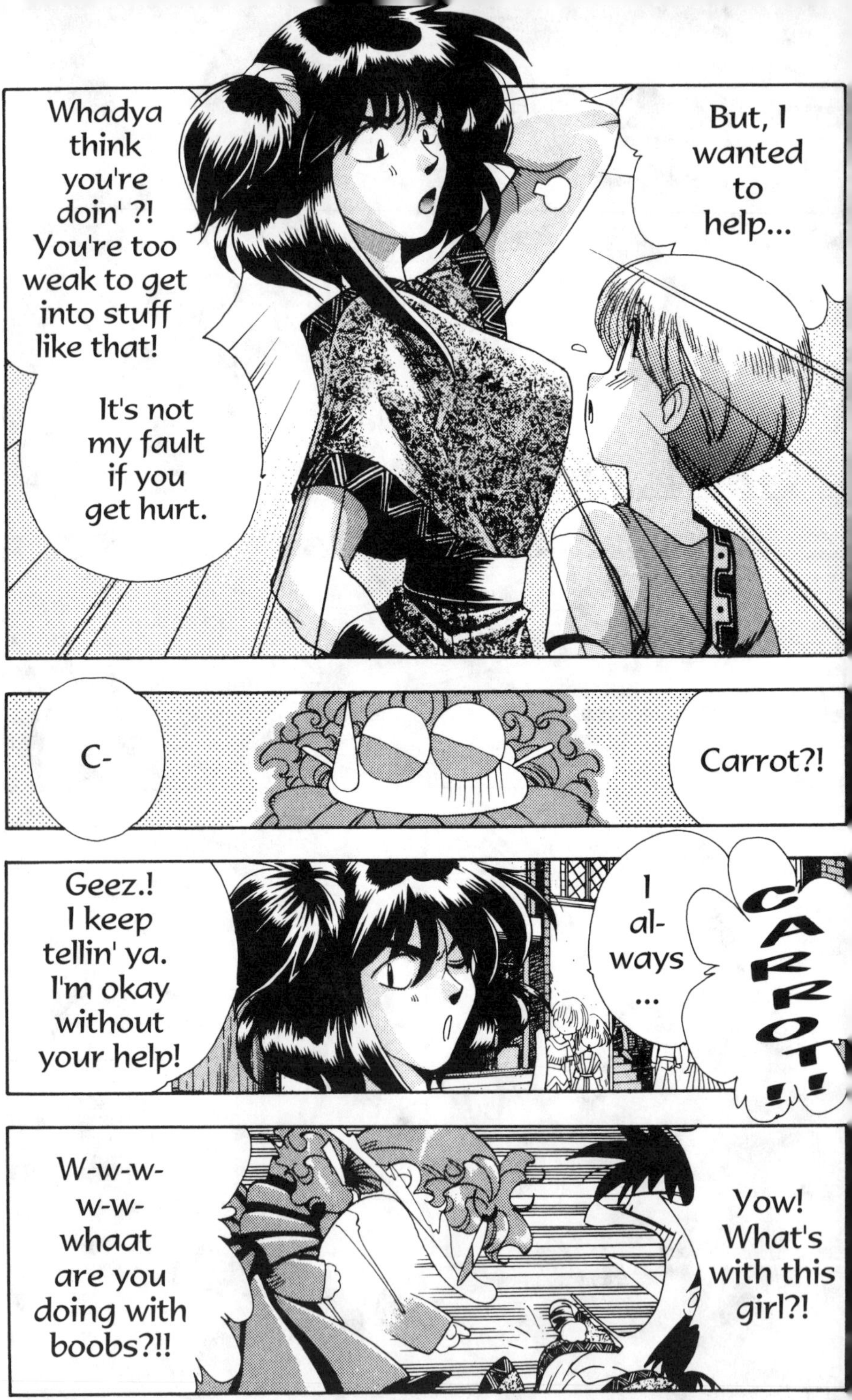
Whadya think you're doin' ?! You're too weak to get into stuff like that!
It's not my fault if you get hurt.
But, I wanted to help...
C-
Carrot?!
Geez.! I keep tellin' ya. I'm okay without your help!
I al-ways ...
CARROT!!
W-w-w-w-w-whaat are you doing with boobs?!!
Yow! What's with this girl?!

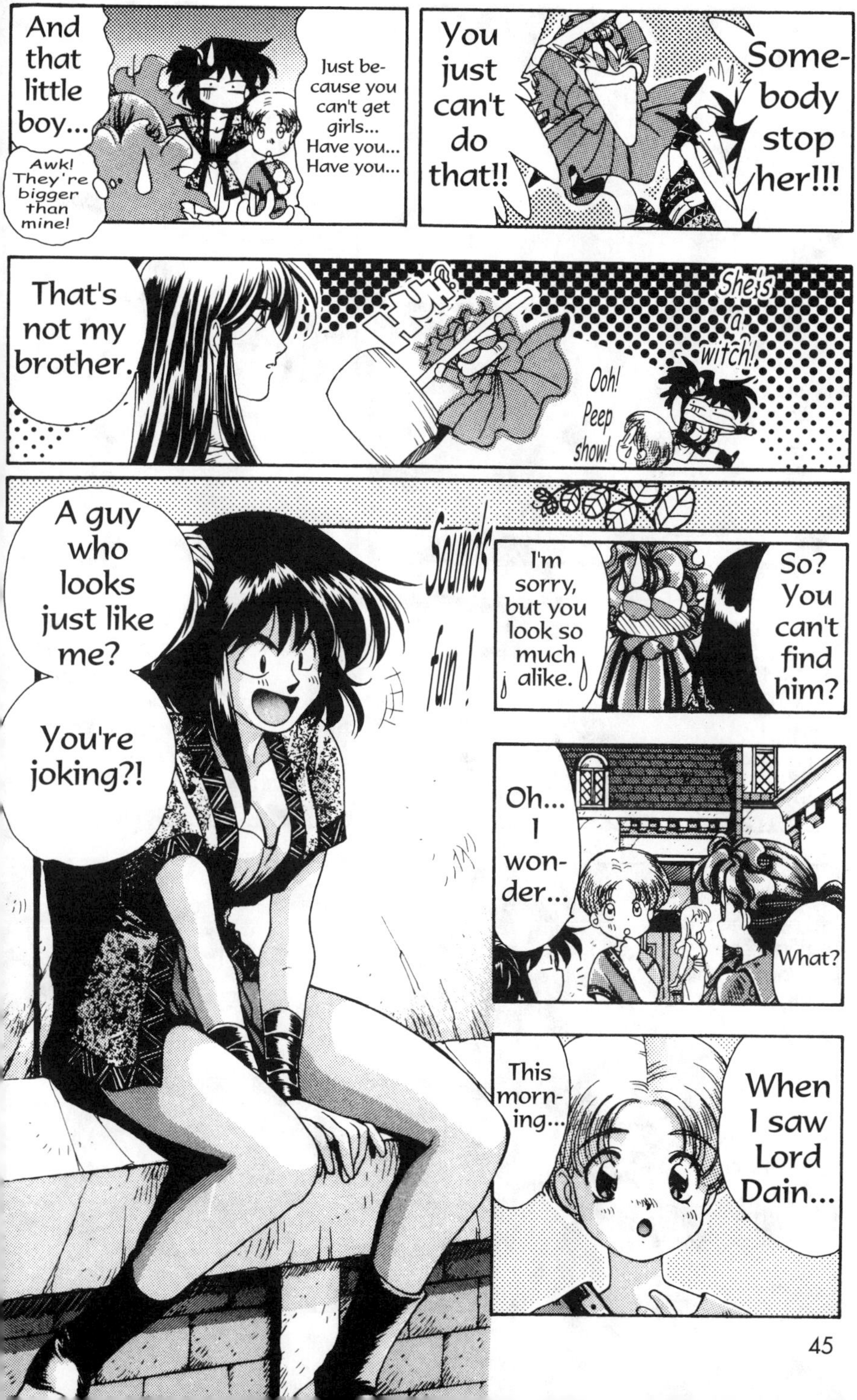
And that little boy...
Awk! They're bigger than mine!
Just because you can't get girls... Have you... Have you...
You just can't do that!!
Somebody stop her!!!
That's not my brother.
HUH?
She's a witch!
Ooh! Peep show!
A guy who looks just like me?
You're joking?!
Sounds fun!
I'm sorry, but you look so much alike.
So? You can't find him?
Oh... I wonder...
What?
This morning...
When I saw Lord Dain...

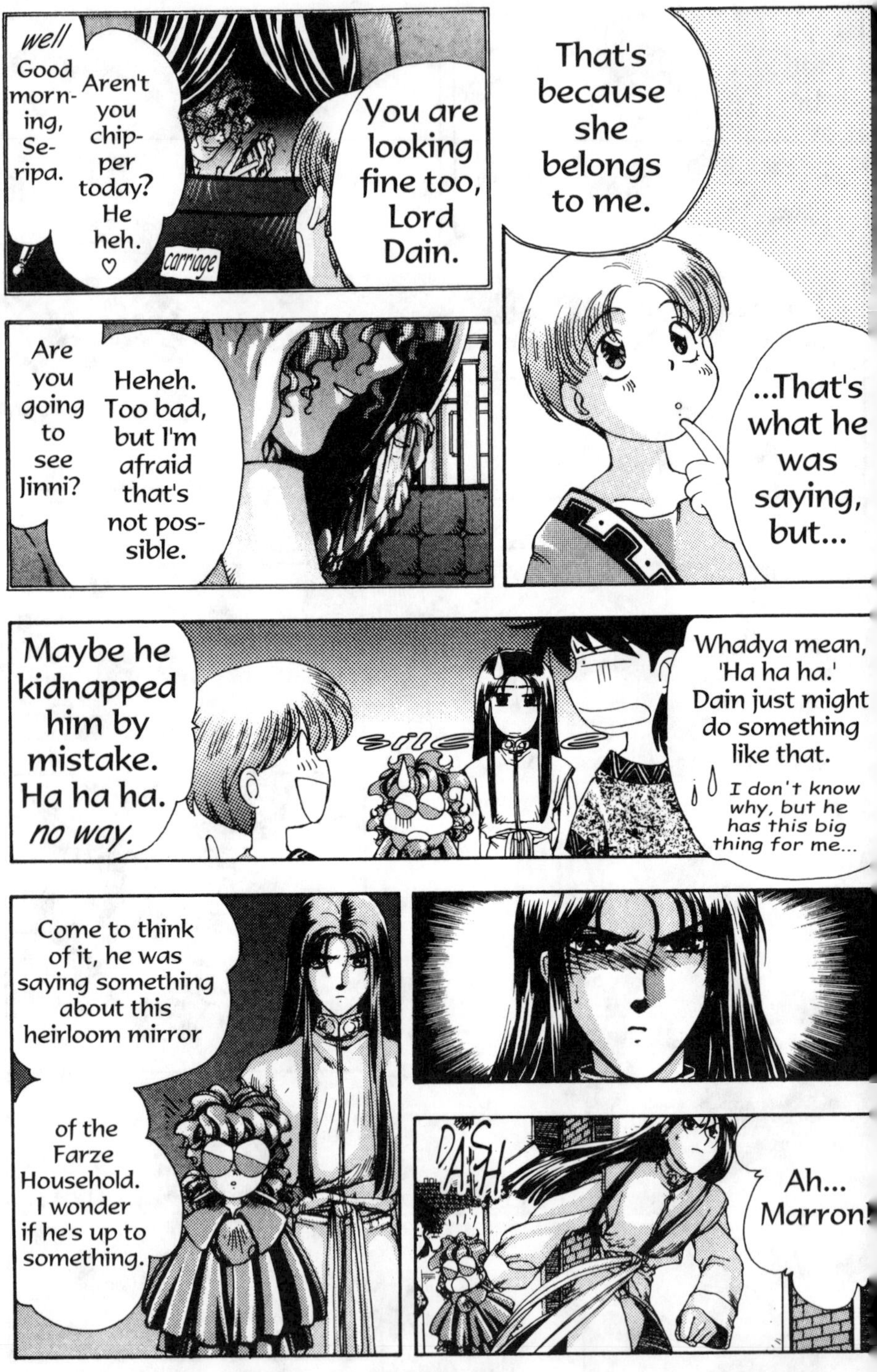
well
Good morn-ing, Se-ripa.
Aren't you chip-per today? He heh. ♡
carriage
You are looking fine too, Lord Dain.
Are you going to see Jinni?
Heheh. Too bad, but I'm afraid that's not pos-sible.
That's because she belongs to me.
...That's what he was saying, but...
Maybe he kidnapped him by mistake. Ha ha ha.
no way.
Whadya mean, 'Ha ha ha.' Dain just might do something like that.
I don't know why, but he has this big thing for me...
Come to think of it, he was saying something about this heirloom mirror
of the Farze Household. I wonder if he's up to something.
DASH
Ah... Marron!

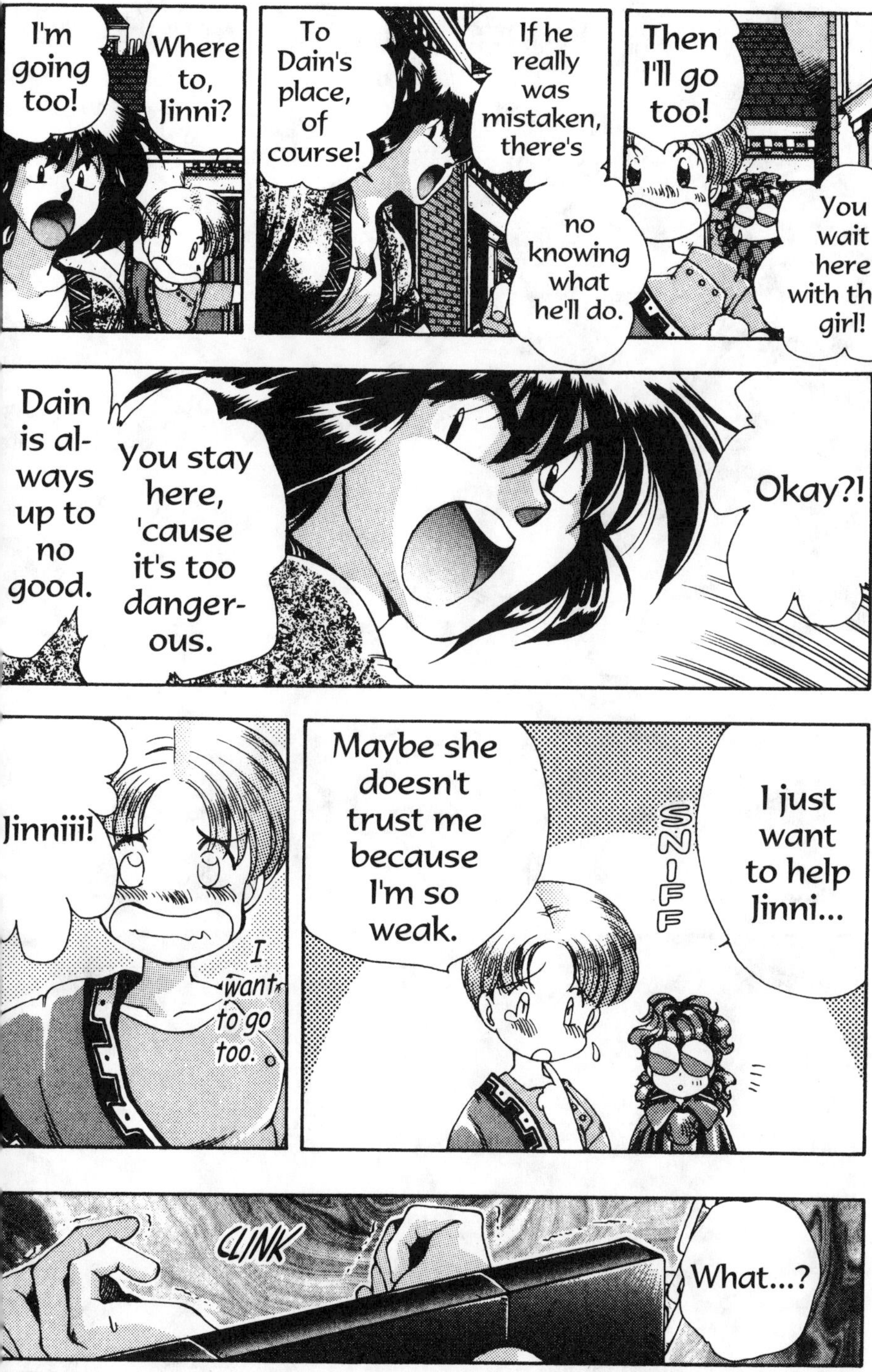
I'm going too!
Where to, Jinni?
To Dain's place, of course!
If he really was mistaken, there's
no knowing what he'll do.
Then I'll go too!
You wait here with that girl!
Dain is al-ways up to no good.
You stay here, 'cause it's too danger-ous.
Okay?!
Jinniii!
I want to go too.
Maybe she doesn't trust me because I'm so weak.
SNIFF
I just want to help Jinni...
CLINK
What...?

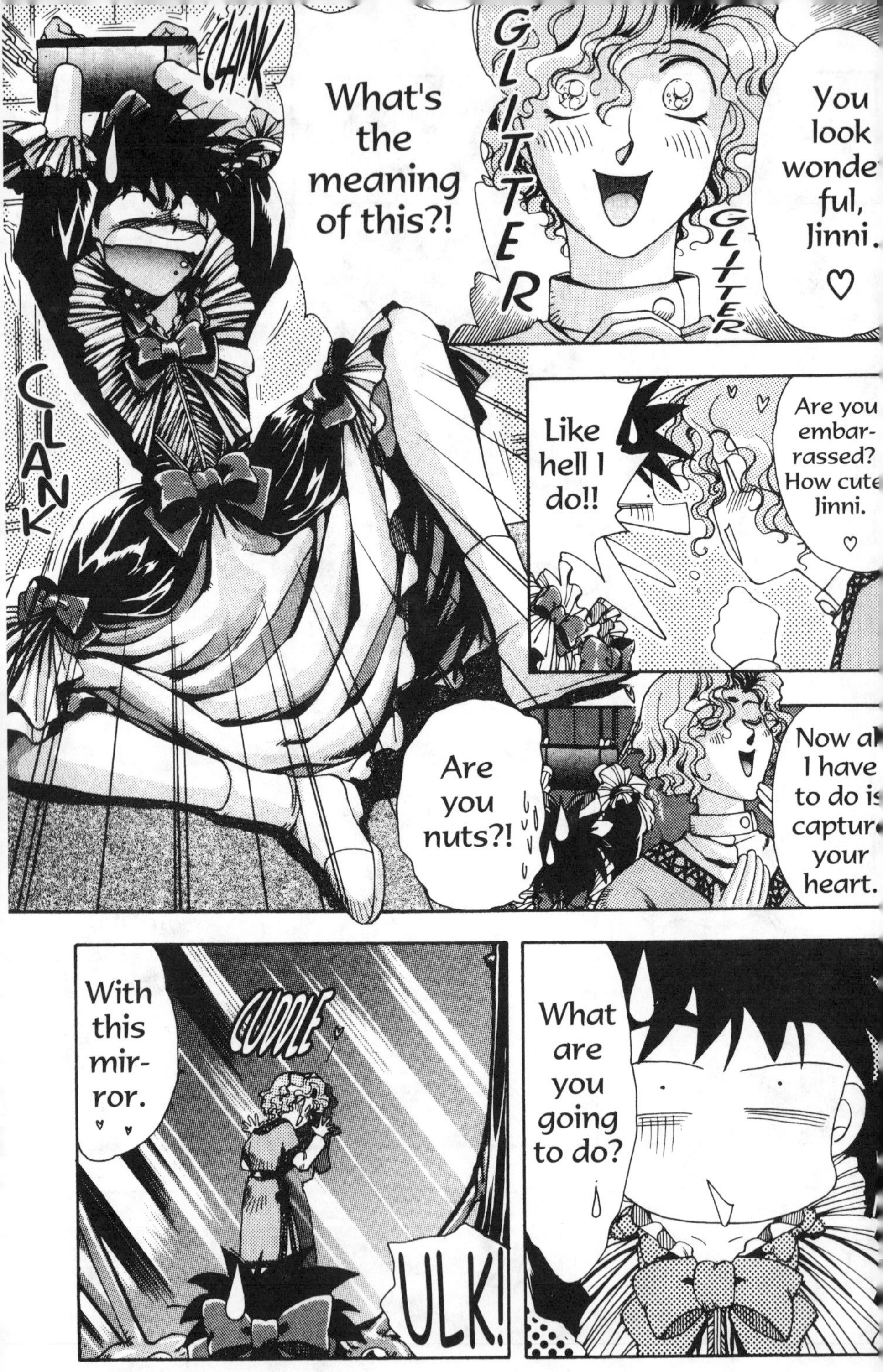
CLANK
What's the meaning of this?!
CLANK
GLITTER
GLITTER
You look wonde ful, Jinni. ♡
Like hell I do!!
Are you embar-rassed? How cute Jinni. ♡
Are you nuts?!
Now al I have to do is captur your heart.
With this mir-ror. ♡ ♡
CUDDLE
ULK!
What are you going to do?

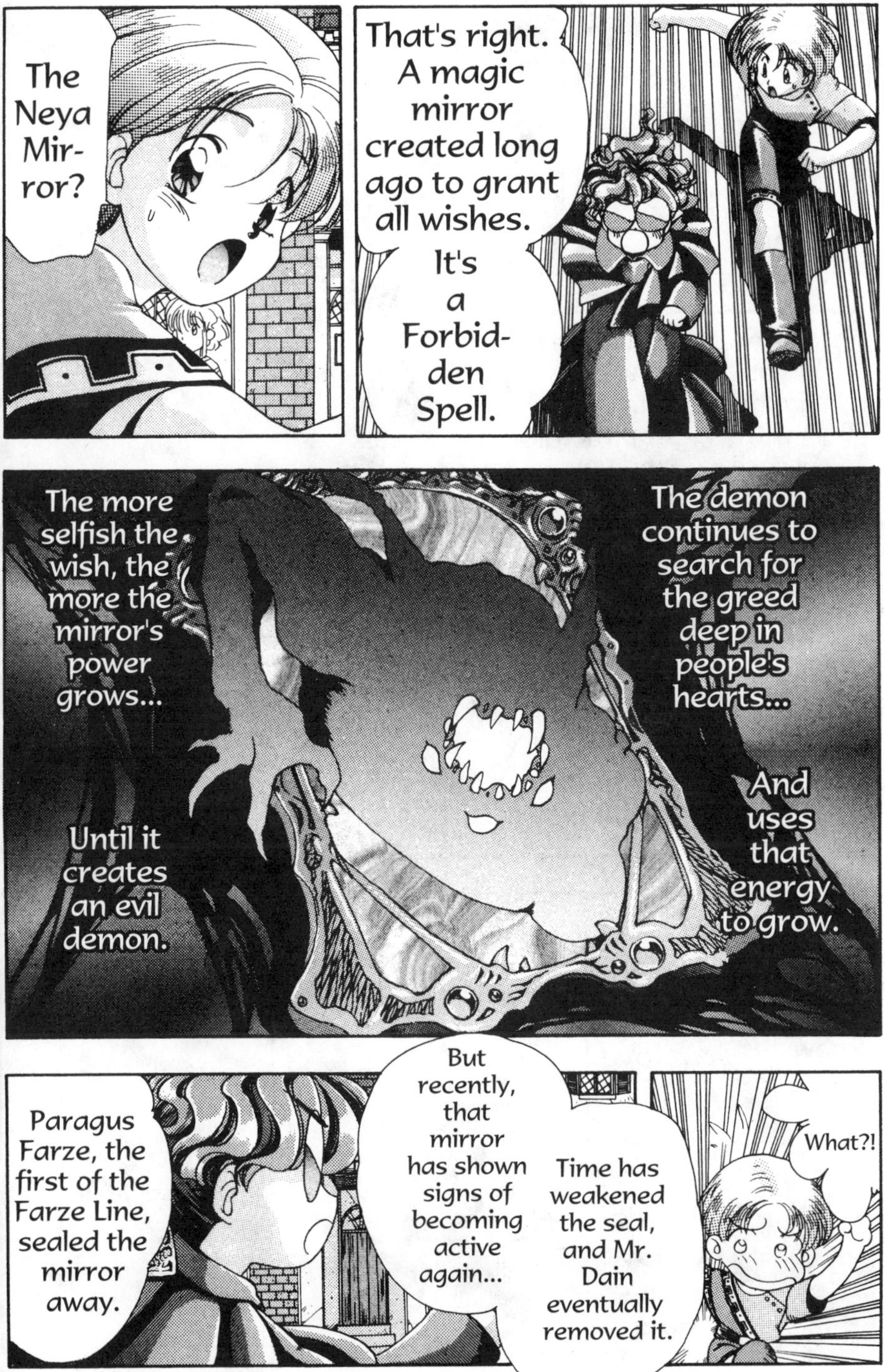
The Neya Mir-ror?
That's right. A magic mirror created long ago to grant all wishes.
It's a Forbid-den Spell.
The more selfish the wish, the more the mirror's power grows...
Until it creates an evil demon.
The demon continues to search for the greed deep in people's hearts...
And uses that energy to grow.
Paragus Farze, the first of the Farze Line, sealed the mirror away.
But recently, that mirror has shown signs of becoming active again...
Time has weakened the seal, and Mr. Dain eventually removed it.
What?!

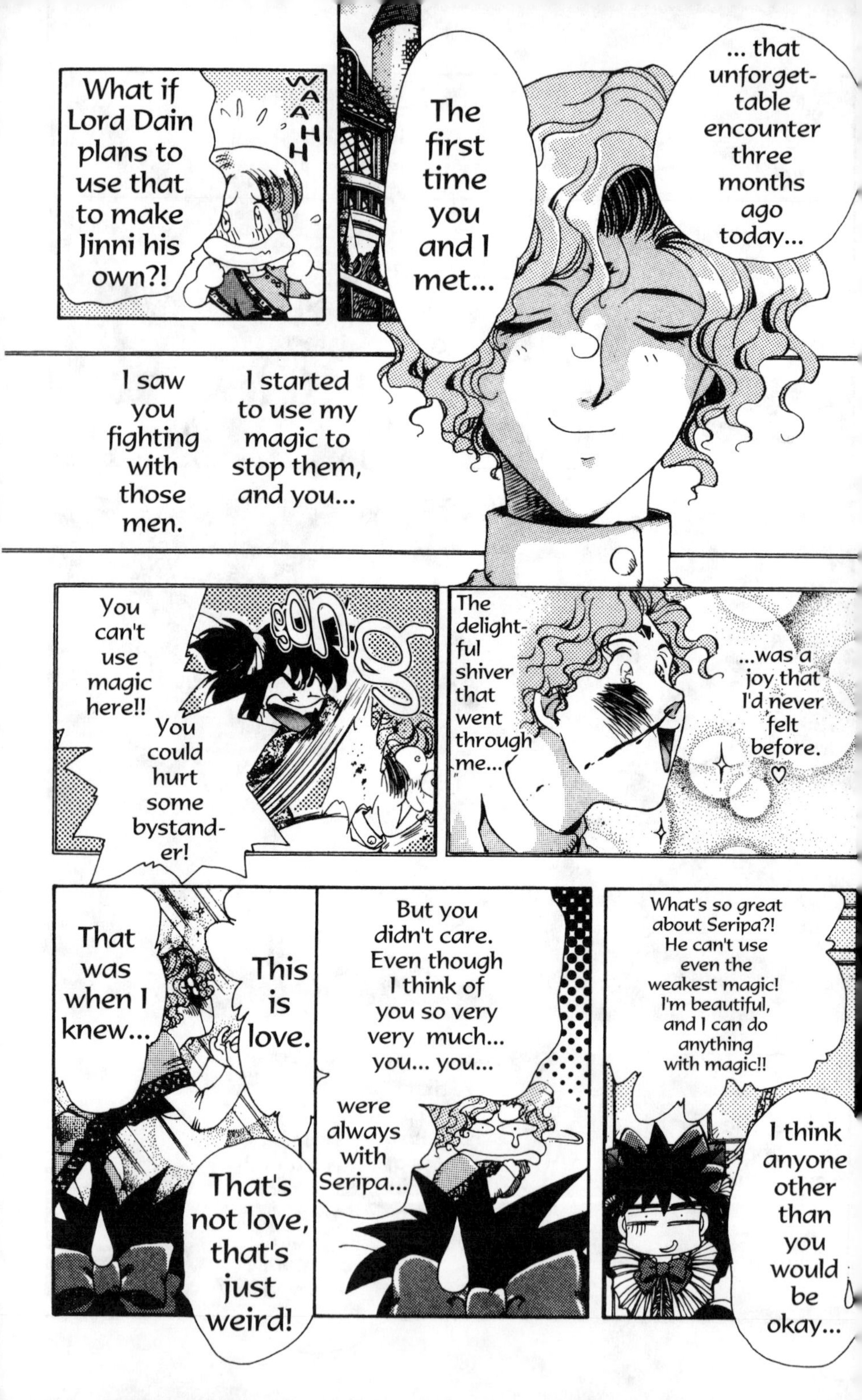

What if Lord Dain plans to use that to make Jinni his own?!
WAAHH
The first time you and I met...
... that unforget-table encounter three months ago today...
I saw you fighting with those men.
I started to use my magic to stop them, and you...
You can't use magic here!!
You could hurt some bystand-er!
gong
The delight-ful shiver that went through me...
...was a joy that I'd never felt before. ♡
That was when I knew...
This is love.
That's not love, that's just weird!
But you didn't care. Even though I think of you so very very much... you... you...
were always with Seripa...
What's so great about Seripa?! He can't use even the weakest magic! I'm beautiful, and I can do anything with magic!!
I think anyone other than you would be okay...

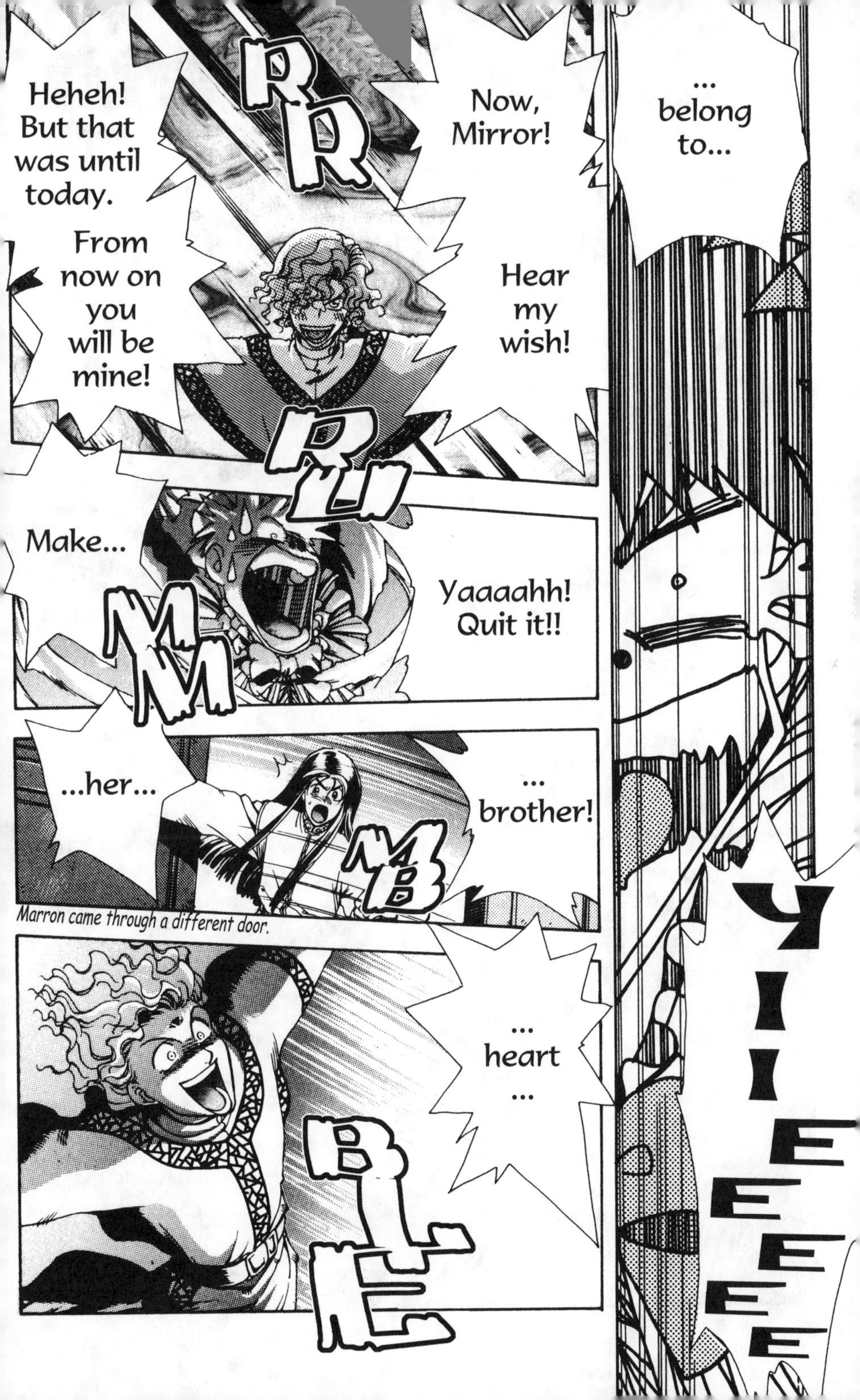
Heheh! But that was until today.
RR
From now on you will be mine!
Now, Mirror!
Hear my wish!
RU
Make...
MM
Yaaaahh! Quit it!!
...her...
... brother!
MB
Marron came through a different door.
BLE
... heart ...
... belong to...
YIIEEEEE

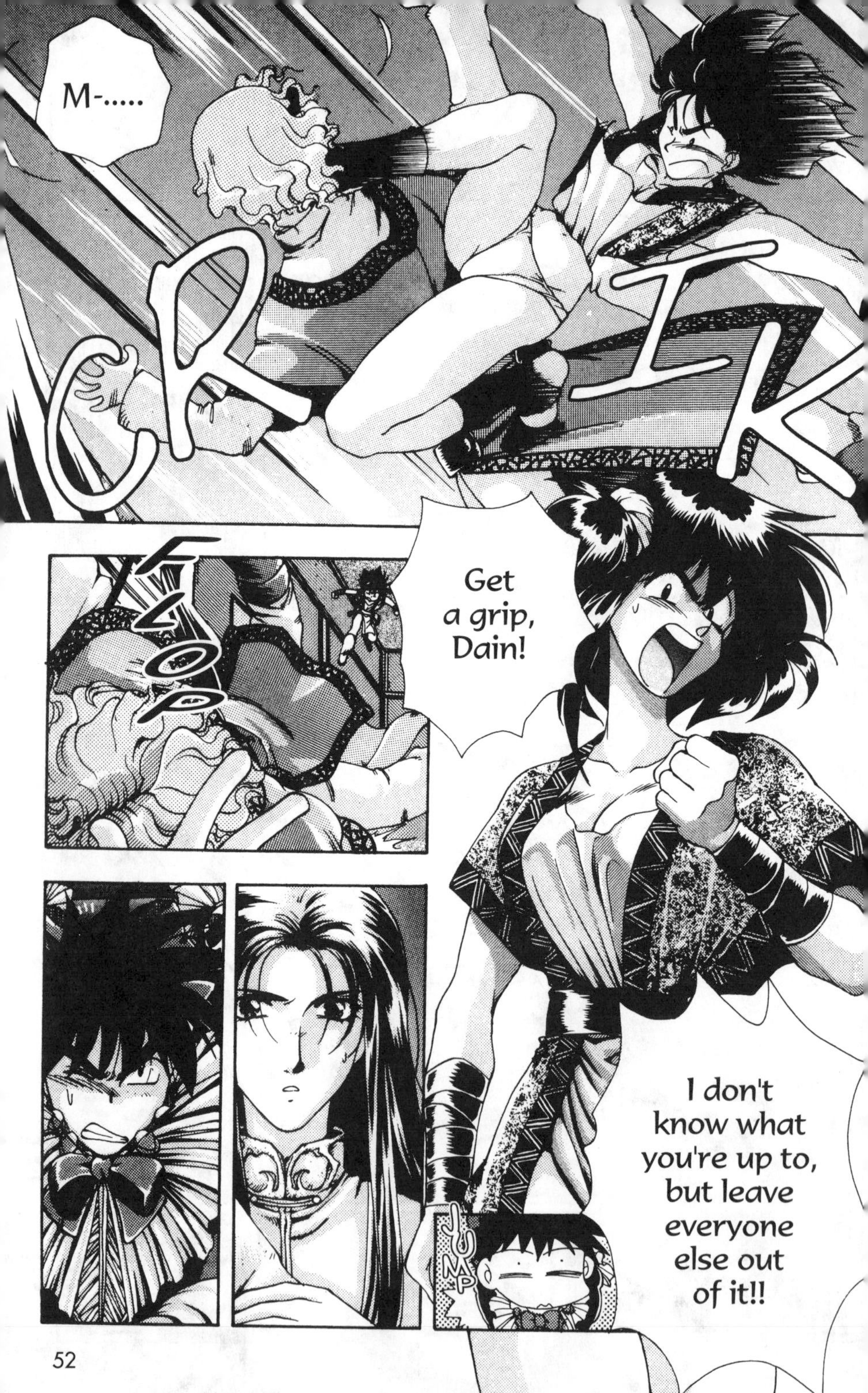
M-.....
CRIK
FLOP
Get a grip, Dain!
JUMP
I don't know what you're up to, but leave everyone else out of it!!

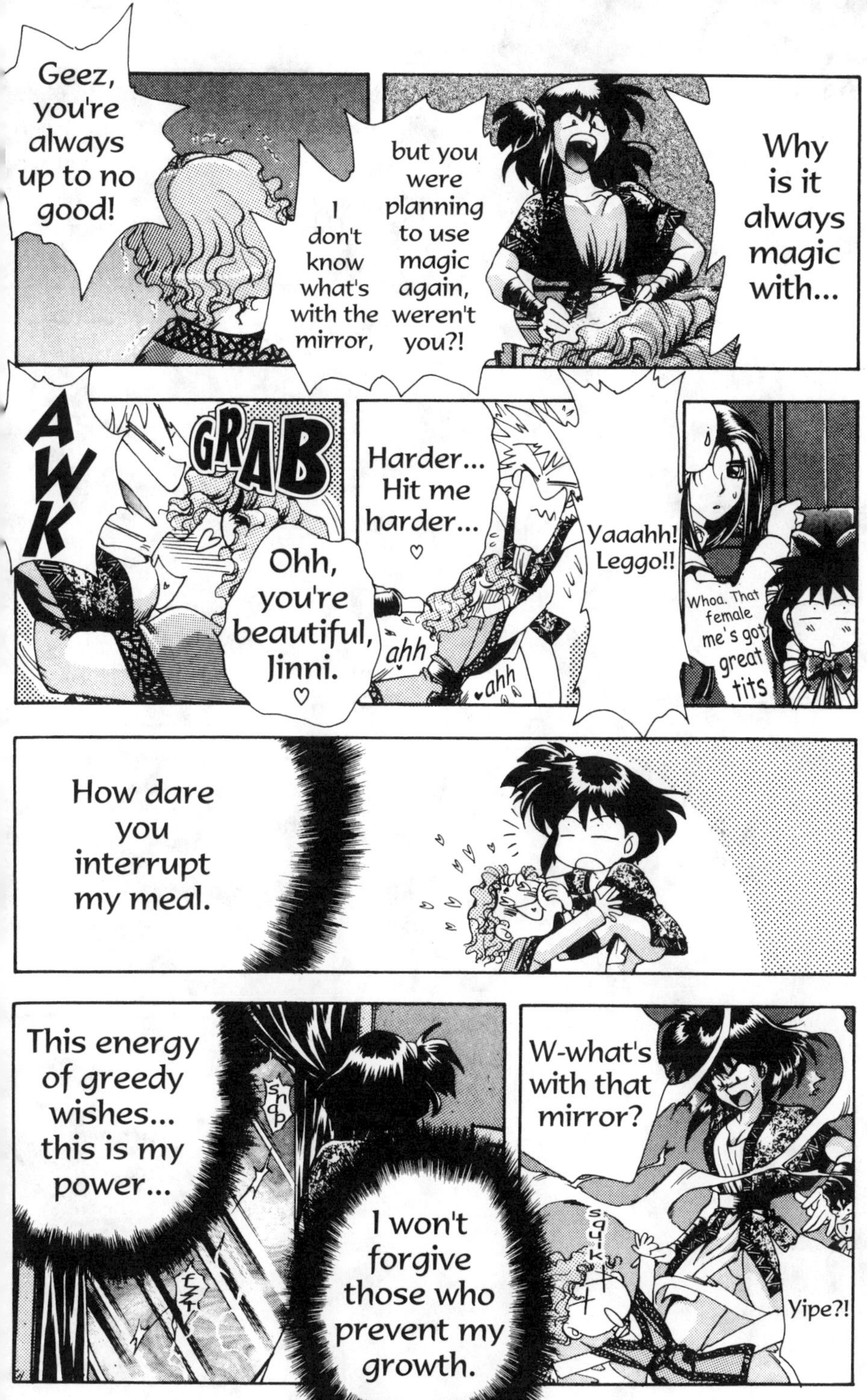

Geez, you're always up to no good!
I don't know what's with the mirror,
but you were planning to use magic again, weren't you?!
Why is it always magic with...
AWK
GRAB
Harder... Hit me harder... ♡
Ohh, you're beautiful, Jinni. ♡
ahh
ahh
Yaaahh! Leggo!!
Whoa. That female me's got great tits
How dare you interrupt my meal.
This energy of greedy wishes... this is my power...
I won't forgive those who prevent my growth.
W-what's with that mirror?
squik
Yipe?!

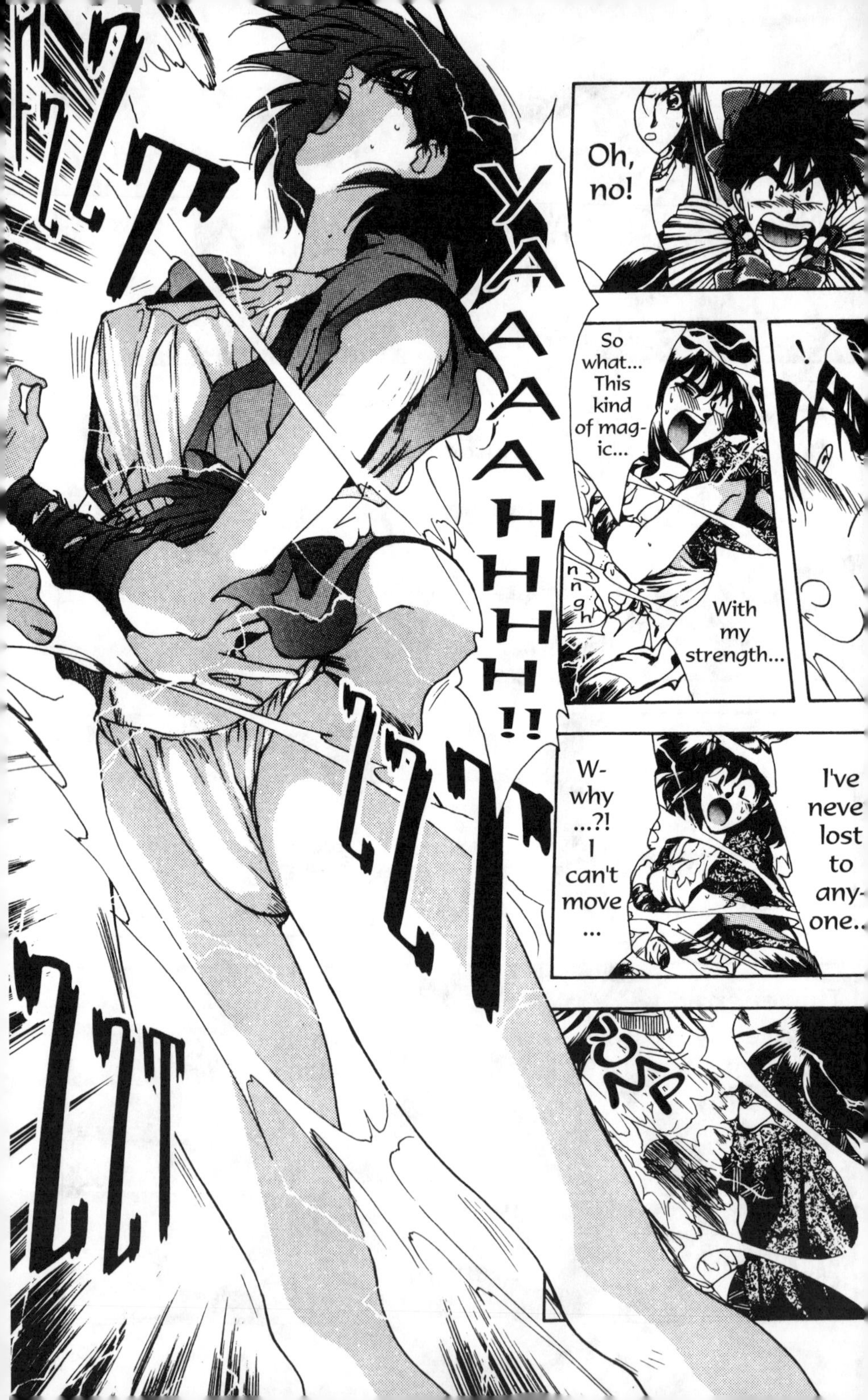
FZZT
YAAAAHHHH!!
ZZT
ZZT
Oh, no!
So what... This kind of mag-ic...
nngh
With my strength...
!
W-why ...?! I can't move ...
I've neve lost to any-one..

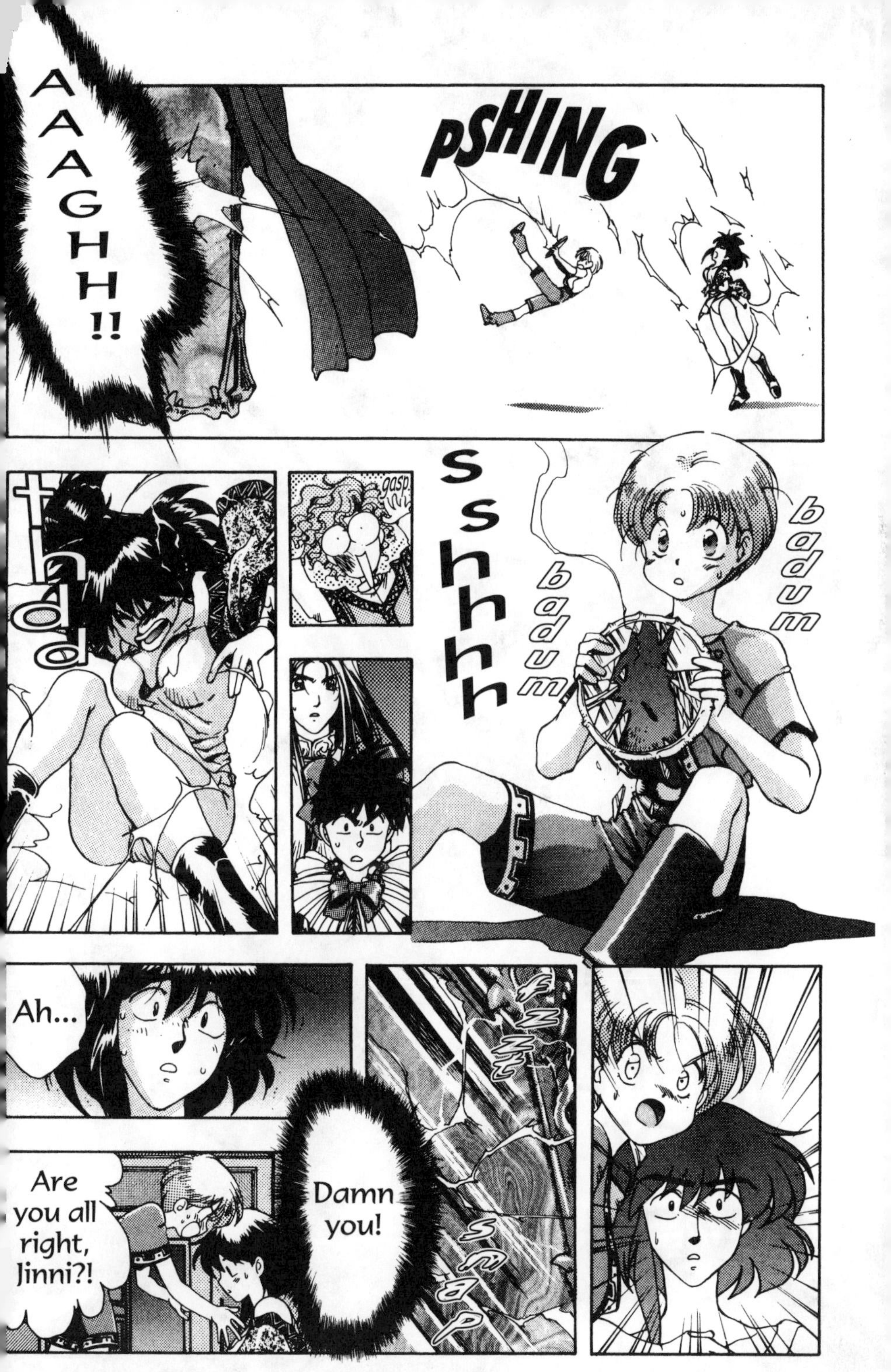

AAAGHH!!
PSHING
thdd
gasp
sshhhh
badum
badum
Ah...
Are you all right, Jinni?!
Damn you!
fzzzt
scrp

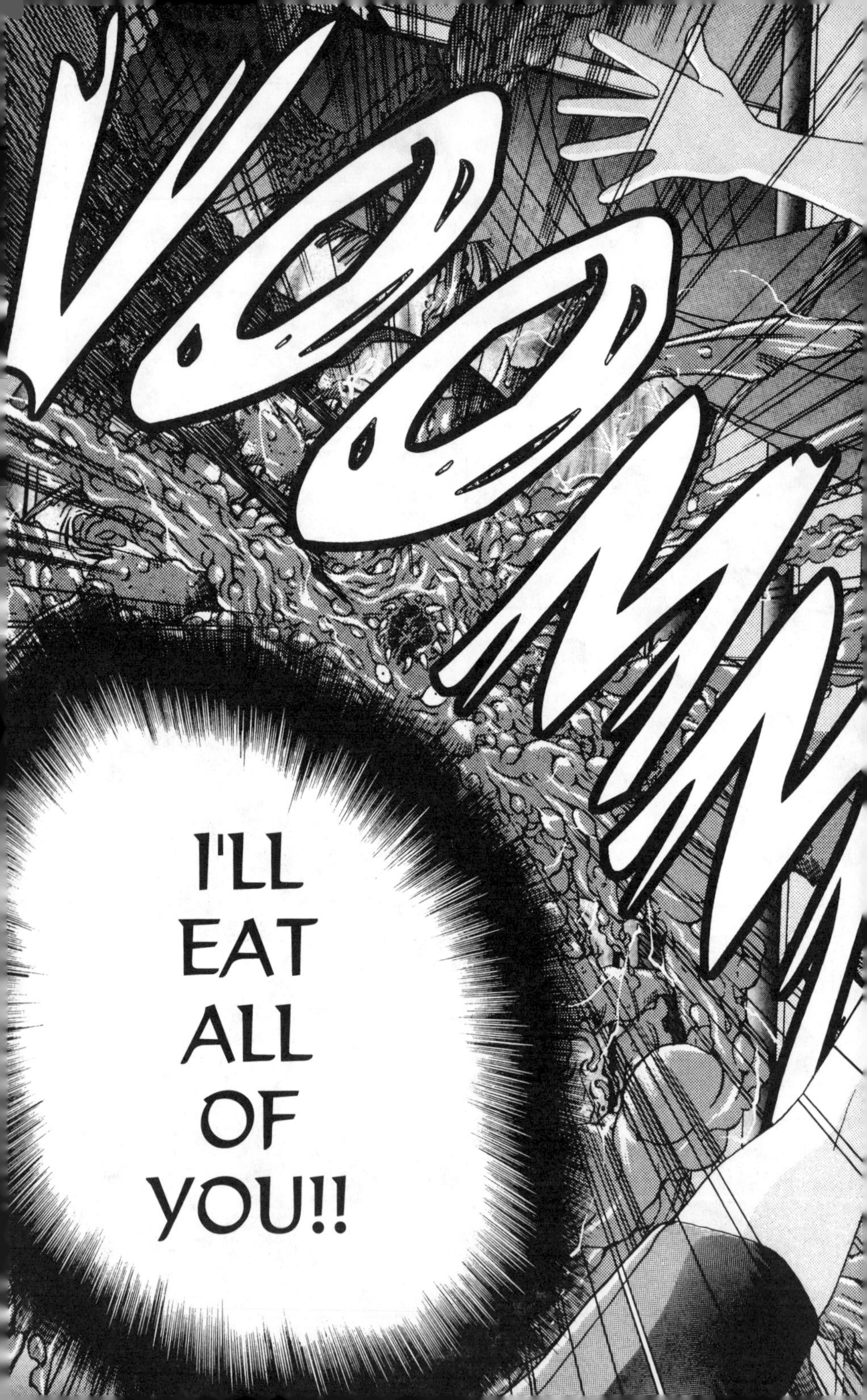
I'LL EAT ALL OF YOU!!

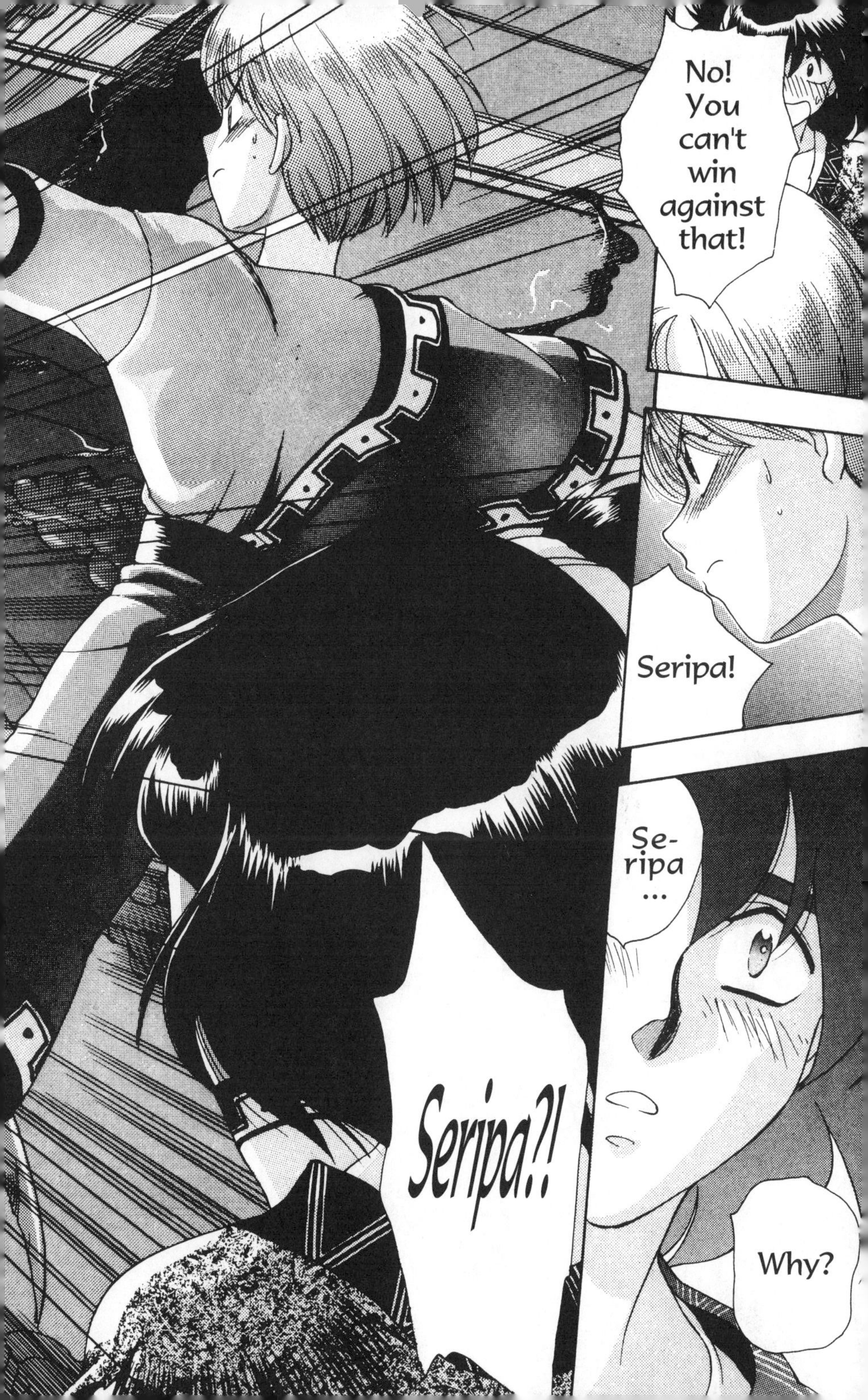
No! You can't win against that!
Seripa!
Se-ripa...
Why?
Seripa?!

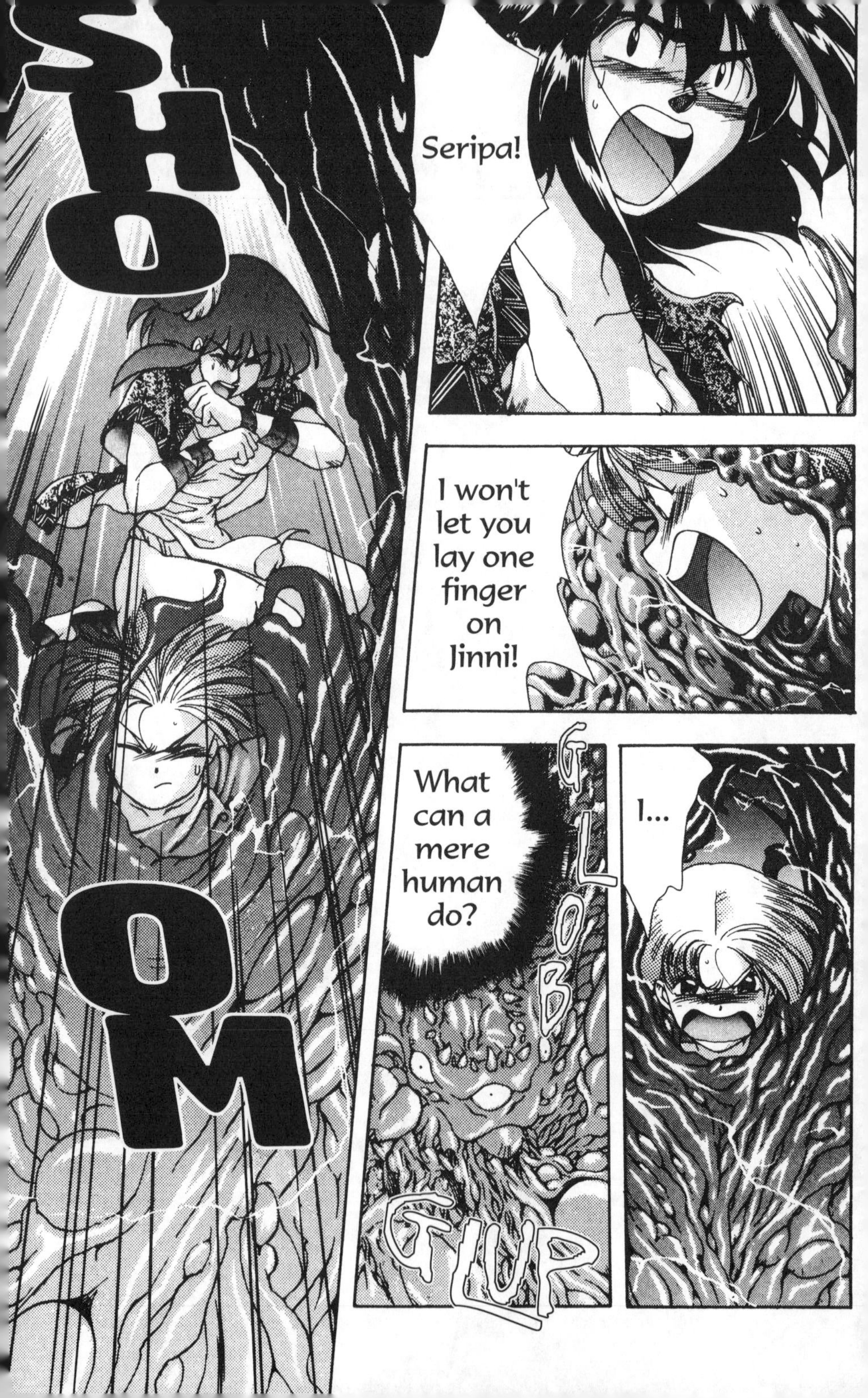
SHOOOM
Seripa!
I won't let you lay one finger on Jinni!
What can a mere human do?
GLOB
GLUP
I...

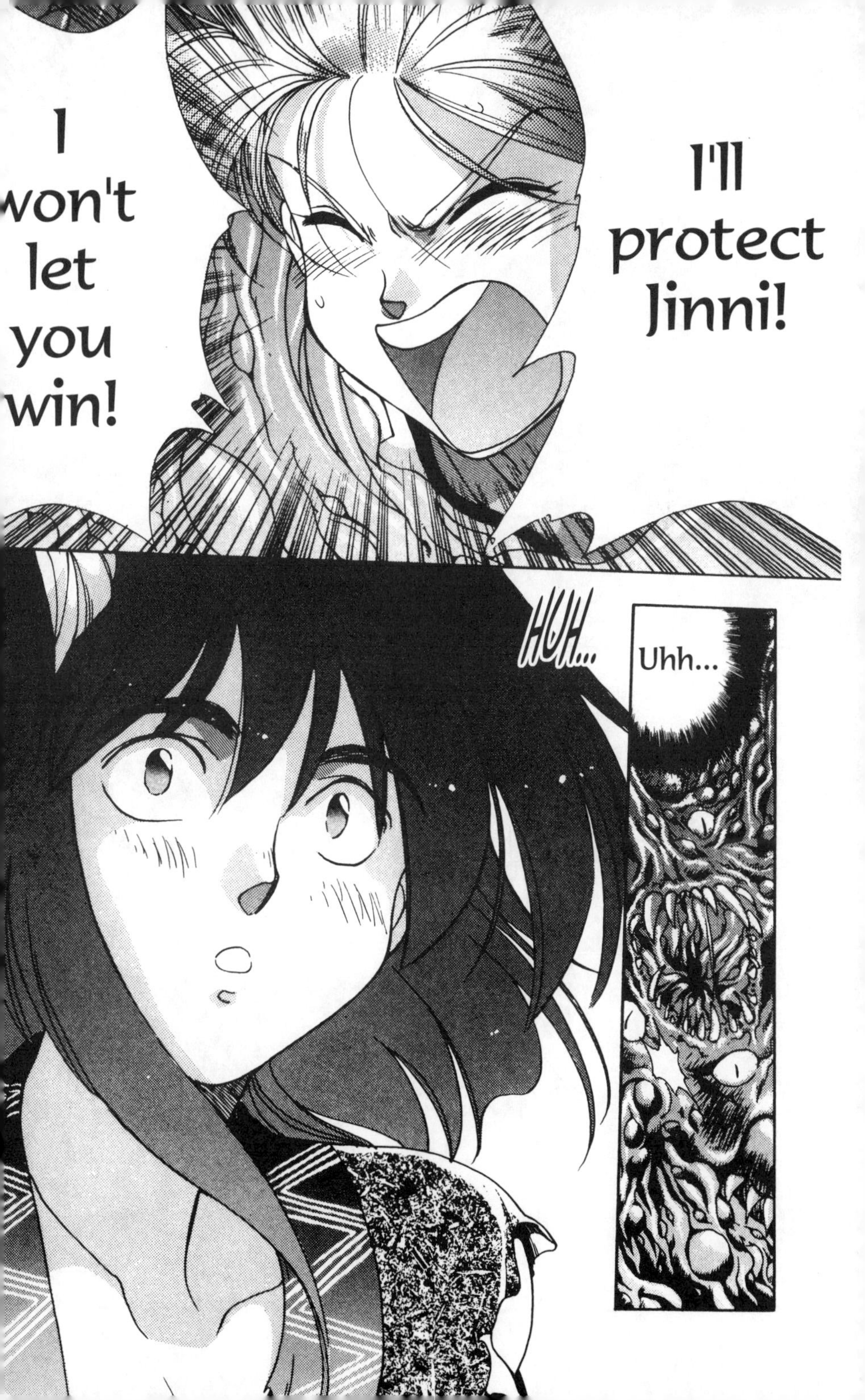
I won't let you win!
I'll protect Jinni!
HUH...
Uhh...

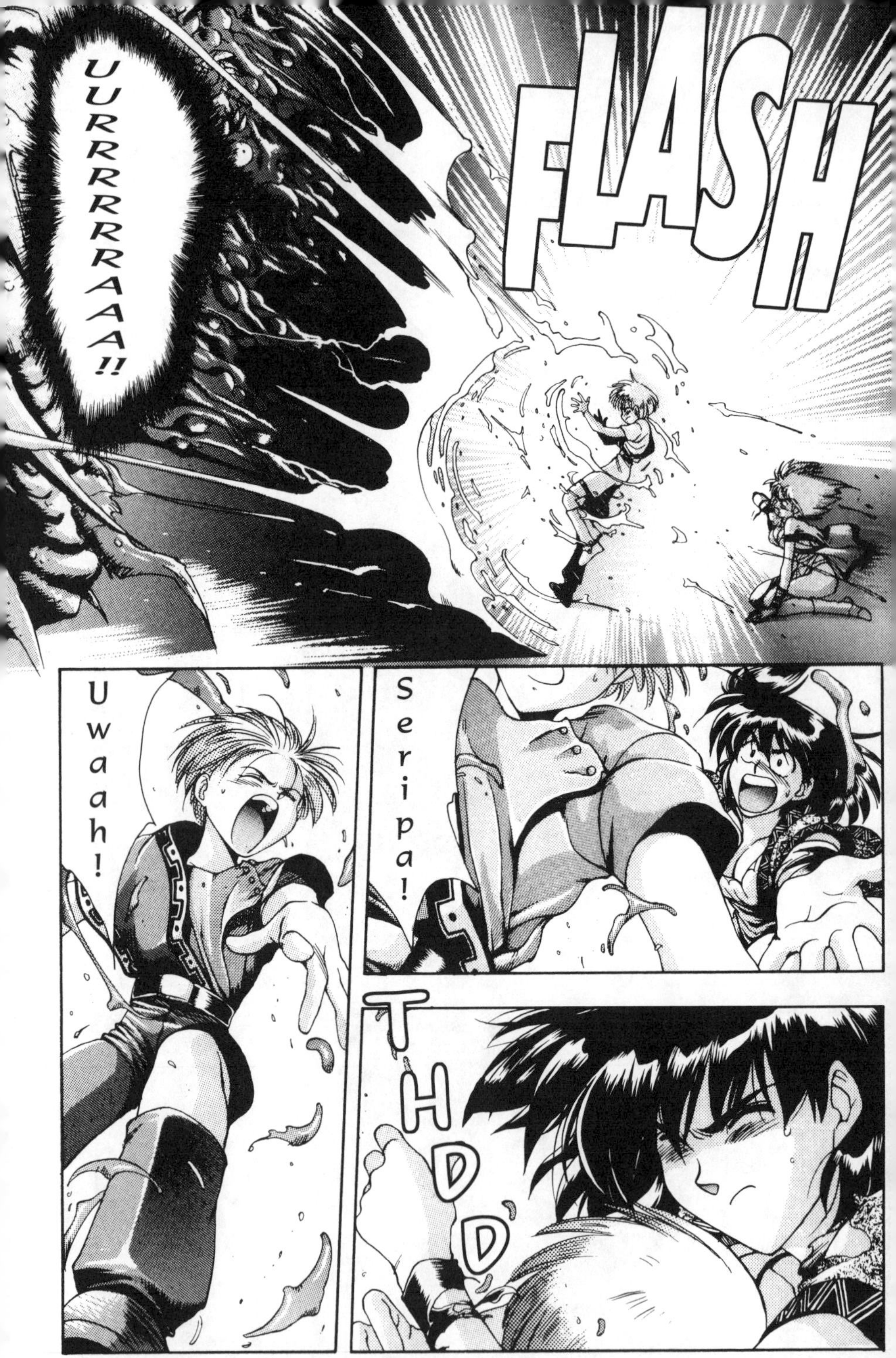
UURRRRRAAA!!
FLASH
Uwaah!
Seripa!
THDD

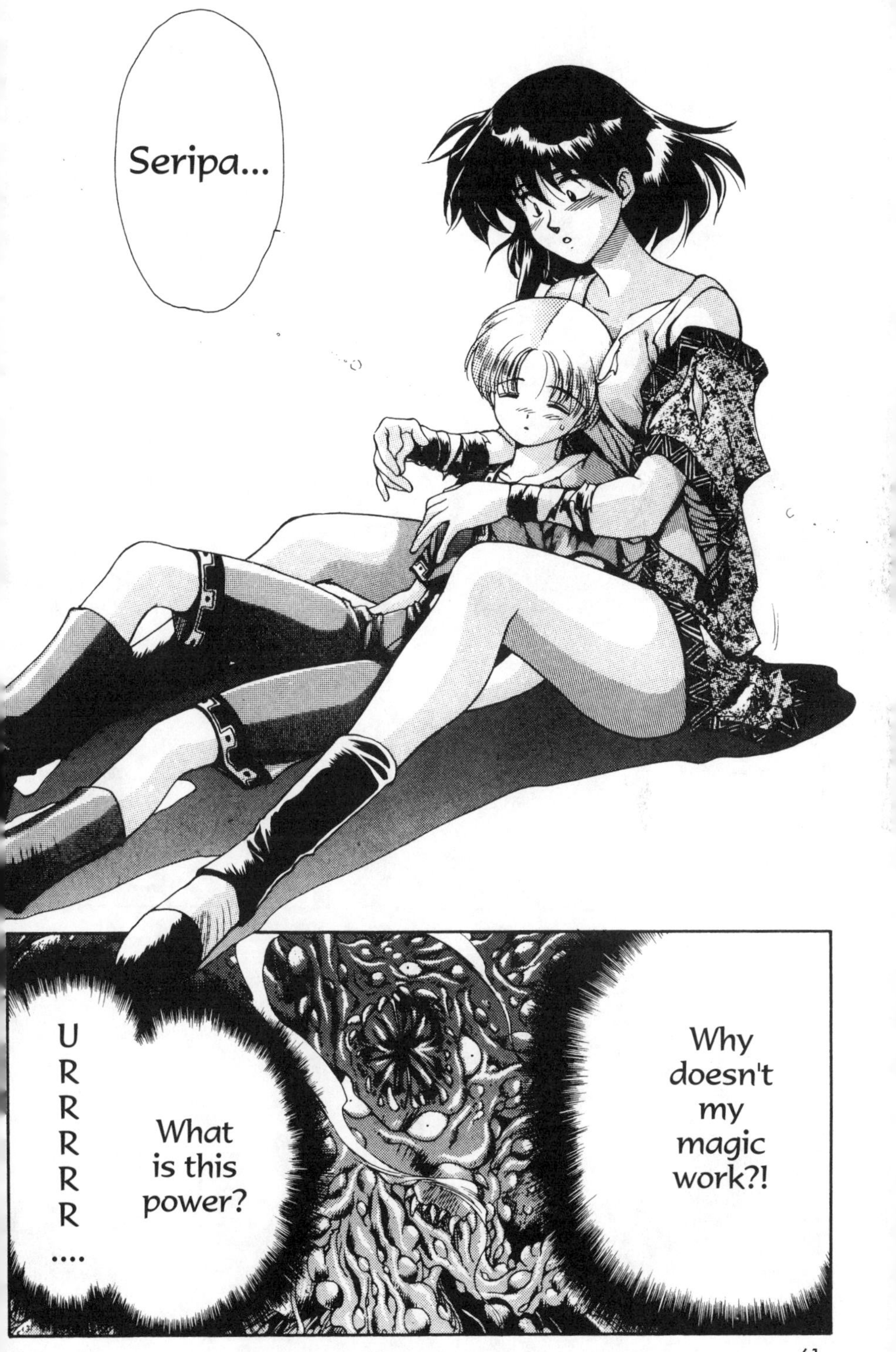
Seripa...
URRRRR....
What is this power?
Why doesn't my magic work?!

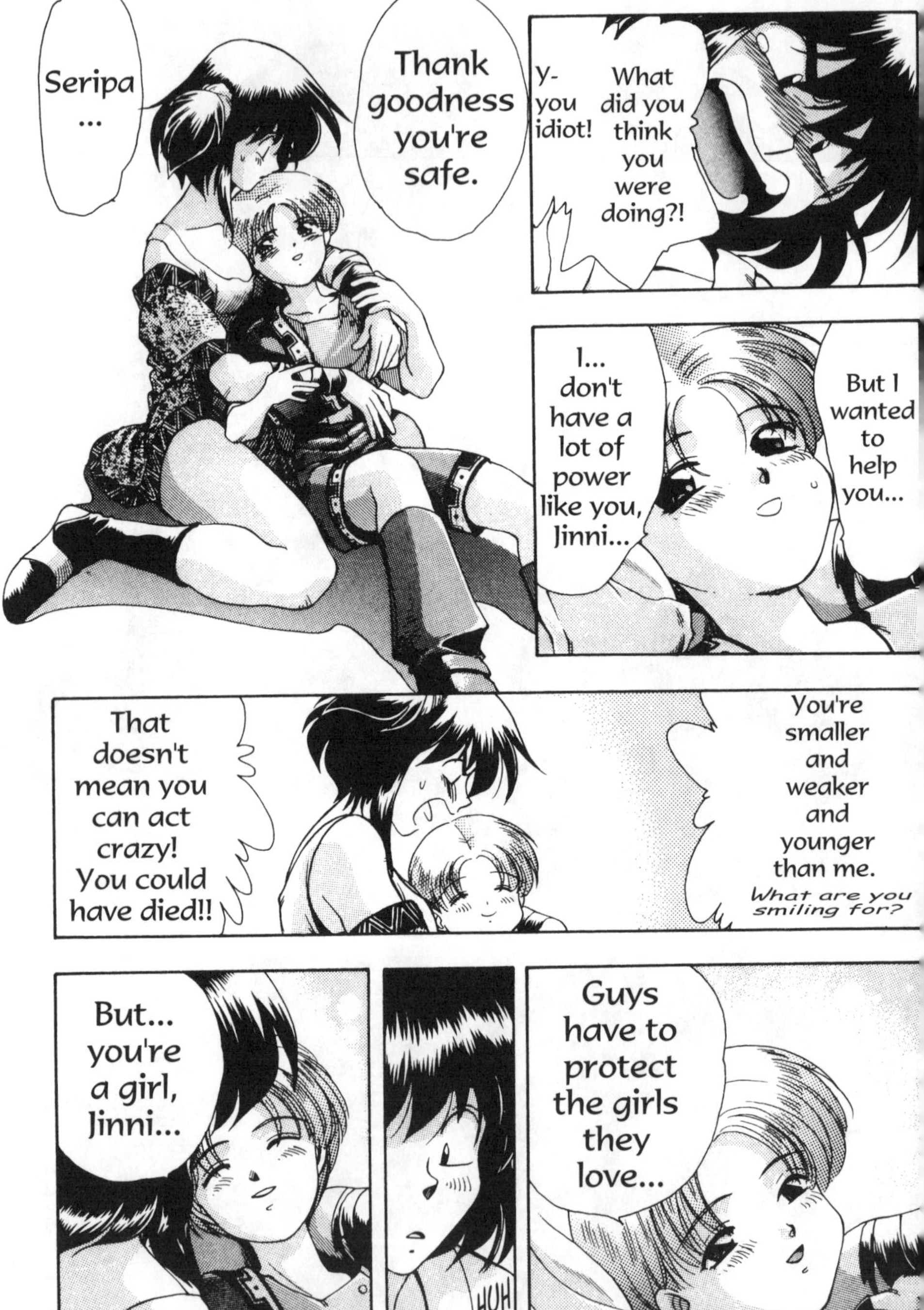
Seripa ...
Thank goodness you're safe.
Y- you idiot!
What did you think you were doing?!
I... don't have a lot of power like you, Jinni...
But I wanted to help you...
That doesn't mean you can act crazy! You could have died!!
You're smaller and weaker and younger than me.
What are you smiling for?
But... you're a girl, Jinni...
HUH
Guys have to protect the girls they love...

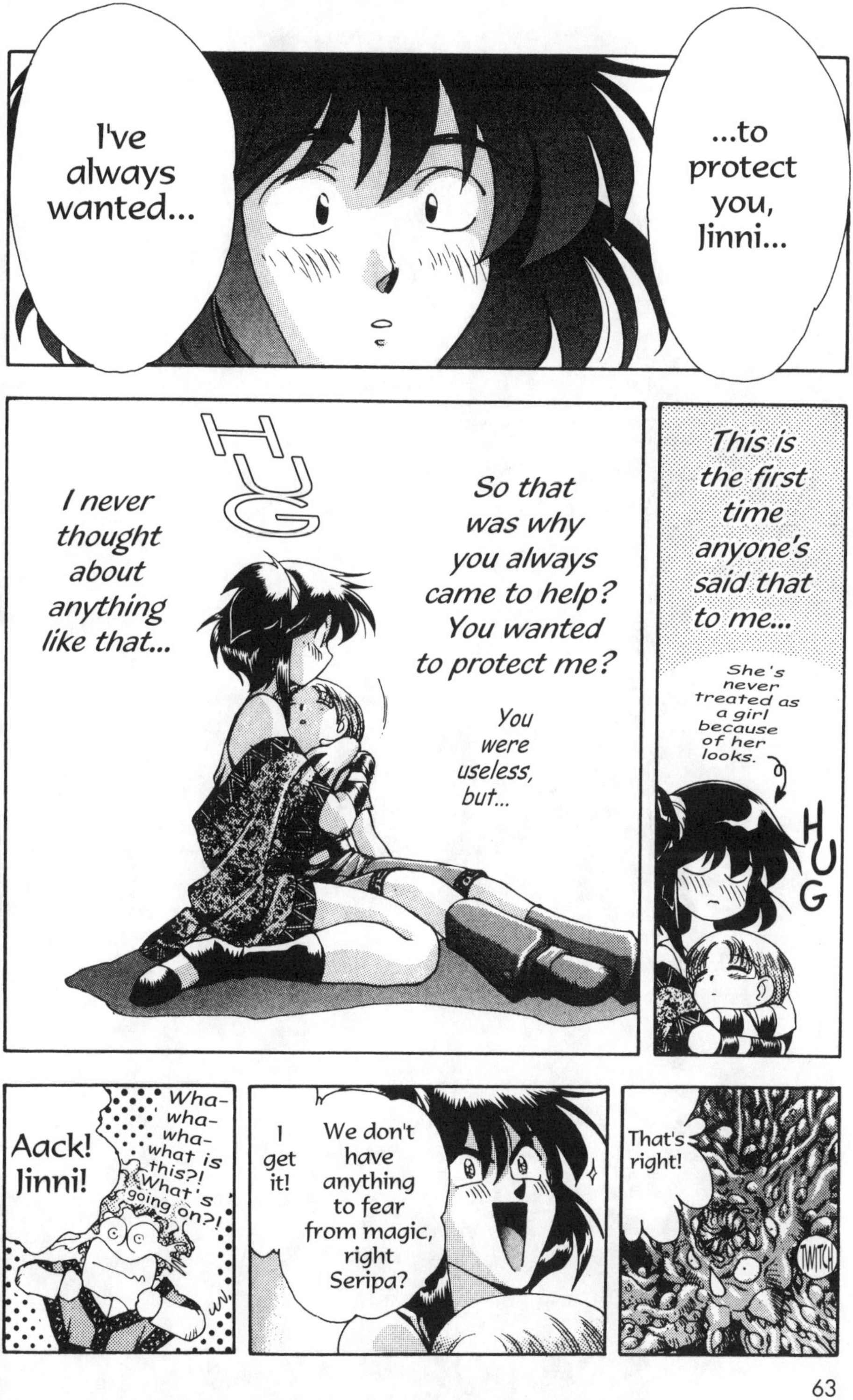

I've always wanted...
...to protect you, Jinni...
HUG
I never thought about anything like that...
So that was why you always came to help? You wanted to protect me?
You were useless, but...
This is the first time anyone's said that to me...
She's never treated as a girl because of her looks.
HUG
Aack! Jinni!
Wha-wha-wha-what is this?! What's going on?!
I get it!
We don't have anything to fear from magic, right Seripa?
That's right!
TWITCH

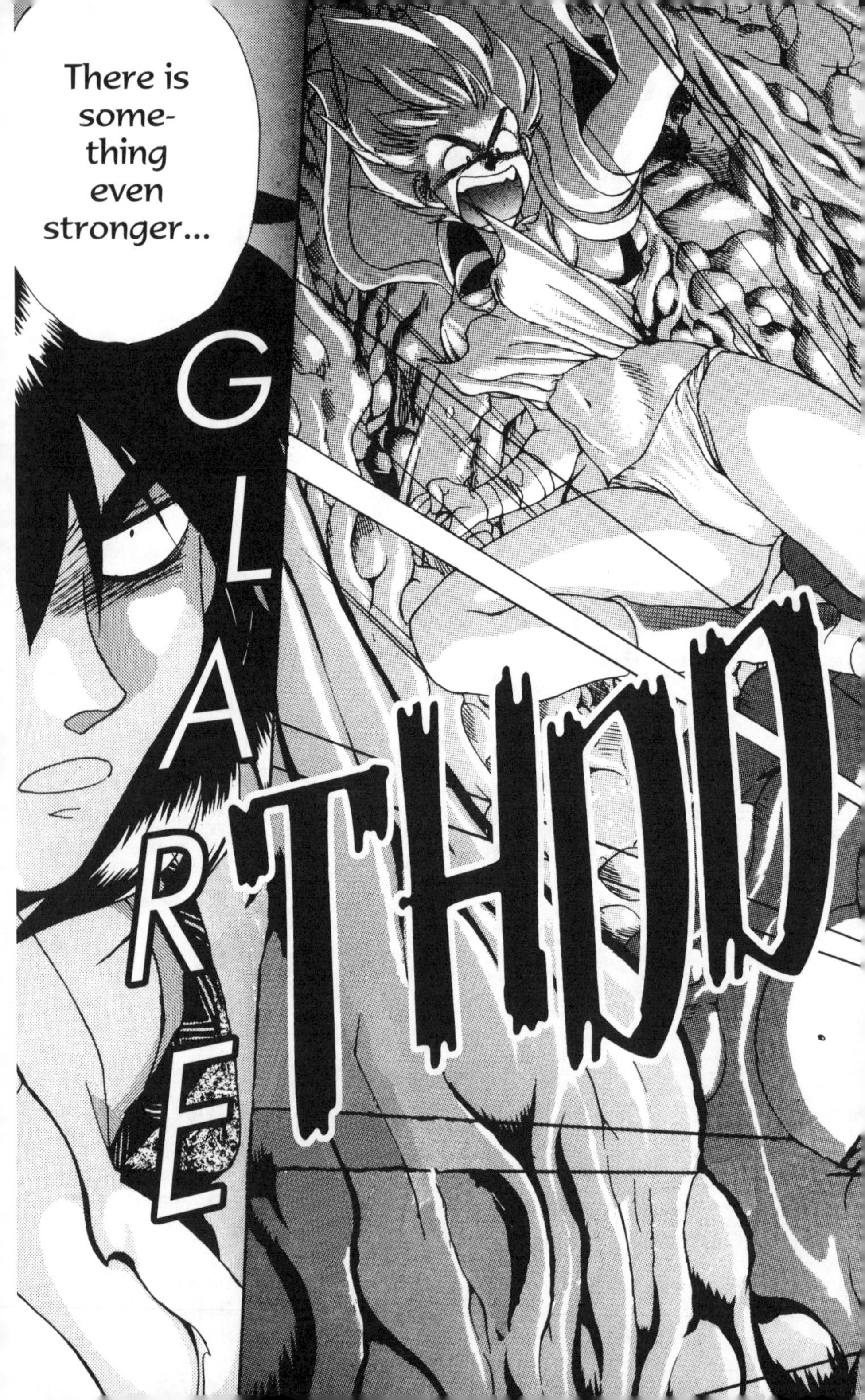
There is some-thing even stronger...
GLARE
THOOM

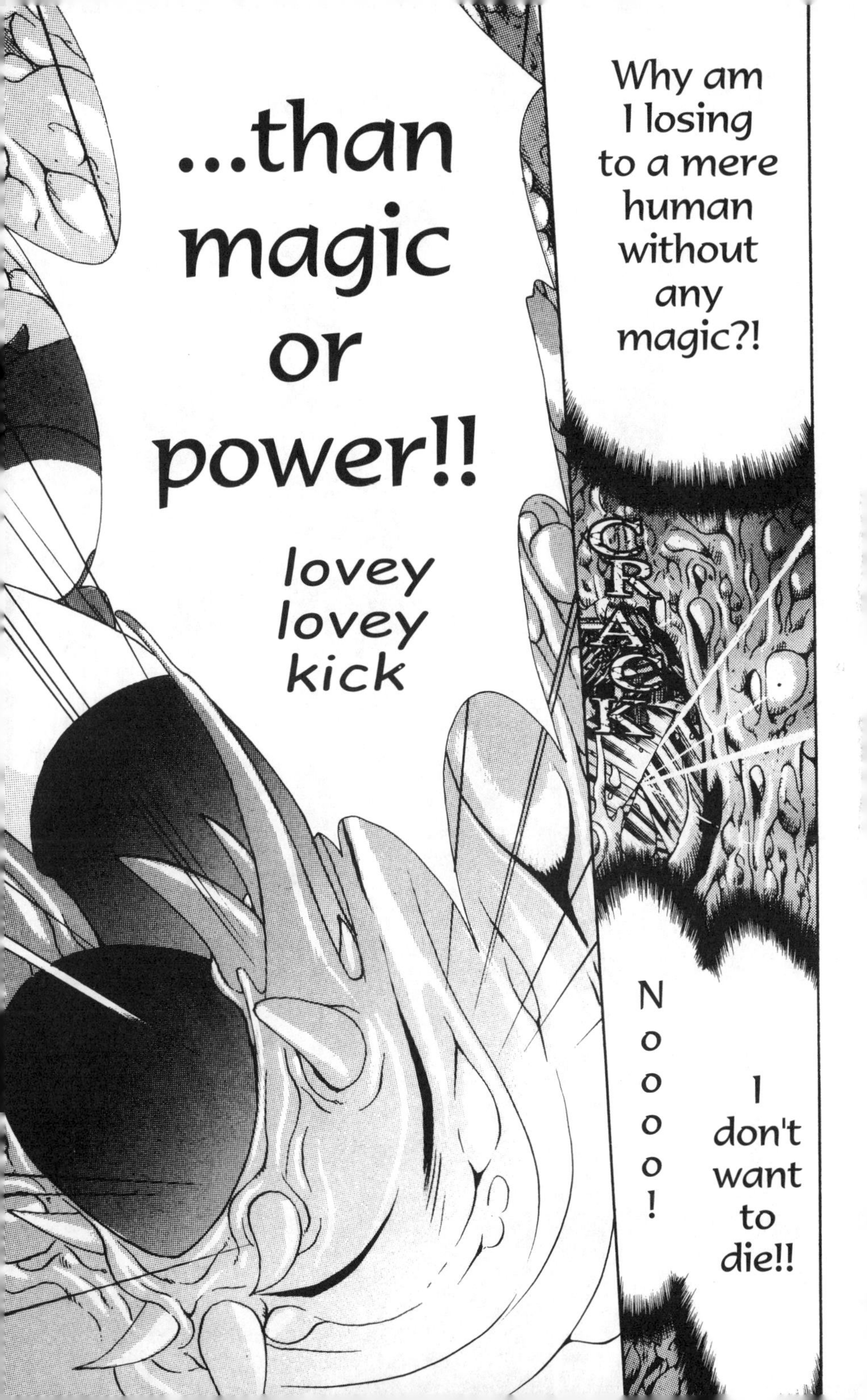
...than magic or power!!
lovey lovey kick
Why am I losing to a mere human without any magic?!
CRACK
Nooooo!
I don't want to die!!

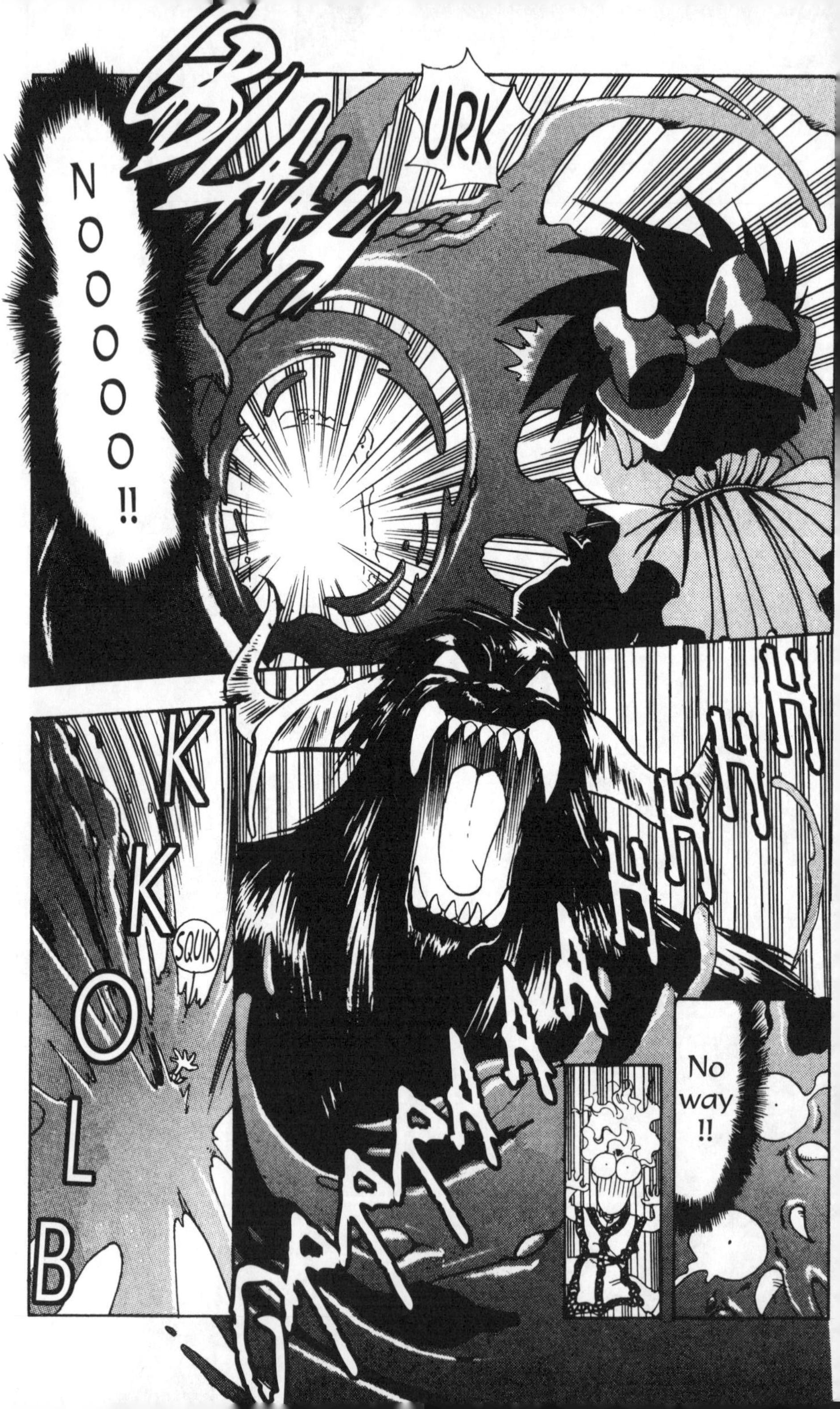
URK
BLAAAH
NOOOOOO!!
KKK
SQUIK
OLB
GRRRAAAAHHHHH
No way!!

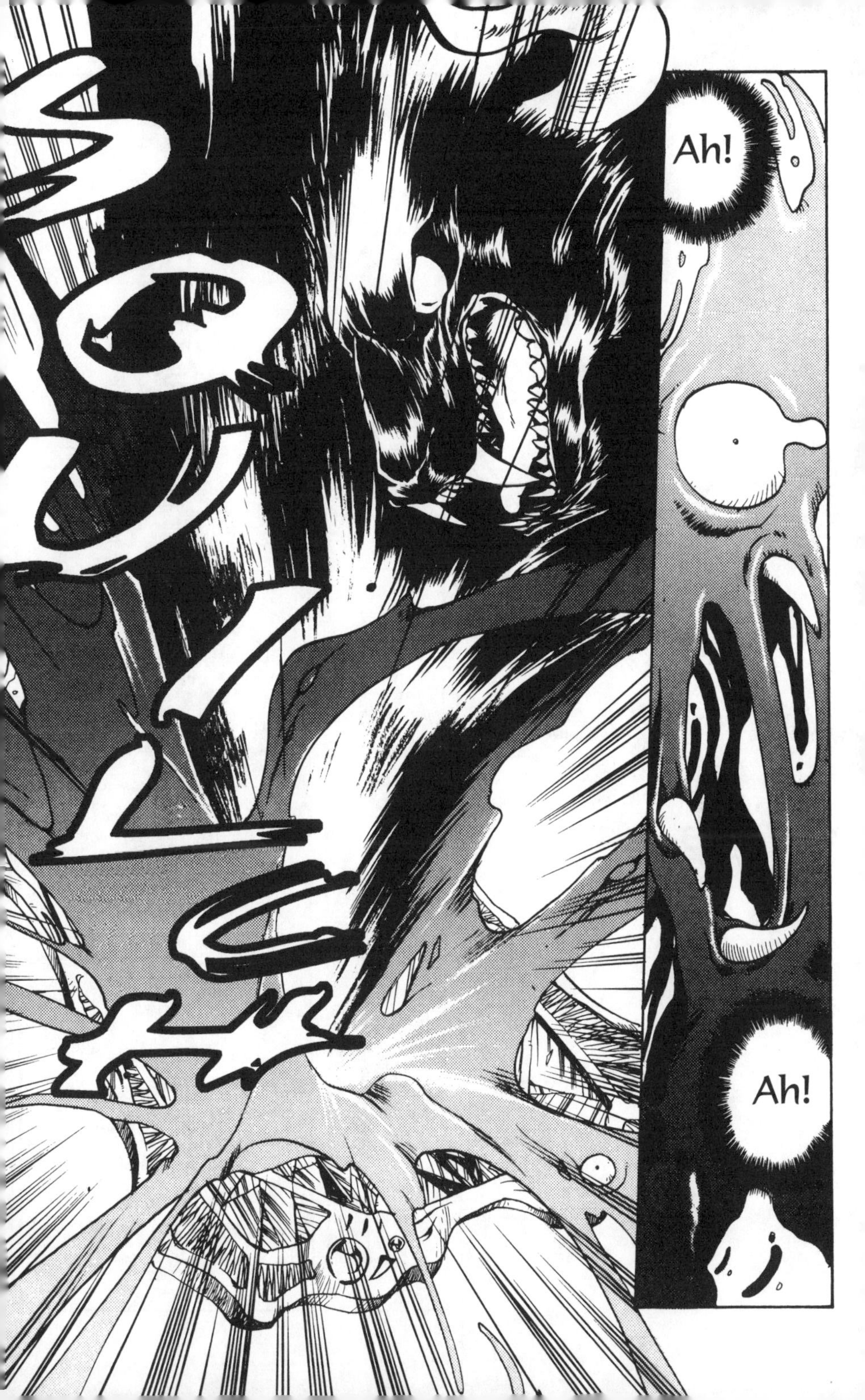
Ah!
Ah!

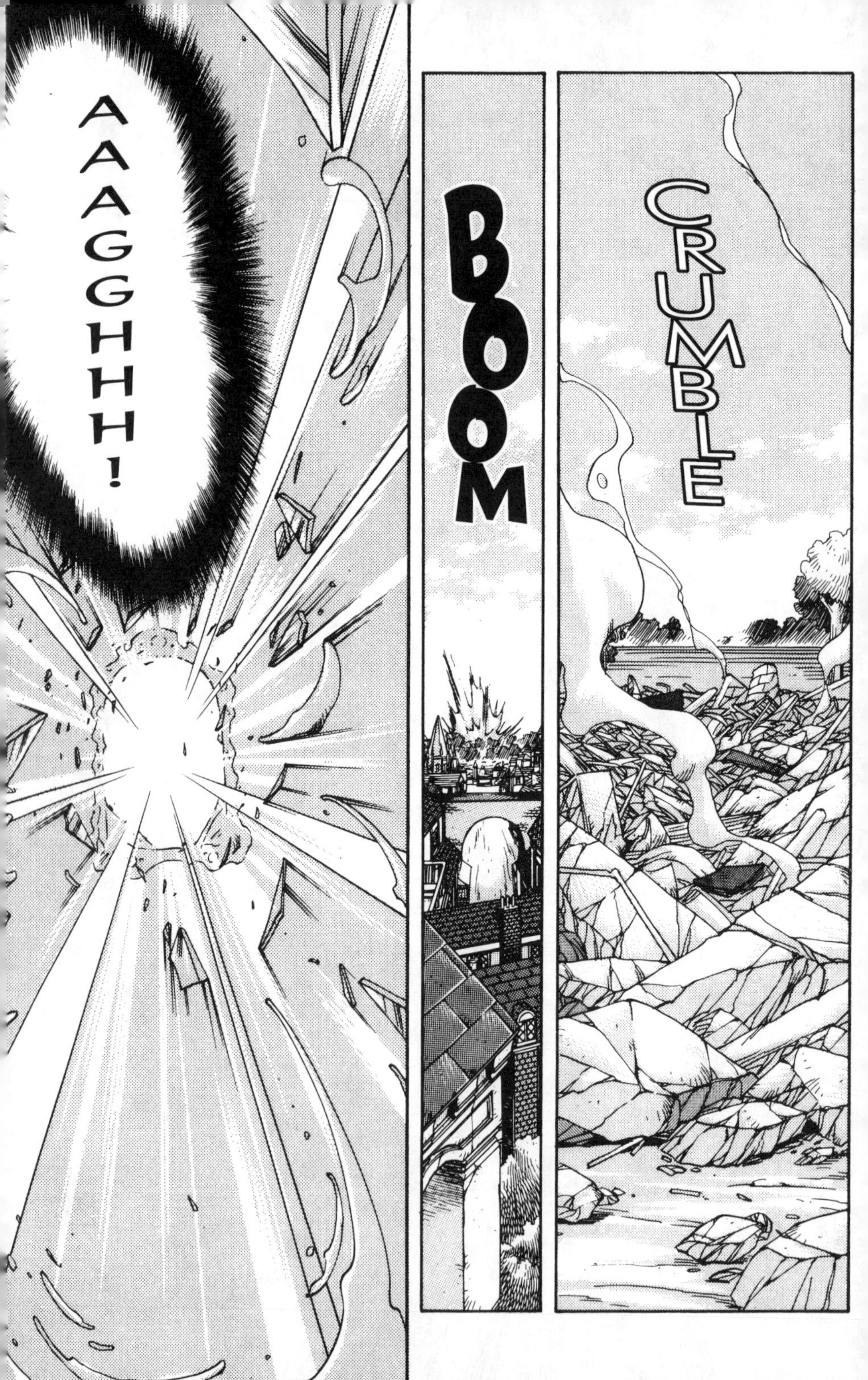
AAAGGHHH!
BOOM
CRUMBLE

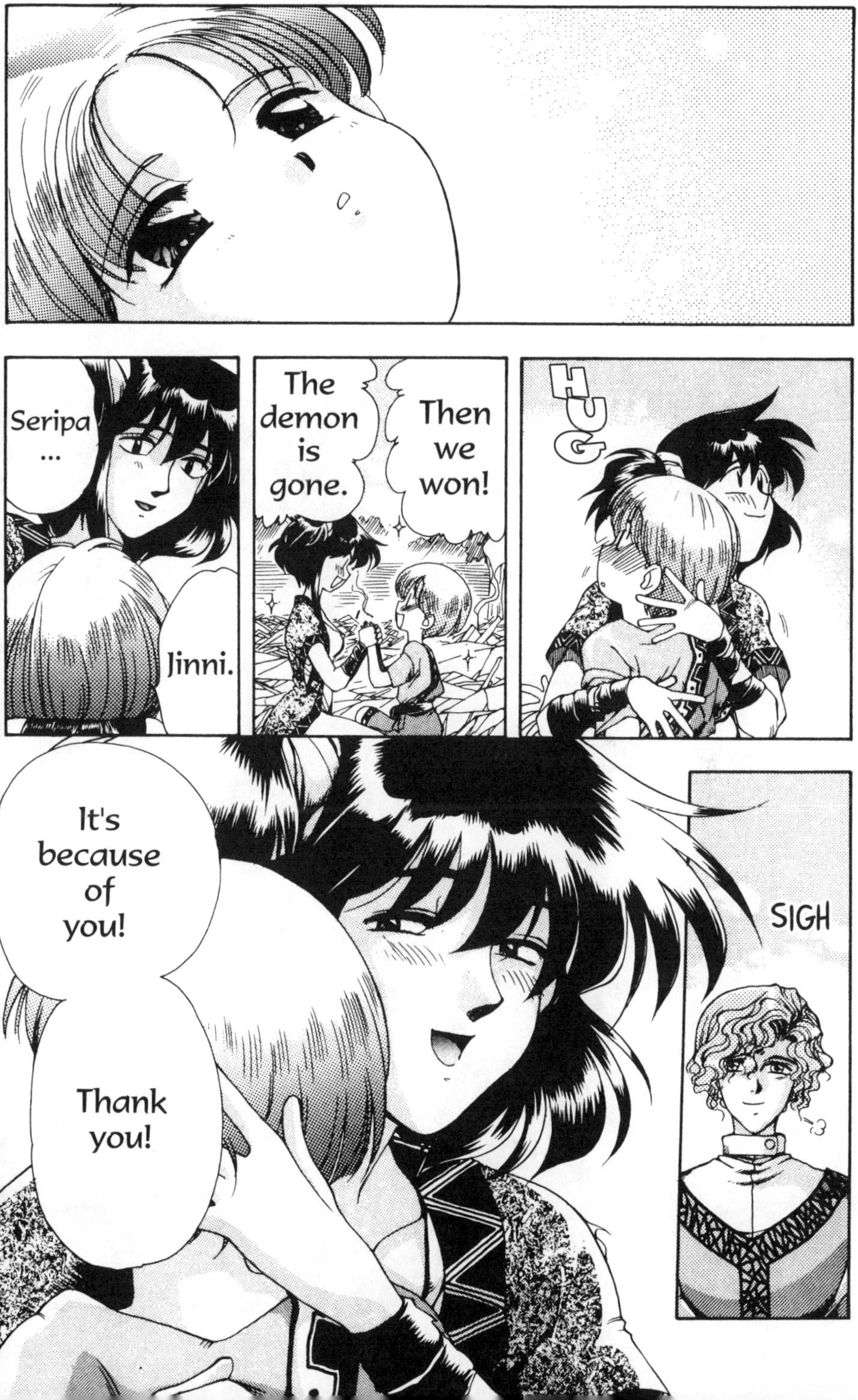

Seripa ...
Jinni.
The demon is gone.
Then we won!
HUG
It's because of you!
Thank you!
SIGH

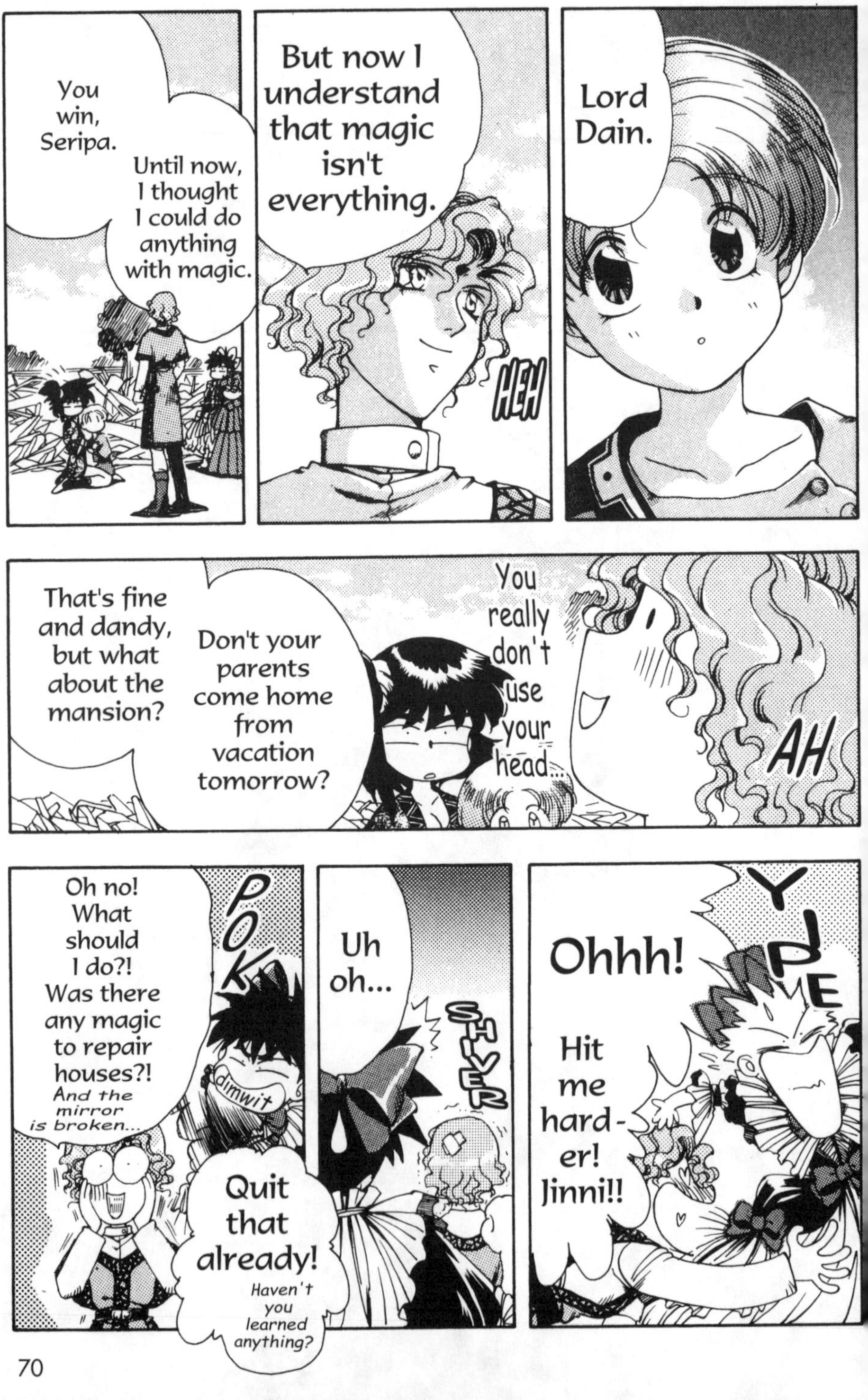

You win, Seripa.
Until now, I thought I could do anything with magic.
But now I understand that magic isn't everything.
HEH
Lord Dain.
That's fine and dandy, but what about the mansion?
Don't your parents come home from vacation tomorrow?
You really don't use your head...
AH
Oh no! What should I do?! Was there any magic to repair houses?!
And the mirror is broken...
POK
dimwit
Quit that already!
Haven't you learned anything?
Uh oh...
SHIVER
Ohhh!
YIPE
Hit me hard-er! Jinni!!

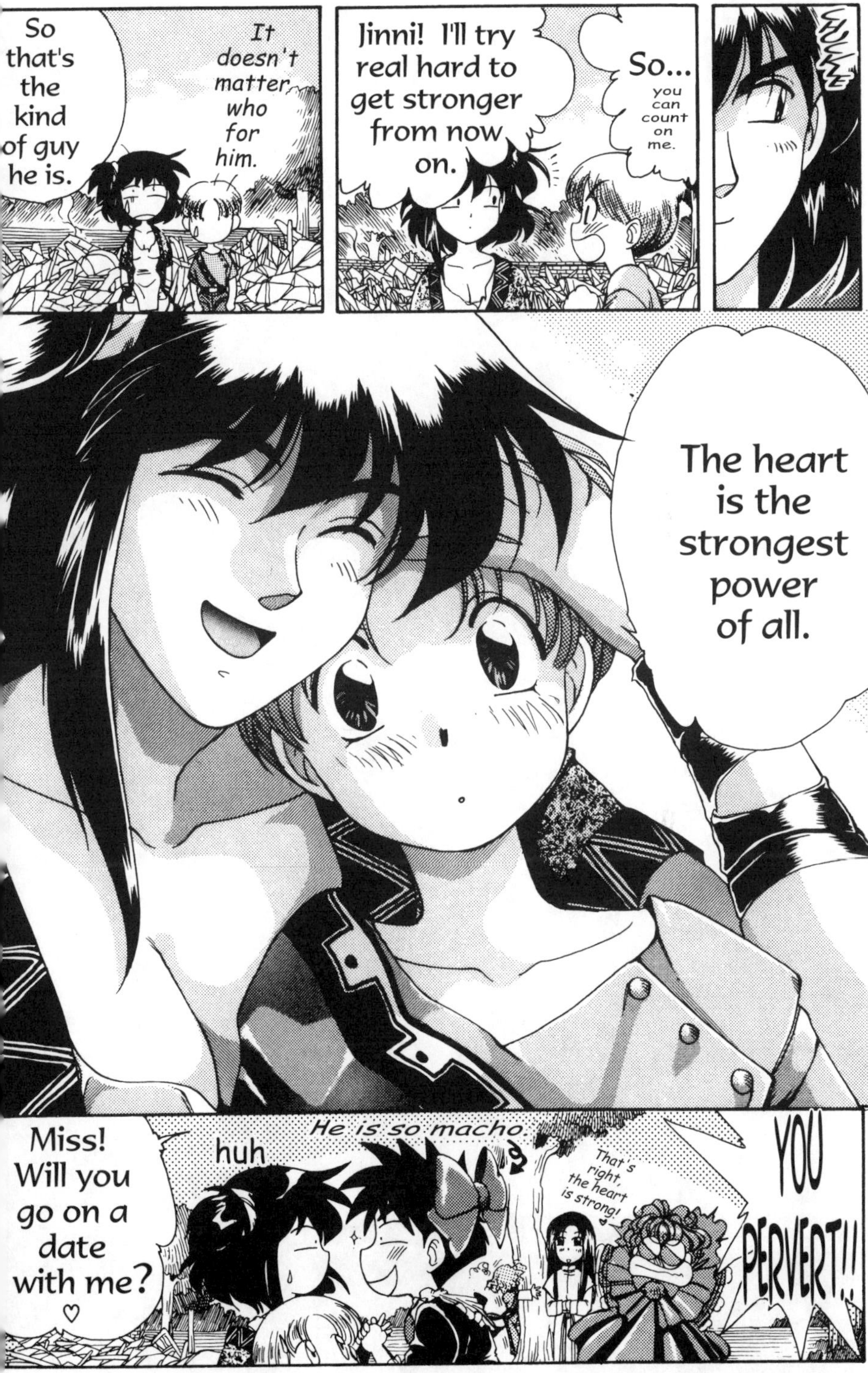
So that's the kind of guy he is.
It doesn't matter who for him.
Jinni! I'll try real hard to get stronger from now on.
So... you can count on me.
The heart is the strongest power of all.
Miss! Will you go on a date with me? ♡
huh
He is so macho.
That's right, the heart is strong! ♡
YOU PERVERT!!

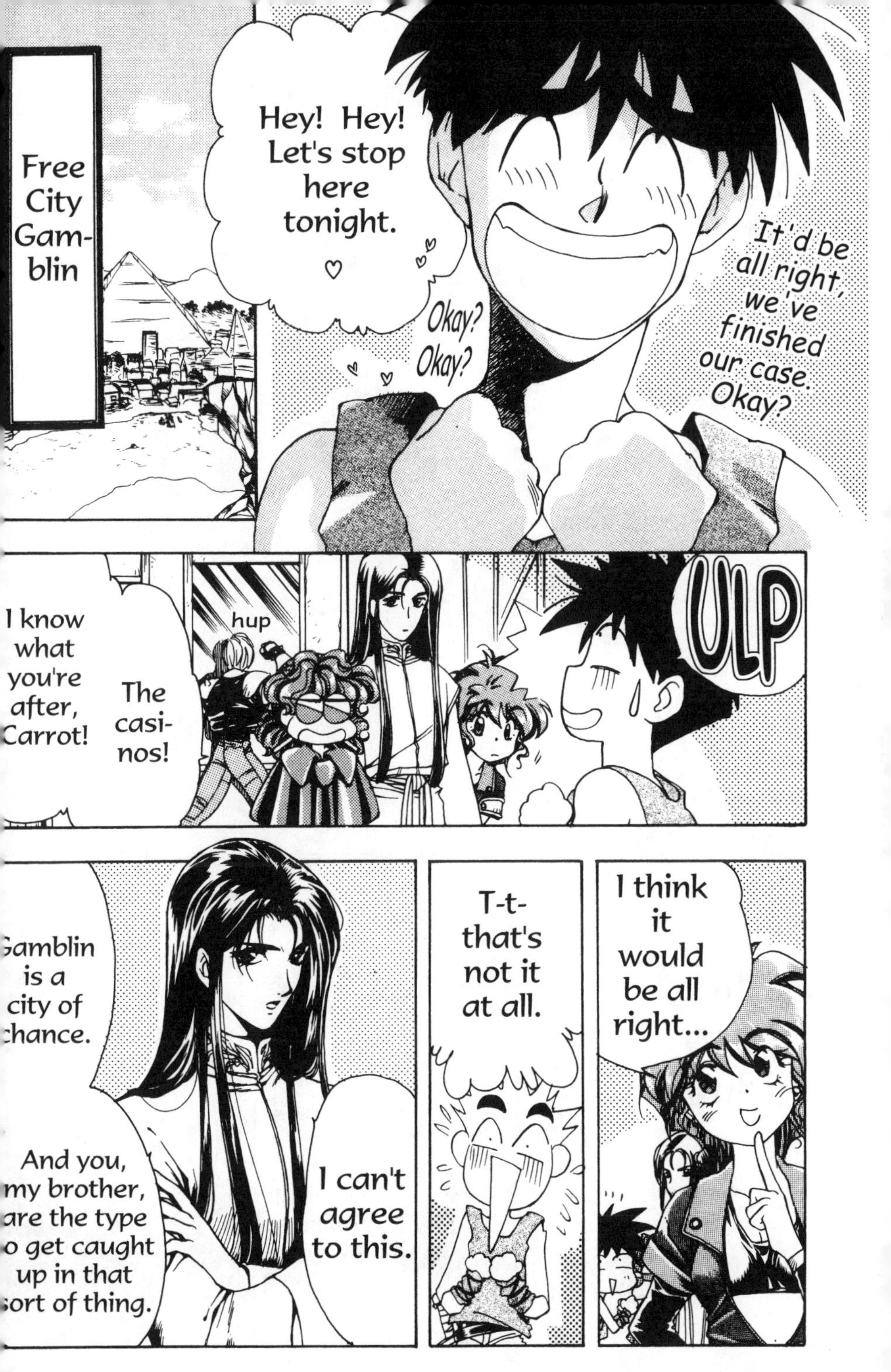
Free City Gamblin
Hey! Hey! Let's stop here tonight.
Okay? Okay?
It'd be all right, we've finished our case. Okay?
I know what you're after, Carrot!
The casinos!
hup
ULP
Gamblin is a city of chance.
And you, my brother, are the type to get caught up in that sort of thing.
I can't agree to this.
T-t-that's not it at all.
I think it would be all right...

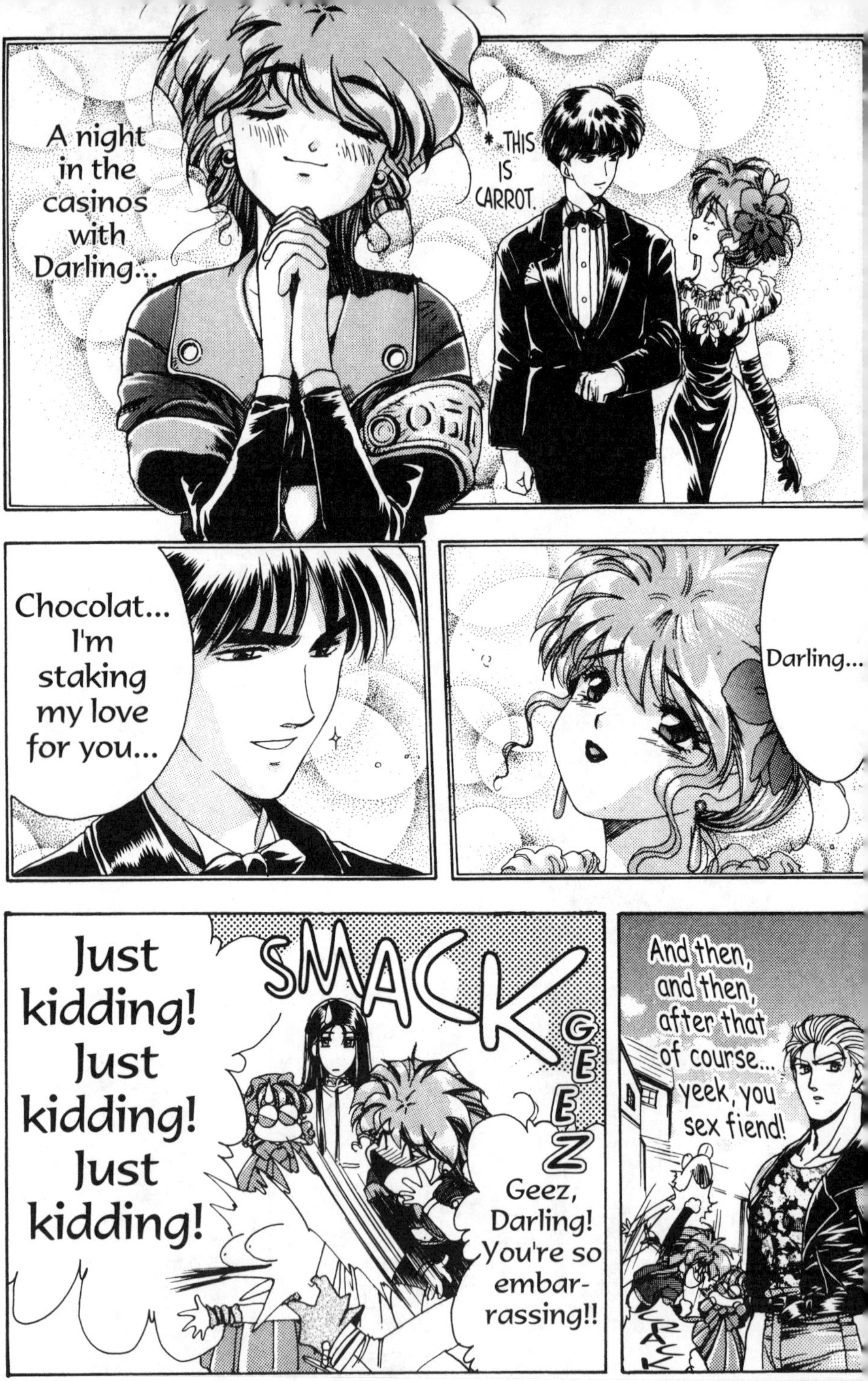
A night in the casinos with Darling...
* THIS IS CARROT.
Chocolat... I'm staking my love for you...
Darling...
Just kidding! Just kidding! Just kidding!
SMACK
GEEZ
Geez, Darling! You're so embar-rassing!!
And then, and then, after that of course... yeek, you sex fiend!
CRACK

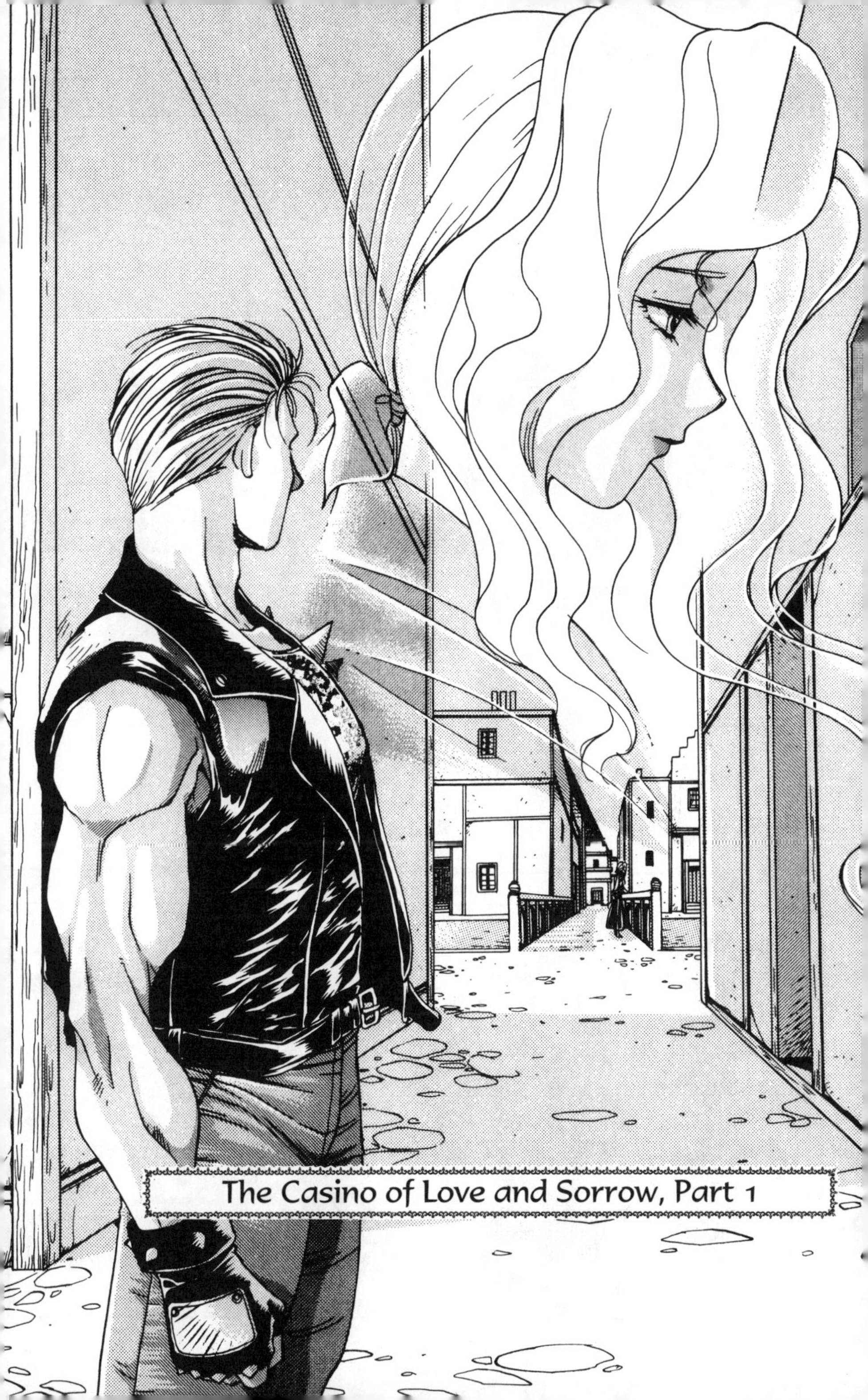
The Casino of Love and Sorrow, Part 1

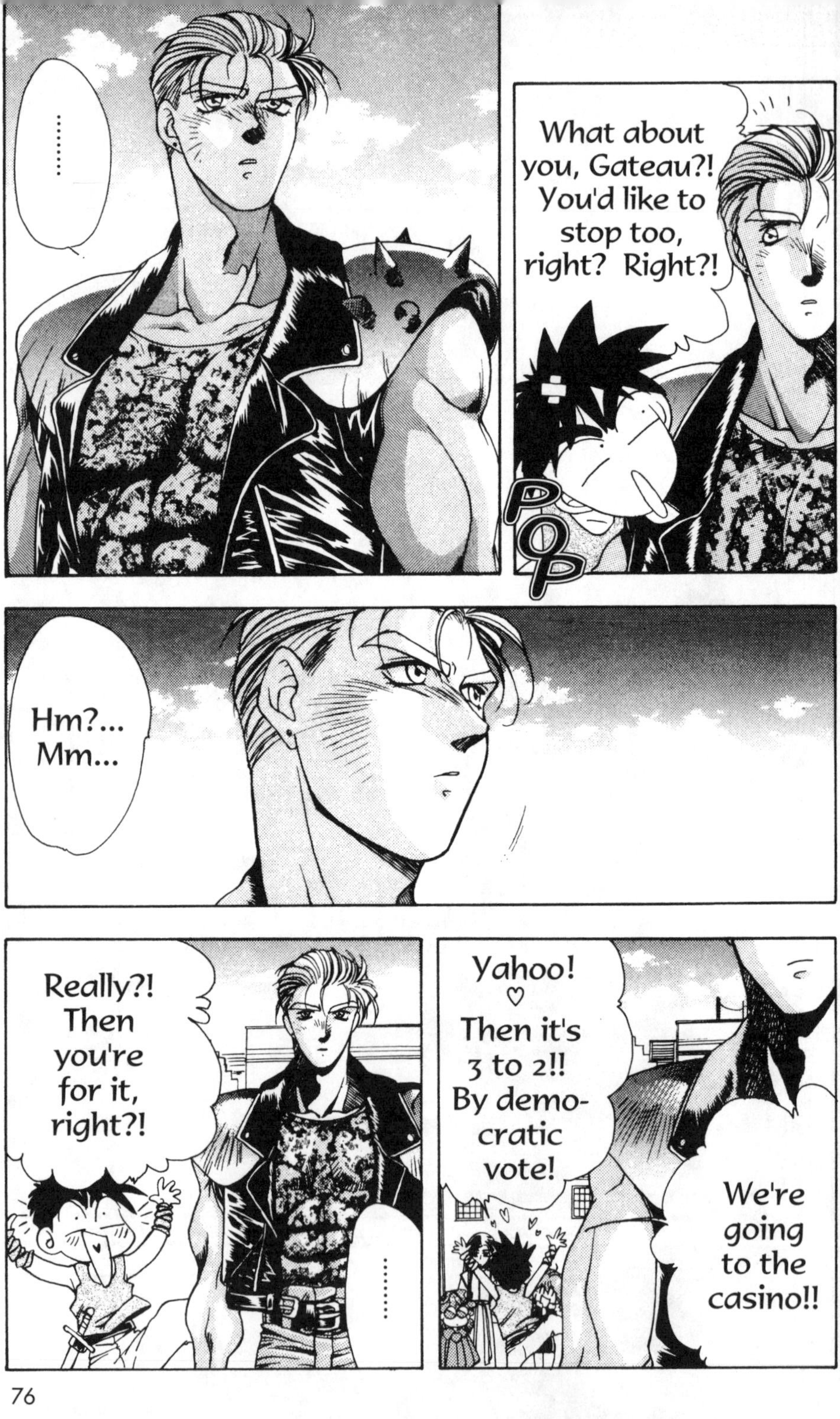
……
What about you, Gateau?! You'd like to stop too, right? Right?!
POP
Hm?... Mm...
Really?! Then you're for it, right?!
……
Yahoo! ♡ Then it's 3 to 2!! By demo-cratic vote!
We're going to the casino!!

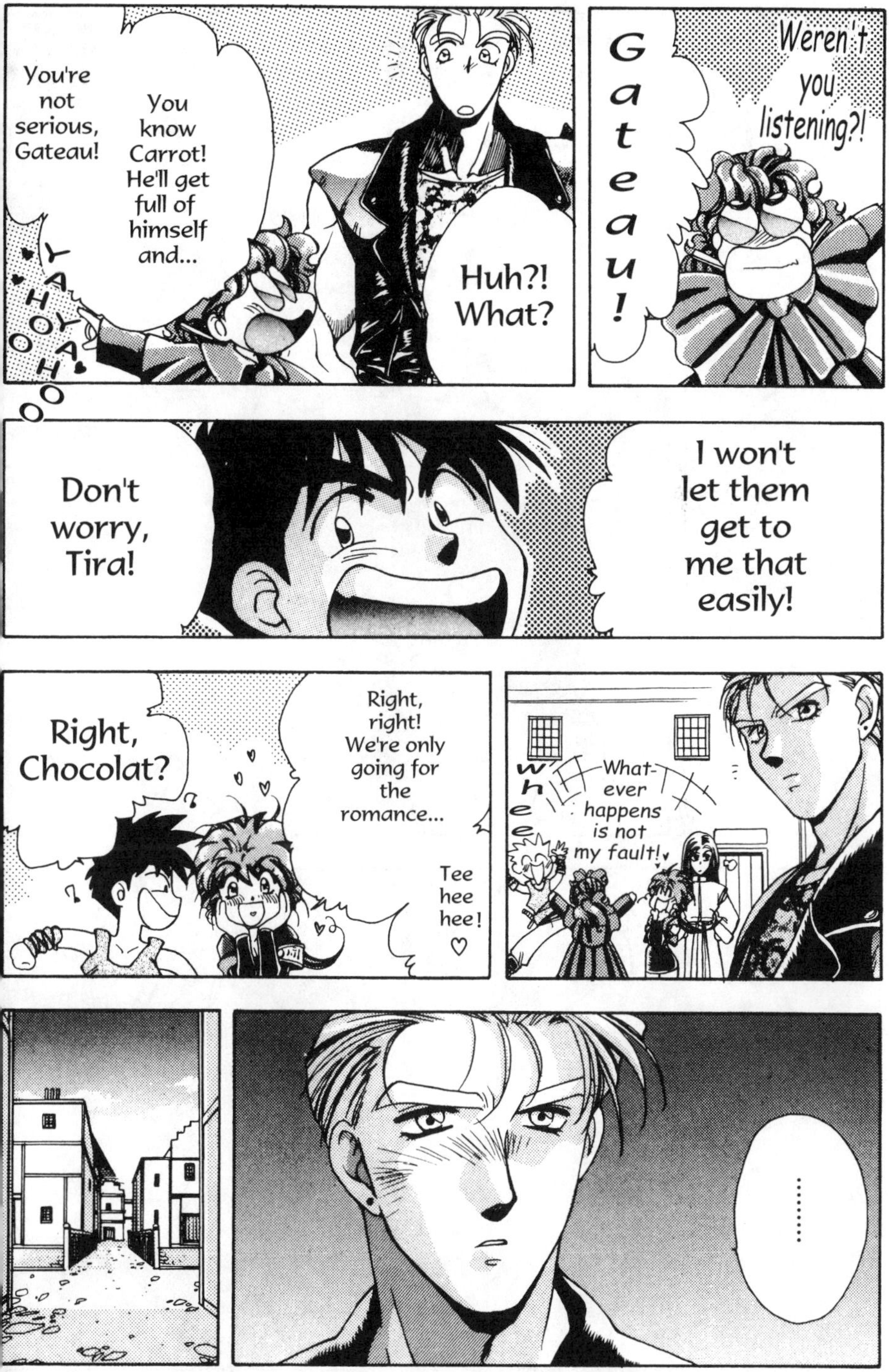
You're not serious, Gateau!
You know Carrot! He'll get full of himself and...
YAHOYAHOOO
Huh?! What?
Gateau!
Weren't you listening?!
Don't worry, Tira!
I won't let them get to me that easily!
Right, Chocolat?
Right, right! We're only going for the romance...
Tee hee hee!
whee
Whatever happens is not my fault!
....

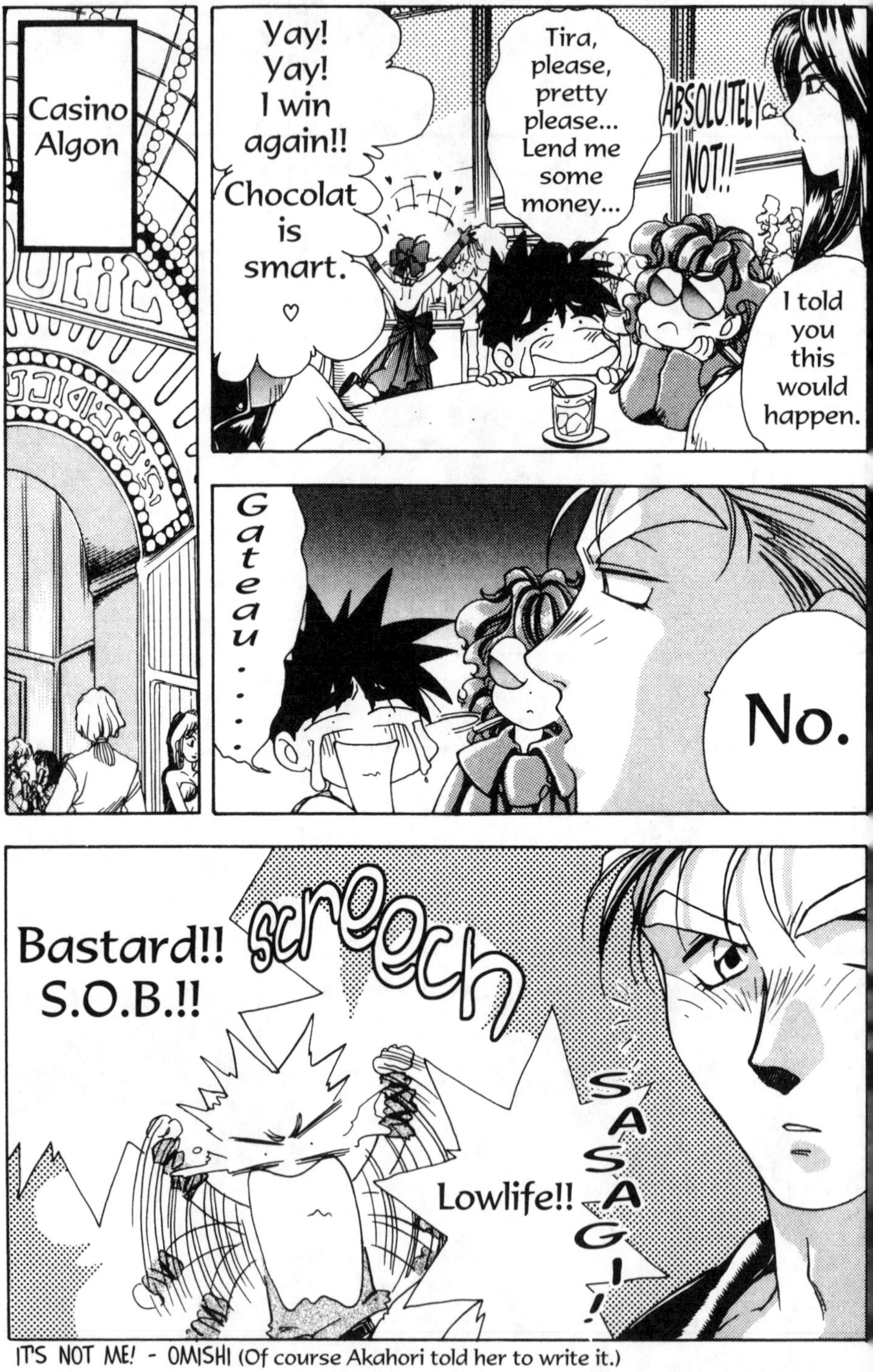
Casino Algon
Yay! Yay! I win again!! Chocolat is smart. ♡
Tira, please, pretty please... Lend me some money...
ABSOLUTELY NOT!!
I told you this would happen.
Gateau.....
No.
screech
Bastard!! S.O.B.!!
Lowlife!!
SASAGI!

IT'S NOT ME! - OMISHI (Of course Akahori told her to write it.)

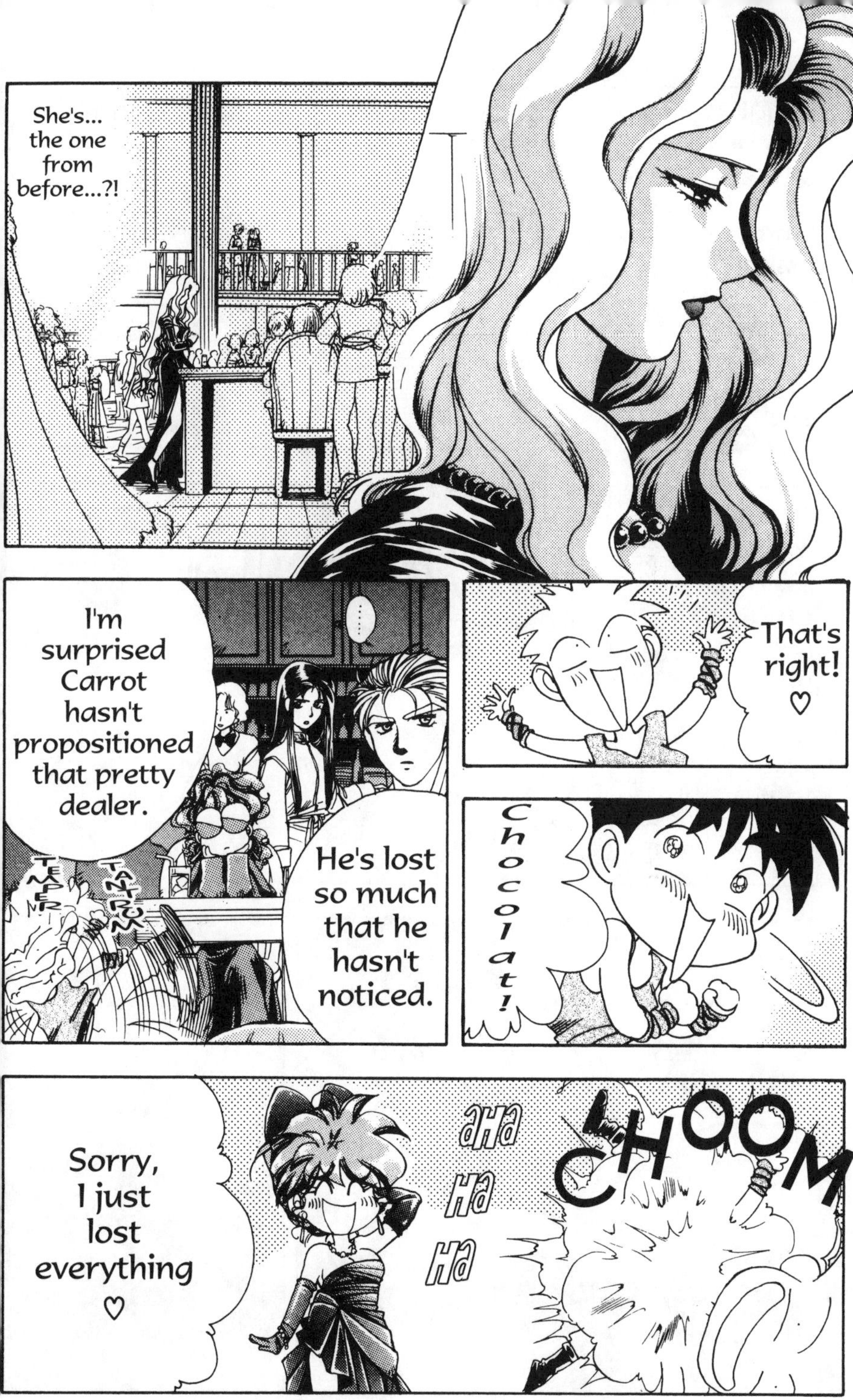
She's... the one from before...?!
I'm surprised Carrot hasn't propositioned that pretty dealer.
......
TEMPER
TANTRUM
He's lost so much that he hasn't noticed.
That's right! ♡
Chocolat!
Sorry, I just lost everything ♡
aHa Ha Ha
CHOOM

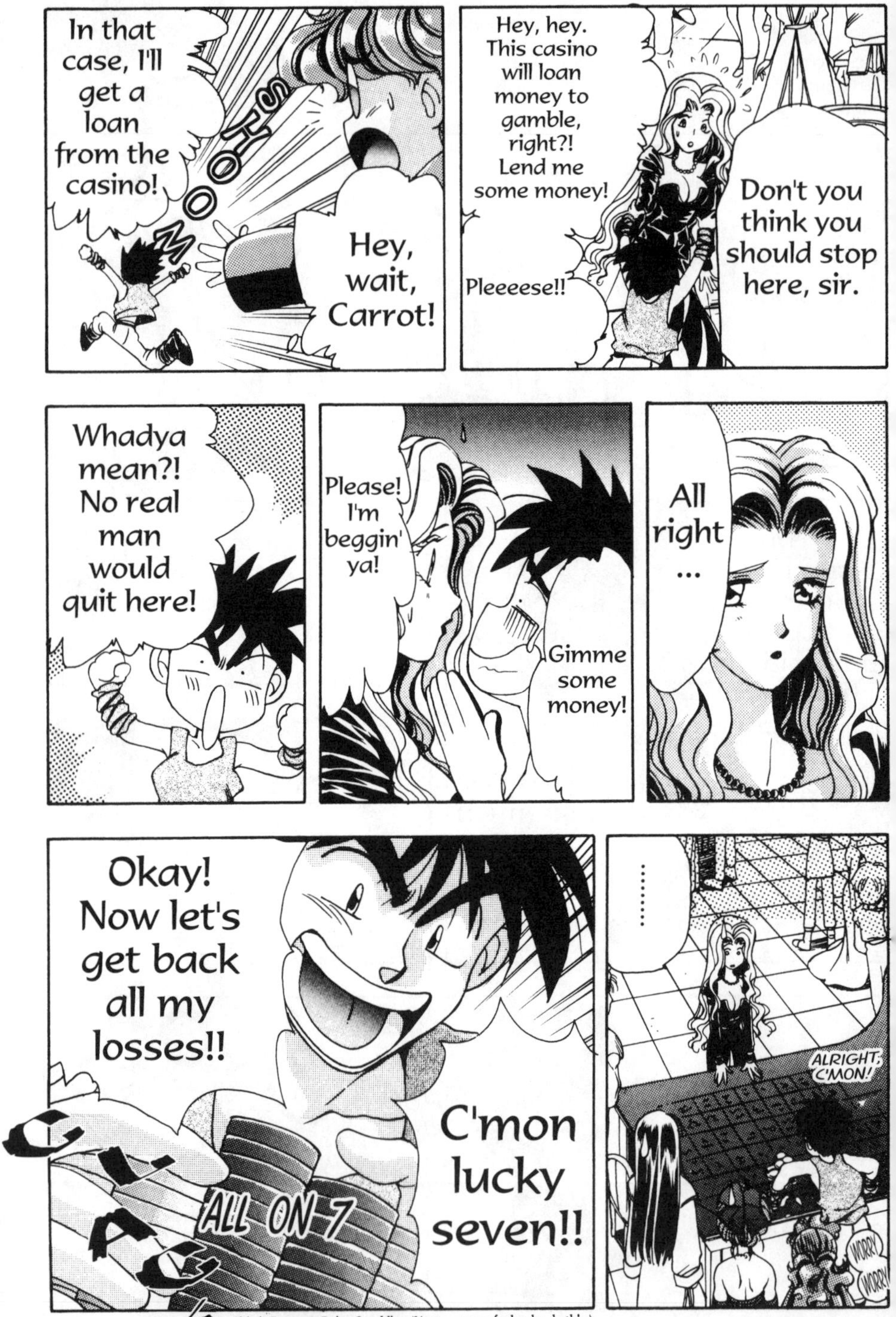
In that case, I'll get a loan from the casino!
SHOOOM
Hey, wait, Carrot!
Hey, hey. This casino will loan money to gamble, right?! Lend me some money!
Pleeeese!!
Don't you think you should stop here, sir.
Whadya mean?! No real man would quit here!
Please! I'm beggin' ya!
Gimme some money!
All right ...
Okay! Now let's get back all my losses!!
ALL ON 7
C'mon lucky seven!!
....
ALRIGHT, C'MON!
WORRY
WORRY
This is Demon's Point Gambling (Not too many fools who do this.)

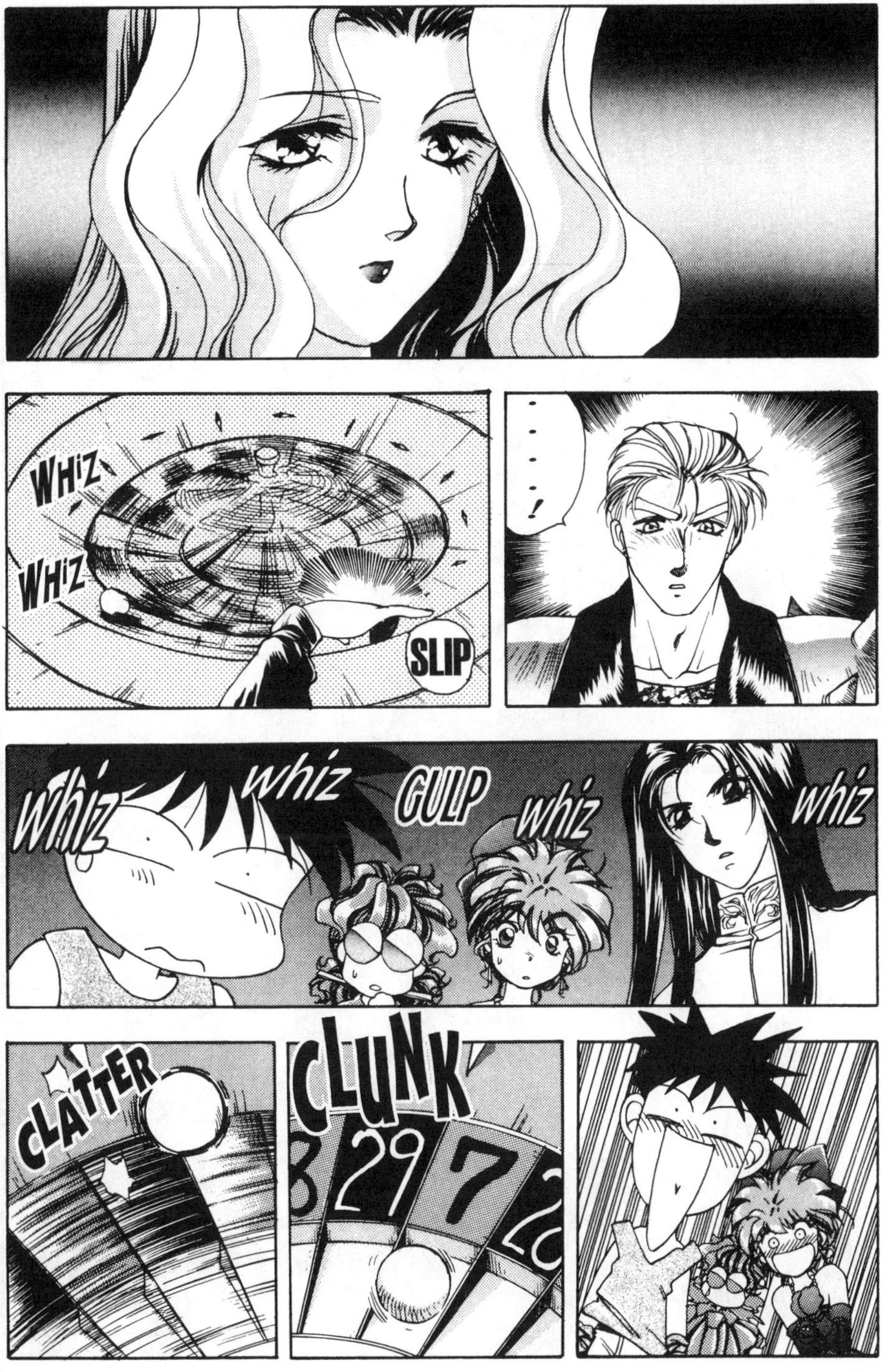
WHIZ
WHIZ
SLIP
.....!
whiz
whiz
GULP
whiz
whiz
CLATTER
CLUNK
8
29
7
28

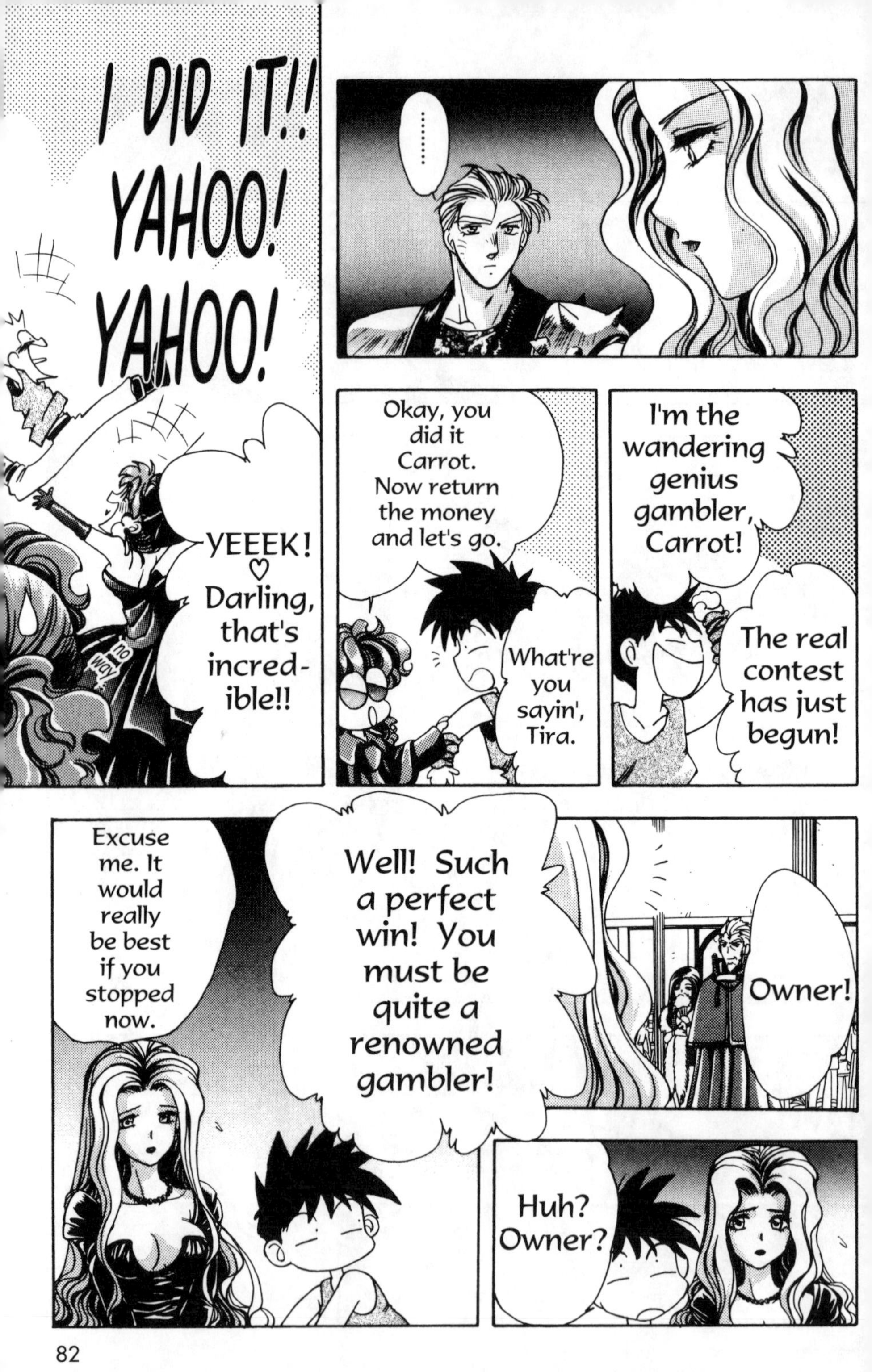
I DID IT!!
YAHOO! YAHOO!
YEEEK! ♡ Darling, that's incred-ible!!
no way
......
Okay, you did it Carrot. Now return the money and let's go.
What're you sayin', Tira.
I'm the wandering genius gambler, Carrot!
The real contest has just begun!
Excuse me. It would really be best if you stopped now.
Well! Such a perfect win! You must be quite a renowned gambler!
Owner!
Huh? Owner?

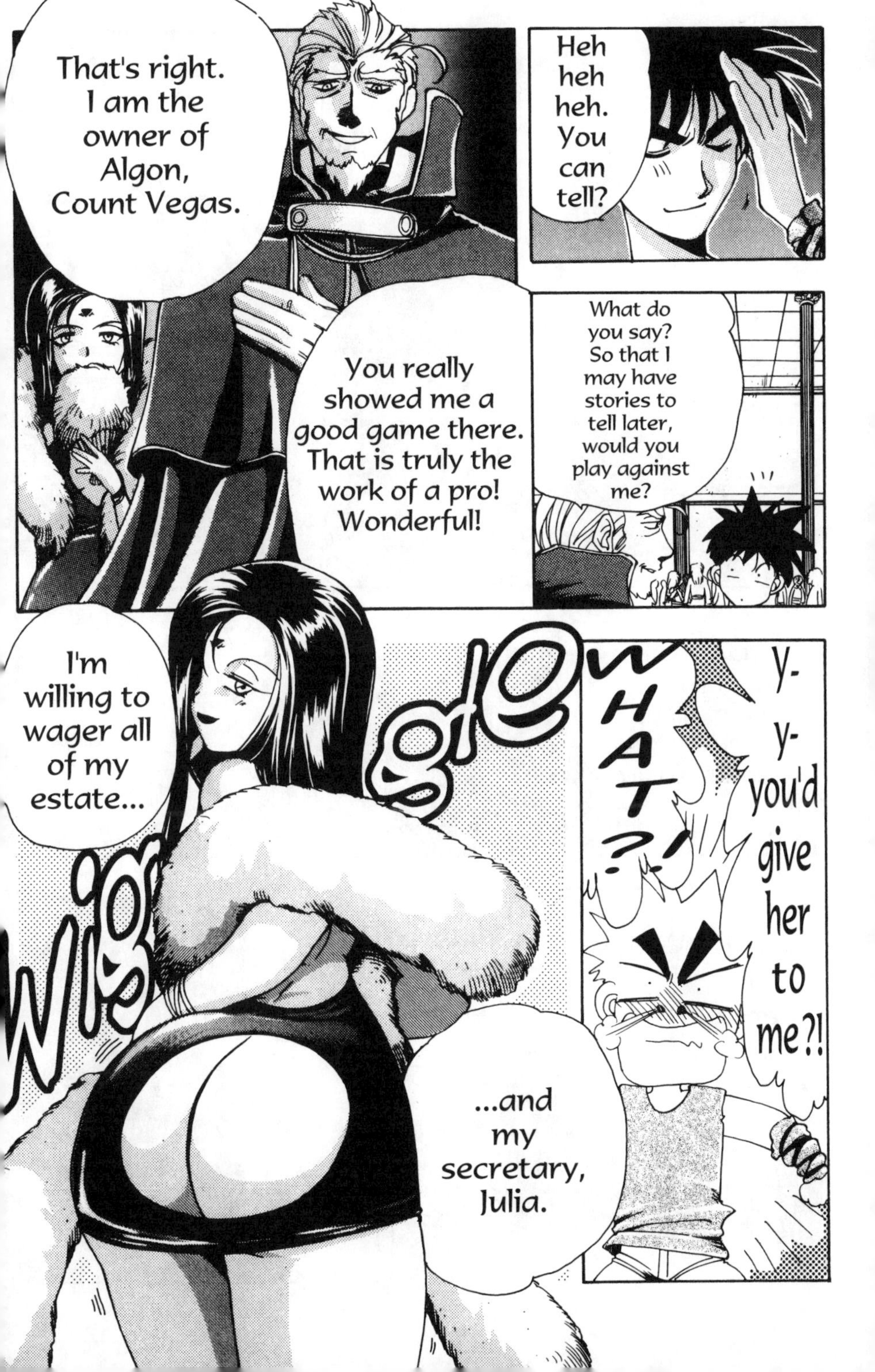

That's right. I am the owner of Algon, Count Vegas.
You really showed me a good game there. That is truly the work of a pro! Wonderful!
Heh heh heh. You can tell?
What do you say? So that I may have stories to tell later, would you play against me?
I'm willing to wager all of my estate...
wiggle
...and my secretary, Julia.
WHAT?!
y-y-you'd give her to me?!

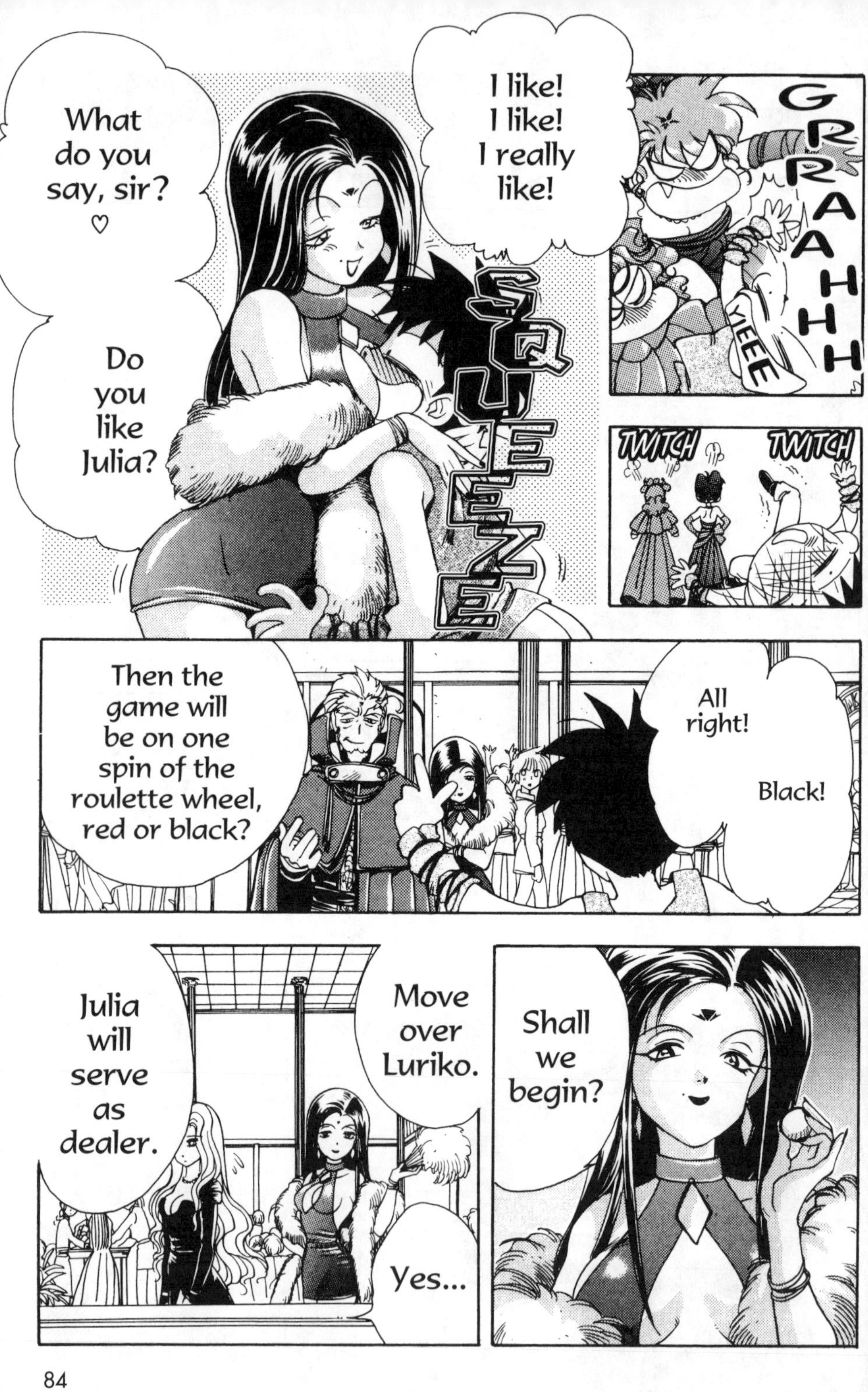

What do you say, sir? ♡
Do you like Julia?
I like! I like! I really like!
SQUEEZE
GRRAAHHH
YIEEE
TWITCH
TWITCH
Then the game will be on one spin of the roulette wheel, red or black?
All right!
Black!
Julia will serve as dealer.
Move over Luriko.
Yes...
Shall we begin?

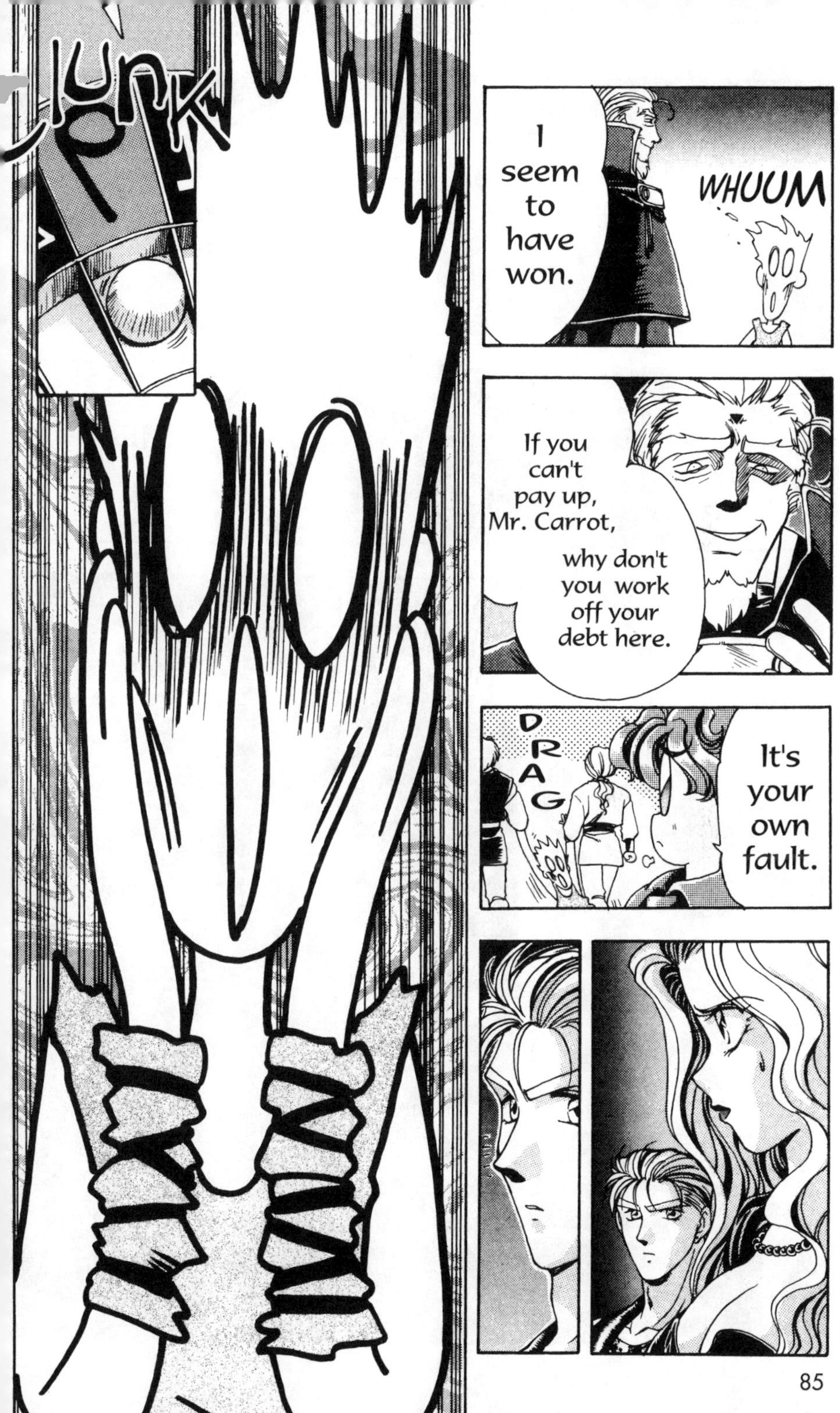
CLUNK
I seem to have won.
WHUUM
If you can't pay up, Mr. Carrot,
why don't you work off your debt here.
DRAG
It's your own fault.

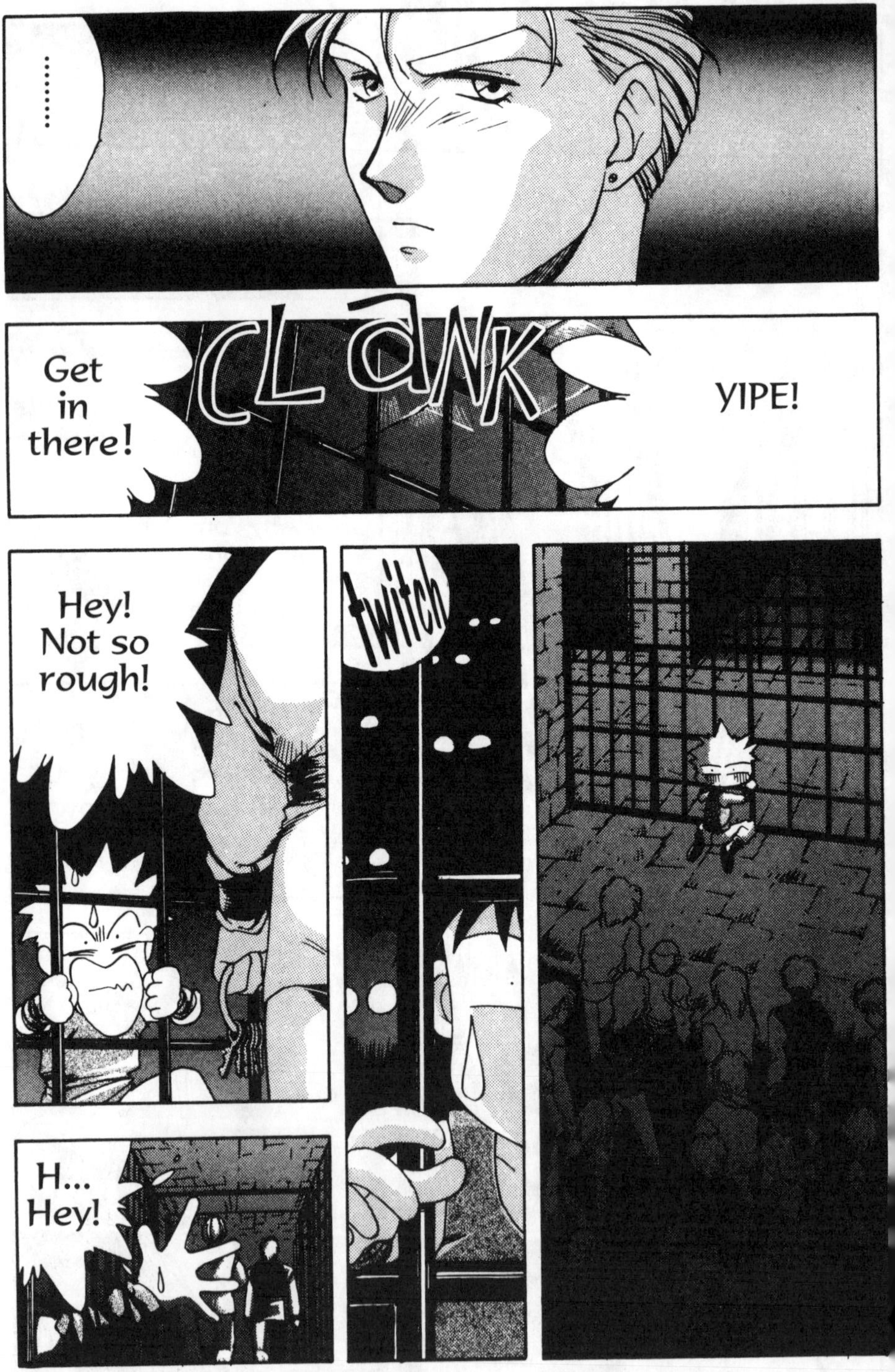
....
Get in there!
CLANK
YIPE!
Hey! Not so rough!
H... Hey!
twitch

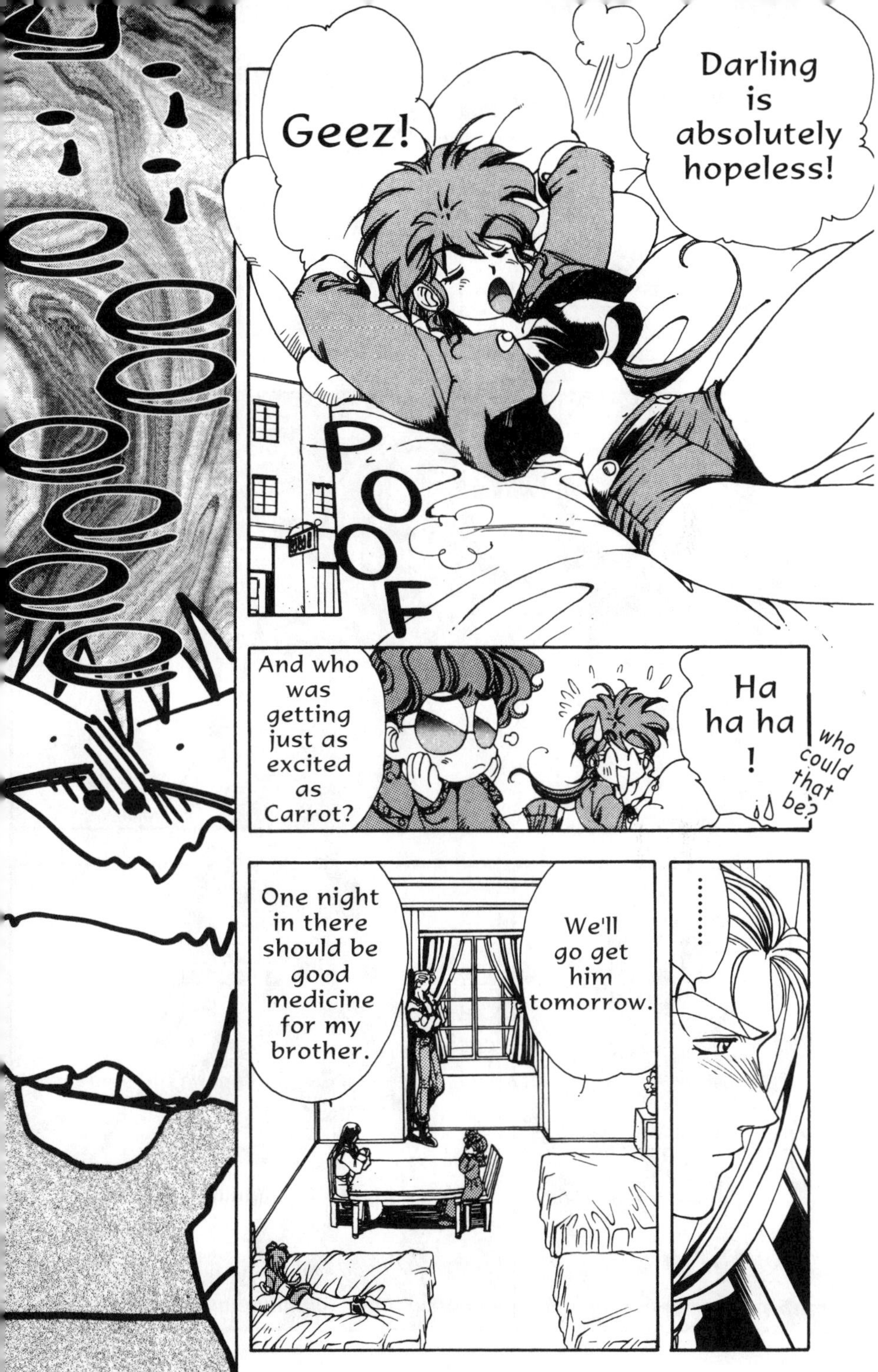

Geez!
Darling is absolutely hopeless!
POOF
And who was getting just as excited as Carrot?
Ha ha ha!
who could that be?
One night in there should be good medicine for my brother.
We'll go get him tomorrow.
....

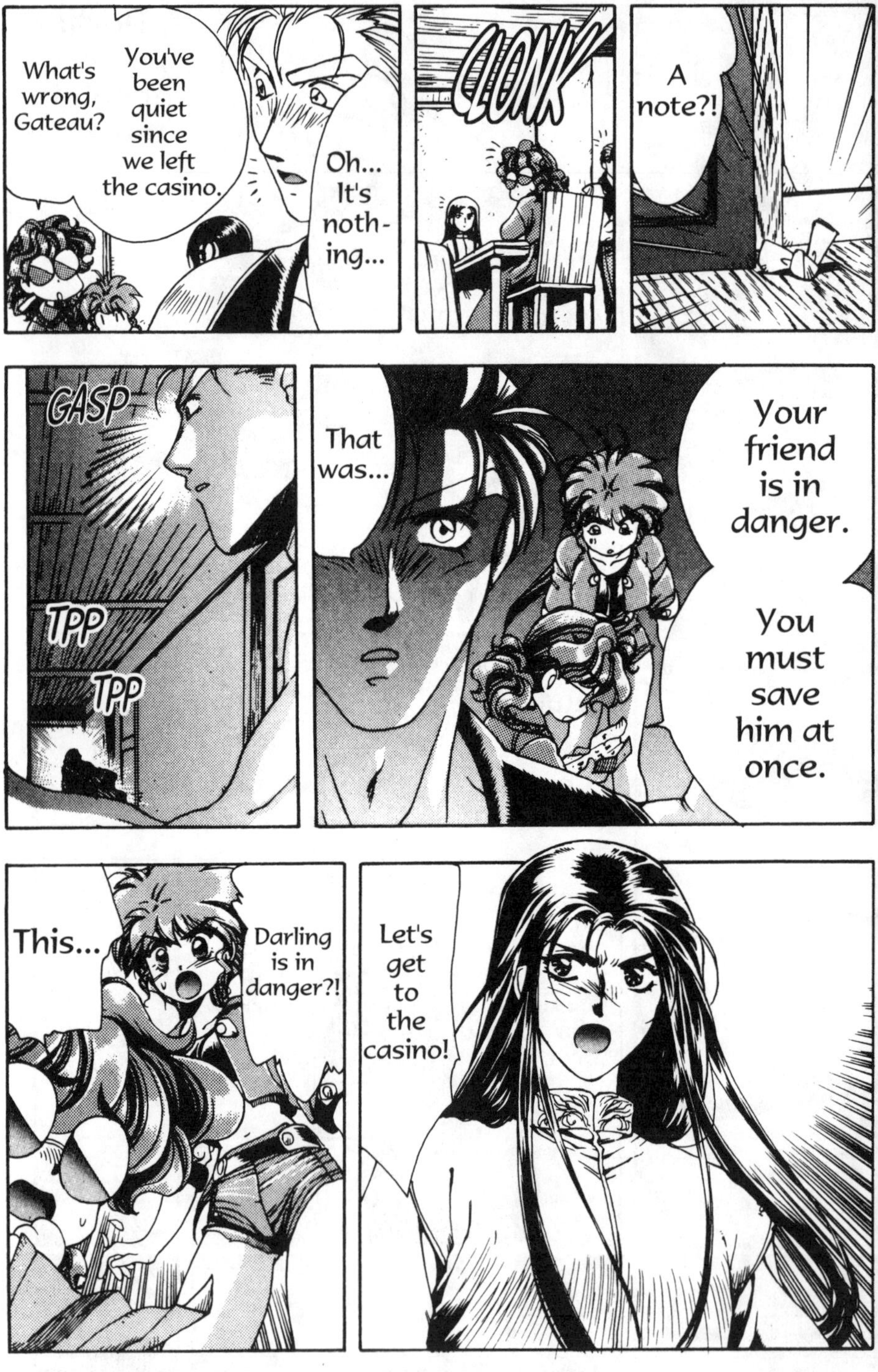

What's wrong, Gateau?
You've been quiet since we left the casino.
Oh... It's noth-ing...
CLONK
A note?!
GASP
TPP
TPP
That was...
Your friend is in danger.
You must save him at once.
This...
Darling is in danger?!
Let's get to the casino!

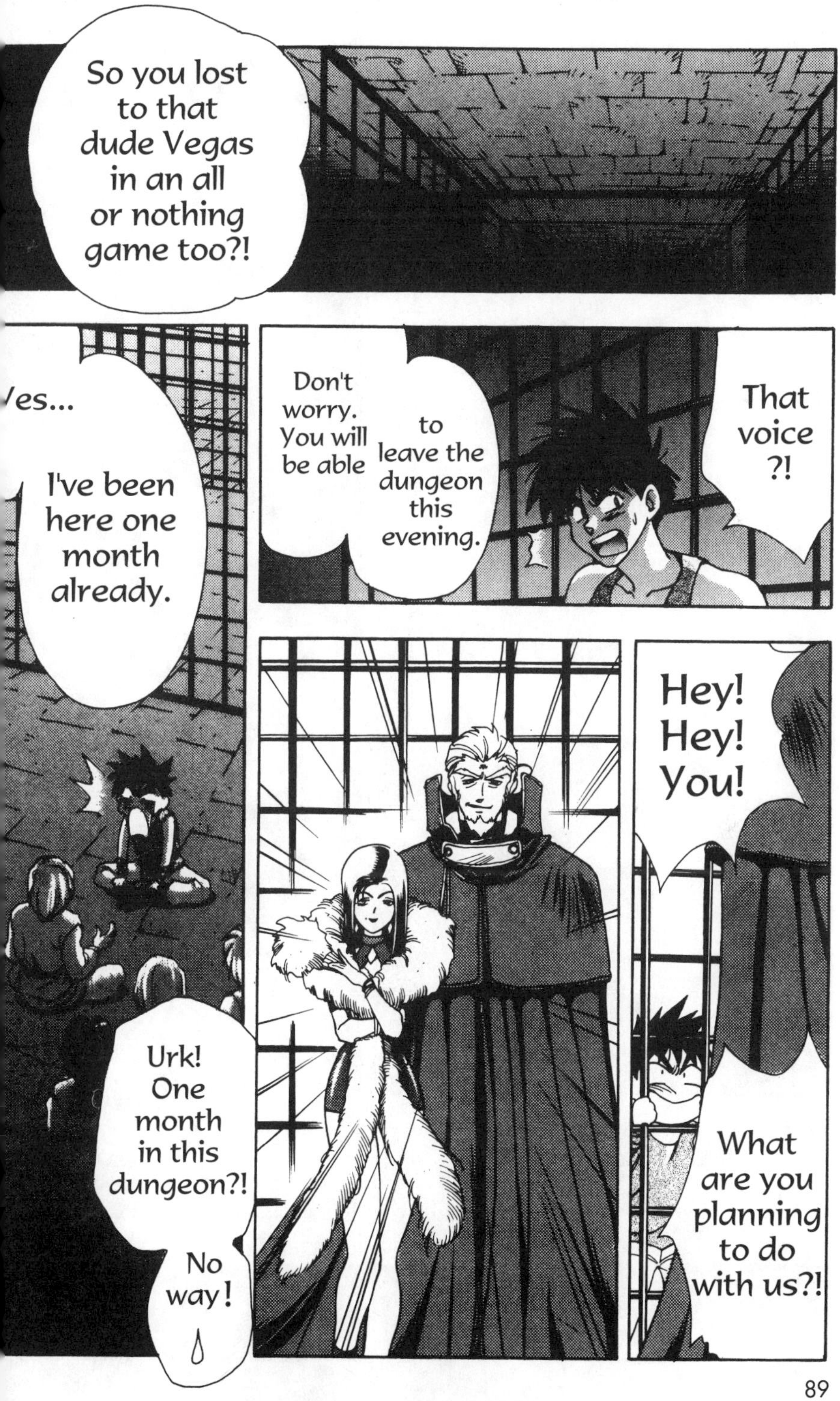
So you lost to that dude Vegas in an all or nothing game too?!
Yes...
I've been here one month already.
Don't worry. You will be able to leave the dungeon this evening.
That voice ?!
Hey! Hey! You!
What are you planning to do with us?!
Urk! One month in this dungeon?!
No way!

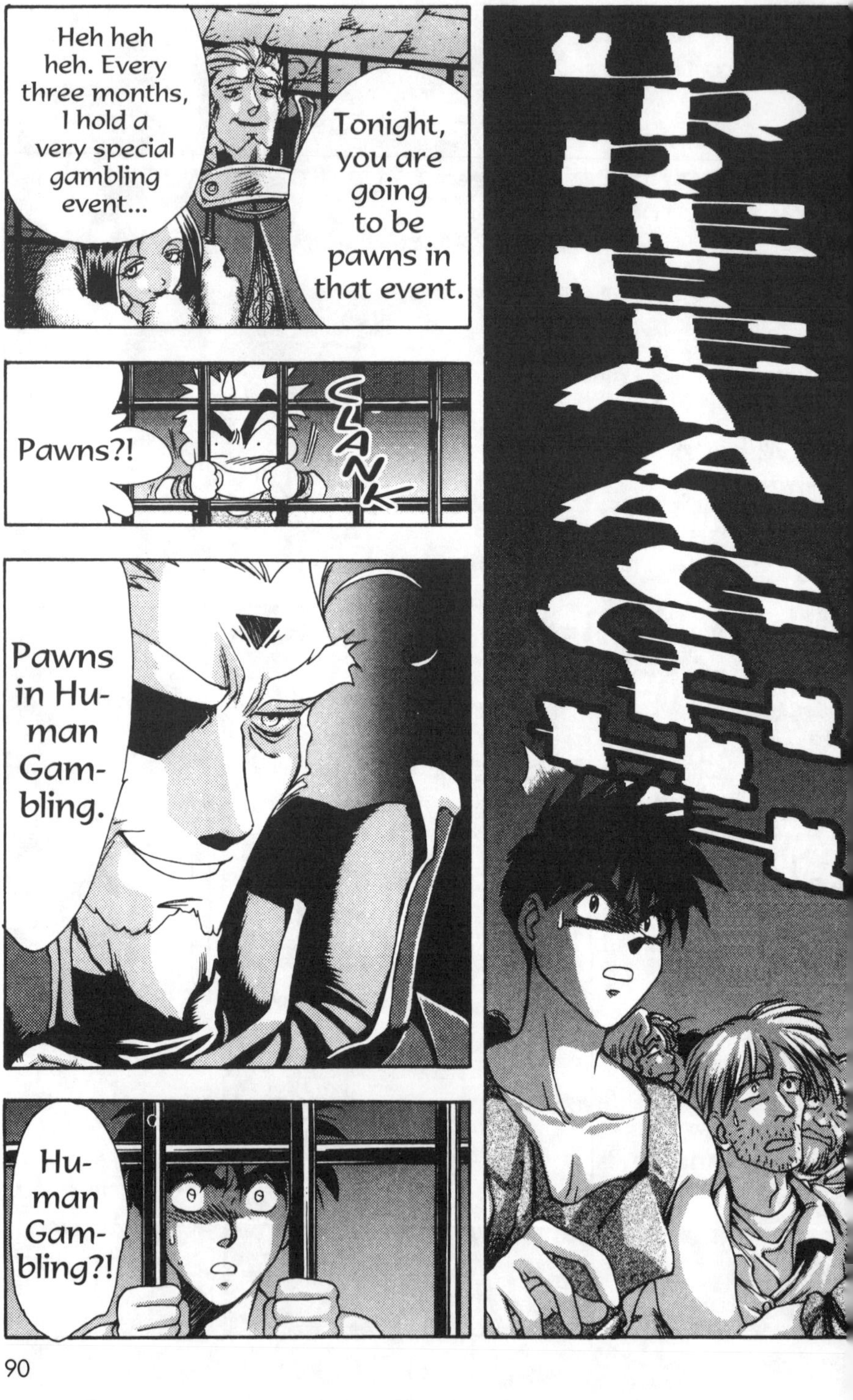
Heh heh heh. Every three months, I hold a very special gambling event...
Tonight, you are going to be pawns in that event.
Pawns?!
CLANK
Pawns in Human Gambling.
Human Gambling?!
URREEEAAASS

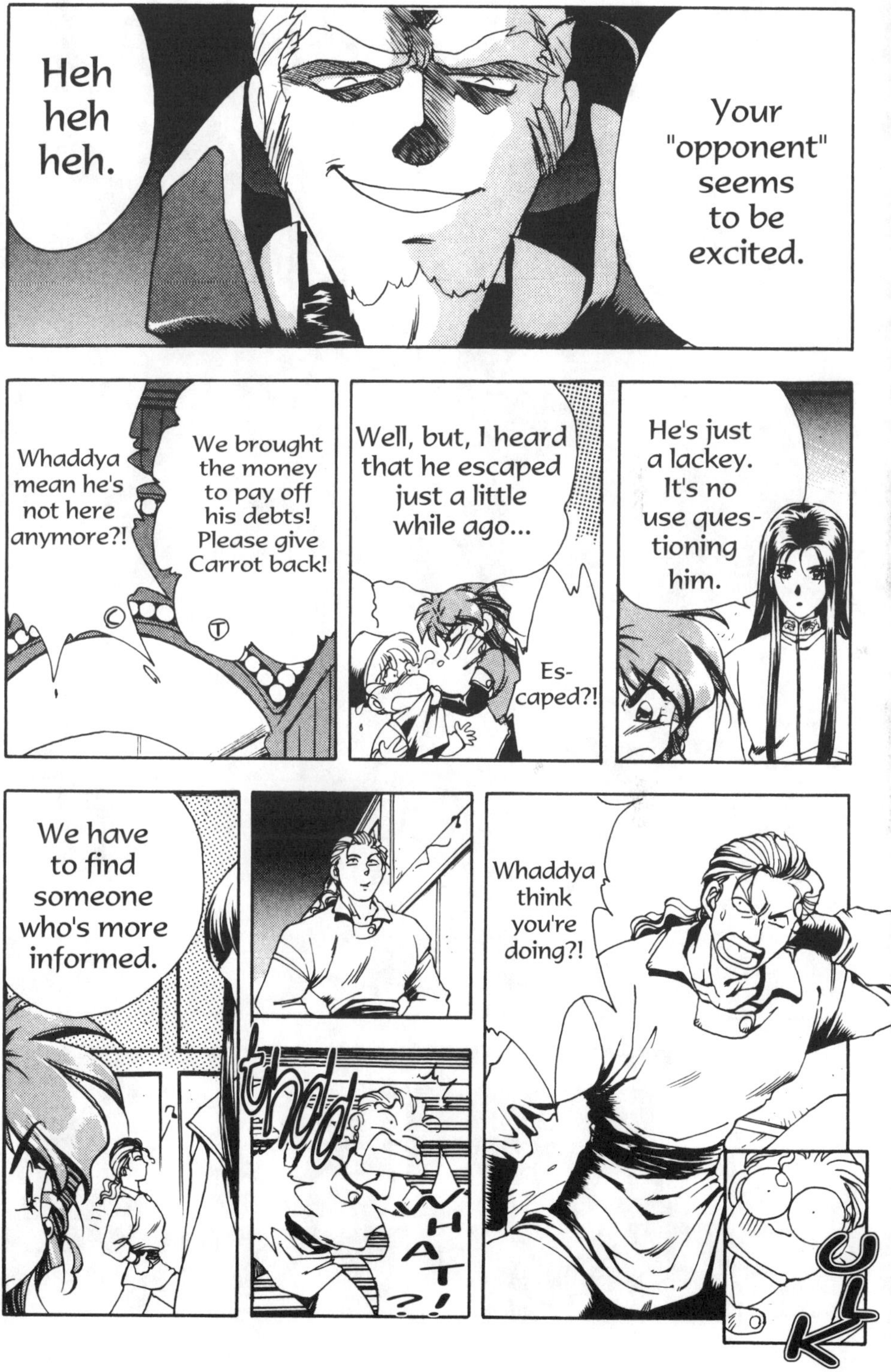
Heh heh heh.
Your "opponent" seems to be excited.
Whaddya mean he's not here anymore?!
We brought the money to pay off his debts! Please give Carrot back!
Well, but, I heard that he escaped just a little while ago...
Es-caped?!
He's just a lackey. It's no use ques-tioning him.
We have to find someone who's more informed.
thdd
WHAT?!
Whaddya think you're doing?!
KLUNK

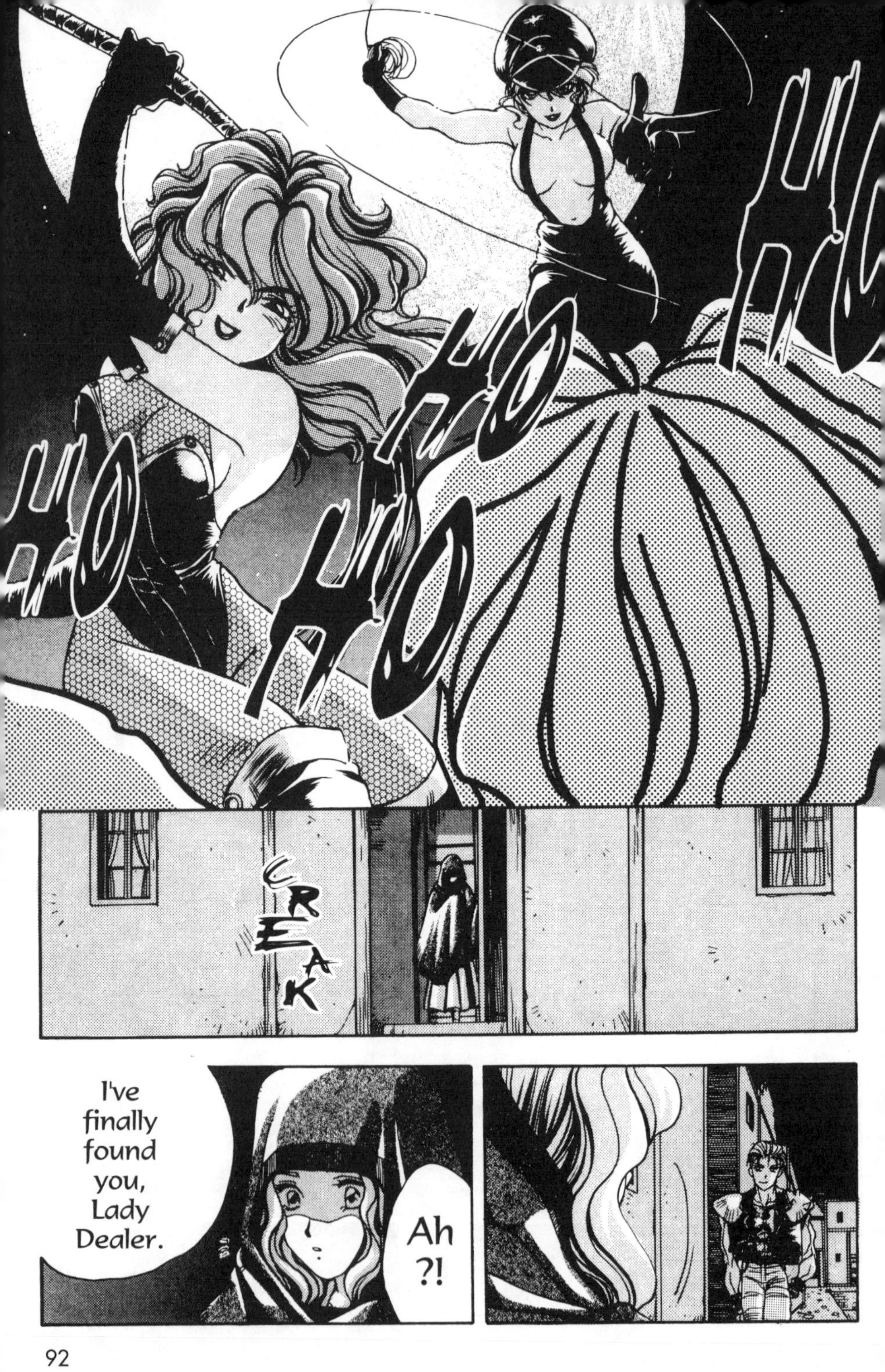
HO HO HO HO
CREAK
I've finally found you, Lady Dealer.
Ah ?!

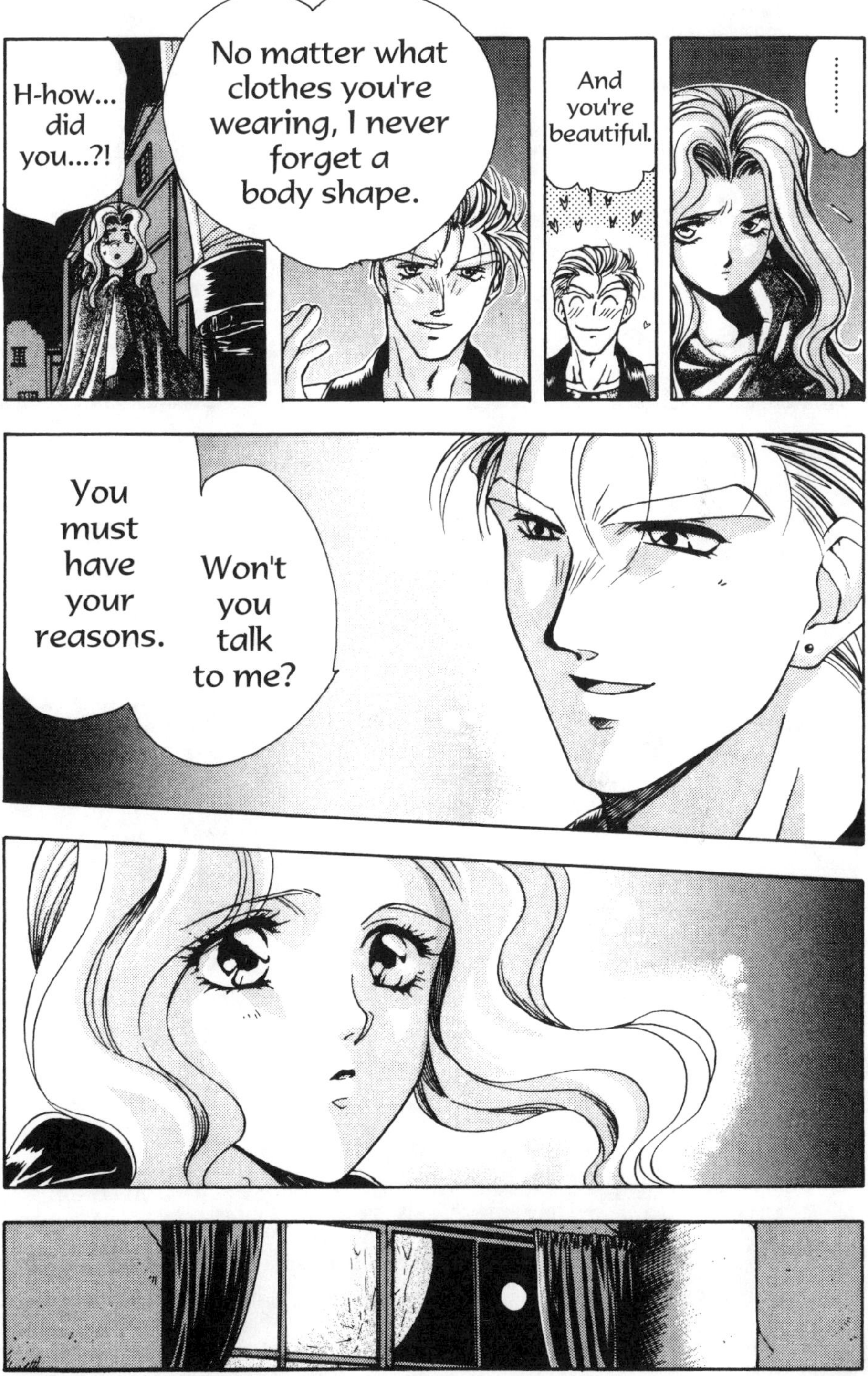
H-how... did you...?!
No matter what clothes you're wearing, I never forget a body shape.
And you're beautiful.
....
You must have your reasons.
Won't you talk to me?

That day...

...he didn't come back from the casino.

• • • • • •

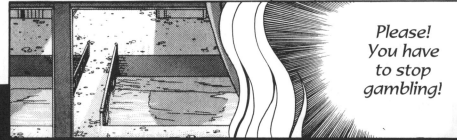

Please! You have to stop gambling!

What are you saying, Luriko! I'm going to have my biggest game today!

Then I'll make you happy, Luriko!

Please, Count Vegas!

Please let Rick go!

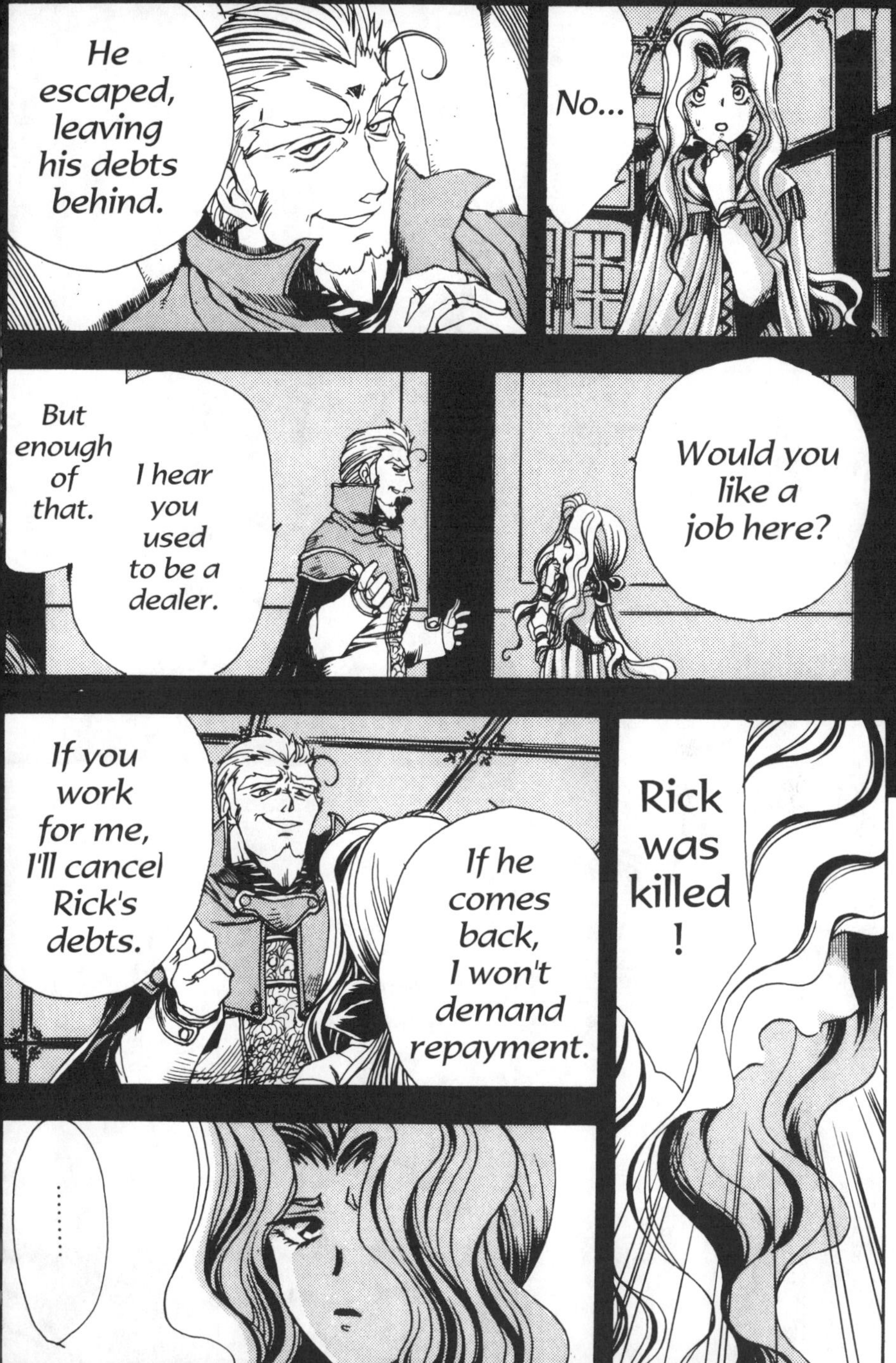
He escaped, leaving his debts behind.
No...
But enough of that.
I hear you used to be a dealer.
Would you like a job here?
If you work for me, I'll cancel Rick's debts.
If he comes back, I won't demand repayment.
....
Rick was killed!

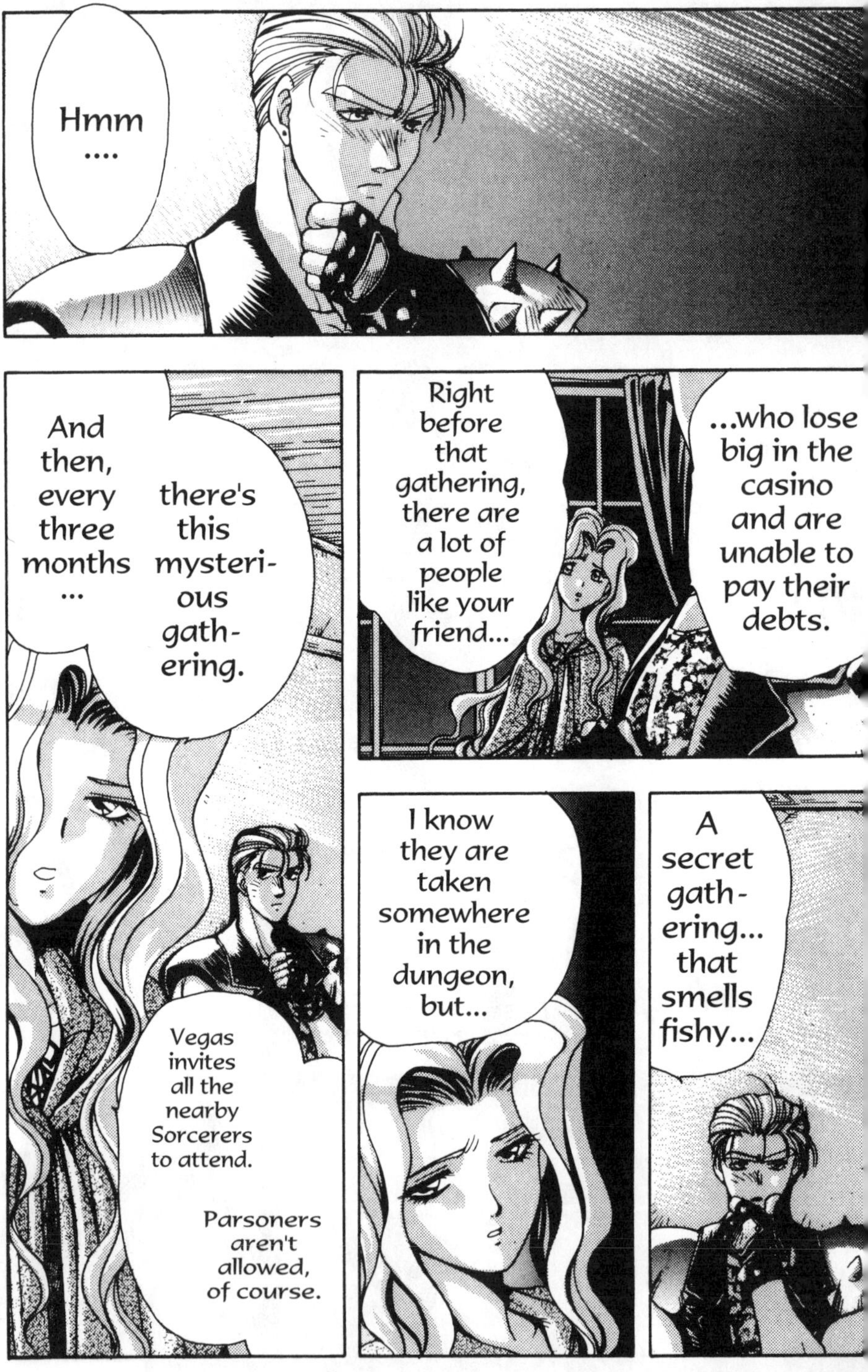
Hmm ....
And then, every three months ...
there's this mysteri-ous gath-ering.
Vegas invites all the nearby Sorcerers to attend.
Parsoners aren't allowed, of course.
Right before that gathering, there are a lot of people like your friend...
...who lose big in the casino and are unable to pay their debts.
I know they are taken somewhere in the dungeon, but...
A secret gath-ering... that smells fishy...

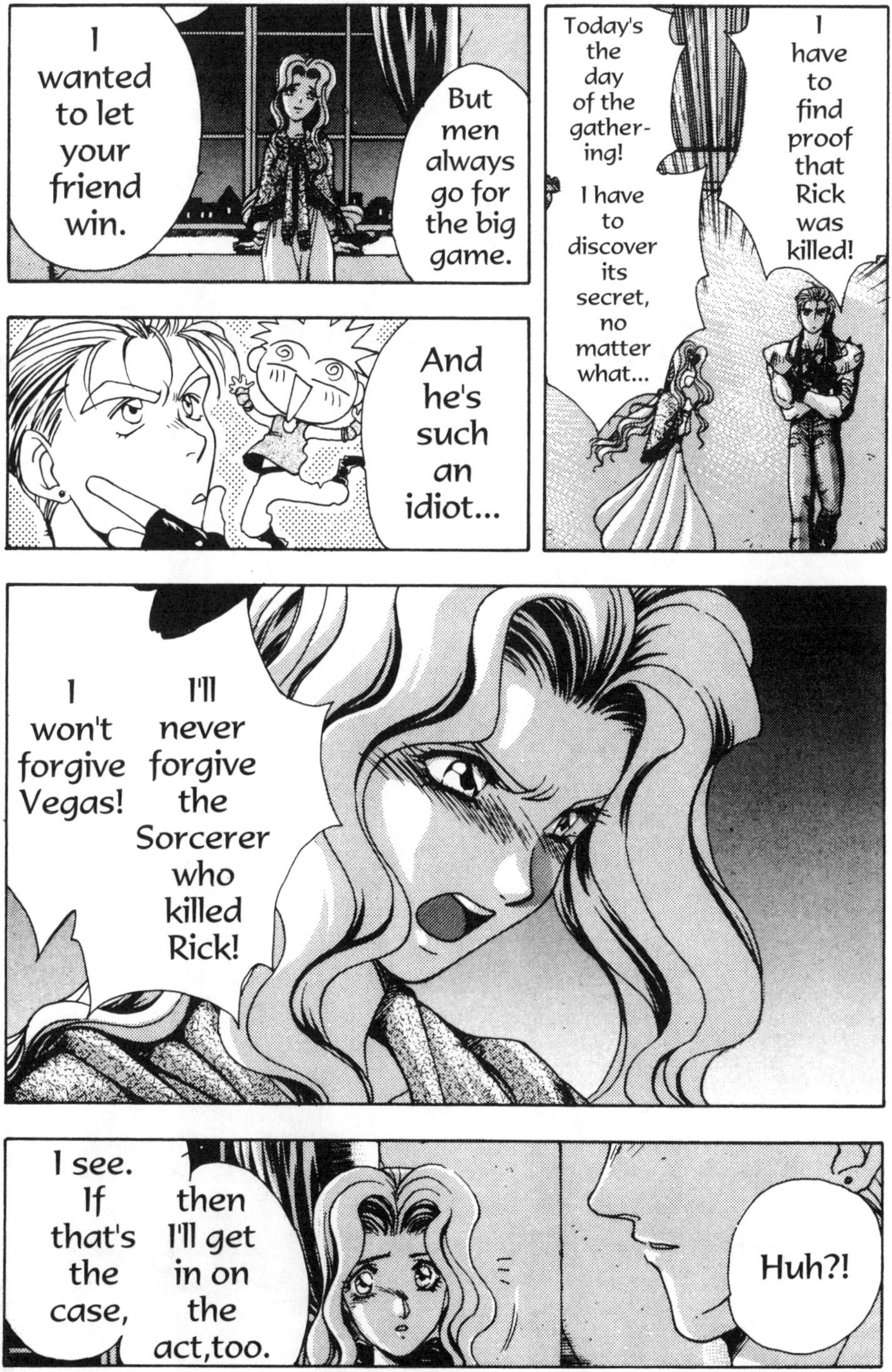

I wanted to let your friend win.
But men always go for the big game.
Today's the day of the gathering!
I have to discover its secret, no matter what...
I have to find proof that Rick was killed!
And he's such an idiot...
I won't forgive Vegas!
I'll never forgive the Sorcerer who killed Rick!
I see. If that's the case,
then I'll get in on the act,too.
Huh?!

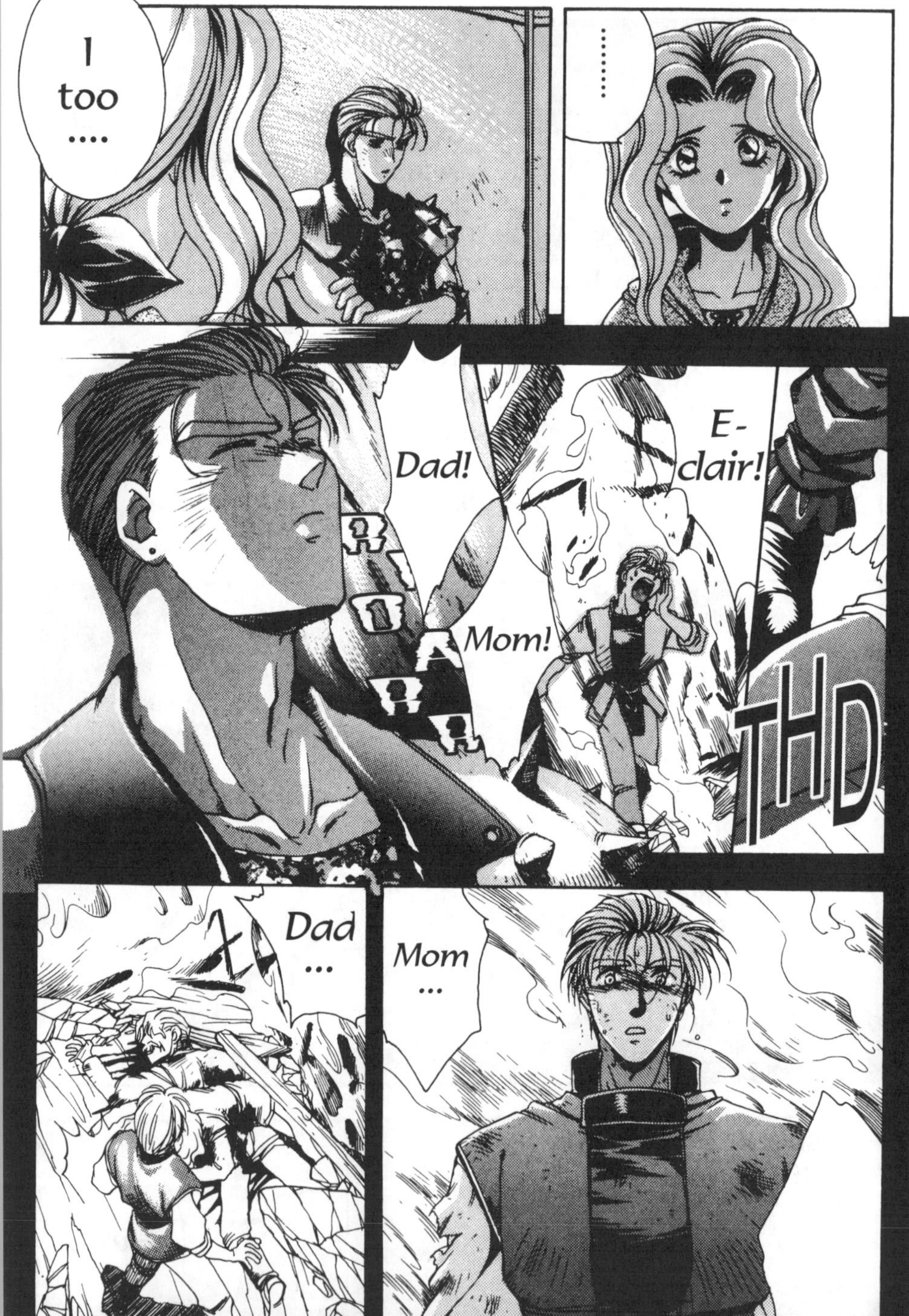
I too ....
......
Dad!
E-clair!
Mom!
THD
Dad ...
Mom ...

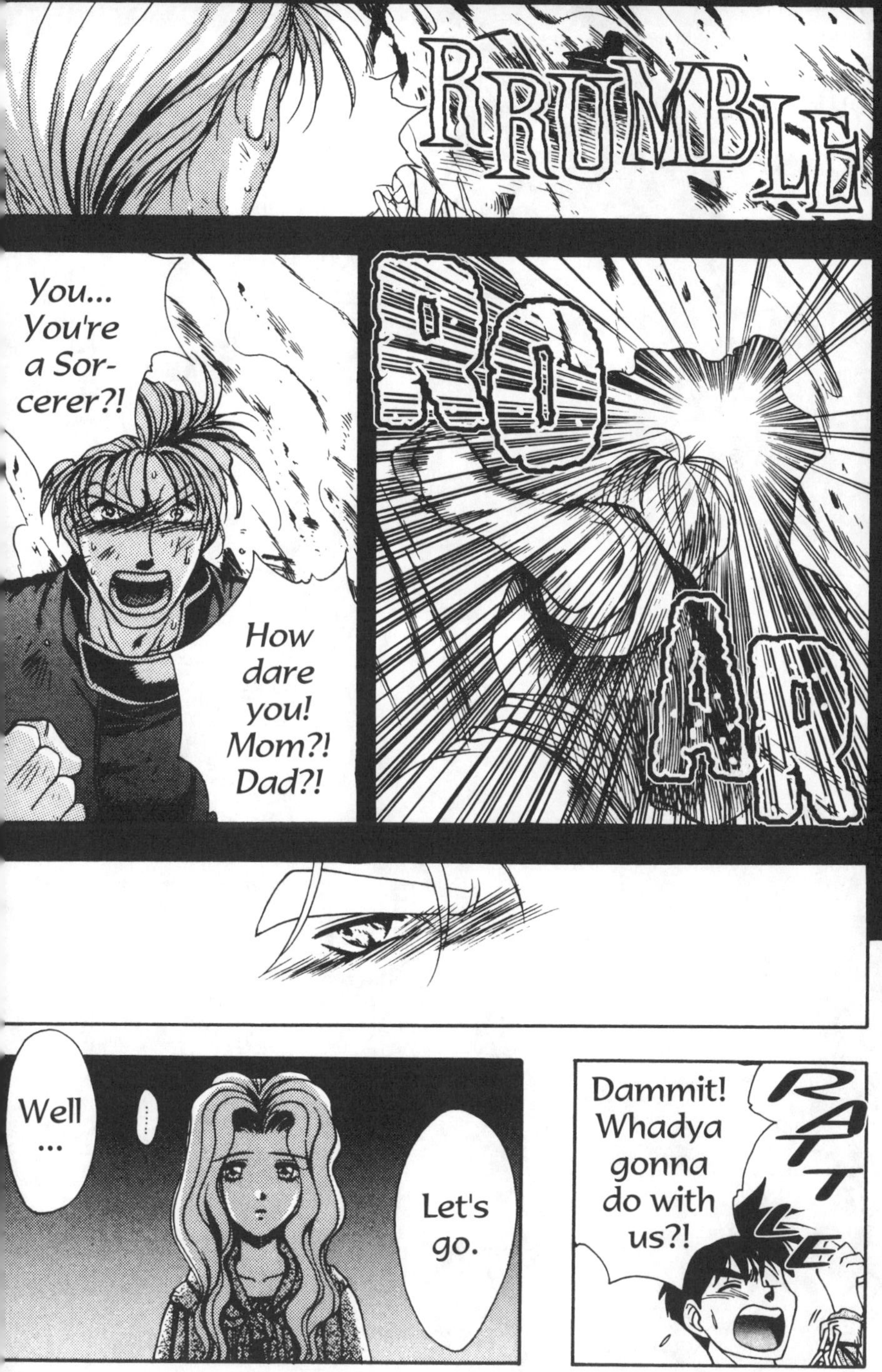
RRUMBLE
You... You're a Sorcerer?!
How dare you! Mom?! Dad?!
ROAR
Well ...
.....
Let's go.
Dammit! Whadya gonna do with us?!
RATTLE

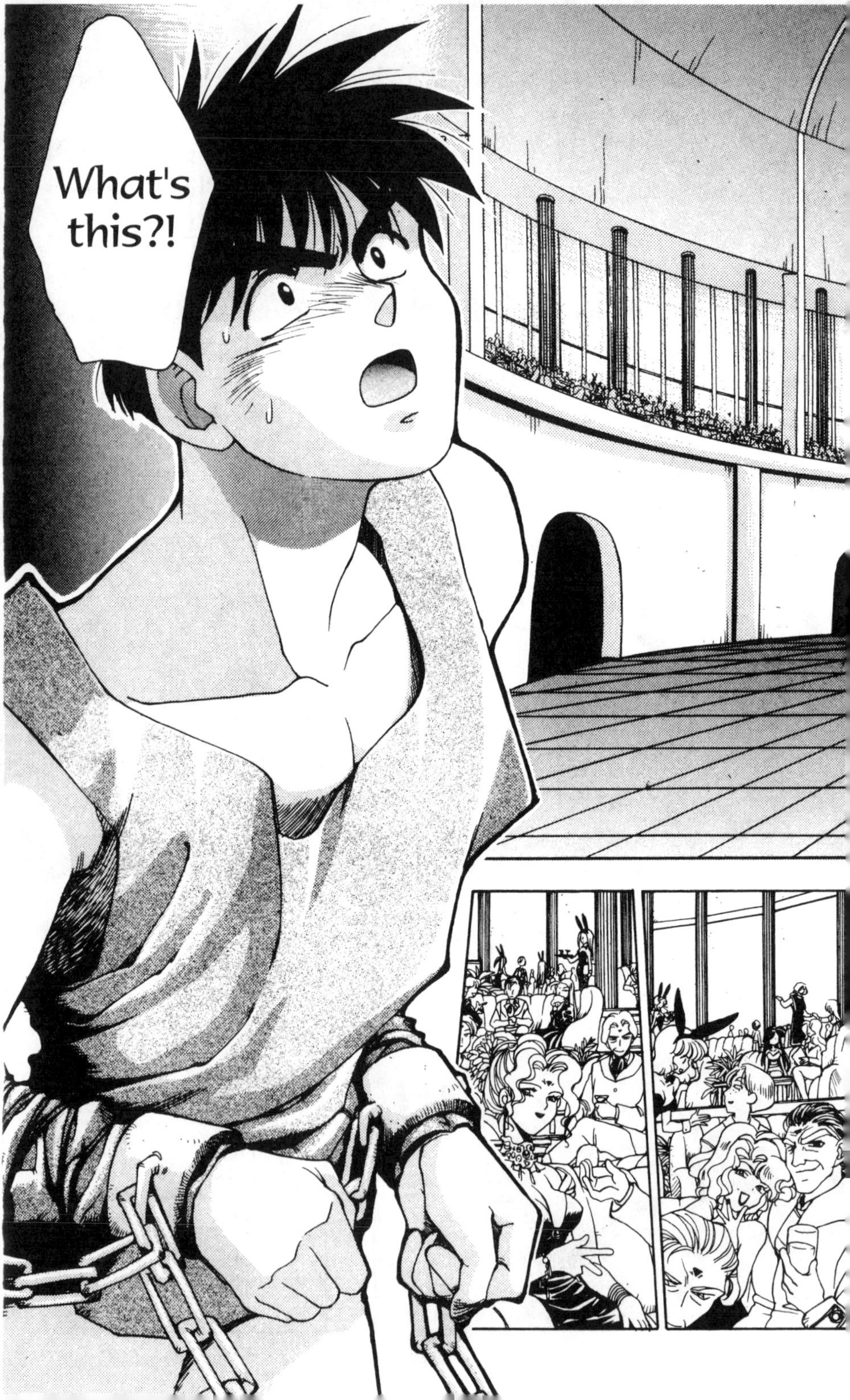
What's this?!

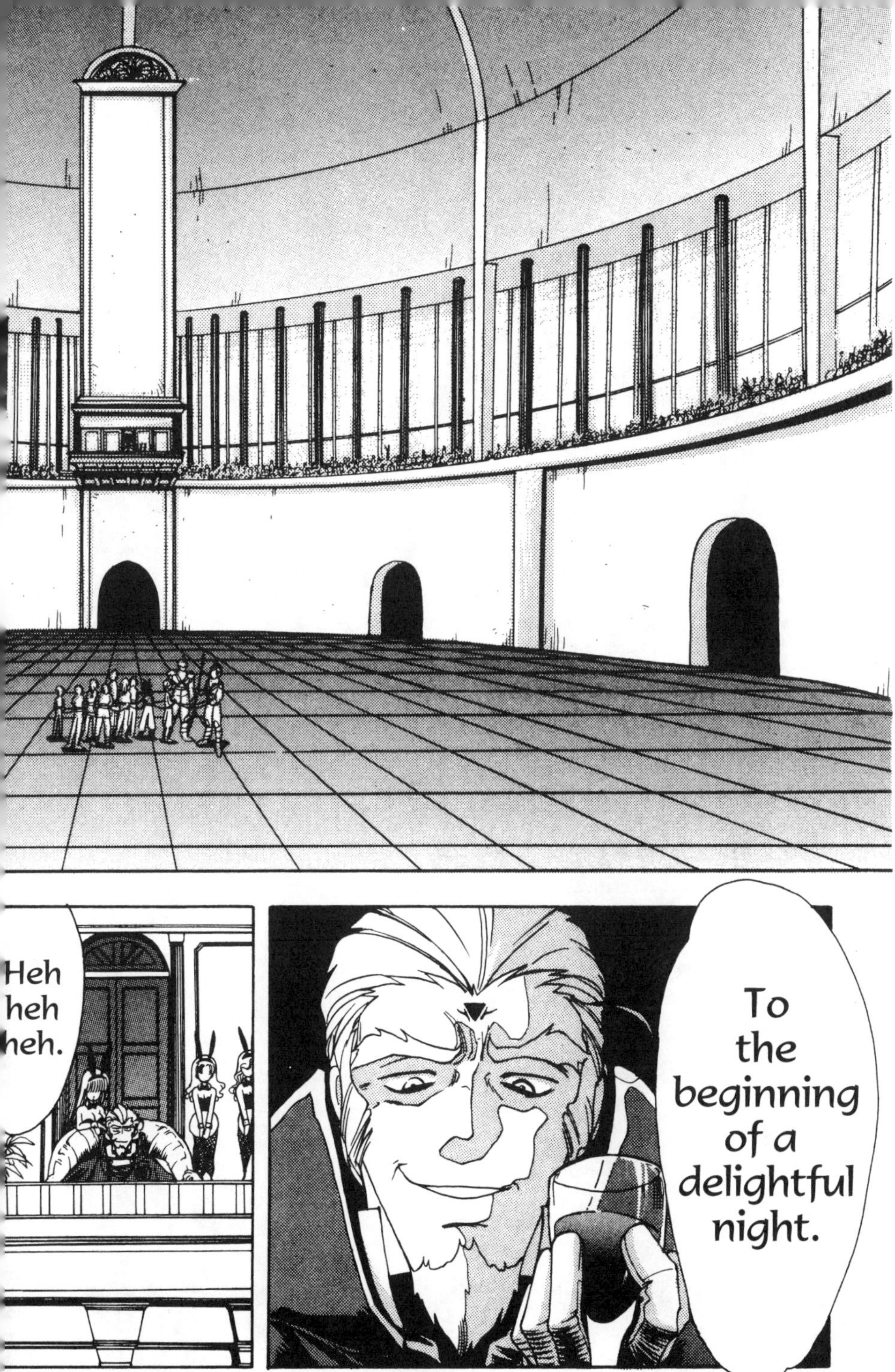
Heh heh heh.
To the beginning of a delightful night.

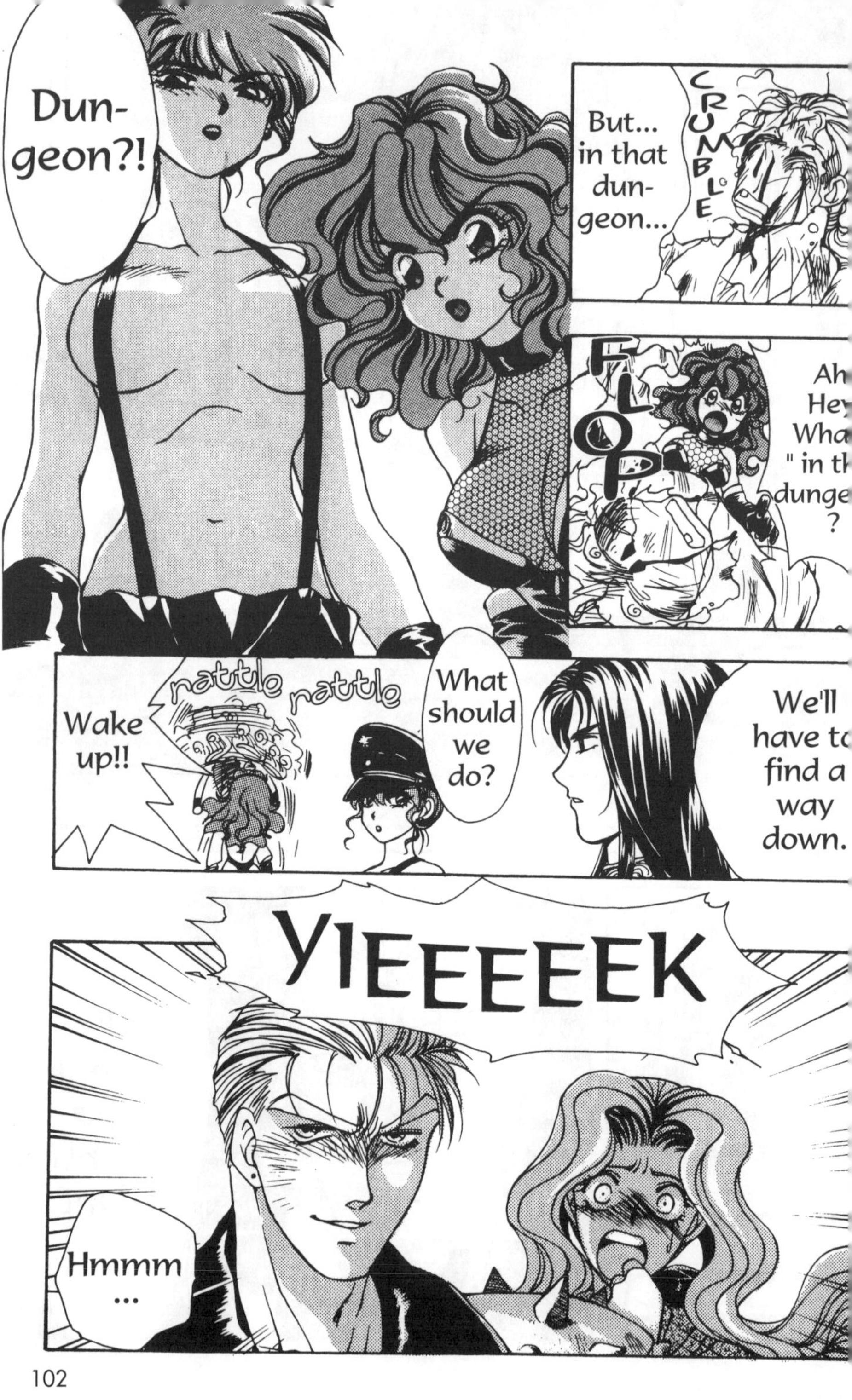

Dun-geon?!
But... in that dun-geon...
CRUMBLE
FLOP
Ah Hey What " in th dunge ?
Wake up!!
rattle rattle
What should we do?
We'll have t find a way down.
YIEEEEEK
Hmmm ...

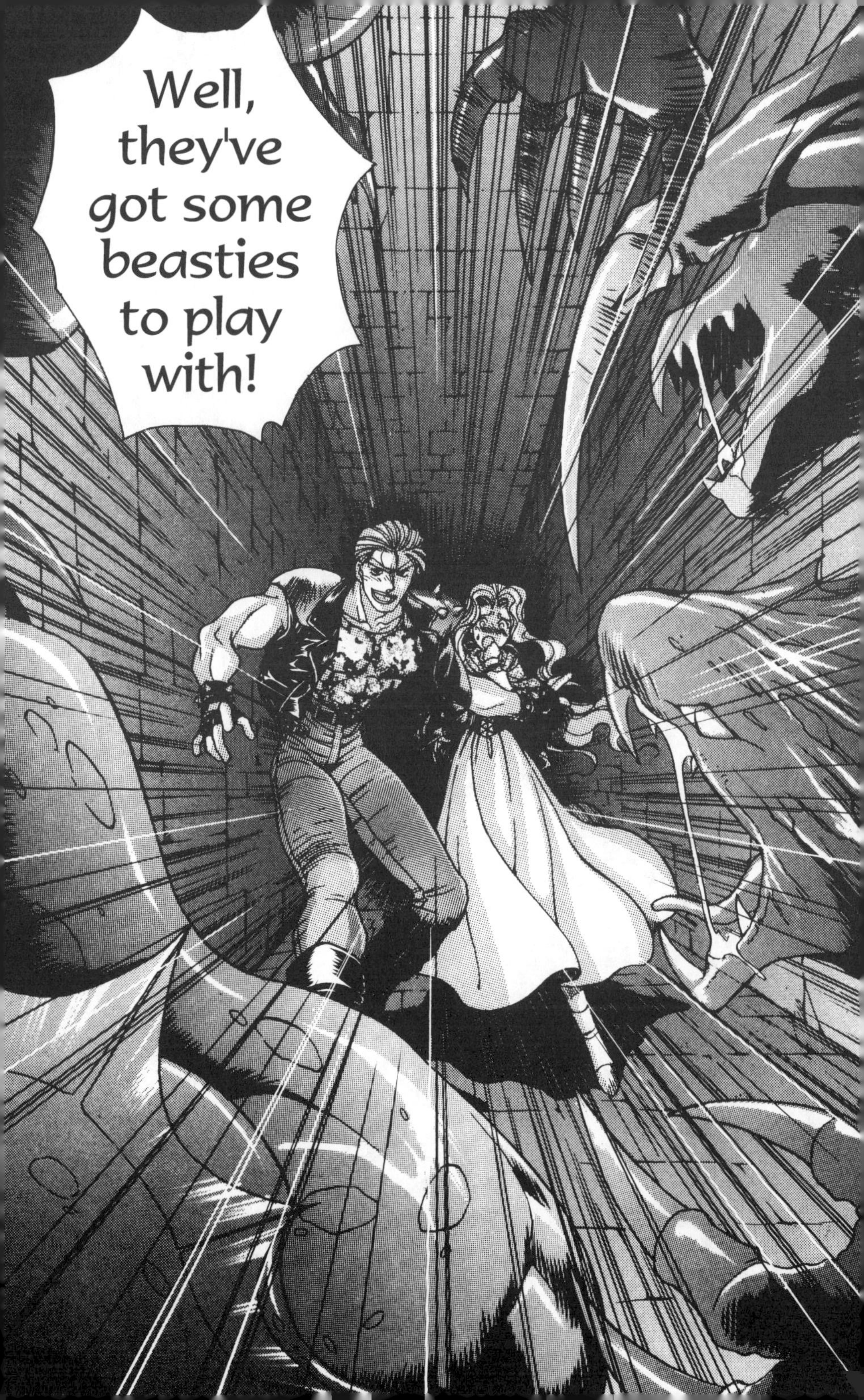
Well, they've got some beasties to play with!

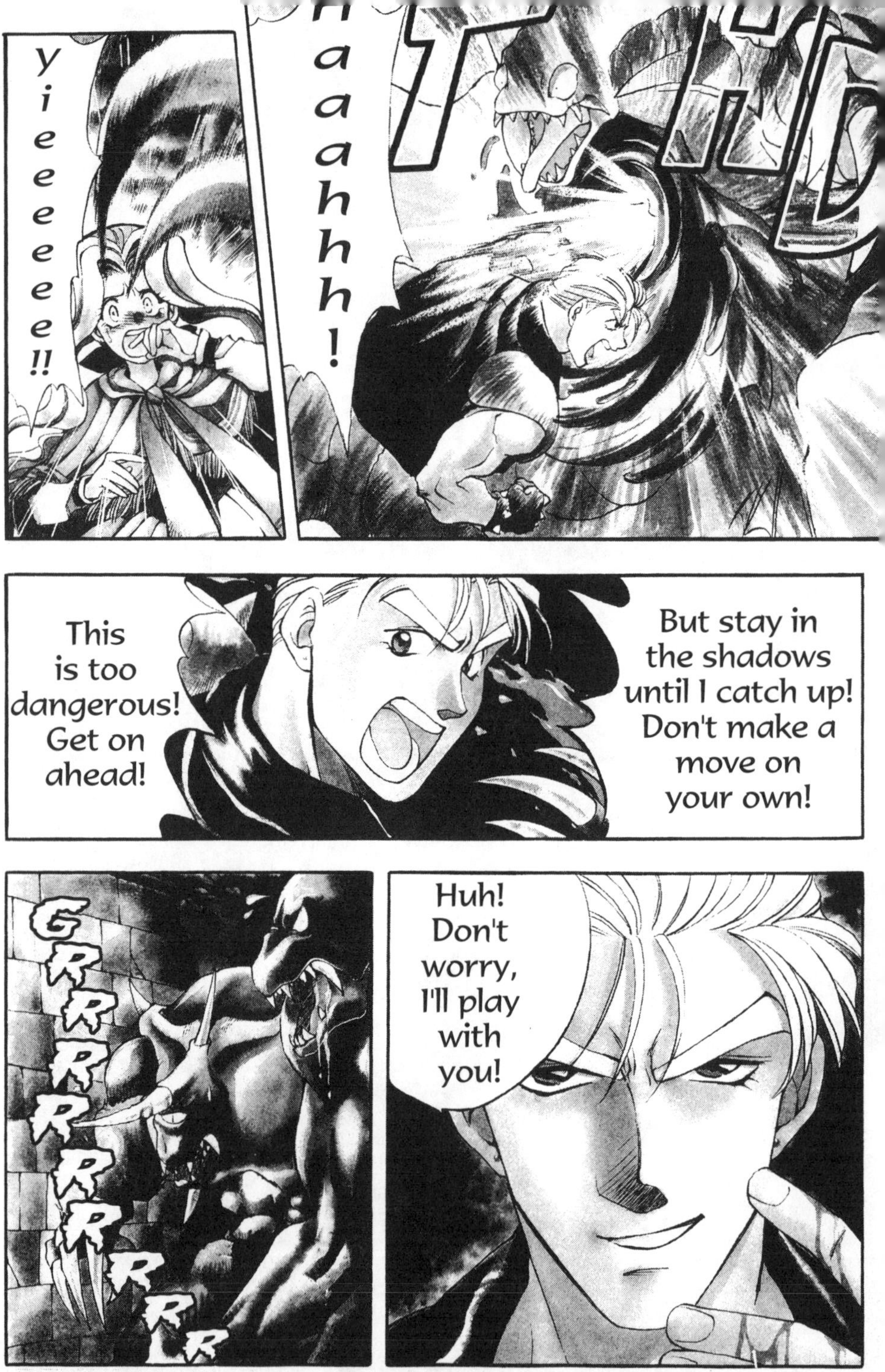
yieeeeeee!!
haaaahhh!
This is too dangerous! Get on ahead!
But stay in the shadows until I catch up! Don't make a move on your own!
GRRRRRRRRR
Huh! Don't worry, I'll play with you!

The Casino of Love and Sorrow, Part 2

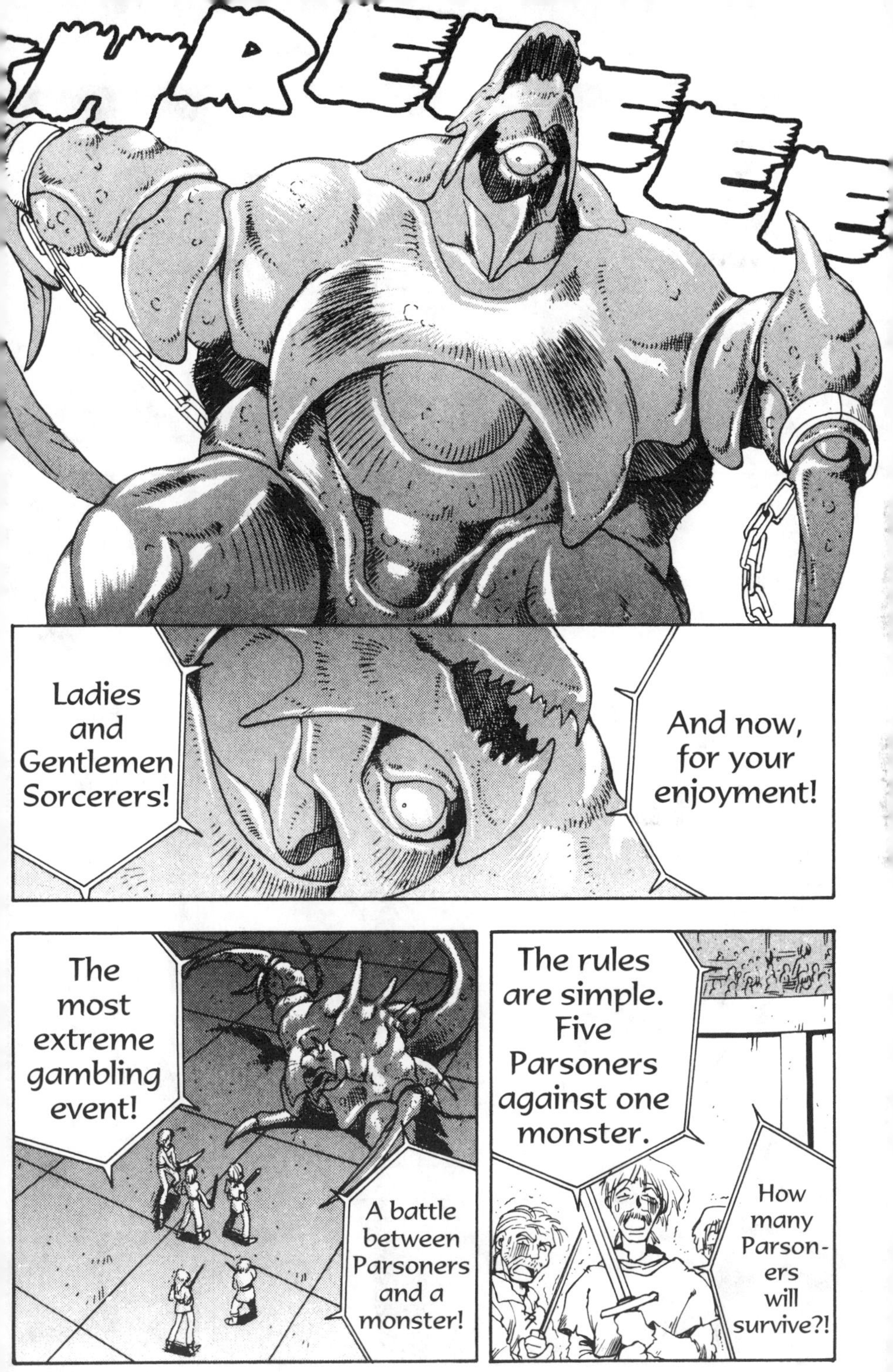
SHREEEEE
Ladies and Gentlemen Sorcerers!
And now, for your enjoyment!
The most extreme gambling event!
A battle between Parsoners and a monster!
The rules are simple. Five Parsoners against one monster.
How many Parson-ers will survive?!

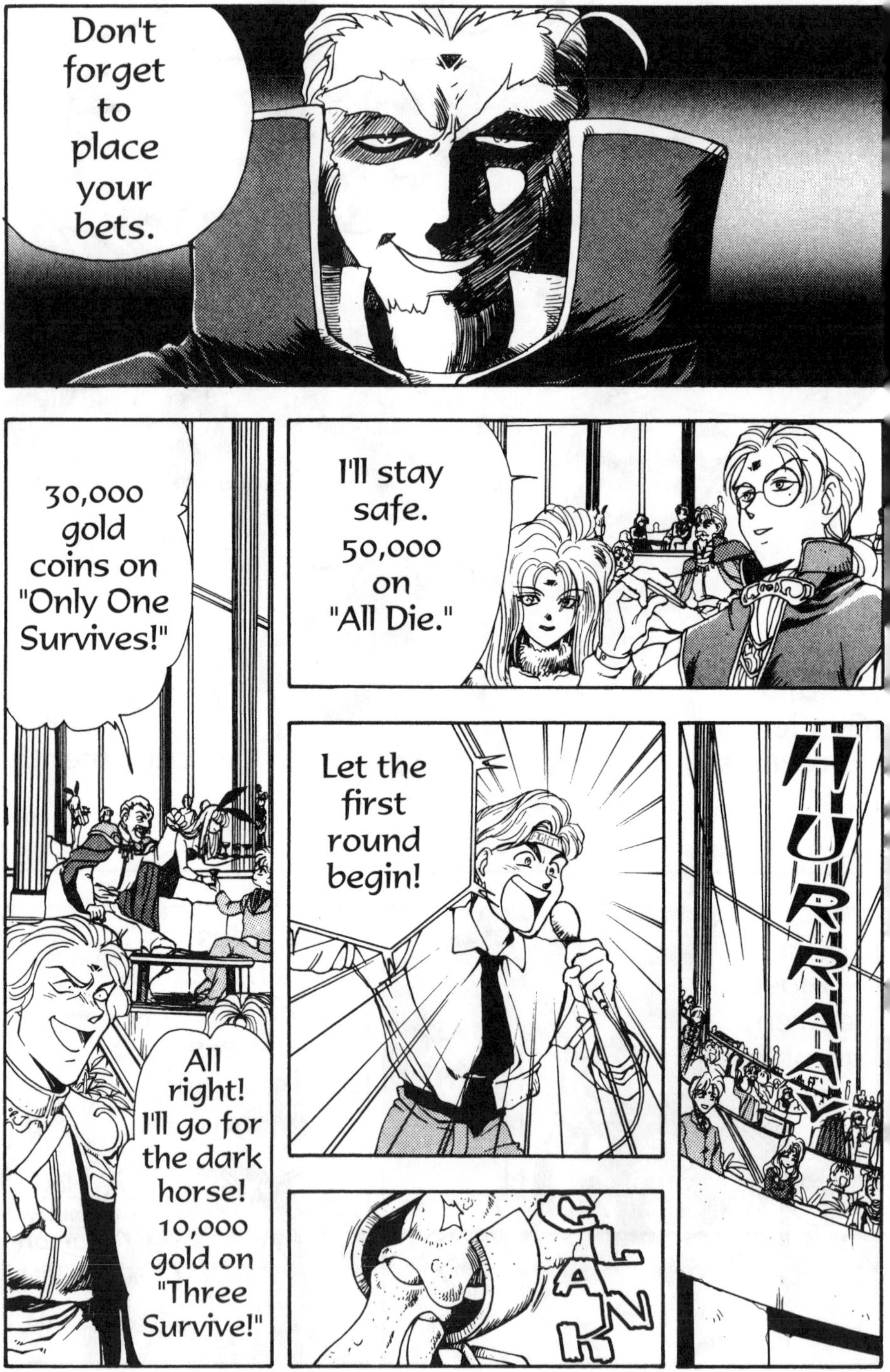
Don't forget to place your bets.
30,000 gold coins on "Only One Survives!"
All right! I'll go for the dark horse! 10,000 gold on "Three Survive!"
I'll stay safe. 50,000 on "All Die."
Let the first round begin!
CLANK
HURRAAY

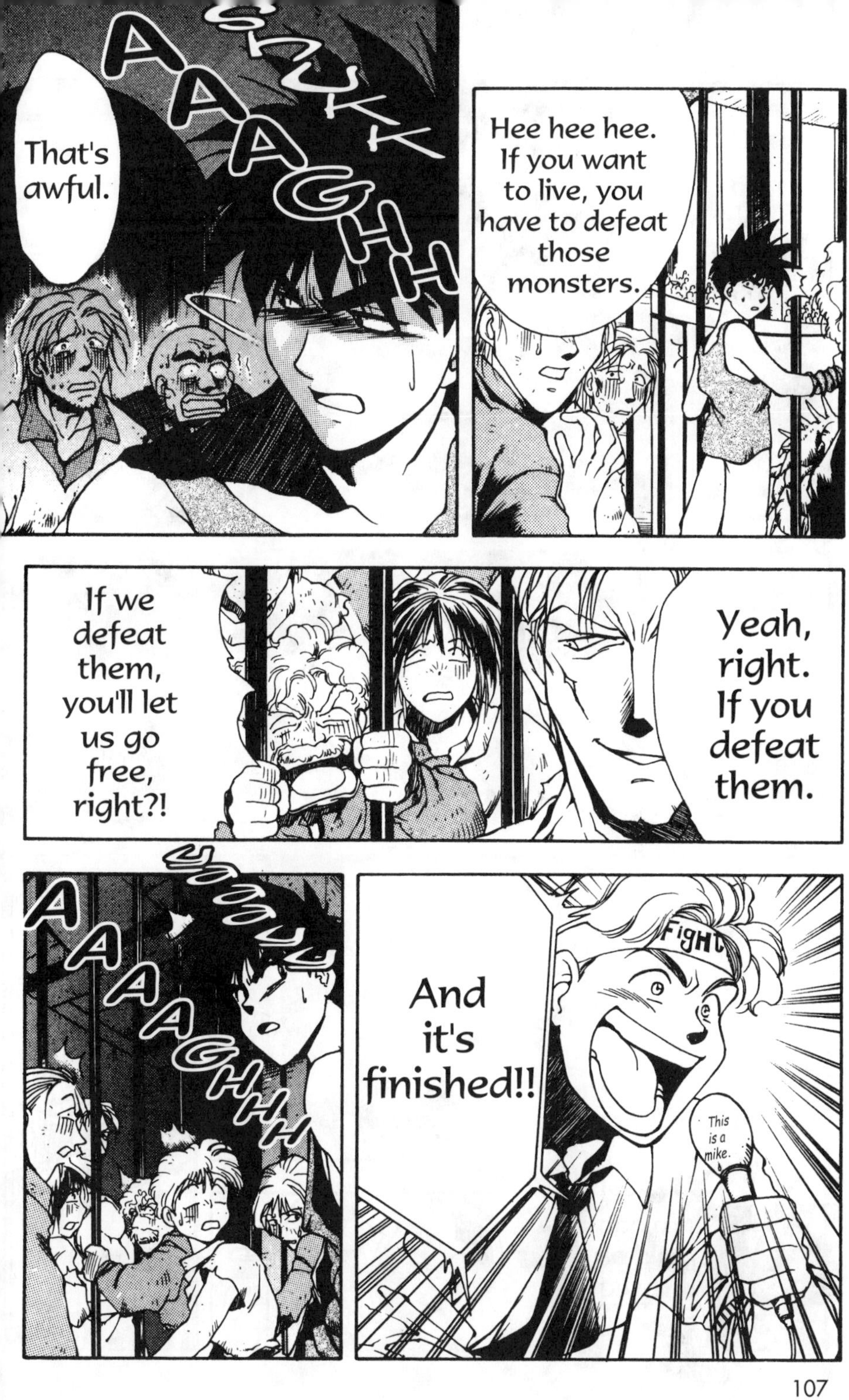
That's awful.
AAAGHH
SHUKK
Hee hee hee. If you want to live, you have to defeat those monsters.
If we defeat them, you'll let us go free, right?!
Yeah, right. If you defeat them.
AAAAGHHH
And it's finished!!
Fight
This is a mike.

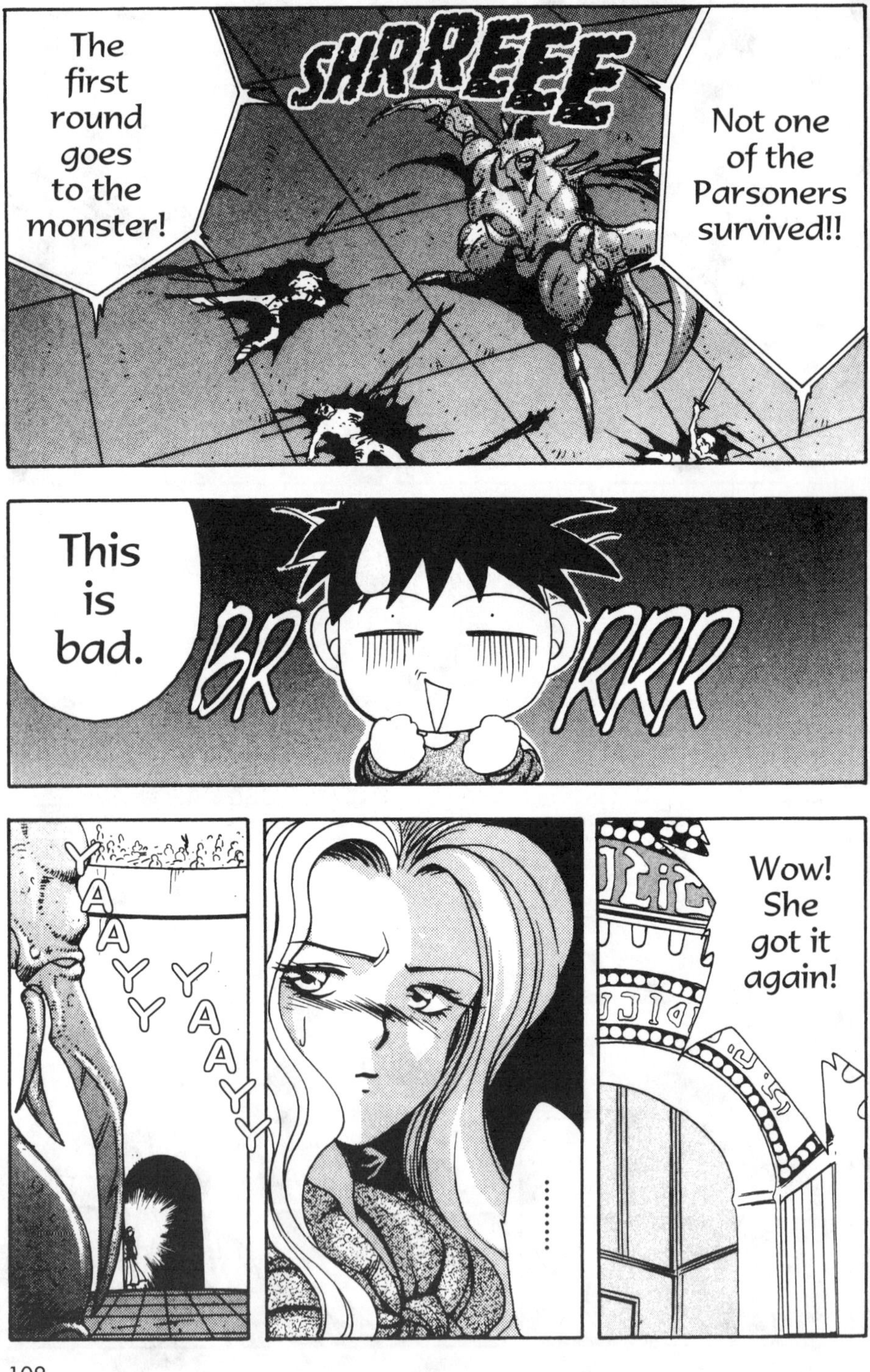
The first round goes to the monster!
SHRREEE
Not one of the Parsoners survived!!
This is bad.
BRRRRR
YAAYYYAAYY
....
Wow! She got it again!

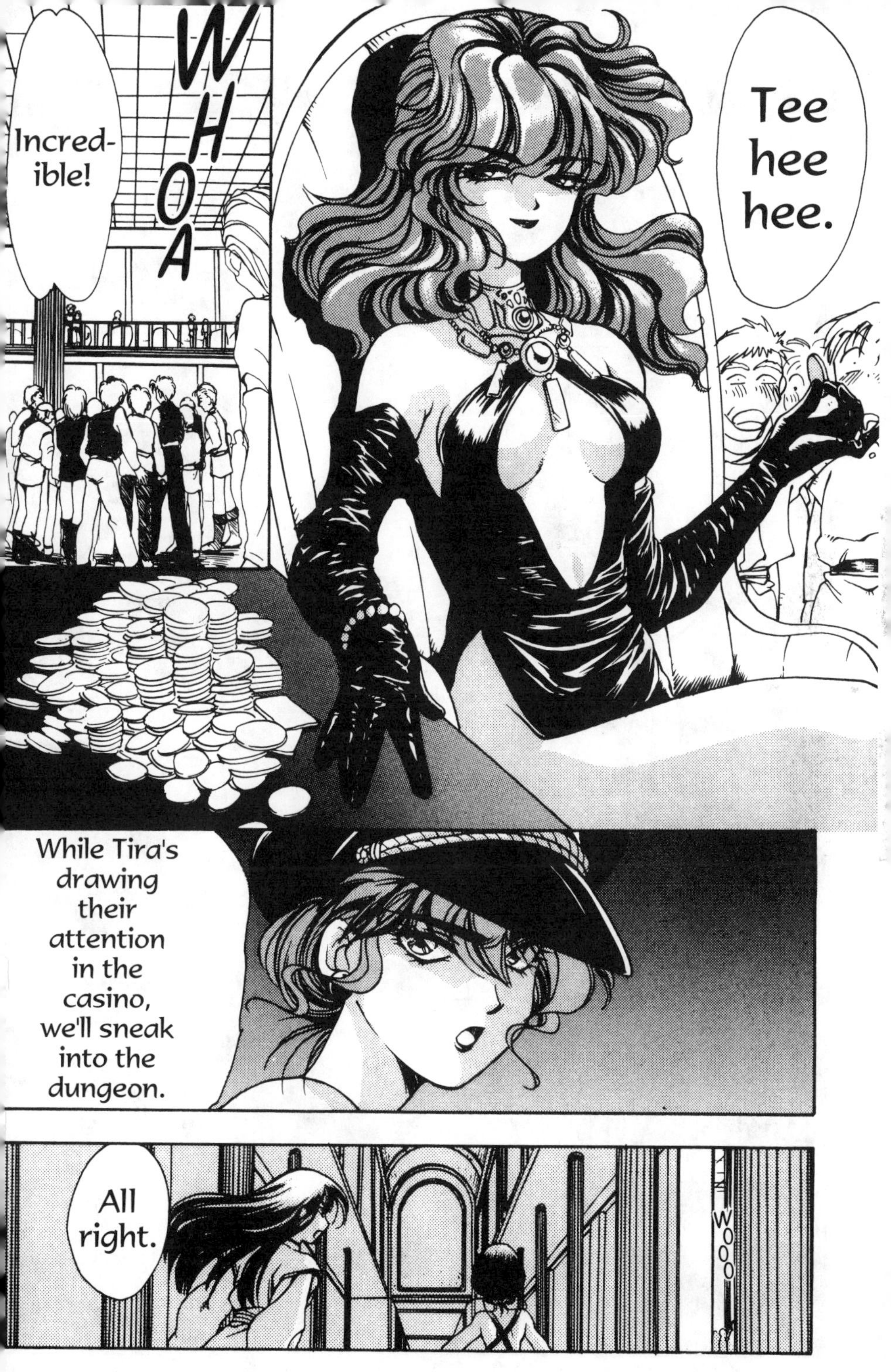
Incred-
ible!
WHOA
Tee hee hee.
While Tira's drawing their attention in the casino, we'll sneak into the dungeon.
All right.
WOOO

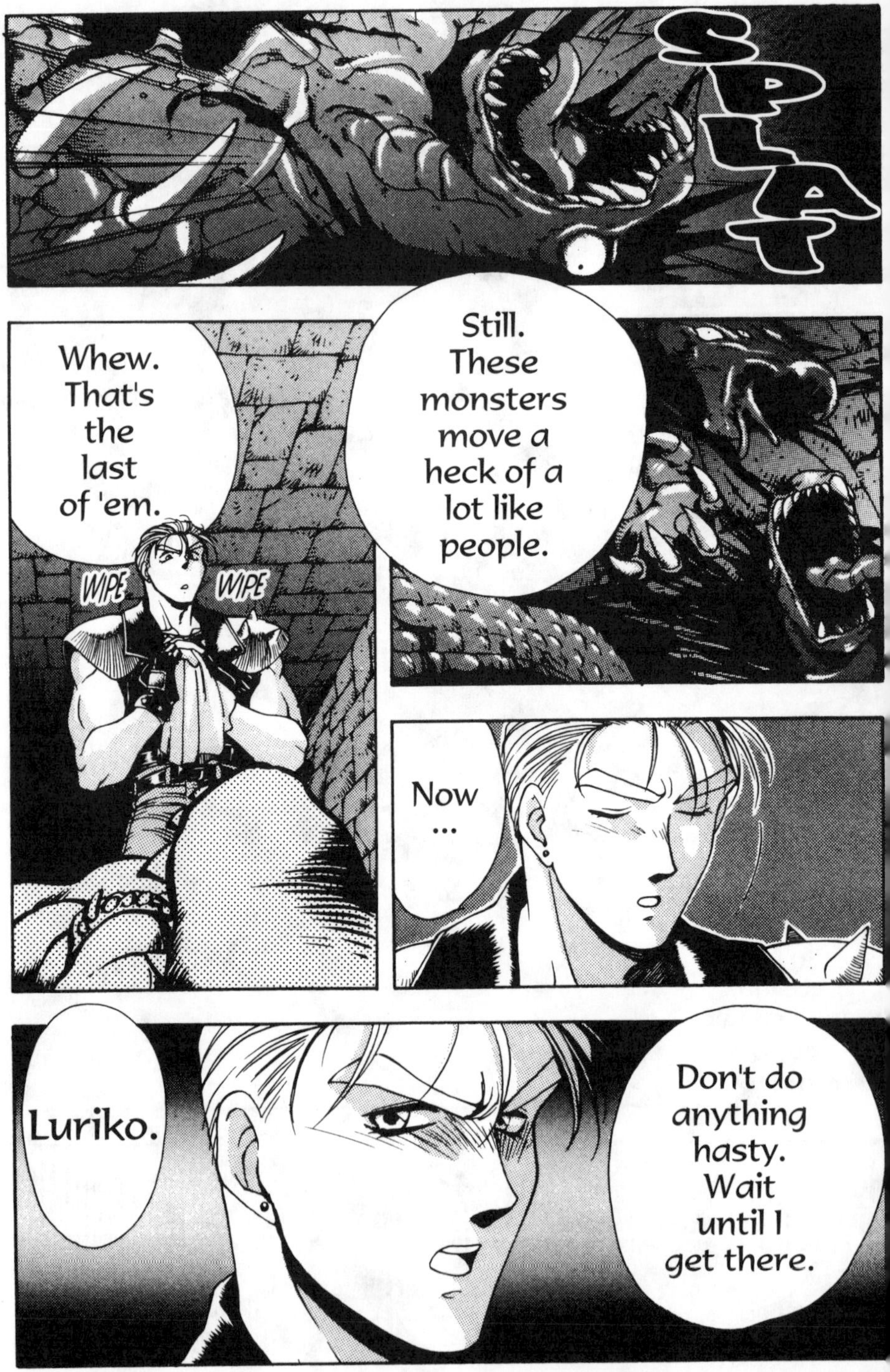
SPLAT
Whew. That's the last of 'em.
WIPE WIPE
Still. These monsters move a heck of a lot like people.
Now ...
Luriko.
Don't do anything hasty. Wait until I get there.

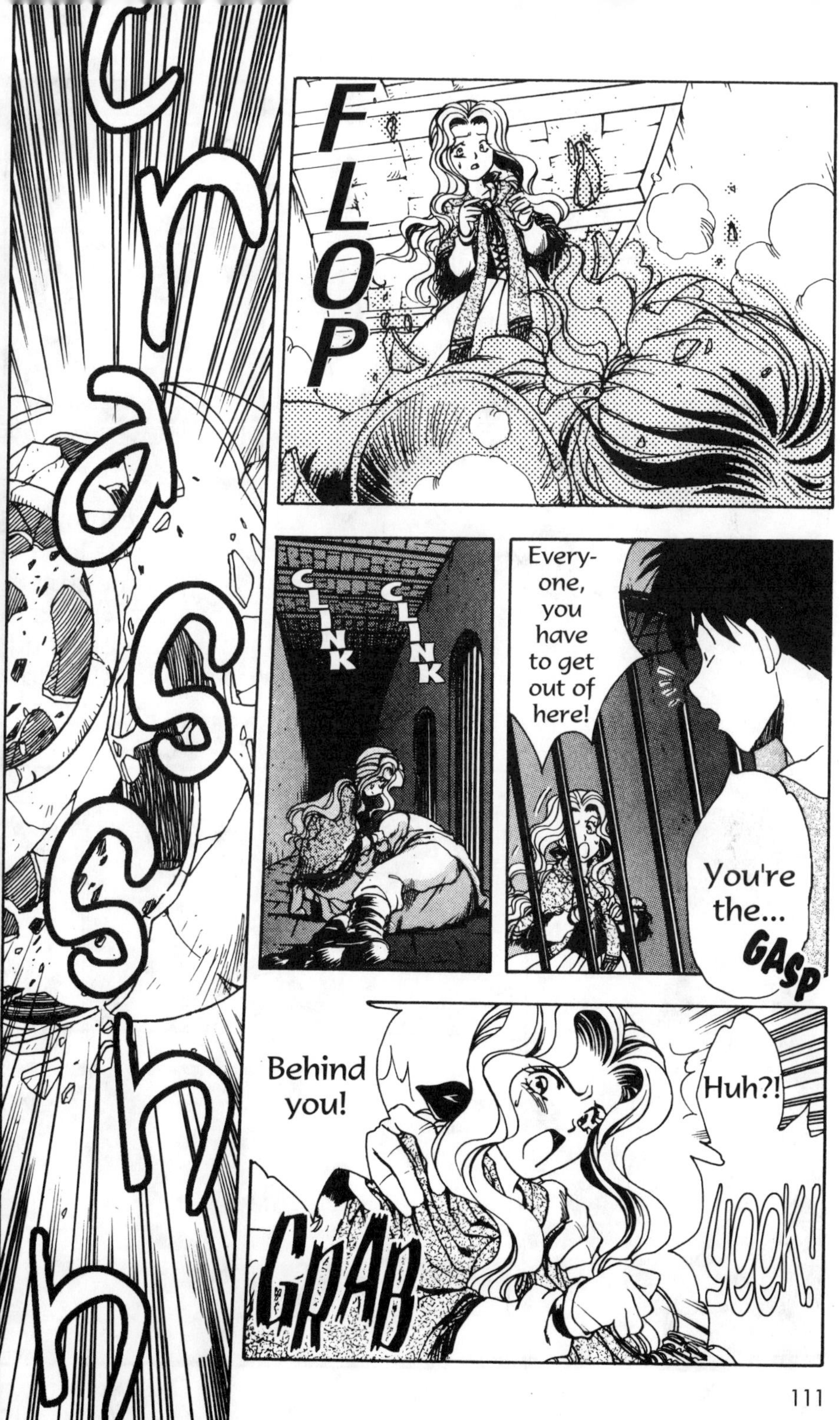
crasshh
FLOP
CLINK
CLINK
Every-one, you have to get out of here!
You're the...
GASP
Behind you!
Huh?!
GRAB
YEEK!

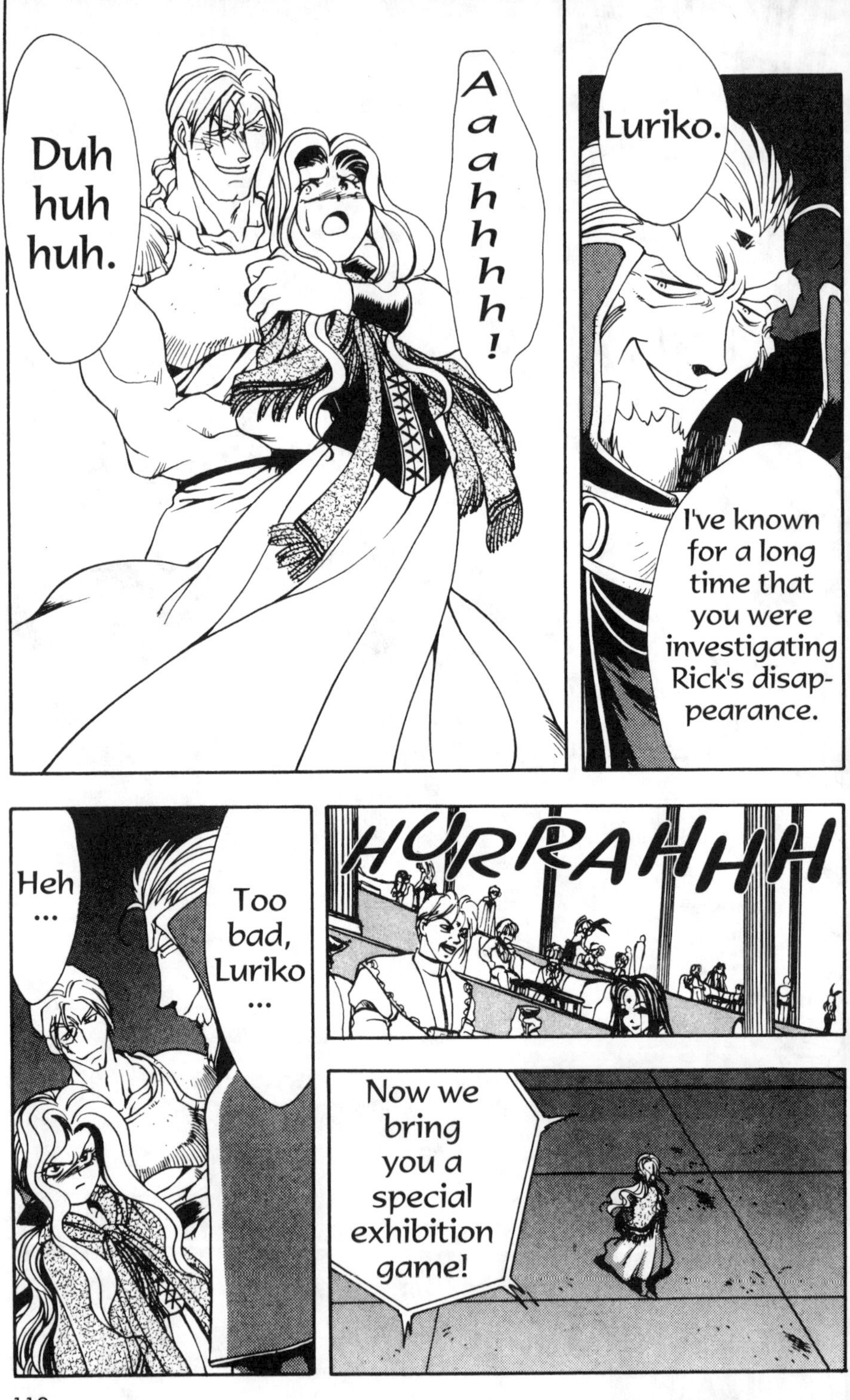
Duh huh huh.
Aaaahhhhh!
Luriko.
I've known for a long time that you were investigating Rick's disap-pearance.
Heh ...
Too bad, Luriko ...
HURRAHHH
Now we bring you a special exhibition game!

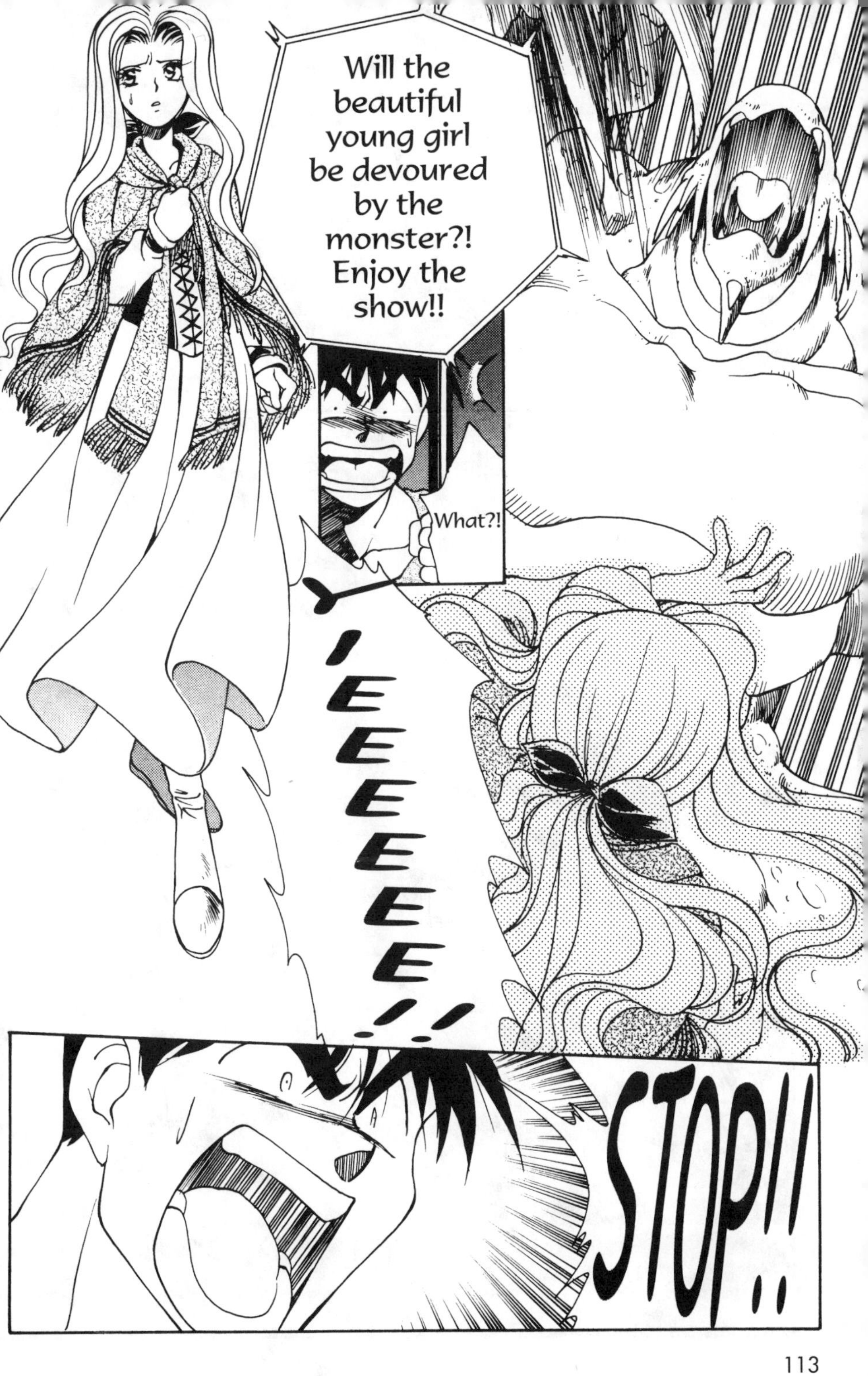

Will the beautiful young girl be devoured by the monster?! Enjoy the show!!
What?!
YIEEEEEE!!
STOP!!

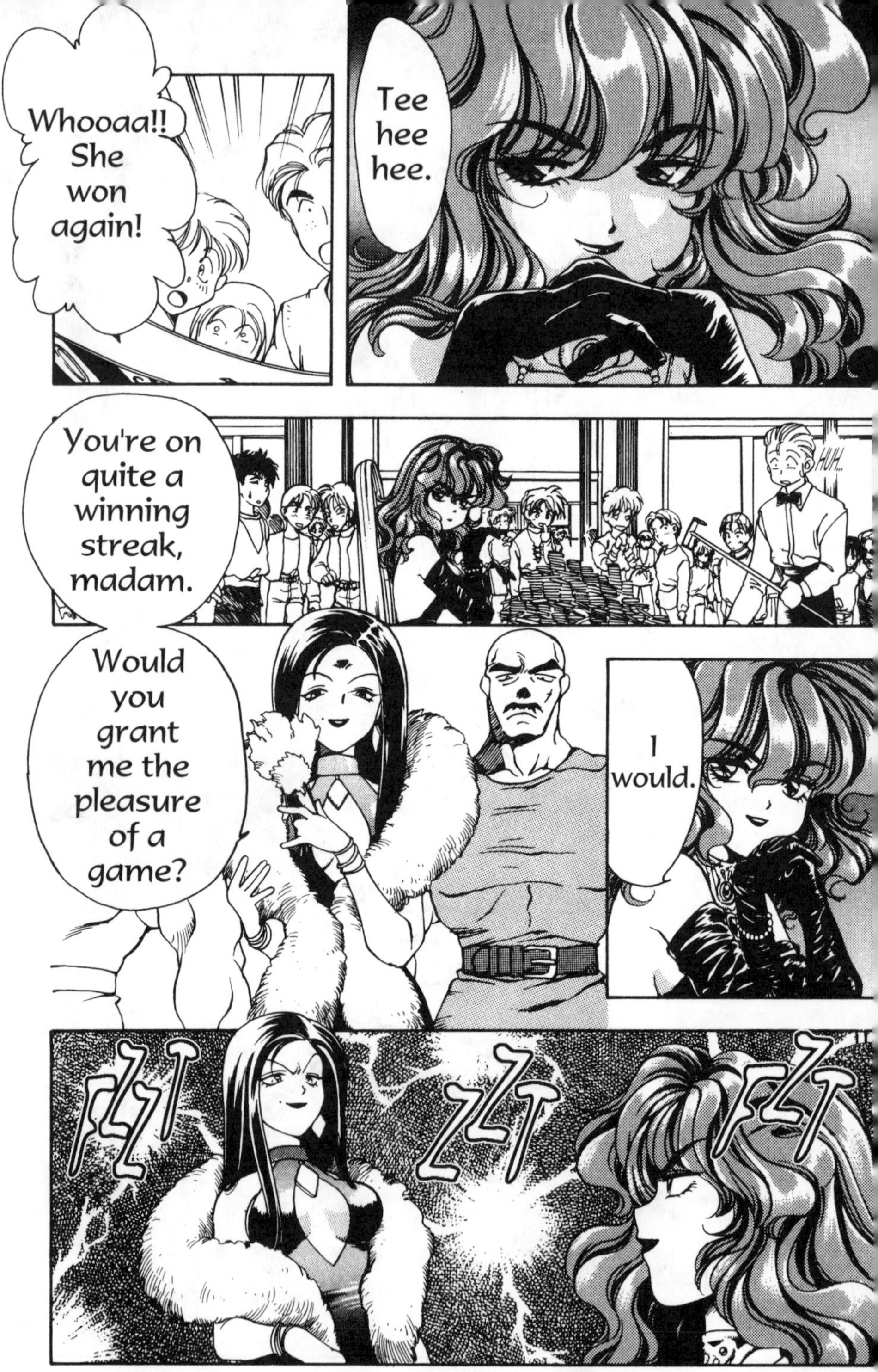
Whooaa!! She won again!
Tee hee hee.
You're on quite a winning streak, madam.
HUH...
Would you grant me the pleasure of a game?
I would.
FZZT
ZZT
FZZT

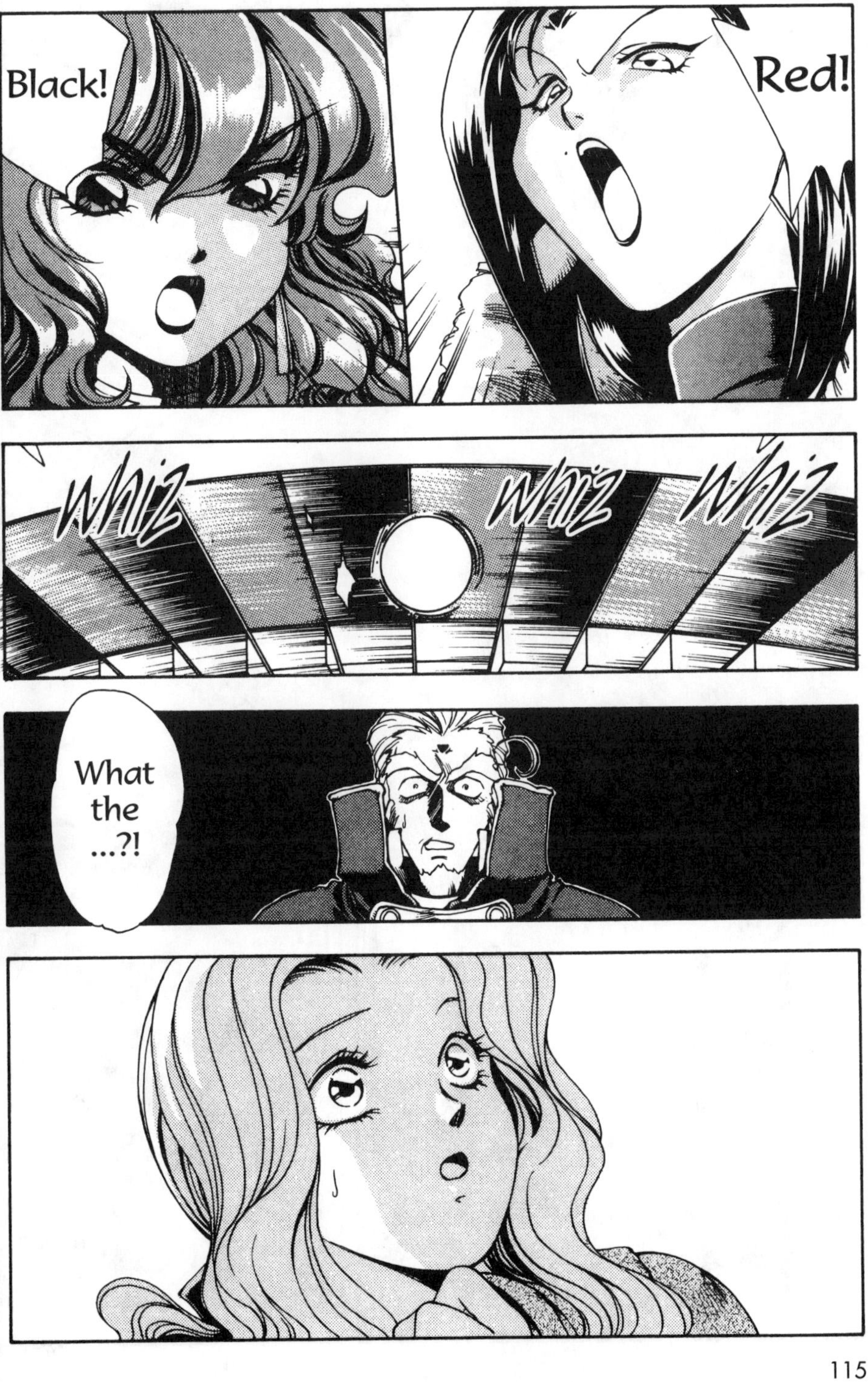
Black!
Red!
whiz
whiz
whiz
What the ...?!

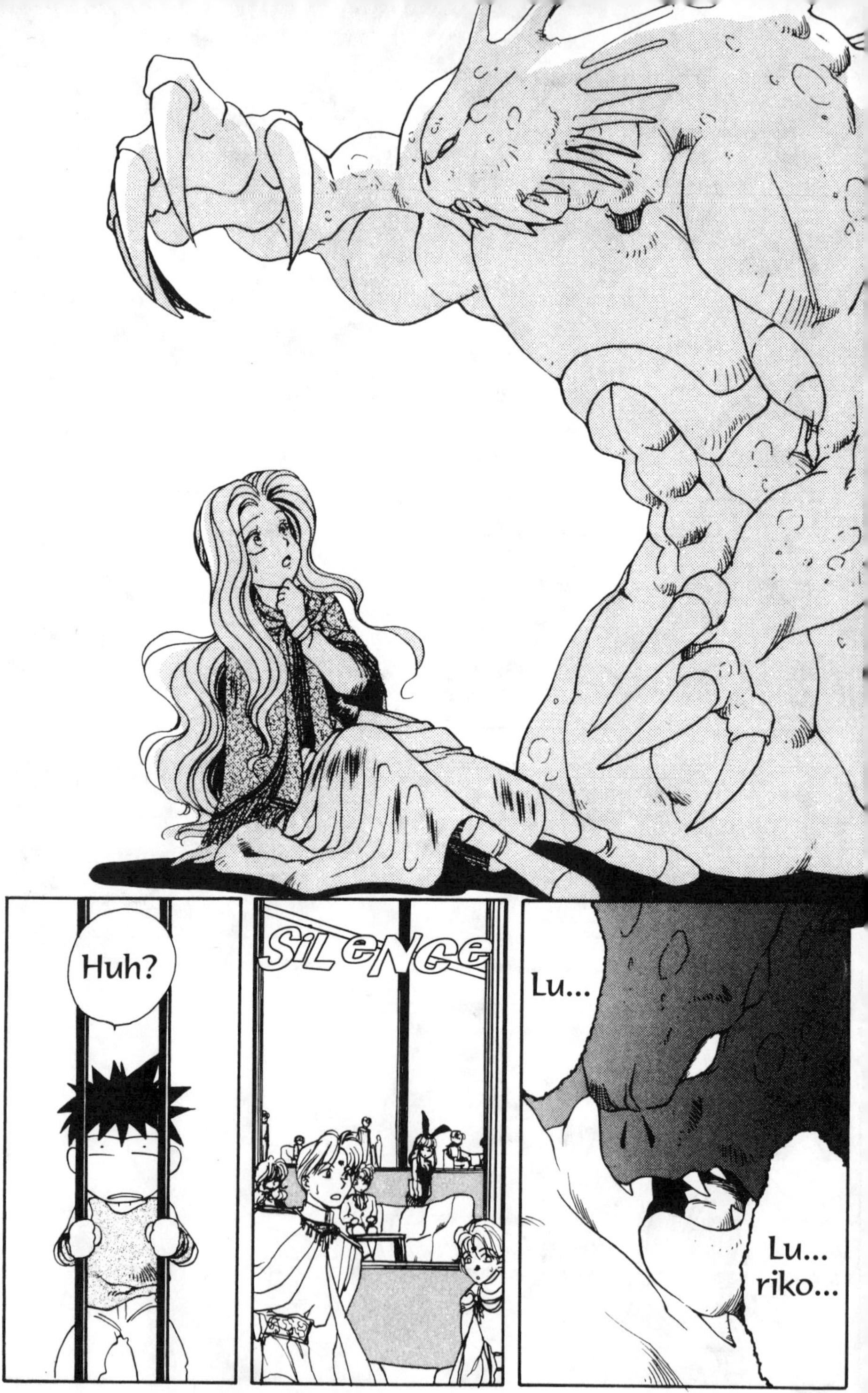
Huh?
SILENCE
Lu...
Lu...
riko...

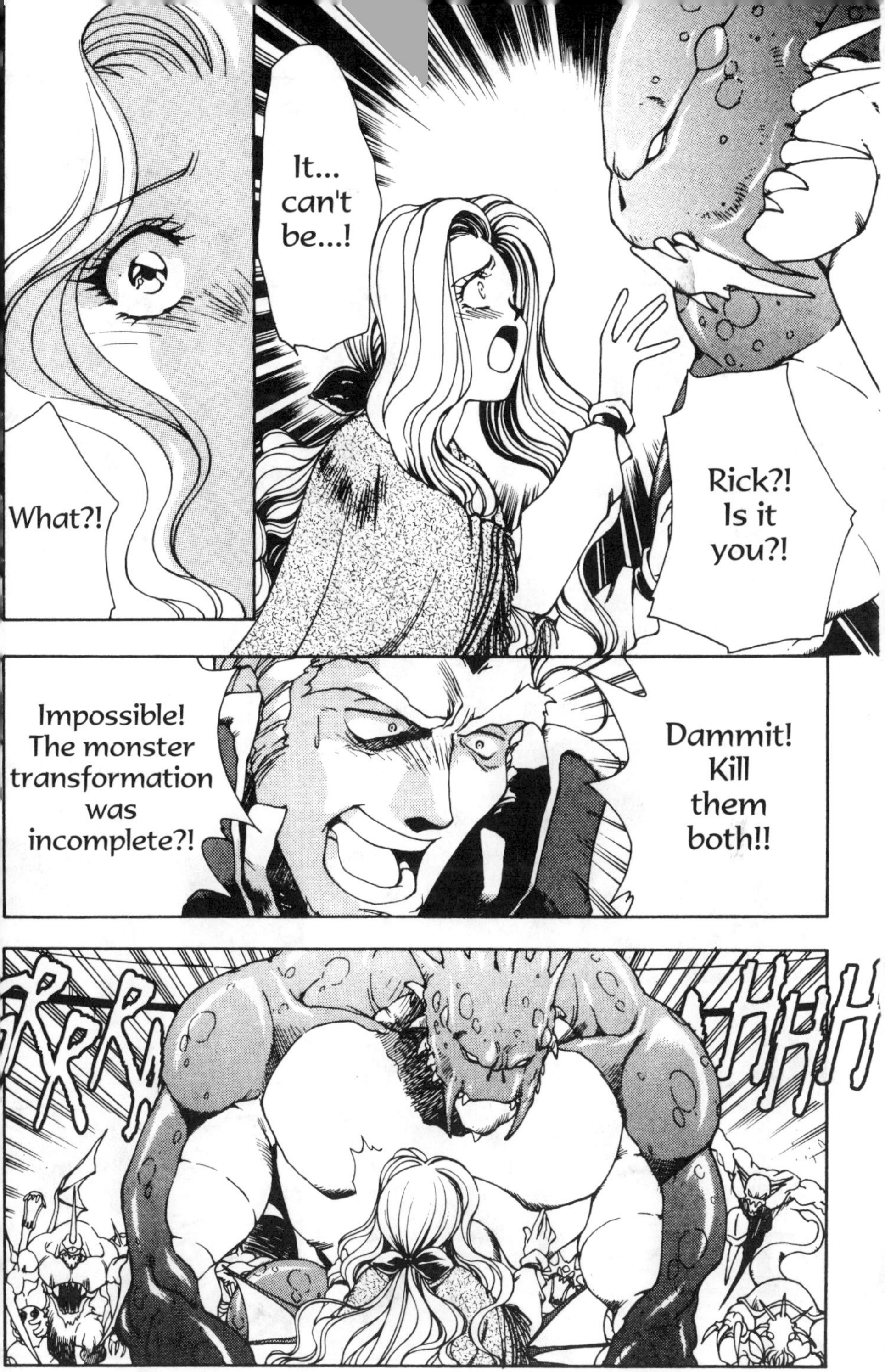
What?!
It... can't be...!
Rick?! Is it you?!
Impossible! The monster transformation was incomplete?!
Dammit! Kill them both!!

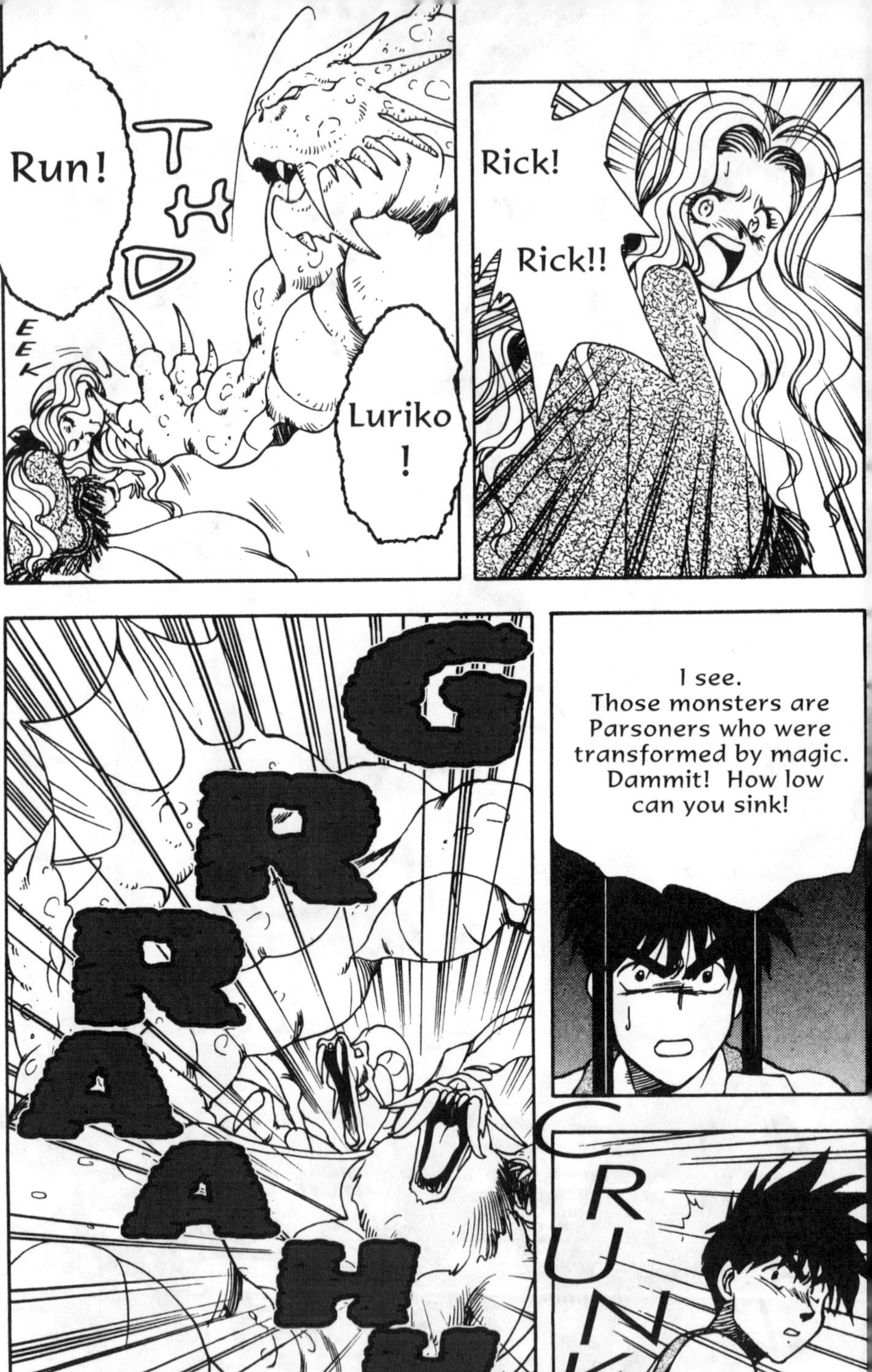
Run!
THD
EEK
Luriko!
Rick!
Rick!!
GRRAAHH
I see.
Those monsters are Parsoners who were transformed by magic.
Dammit! How low can you sink!
CRUNK

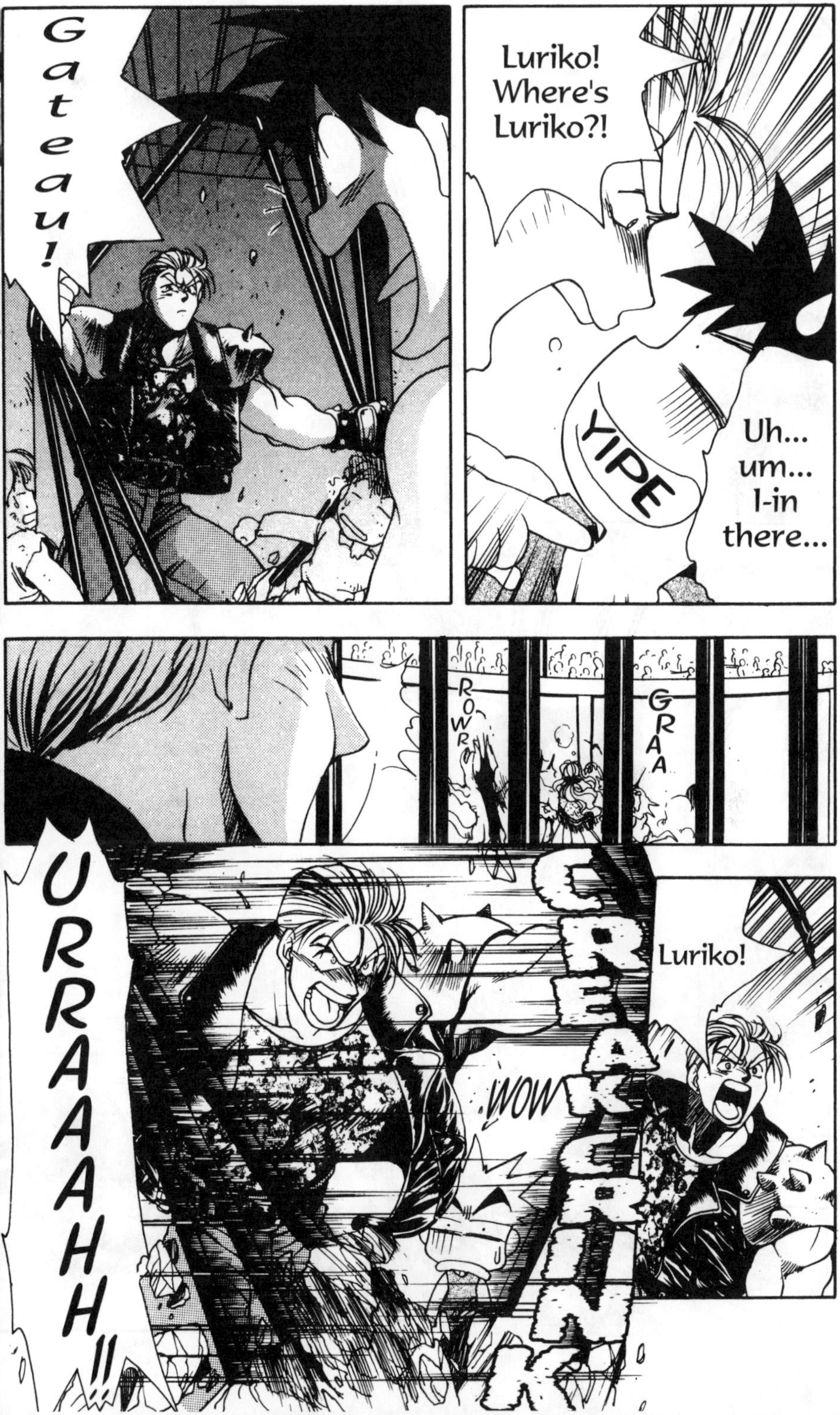
Gateau!
Luriko! Where's Luriko?!
YIPE
Uh... um... I-in there...
ROWR
GRAA
URRAAAAHH!!
CREAKCRINK
WOW
Luriko!

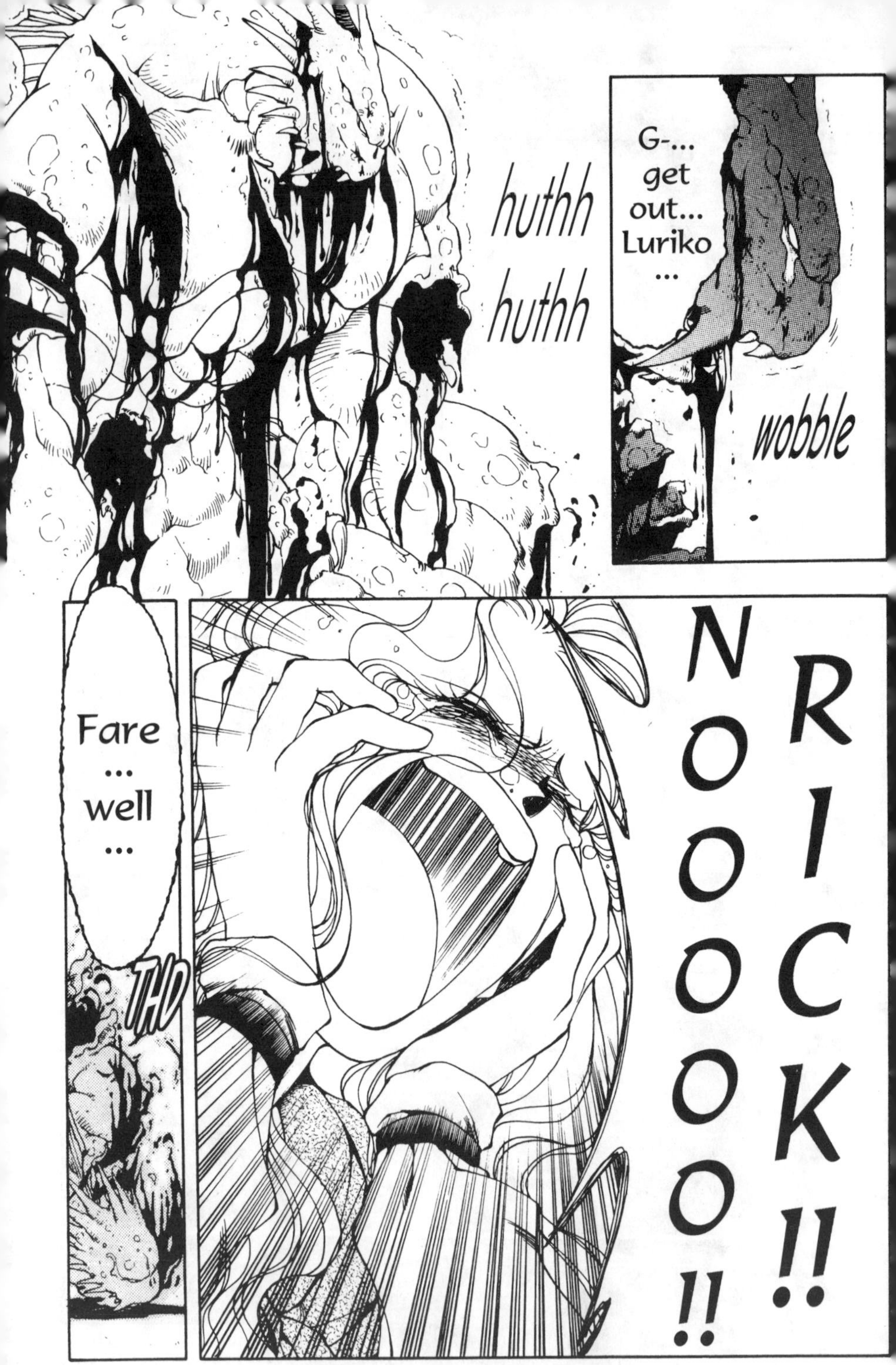
huthh
huthh
G-... get out... Luriko ...
wobble
Fare ... well ...
THD
NOOOOOO!!
RICK!!

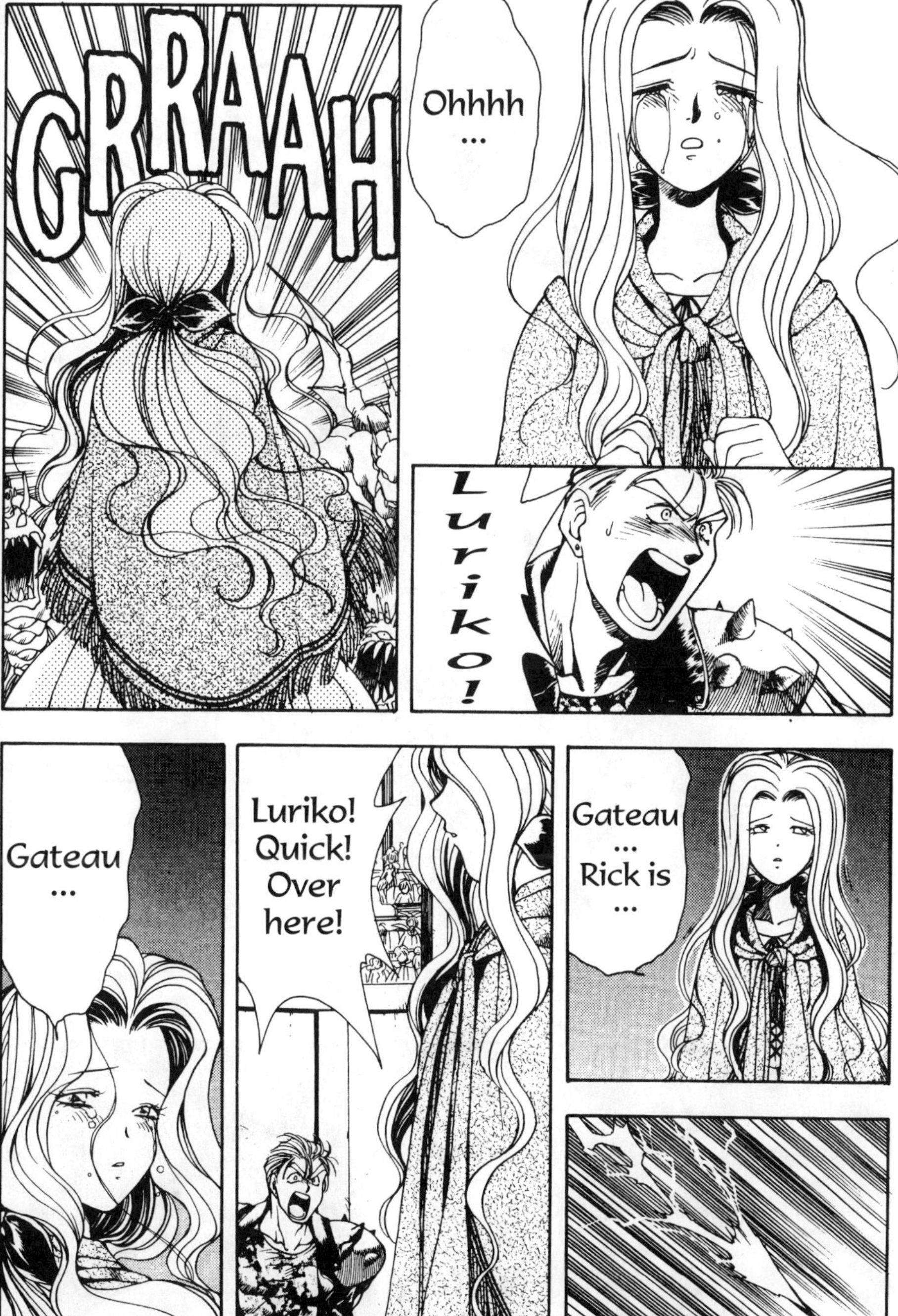
GRRAAH
Ohhhh ...
Luriko!
Gateau ...
Luriko! Quick! Over here!
Gateau ... Rick is ...

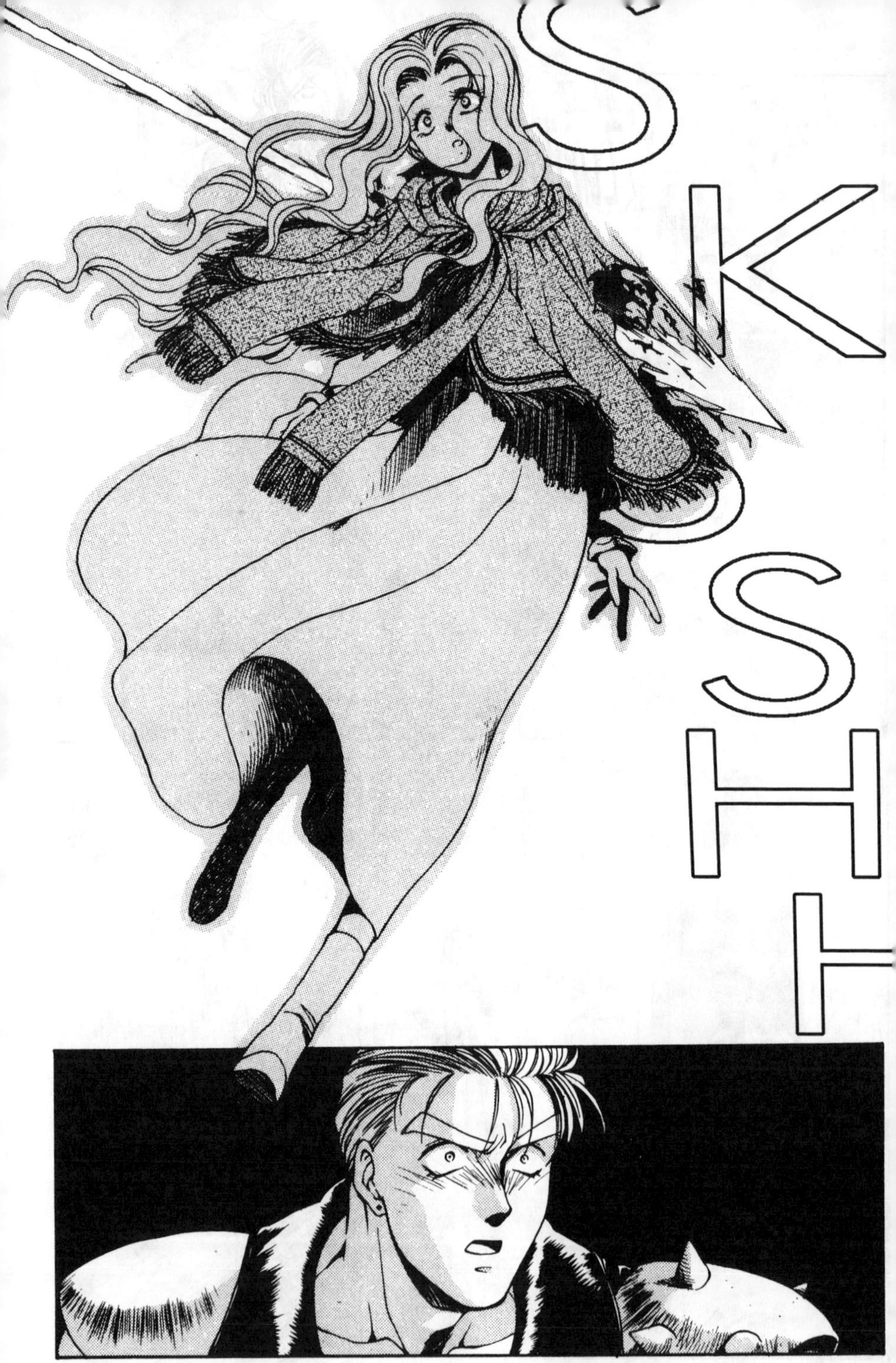
SKSSHH

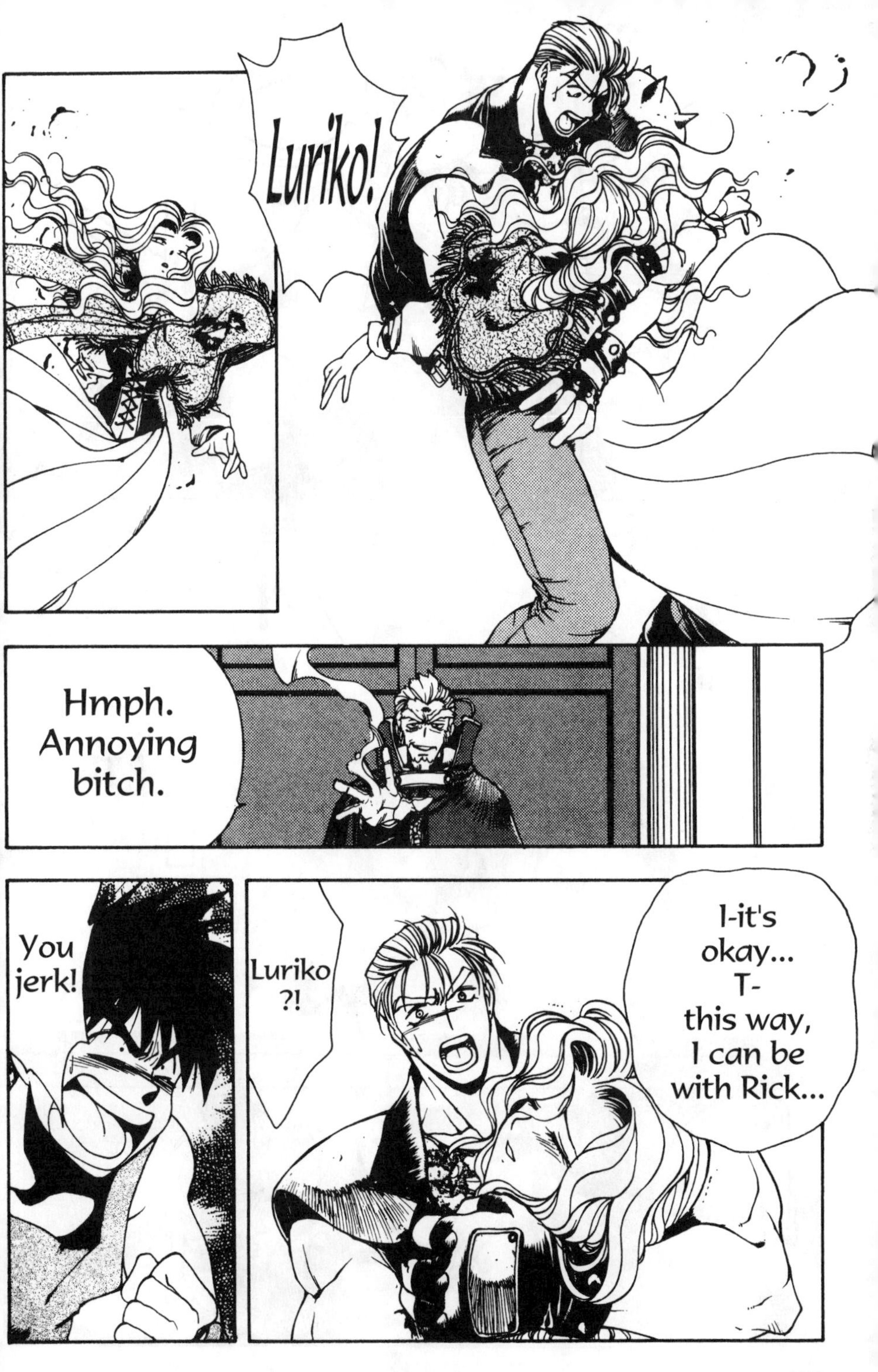

Luriko!
Hmph. Annoying bitch.
You jerk!
Luriko ?!
I-it's okay... T- this way, I can be with Rick...

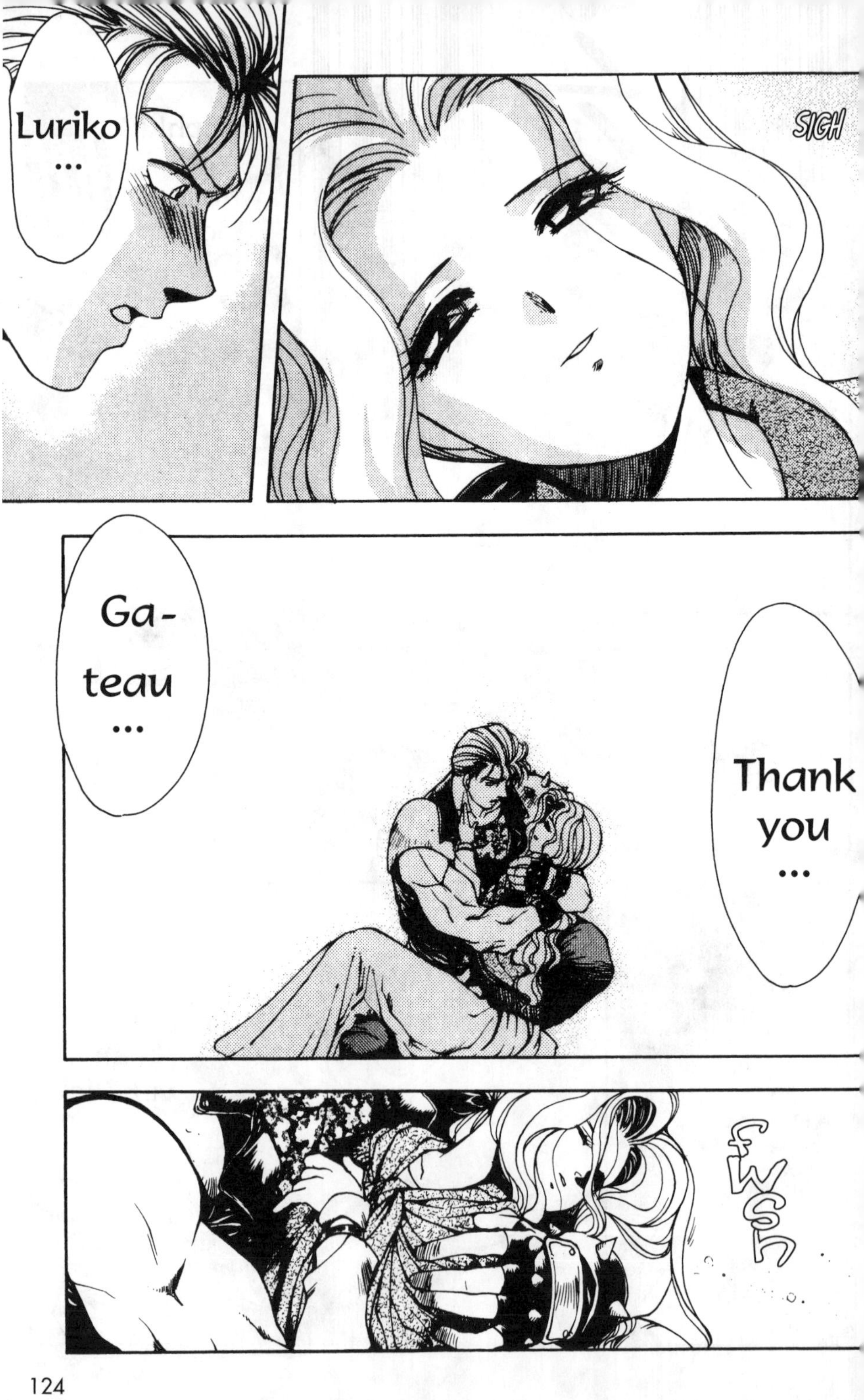
Luriko ...
SIGH
Ga-teau ...
Thank you ...
FWSH

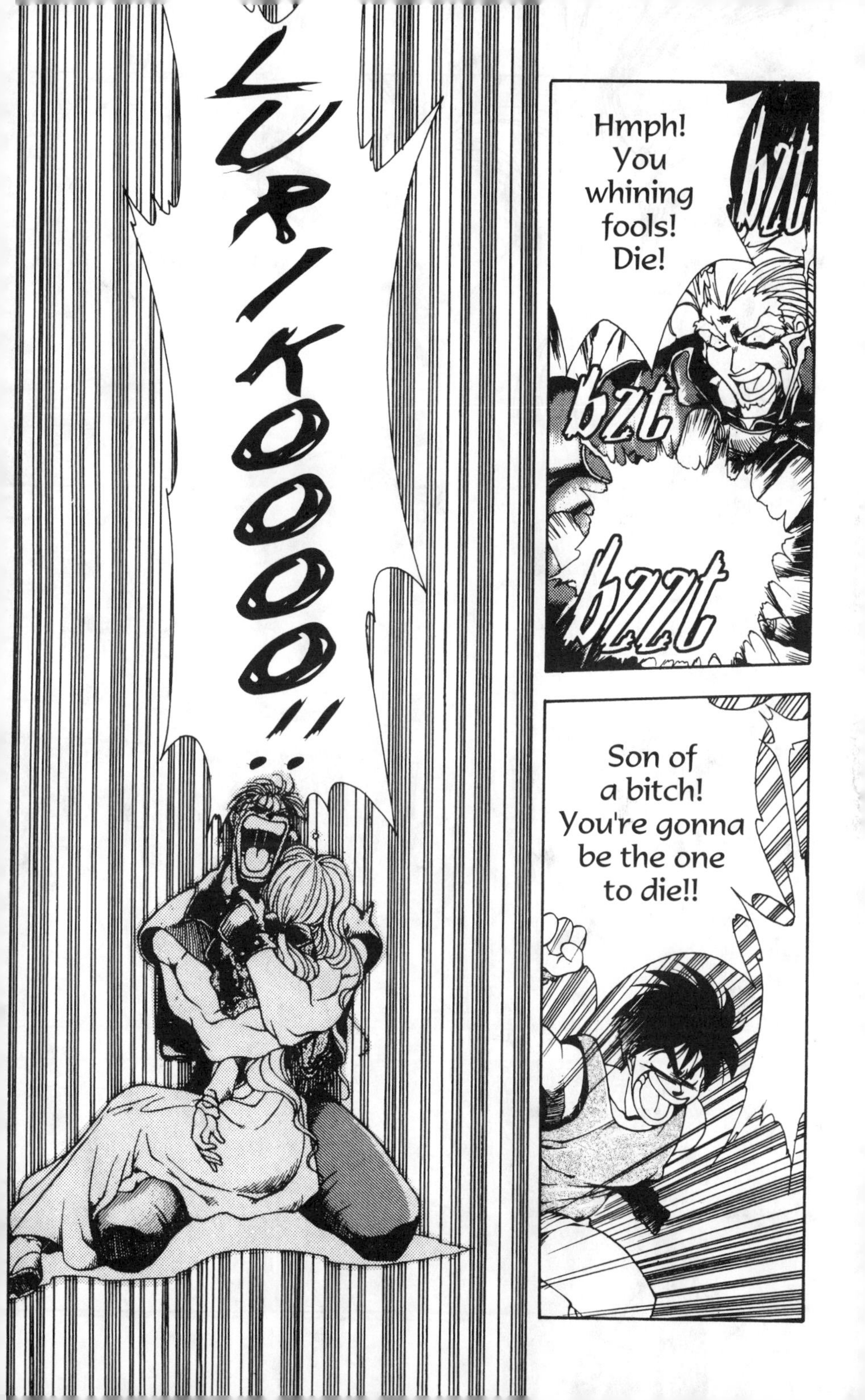
LURIKOOOO!!
Hmph! You whining fools! Die!
bzt
bzt
bzzt
Son of a bitch! You're gonna be the one to die!!

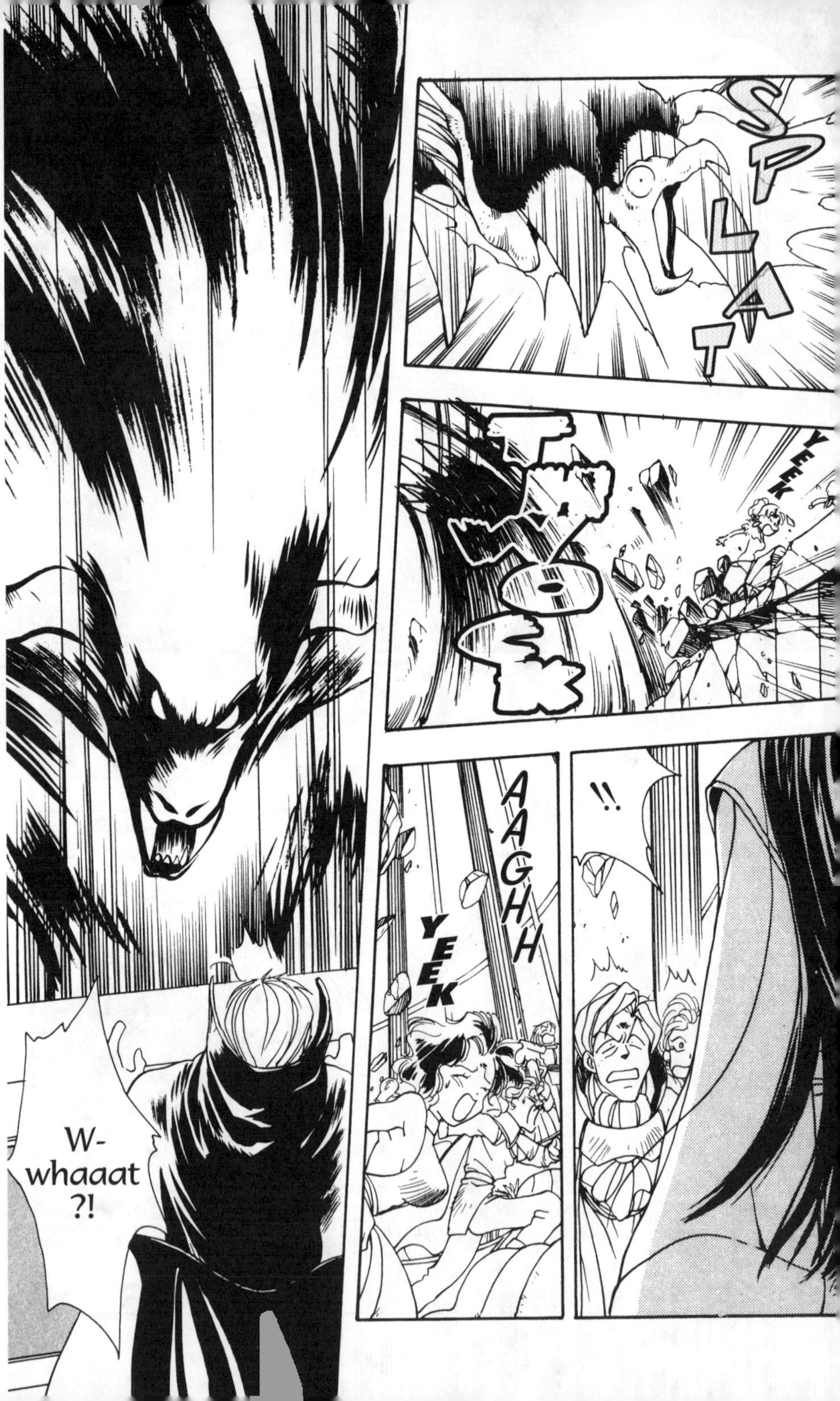
W-
whaaat
?!
SPLAT
THWOCK
YEEK
YEEK
AAAGHH
!!

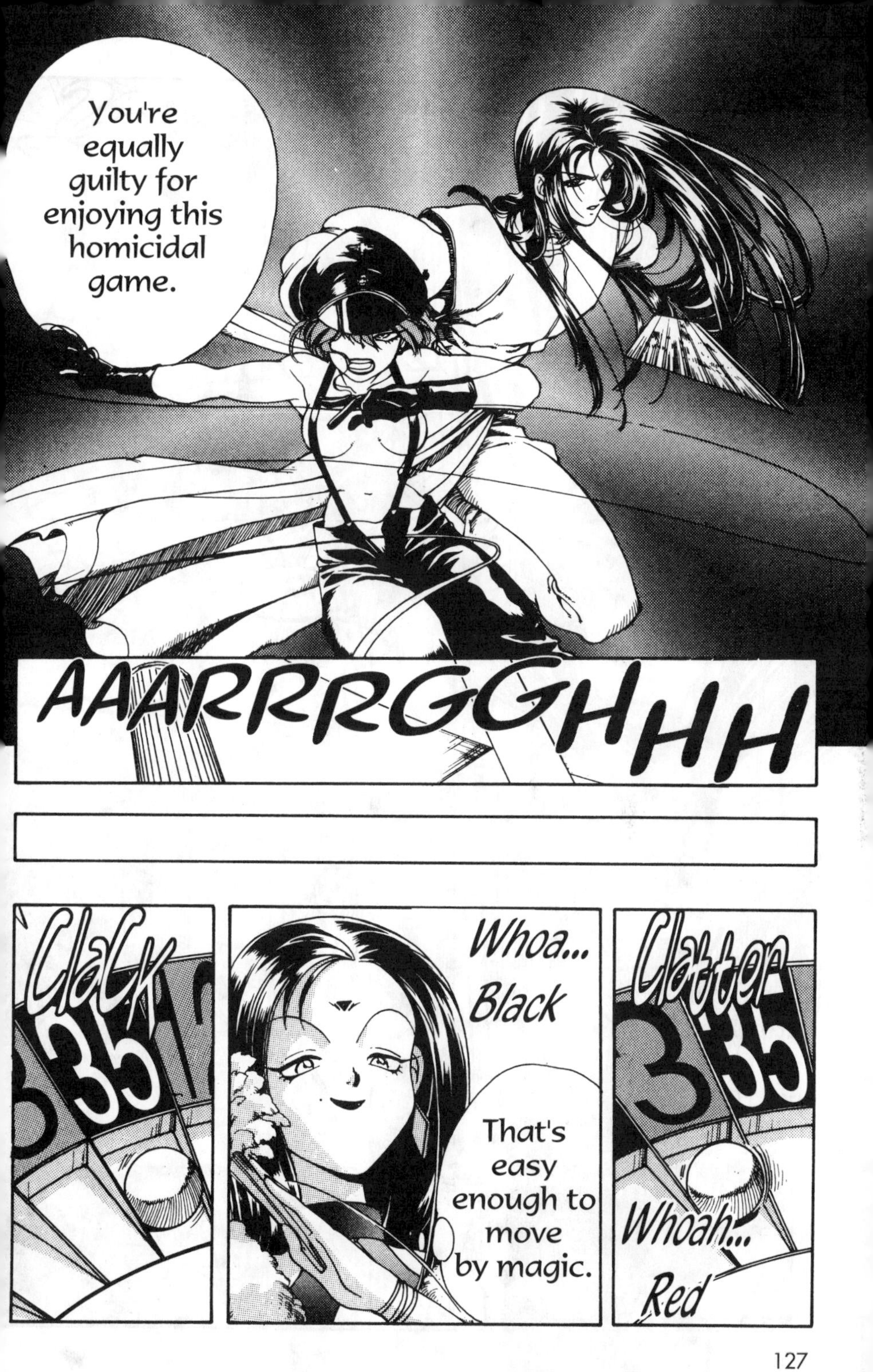
You're equally guilty for enjoying this homicidal game.
AAARRRGGHHH
Clack
Whoa... Black
That's easy enough to move by magic.
Clatter
Whoah... Red

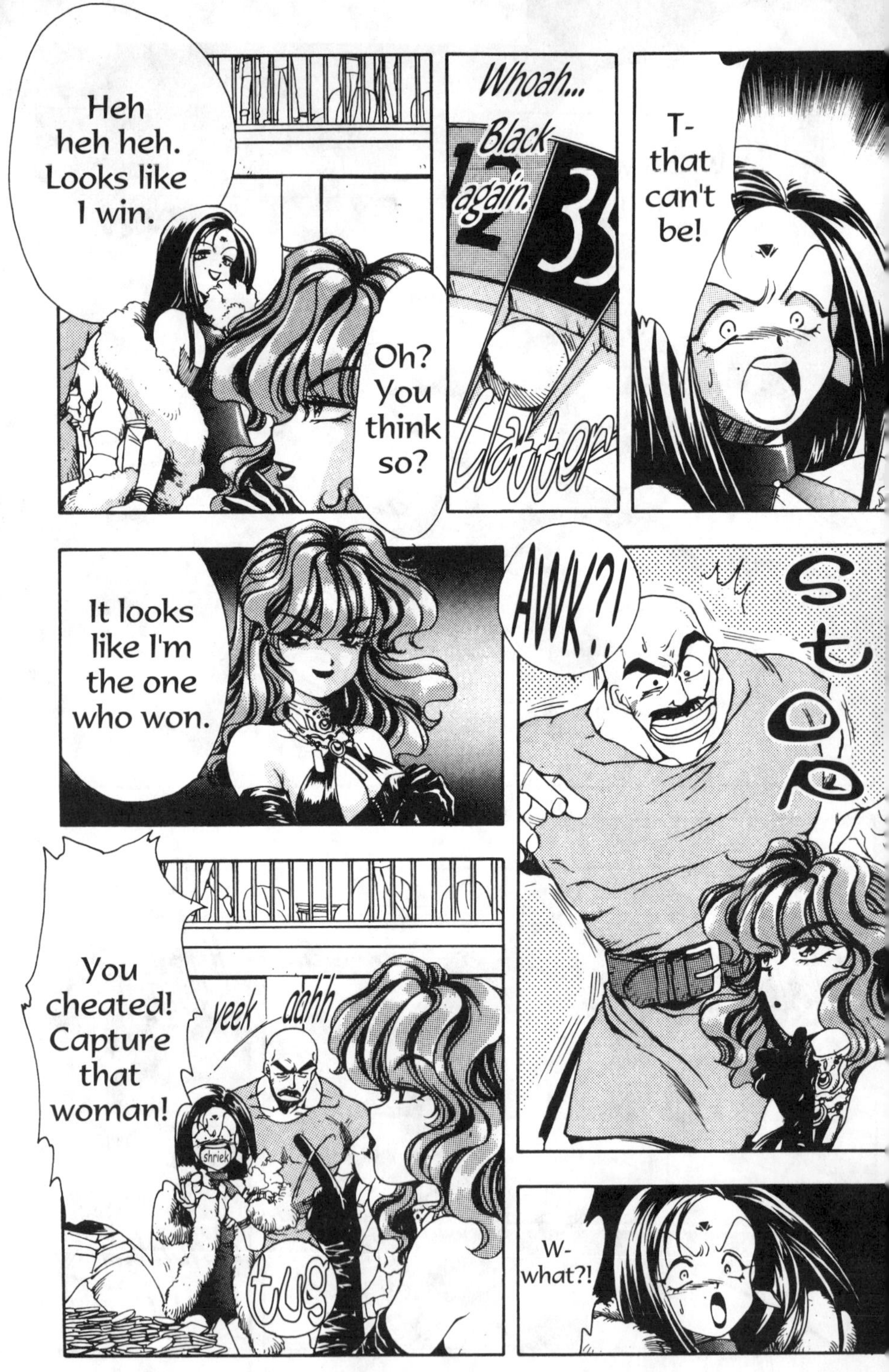
Heh heh heh. Looks like I win.
Oh? You think so?
Whoah... Black again.
12
35
Clatter
T-that can't be!
It looks like I'm the one who won.
AWK?!
STOP
You cheated! Capture that woman!
yeek
aahh
shriek
tug
W-what?!

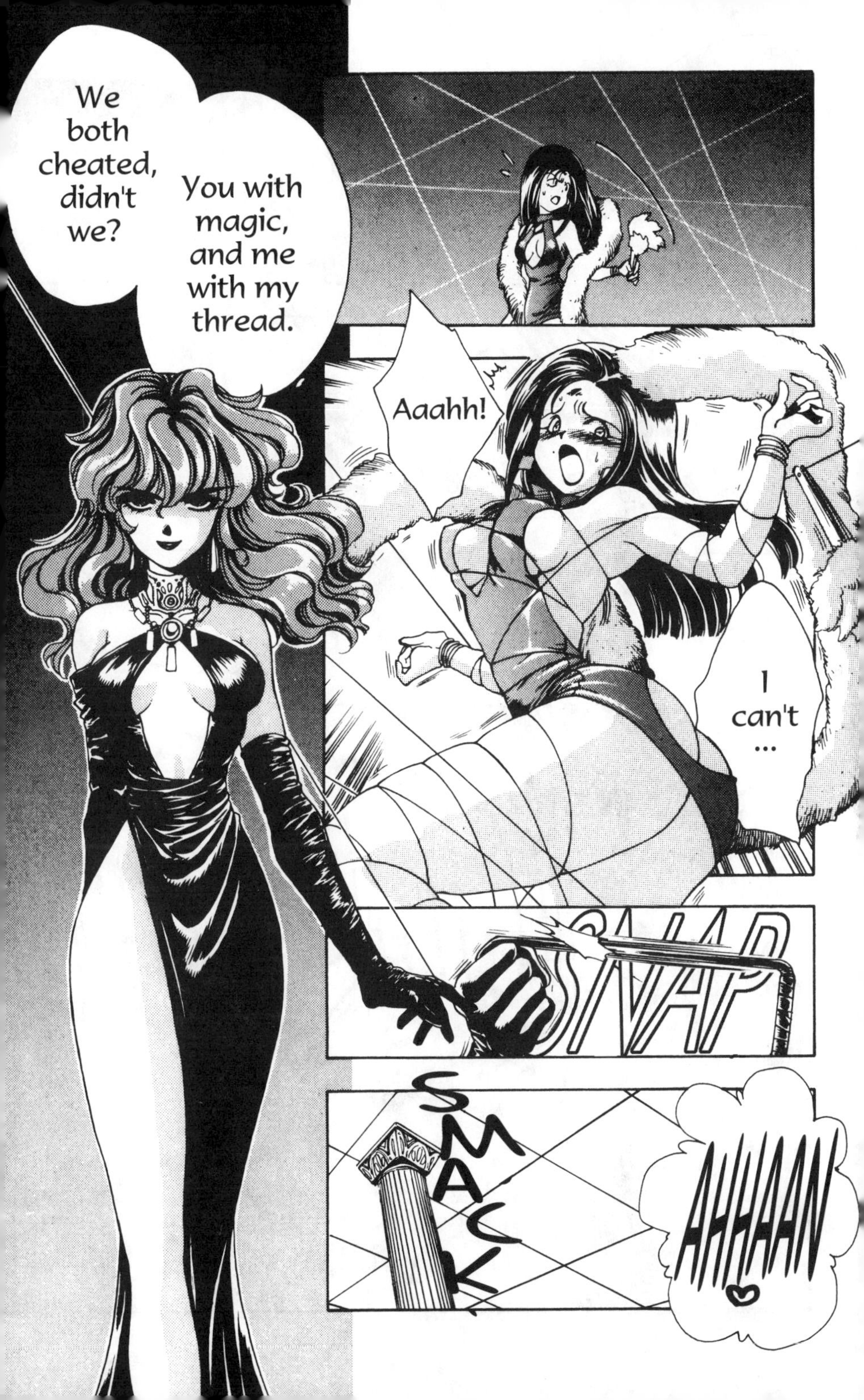
We both cheated, didn't we?
You with magic, and me with my thread.
Aaahh!
I can't ...
SNAP
SMACK
AHHAAN

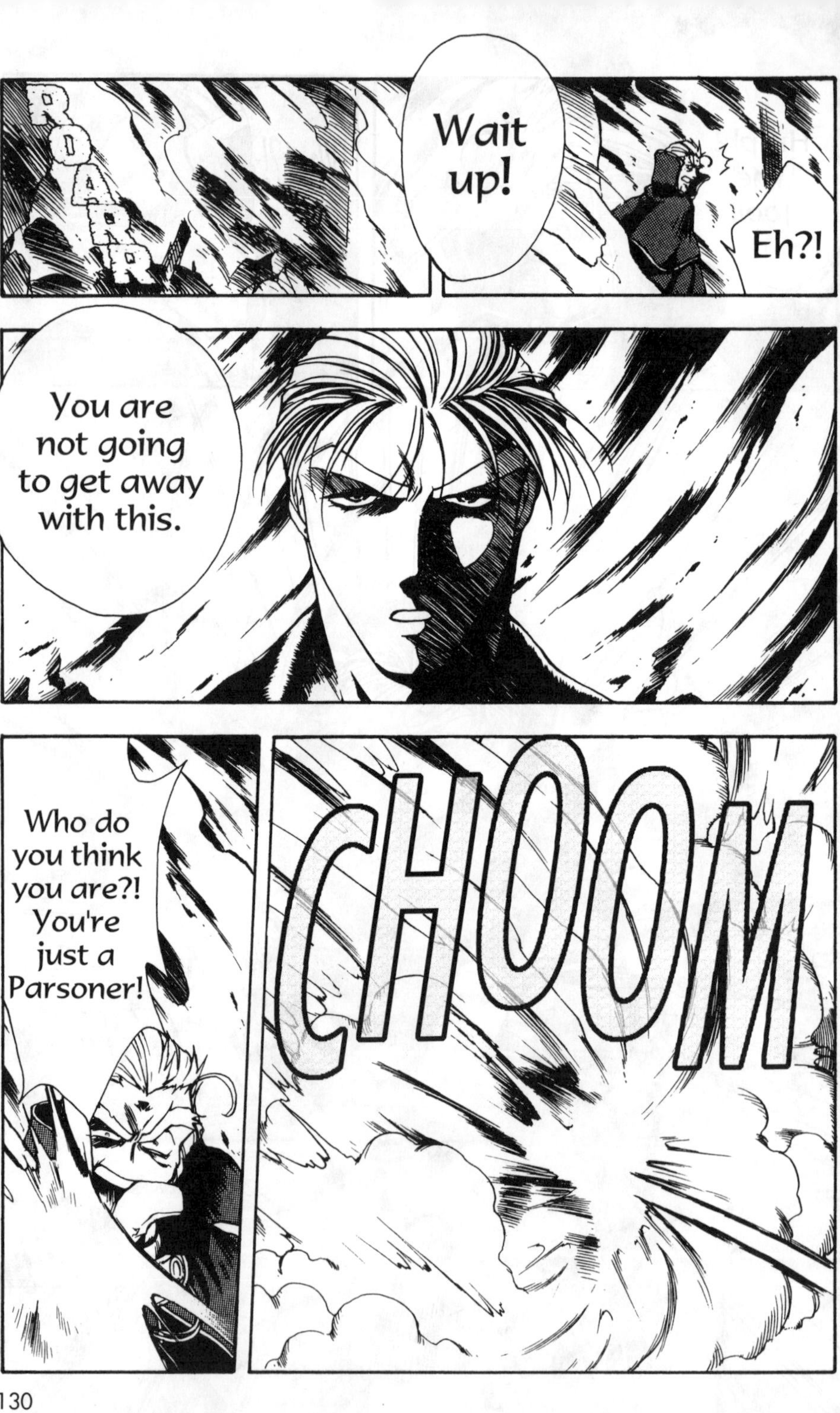
ROAR
Wait up!
Eh?!
You are not going to get away with this.
Who do you think you are?! You're just a Parsoner!
CHOOM

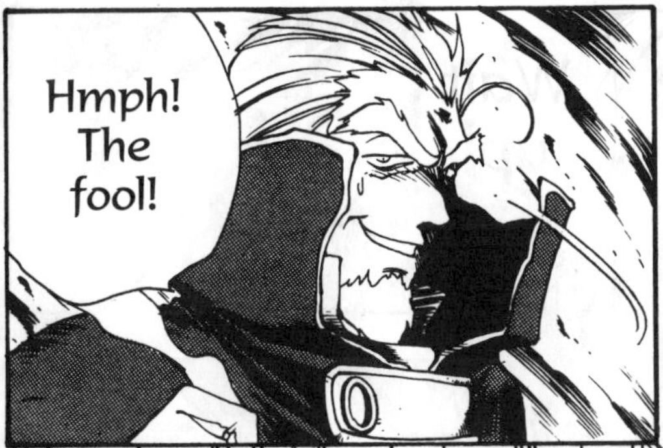
Hmph! The fool!
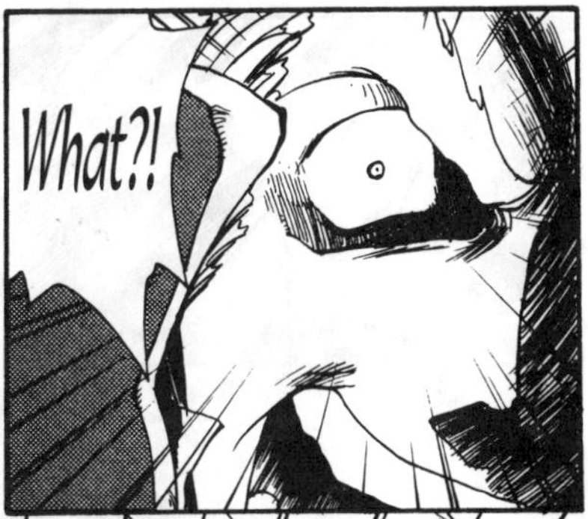
What?!
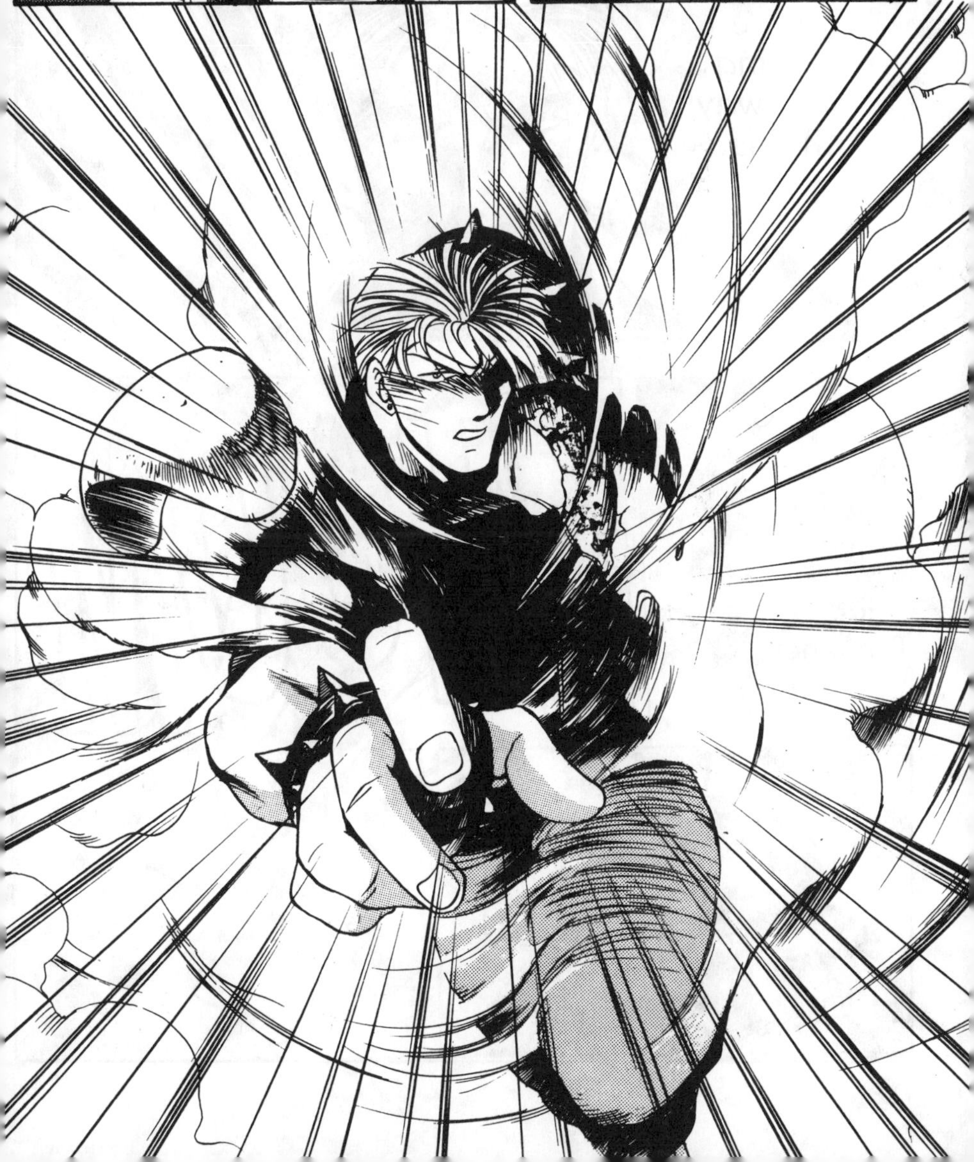

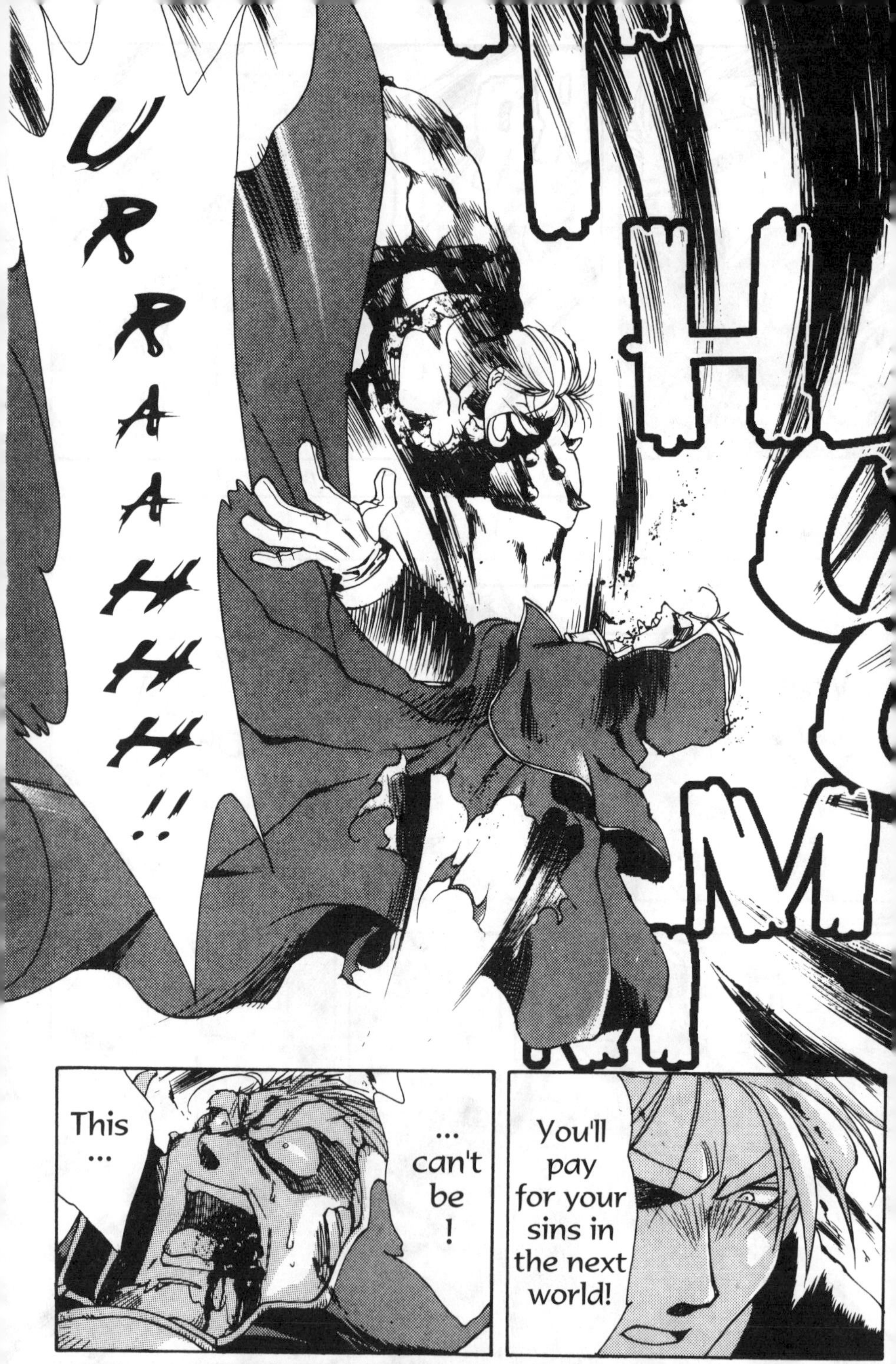
URRAAHHH!!
This ...
... can't be !
You'll pay for your sins in the next world!

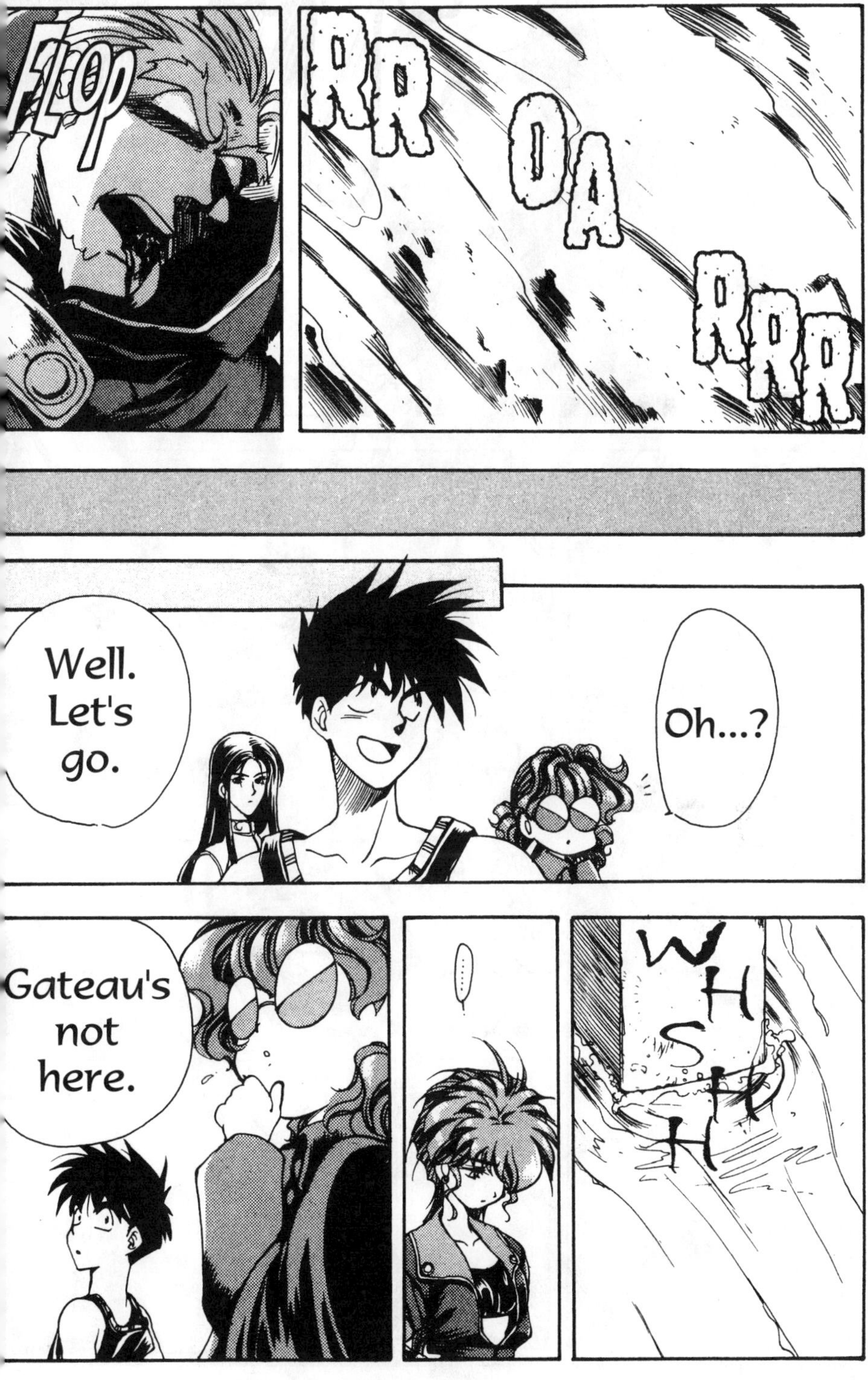
FLOP
RROARRR
Well. Let's go.
Oh...?
Gateau's not here.
!
.....
WHSHH

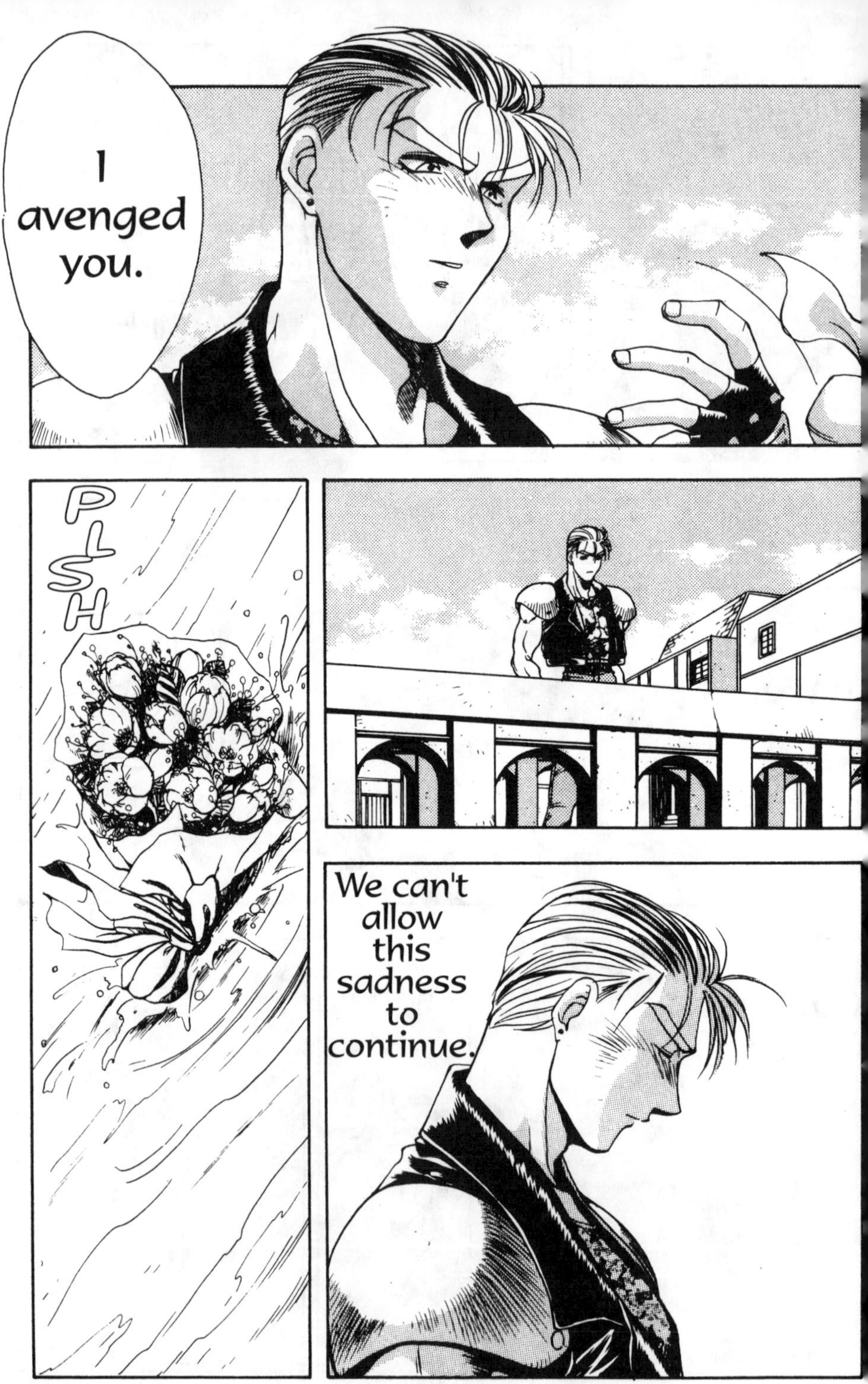

I avenged you.
PLSH
We can't allow this sadness to continue.

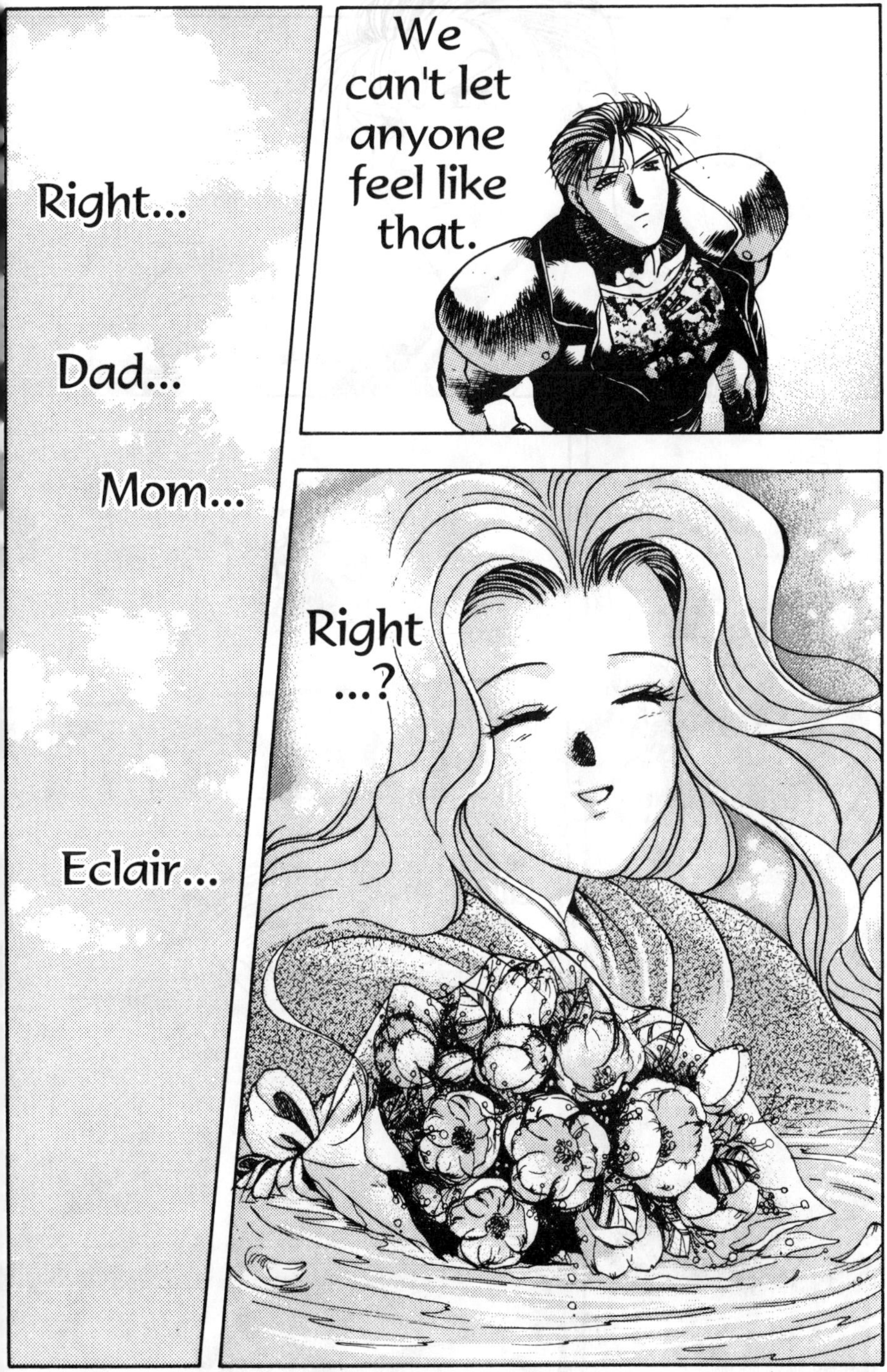

Right...
Dad...
Mom...
Eclair...
We can't let anyone feel like that.
Right ...?

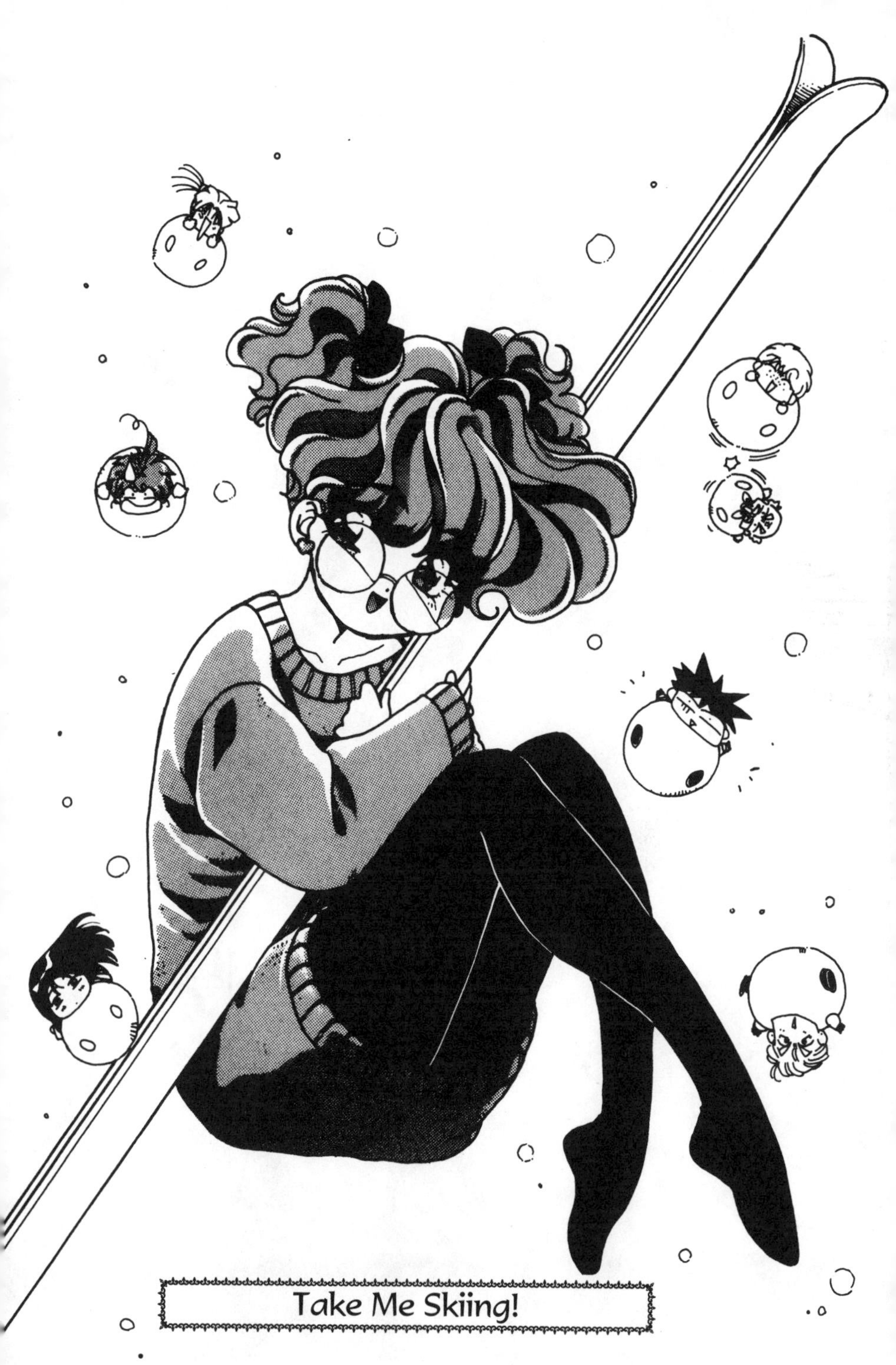

Take Me Skiing!

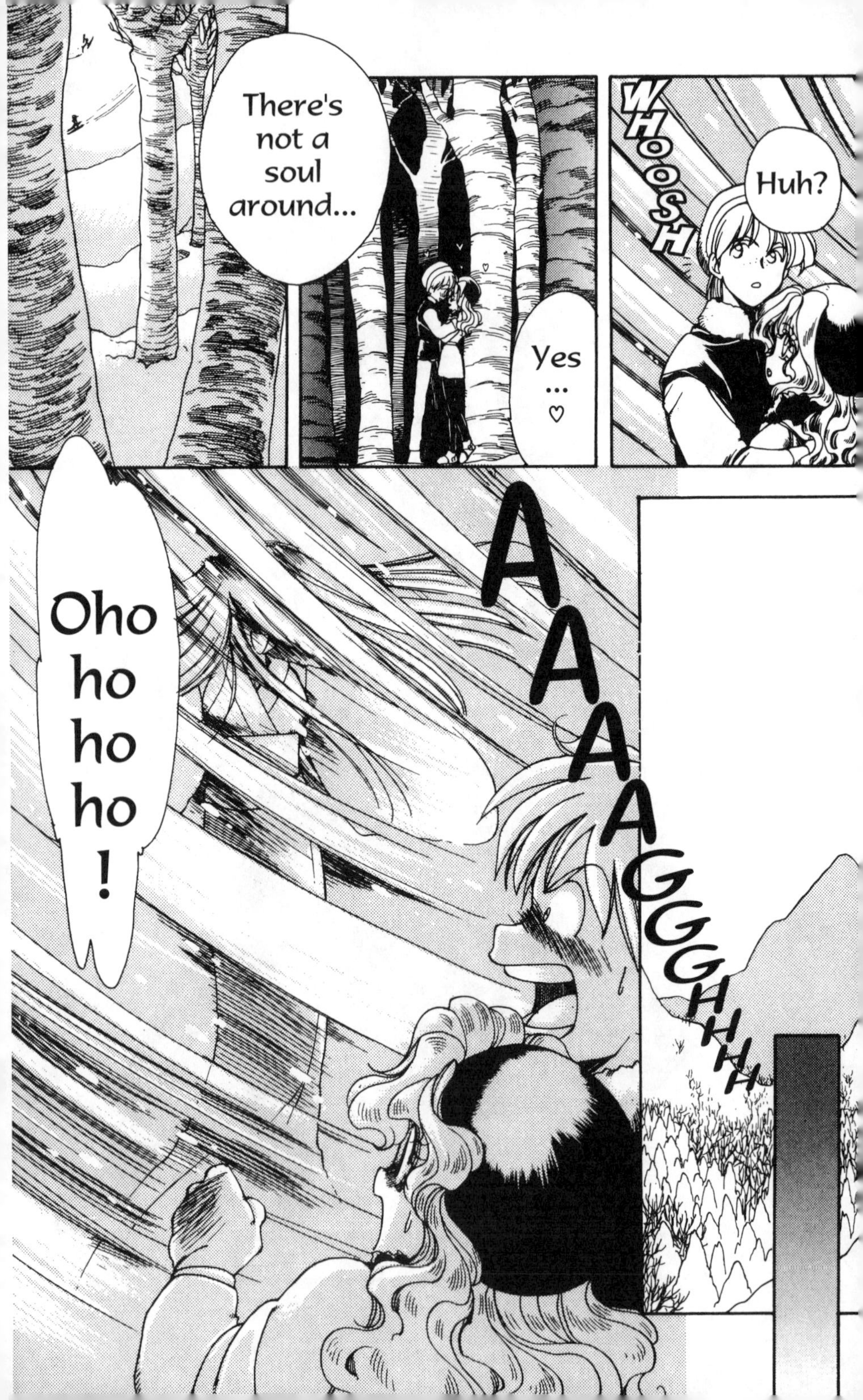
There's not a soul around...
Yes ... ♡
WHOOSH
Huh?
Oho ho ho ho !
AAAAAGGGHHHH

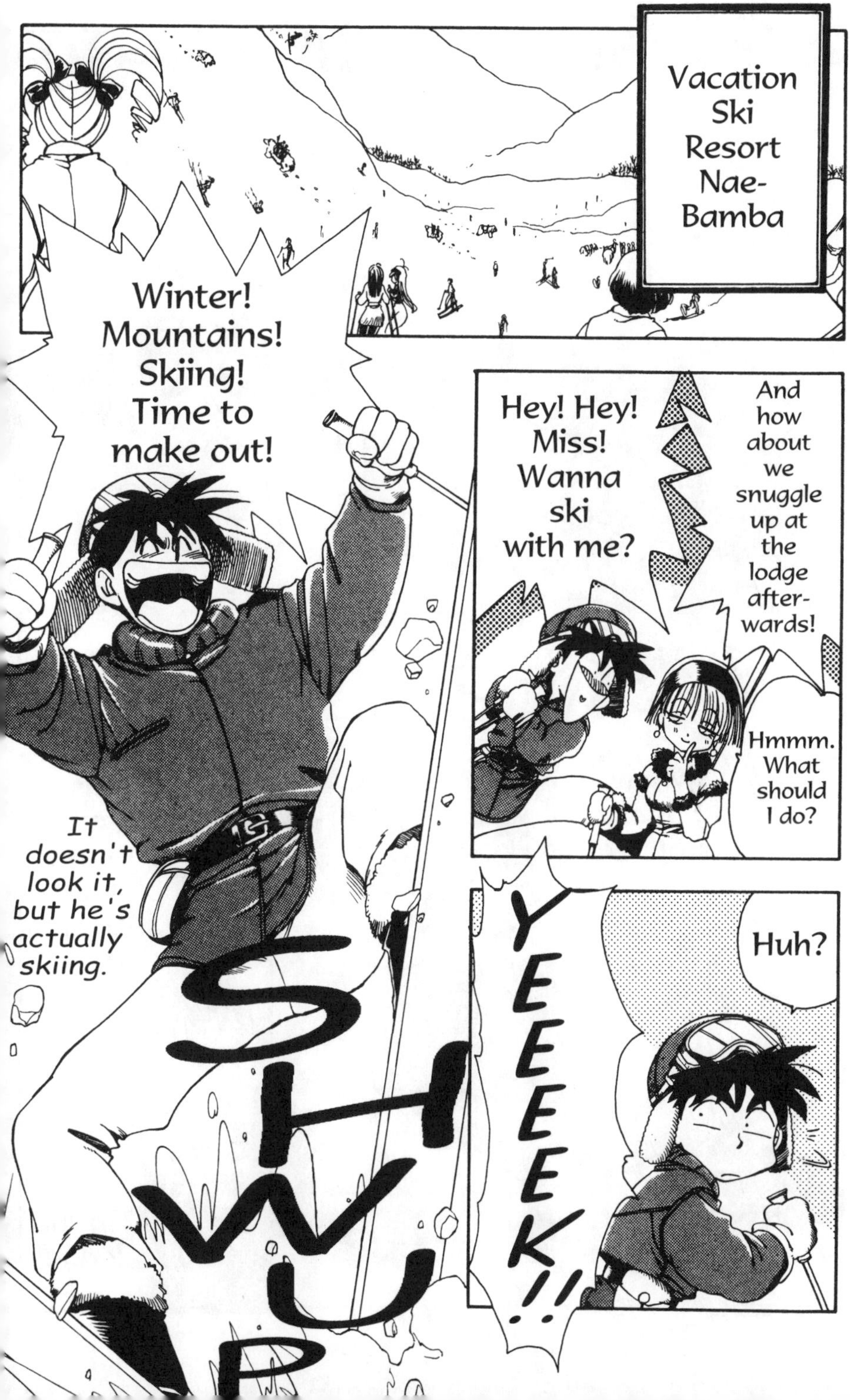
Vacation Ski Resort Nae-Bamba
Winter! Mountains! Skiing! Time to make out!
It doesn't look it, but he's actually skiing.
SHWUP
Hey! Hey! Miss! Wanna ski with me?
And how about we snuggle up at the lodge afterwards!
Hmmm. What should I do?
YEEEEK!!
Huh?

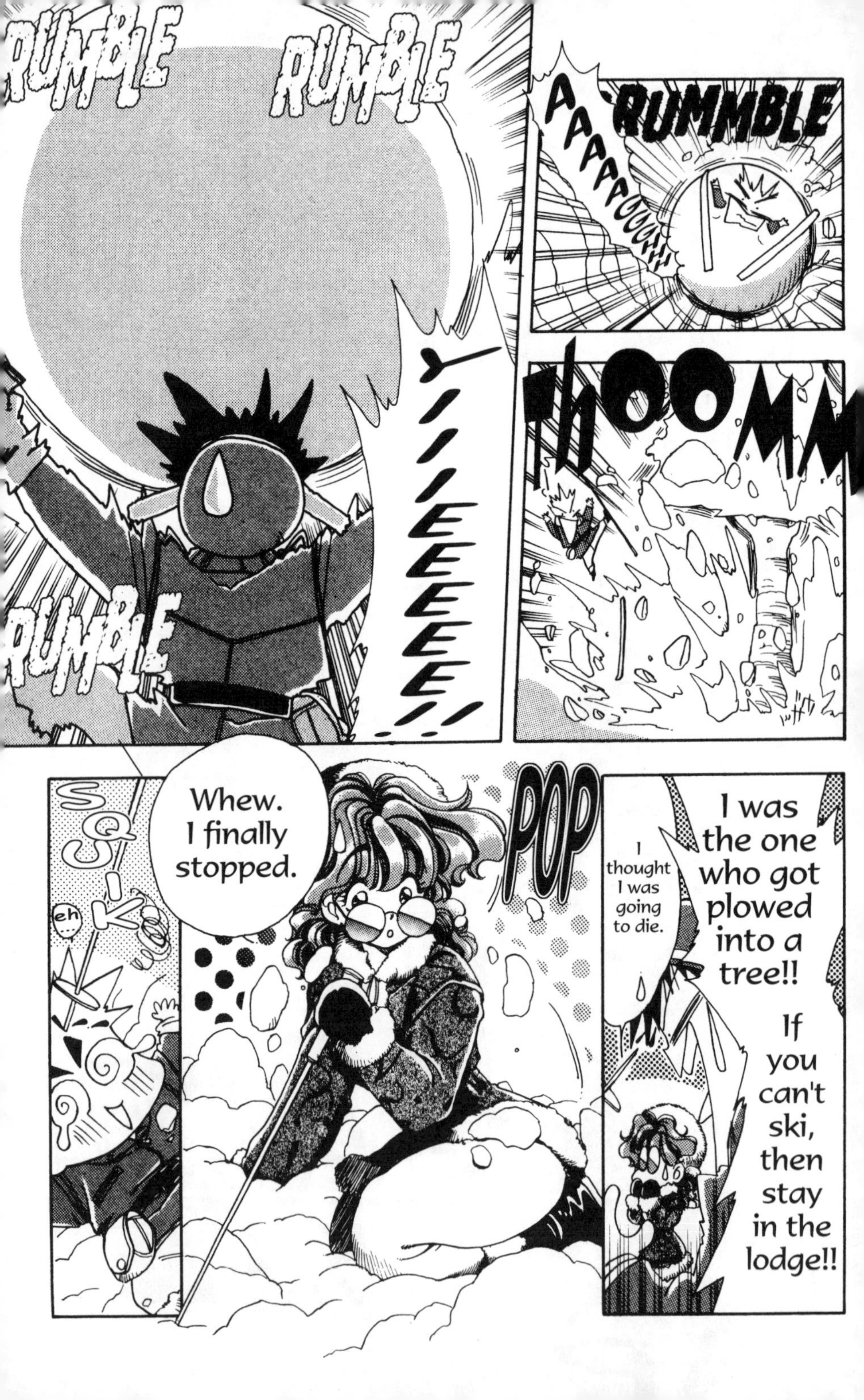
RUMBLE
RUMBLE
RUMBLE
YIIIIEEEEEEE!!
AAAAAAGGGHHHH
RUMMBLE
THOOMM
SQUIK
eh...
Whew. I finally stopped.
POP
I thought I was going to die.
I was the one who got plowed into a tree!!
If you can't ski, then stay in the lodge!!

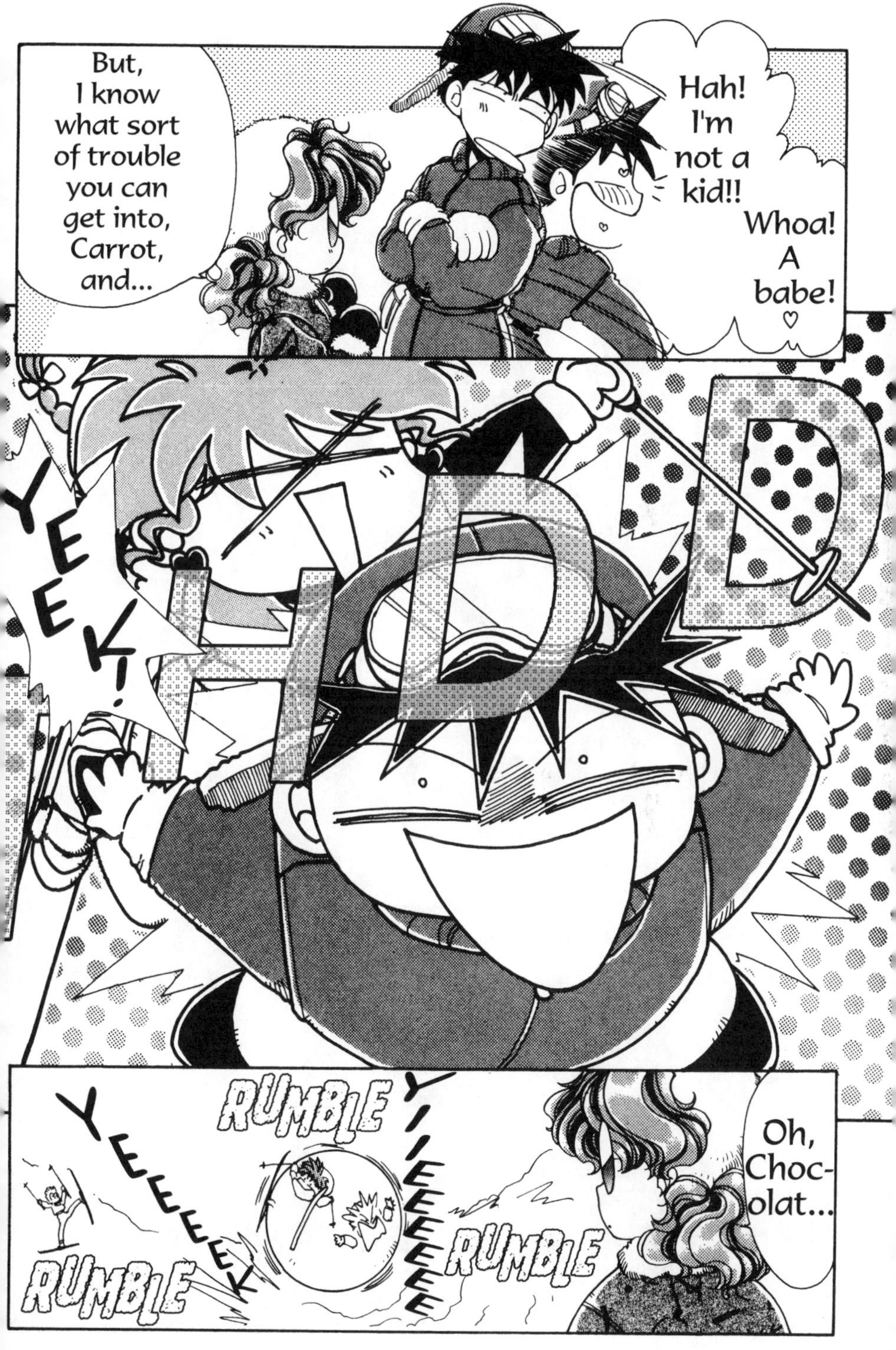
Hah! I'm not a kid!!
Whoa! A babe! ♡
But, I know what sort of trouble you can get into, Carrot, and...
YEEK!
Oh, Chocolat...
RUMBLE
YIIEEEEEEE
RUMBLE
YEEEEEEK
RUMBLE

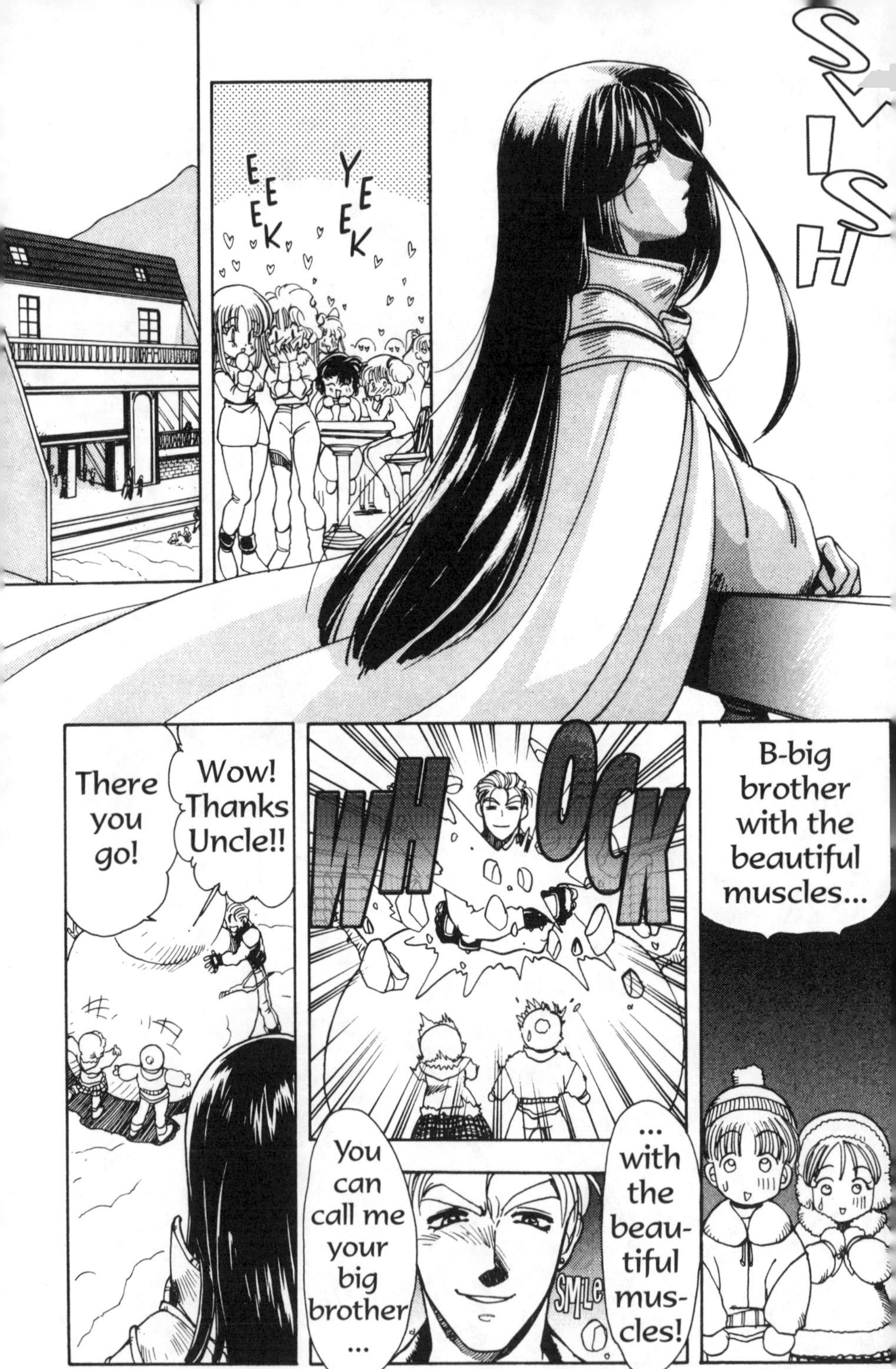
EEEK
YEEEK
SWISH
There you go!
Wow! Thanks Uncle!!
WHOCK
You can call me your big brother...
...with the beautiful muscles!
SMILE
B-big brother with the beautiful muscles...

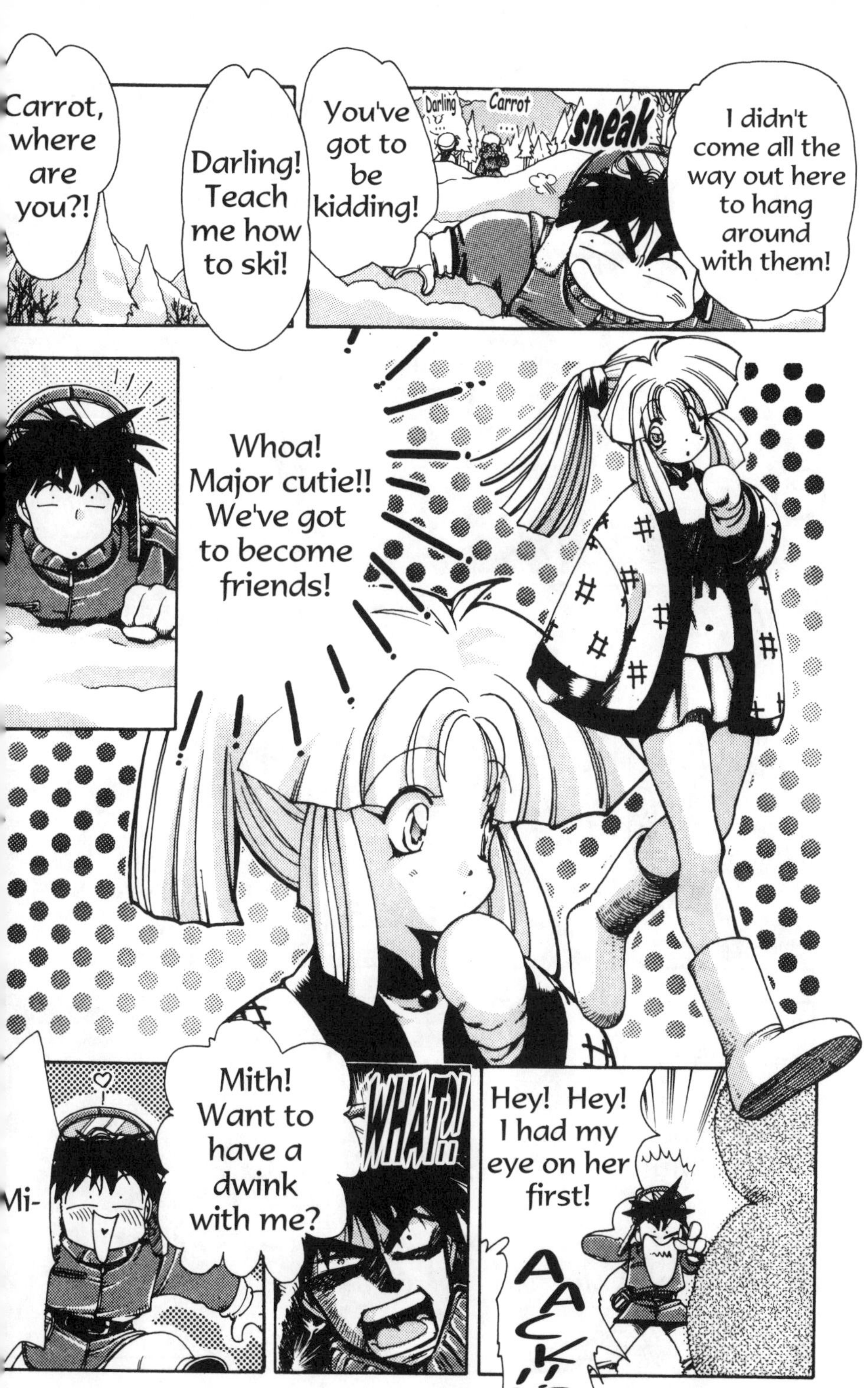
Carrot, where are you?!
Darling! Teach me how to ski!
You've got to be kidding!
Darling
Carrot
sneak
I didn't come all the way out here to hang around with them!
Whoa! Major cutie!! We've got to become friends!
Mi-
Mith! Want to have a dwink with me?
WHAT!!
Hey! Hey! I had my eye on her first!
AACK!!

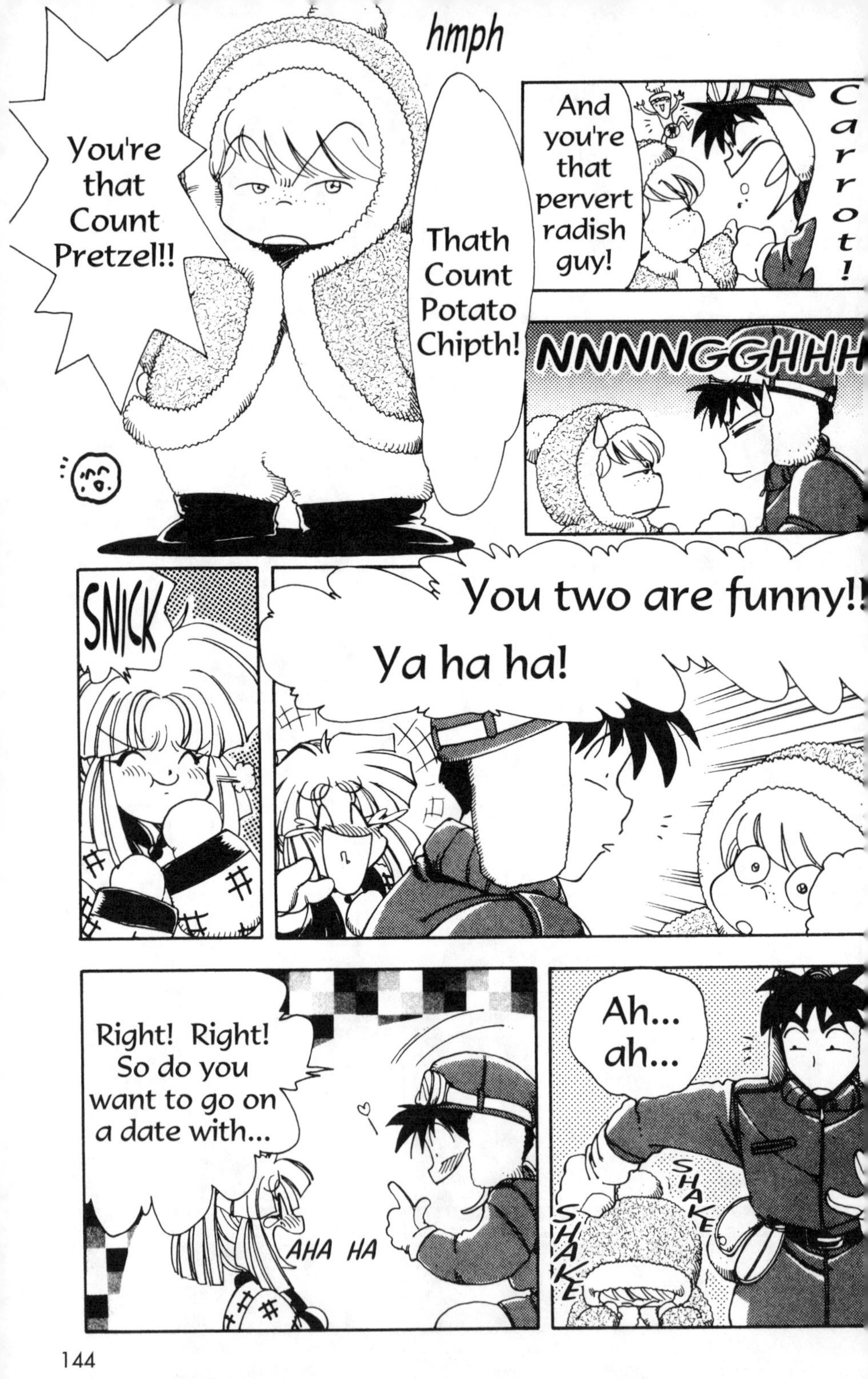
You're that Count Pretzel!!
hmph
Thath Count Potato Chipth!
And you're that pervert radish guy!
Carrot!
NNNNGGHHH
SNICK
You two are funny!!
Ya ha ha!
Right! Right! So do you want to go on a date with...
AHA HA
Ah... ah...
SHAKE
SHAKE

She laughed!!

JUMP

The firth time in my 14 yearth, I've made a girl laugh! My life ith complete!!

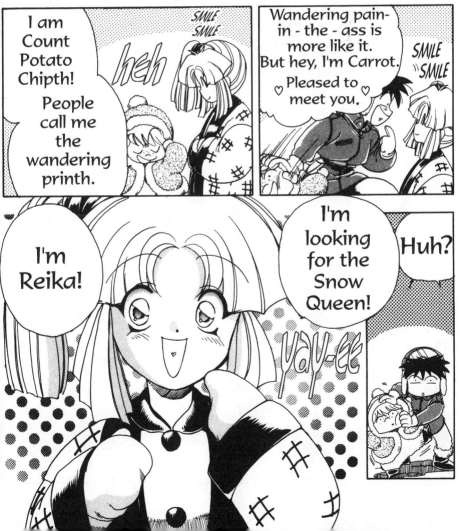

SMILE SMILE

heh

I am Count Potato Chipth!

People call me the wandering printh.

Wandering pain-in-the-ass is more like it. But hey, I'm Carrot.

SMILE SMILE

♡ Pleased to meet you. ♡

I'm Reika!

I'm looking for the Snow Queen!

Huh?

yay-ee

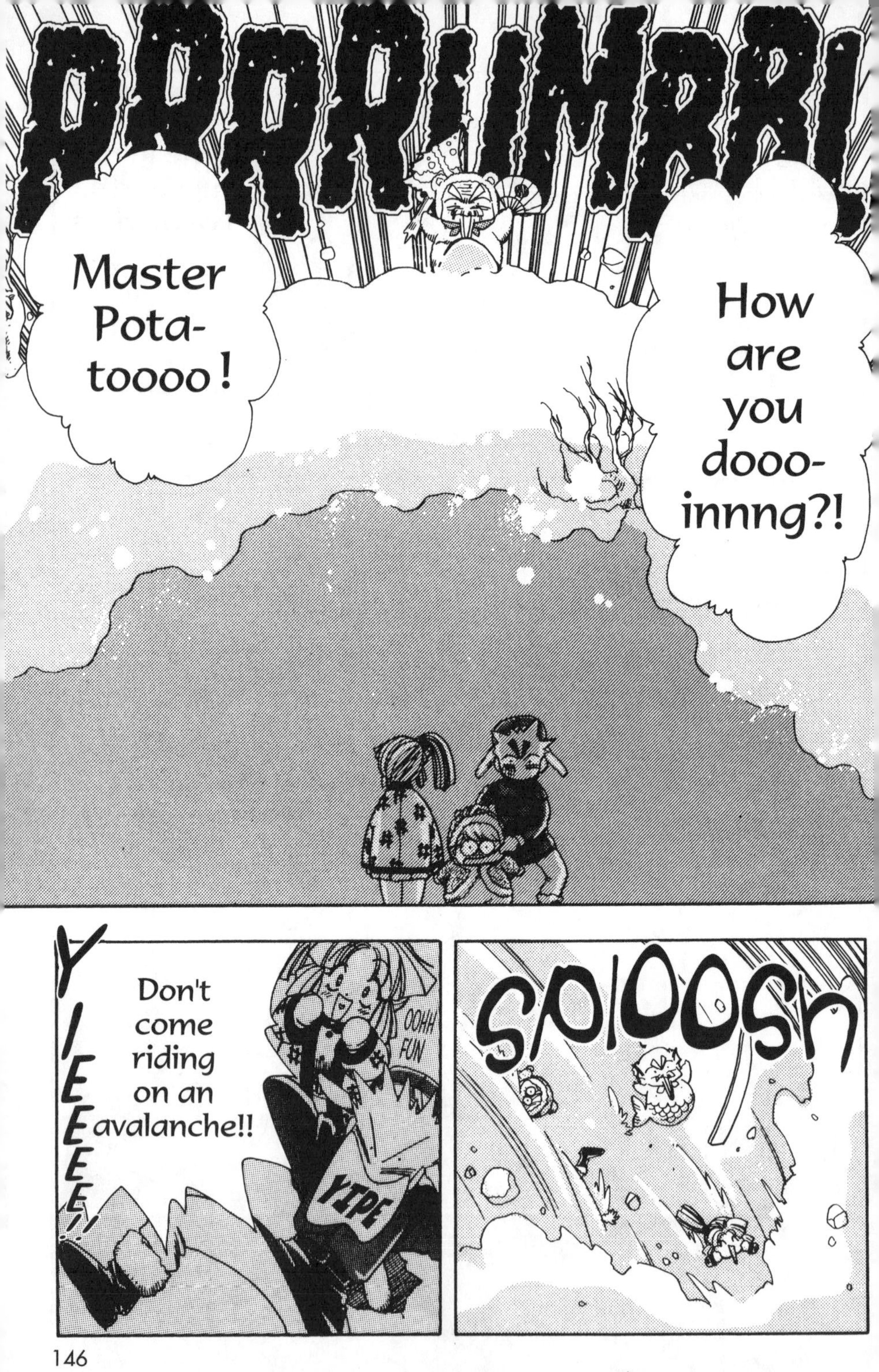

Master Pota-toooo!
How are you dooo-innng?!
YIEEEEE!!
Don't come riding on an avalanche!!
OOHH FUN
YIPE
SPLOOSH

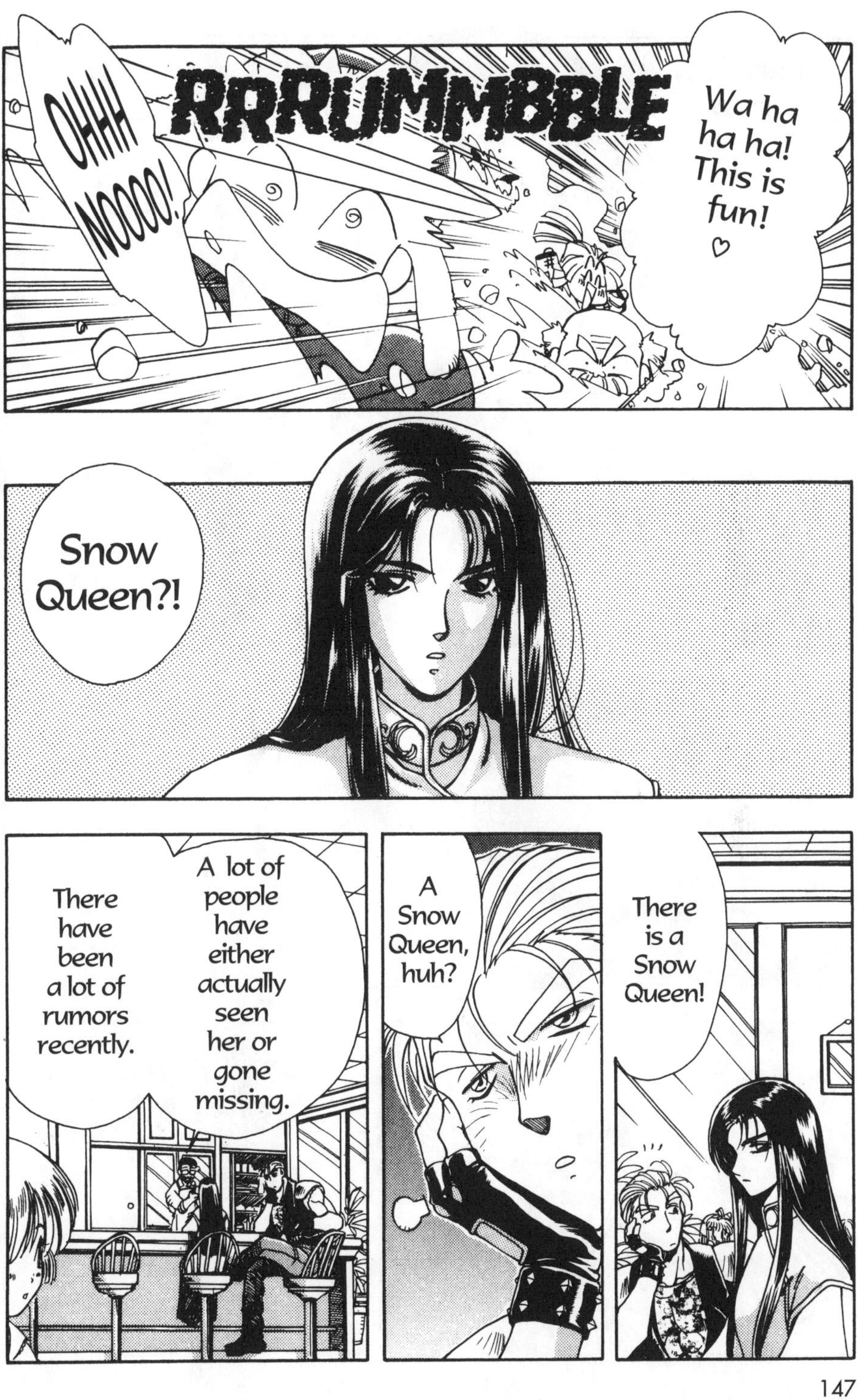
OHHH NOOOO!
RRRUMMBBLE
Wa ha ha ha! This is fun! ♡
Snow Queen?!
There have been a lot of rumors recently.
A lot of people have either actually seen her or gone missing.
A Snow Queen, huh?
There is a Snow Queen!

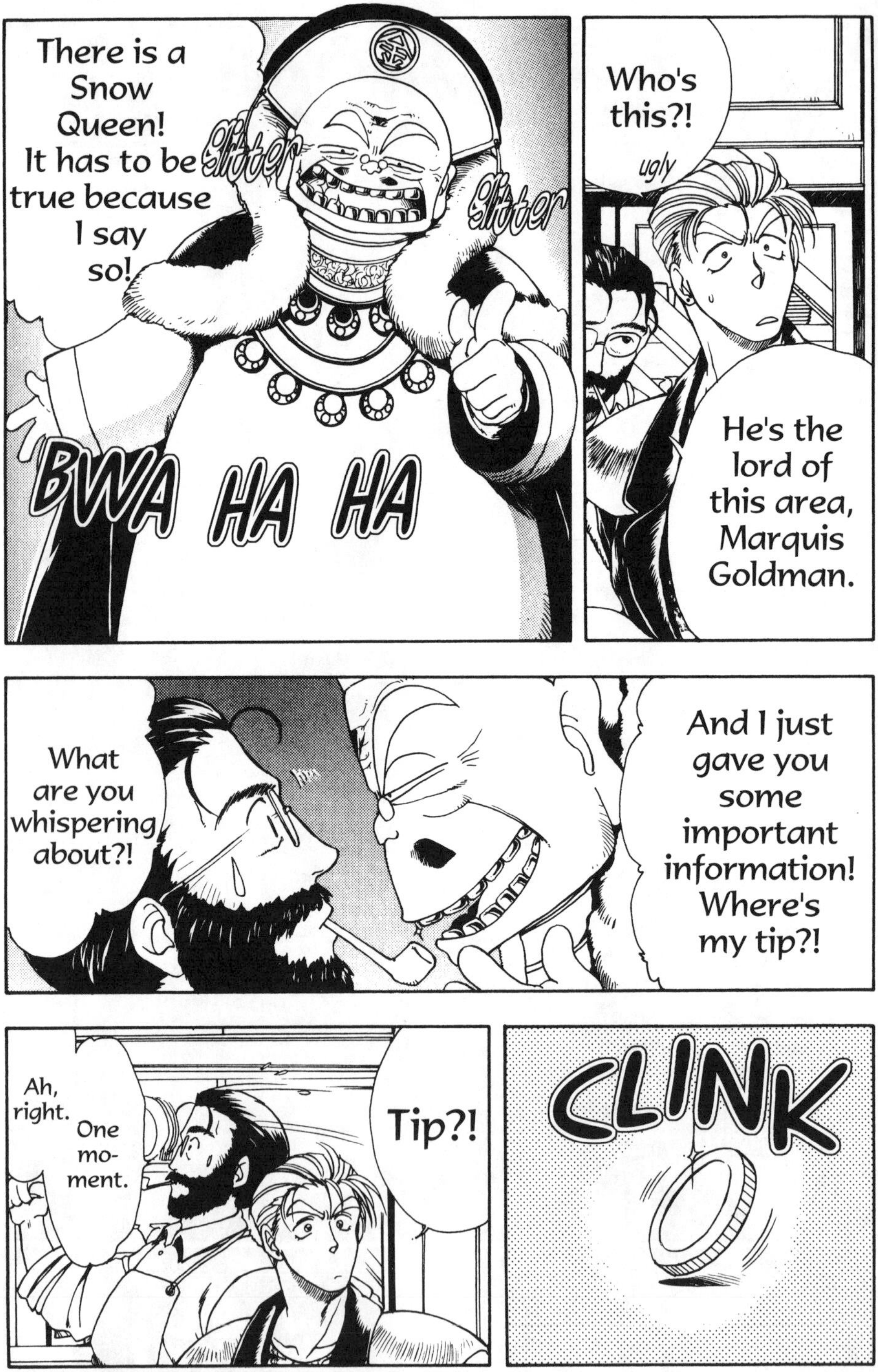
There is a Snow Queen! It has to be true because I say so!
Glitter
Glitter
BWA HA HA
Who's this?!
ugly
He's the lord of this area, Marquis Goldman.
What are you whispering about?!
And I just gave you some important information! Where's my tip?!
Ah, right.
One mo-ment.
Tip?!
CLINK

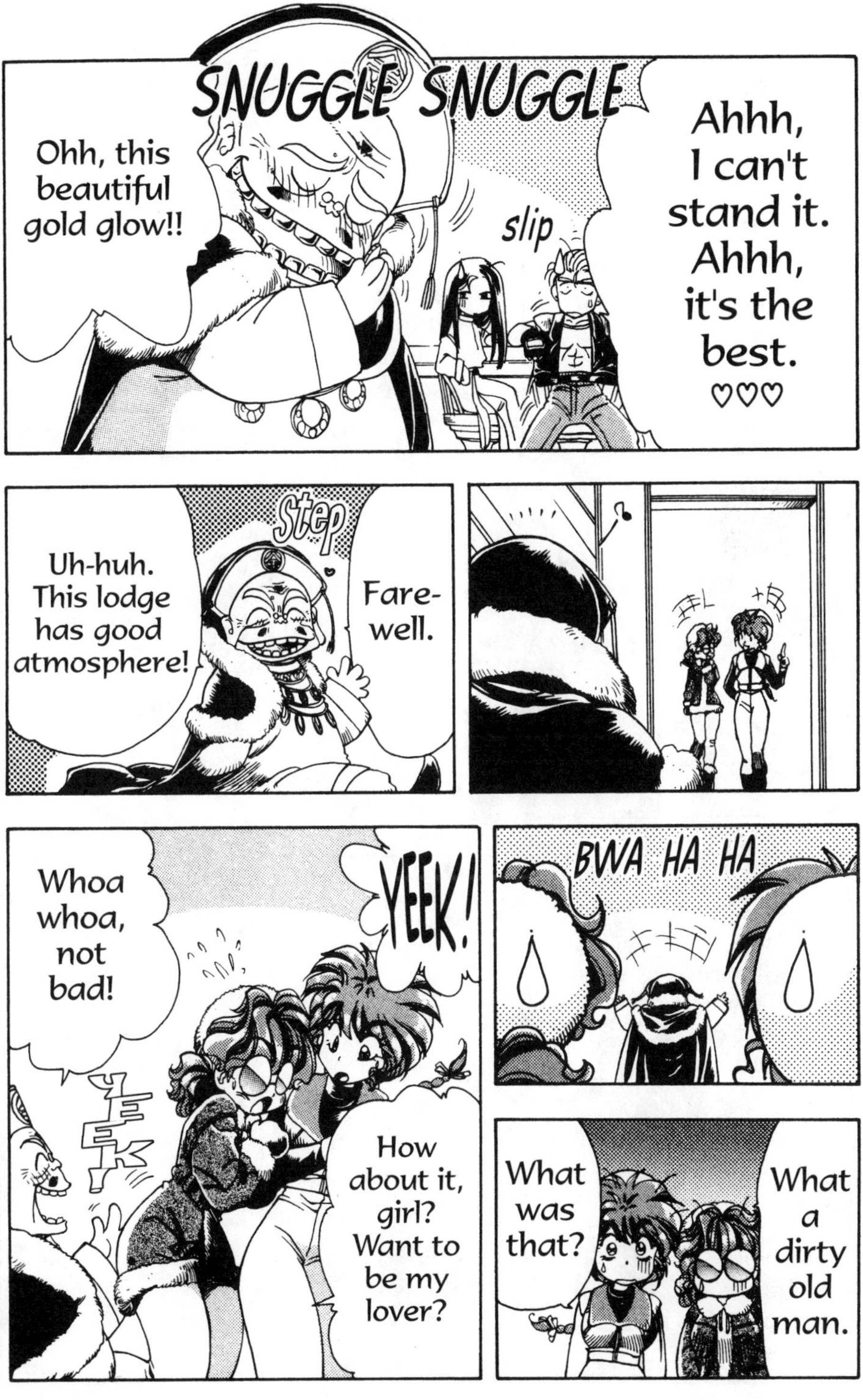
SNUGGLE SNUGGLE
Ohh, this beautiful gold glow!!
slip
Ahhh, I can't stand it. Ahhh, it's the best. ♡♡♡
Uh-huh. This lodge has good atmosphere!
Step
Fare-well.
Whoa whoa, not bad!
YEEK!
YEEK!
How about it, girl? Want to be my lover?
BWA HA HA
What was that?
What a dirty old man.

There was no real reason to give that guy any money.

Yes, but if you don't get him to leave nicely, he can cause a lot of mischief.

Tch! When you think he's the lord of the area...

By the way, where's my brother?

What?! He's not back yet?!

POK

gasp

You know him! He's probably too busy trying to get a date.

Forget about him.

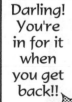

Darling! You're in for it when you get back!!

What are you thinking of, Chocolat?

candle ◄ rough rope ♥ whip ♥

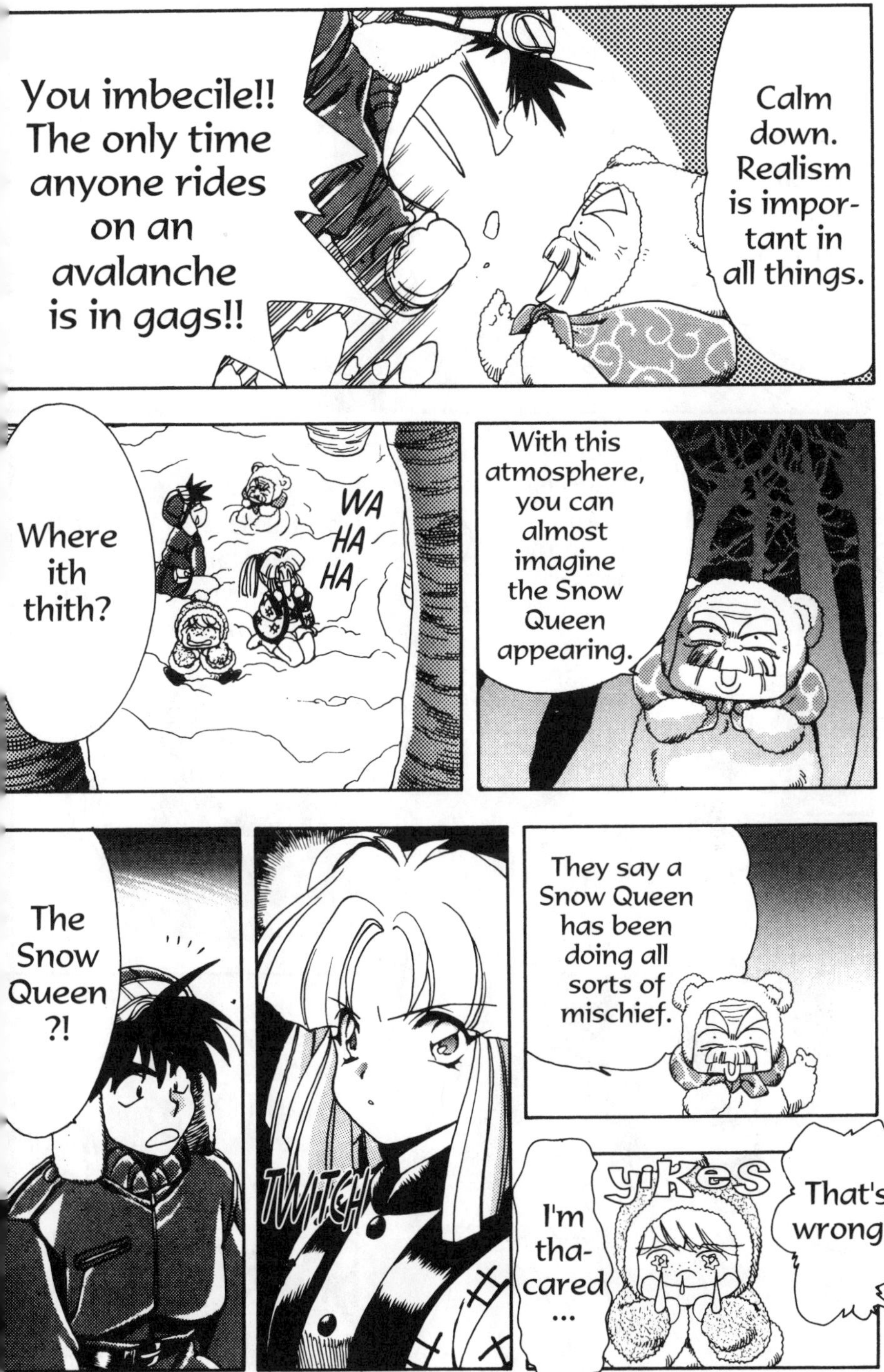
You imbecile!! The only time anyone rides on an avalanche is in gags!!
Calm down. Realism is impor-tant in all things.
Where ith thith?
WA HA HA
With this atmosphere, you can almost imagine the Snow Queen appearing.
The Snow Queen ?!
TWITCH
They say a Snow Queen has been doing all sorts of mischief.
I'm tha-cared ...
yiKeS
That's wrong!!

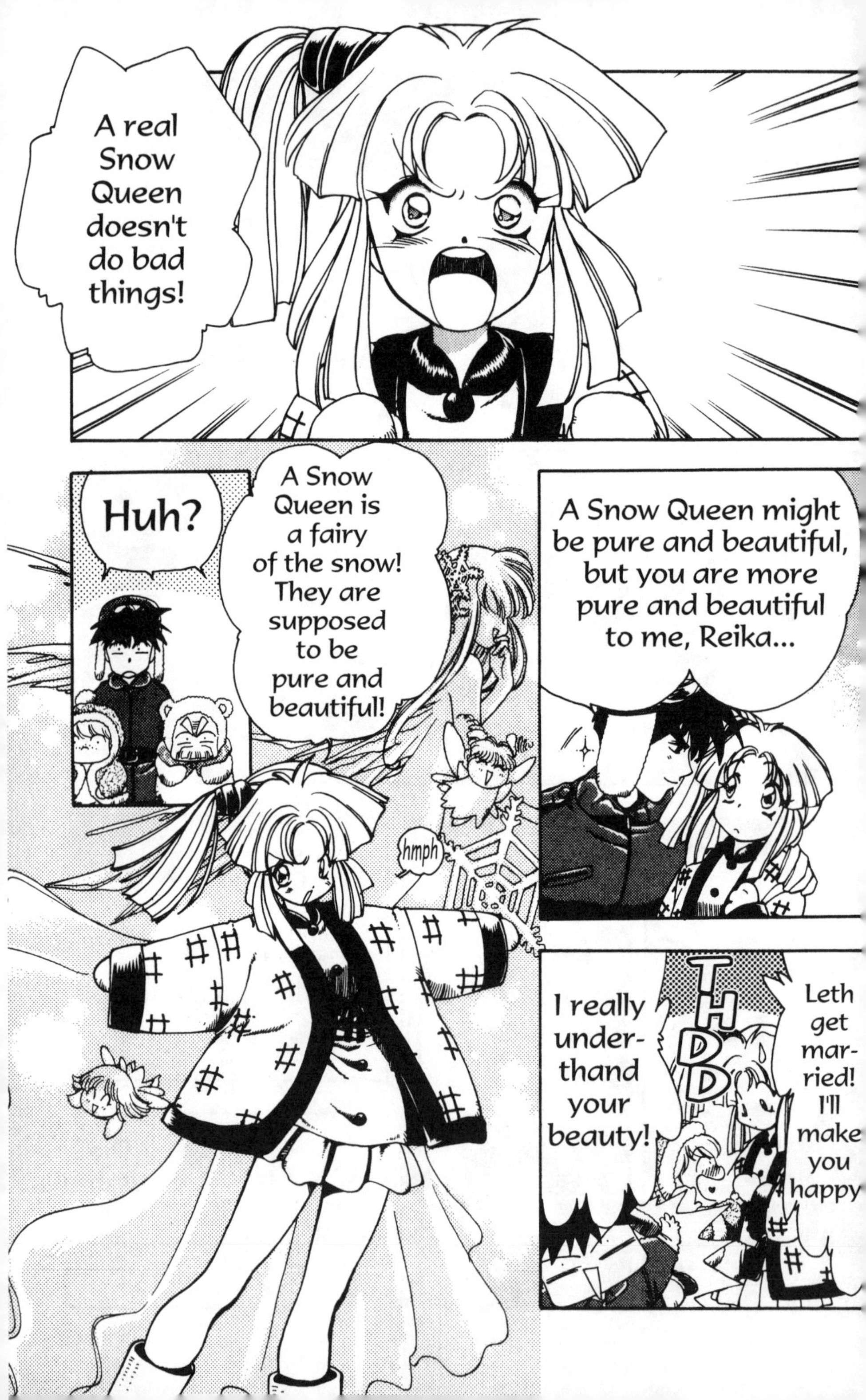
A real Snow Queen doesn't do bad things!
Huh?
A Snow Queen is a fairy of the snow! They are supposed to be pure and beautiful!
hmph
A Snow Queen might be pure and beautiful, but you are more pure and beautiful to me, Reika...
I really under-thand your beauty!
THDD
Leth get mar-ried! I'll make you happy

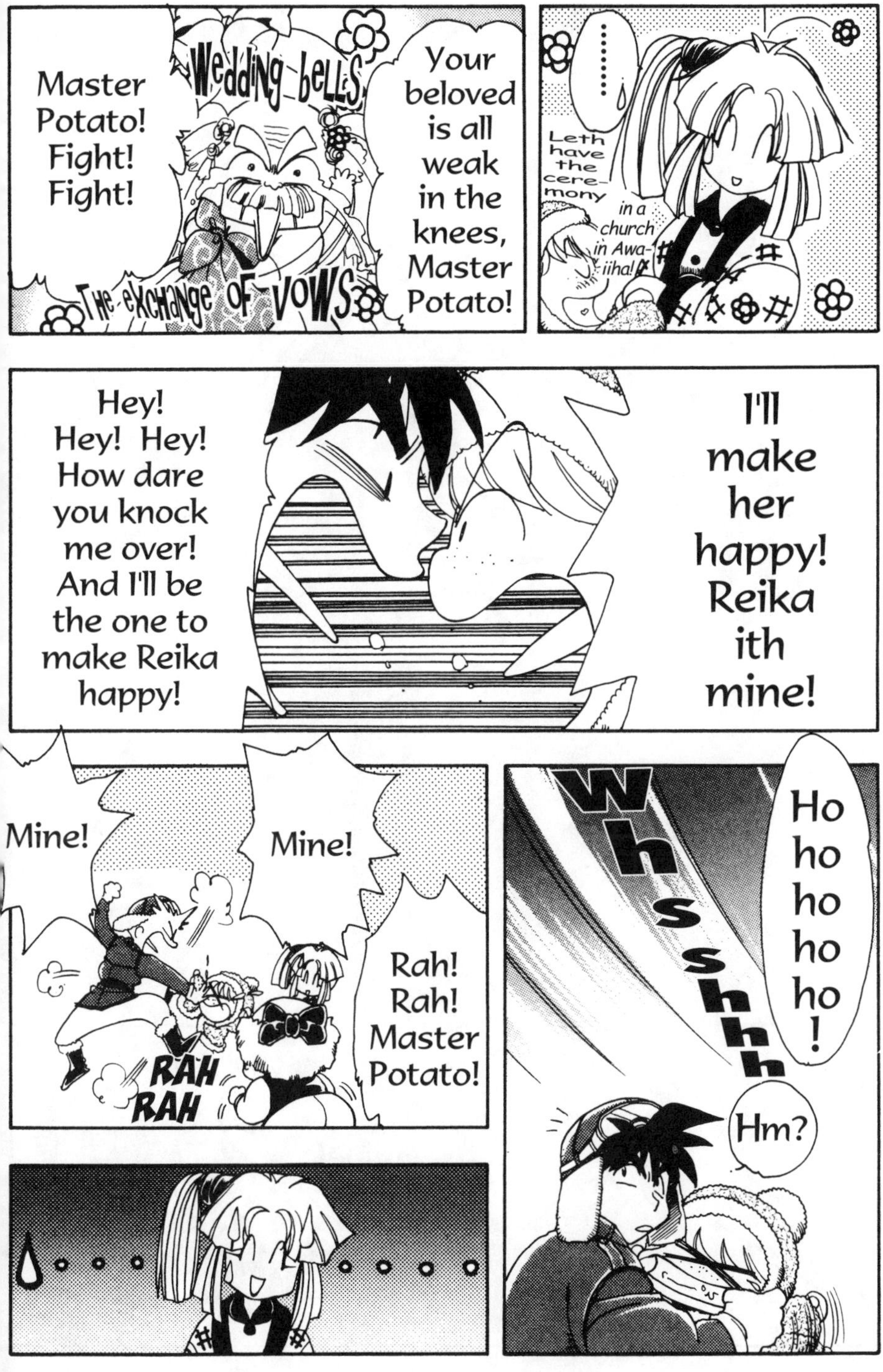
Master Potato! Fight! Fight!
Wedding bells
The exchange of vows
Your beloved is all weak in the knees, Master Potato!
......
Leth have the ceremony in a church in Awa-iiha!
Hey! Hey! Hey! How dare you knock me over! And I'll be the one to make Reika happy!
I'll make her happy! Reika ith mine!
Mine!
Mine!
Rah! Rah! Master Potato!
RAH RAH
....
Whsshhh
Ho ho ho ho ho!
Hm?

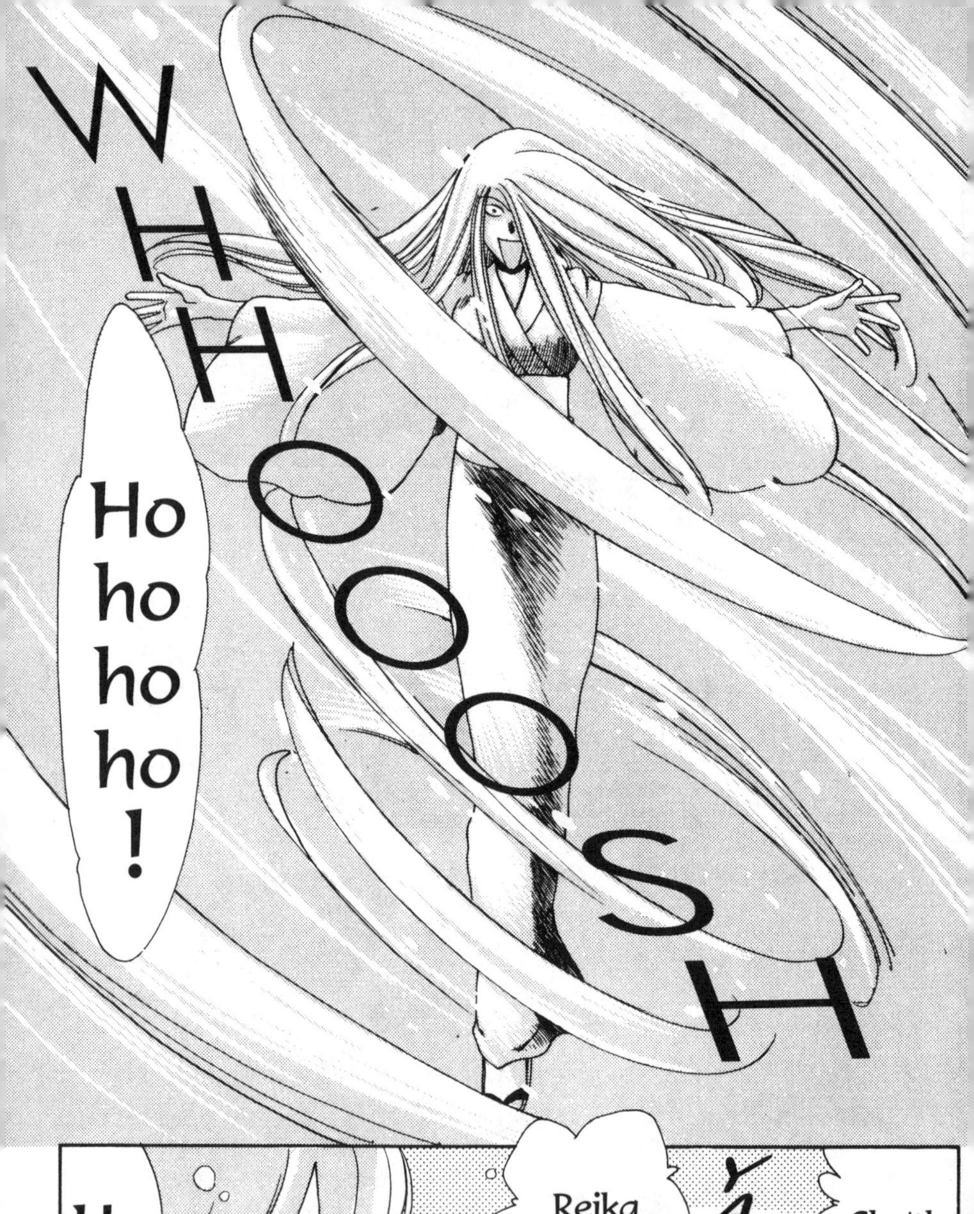

WHOOOOSH
Ho ho ho ho ho!

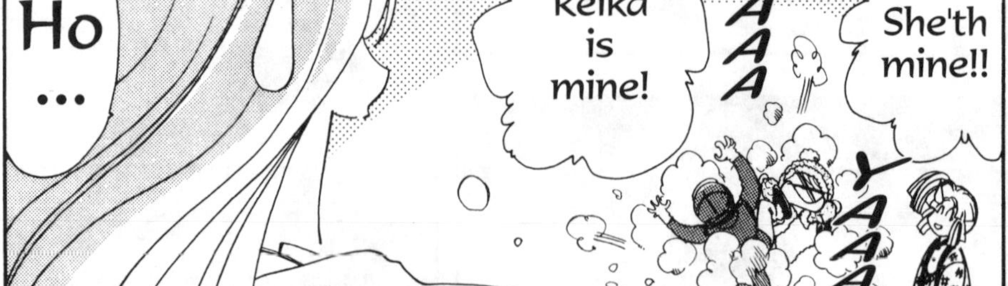

Ho ...
Reika is mine!
YAAAA
She'th mine!!
YAAAA

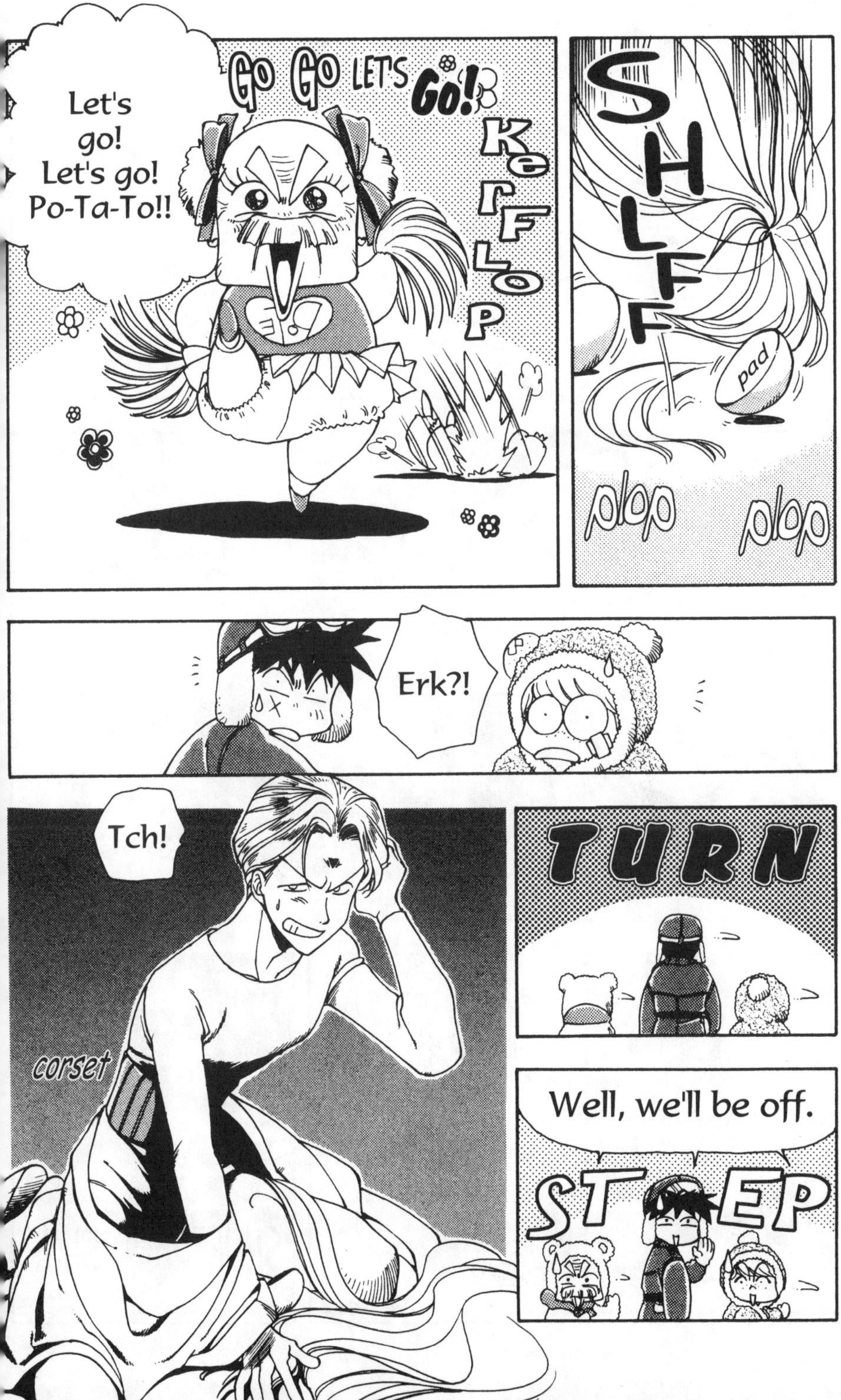

Let's go! Let's go! Po-Ta-To!!
GO GO LET'S GO!
KERFLOP
SHLFFF
pad
plop
plop
Erk?!
Tch!
corset
TURN
Well, we'll be off.
STEP

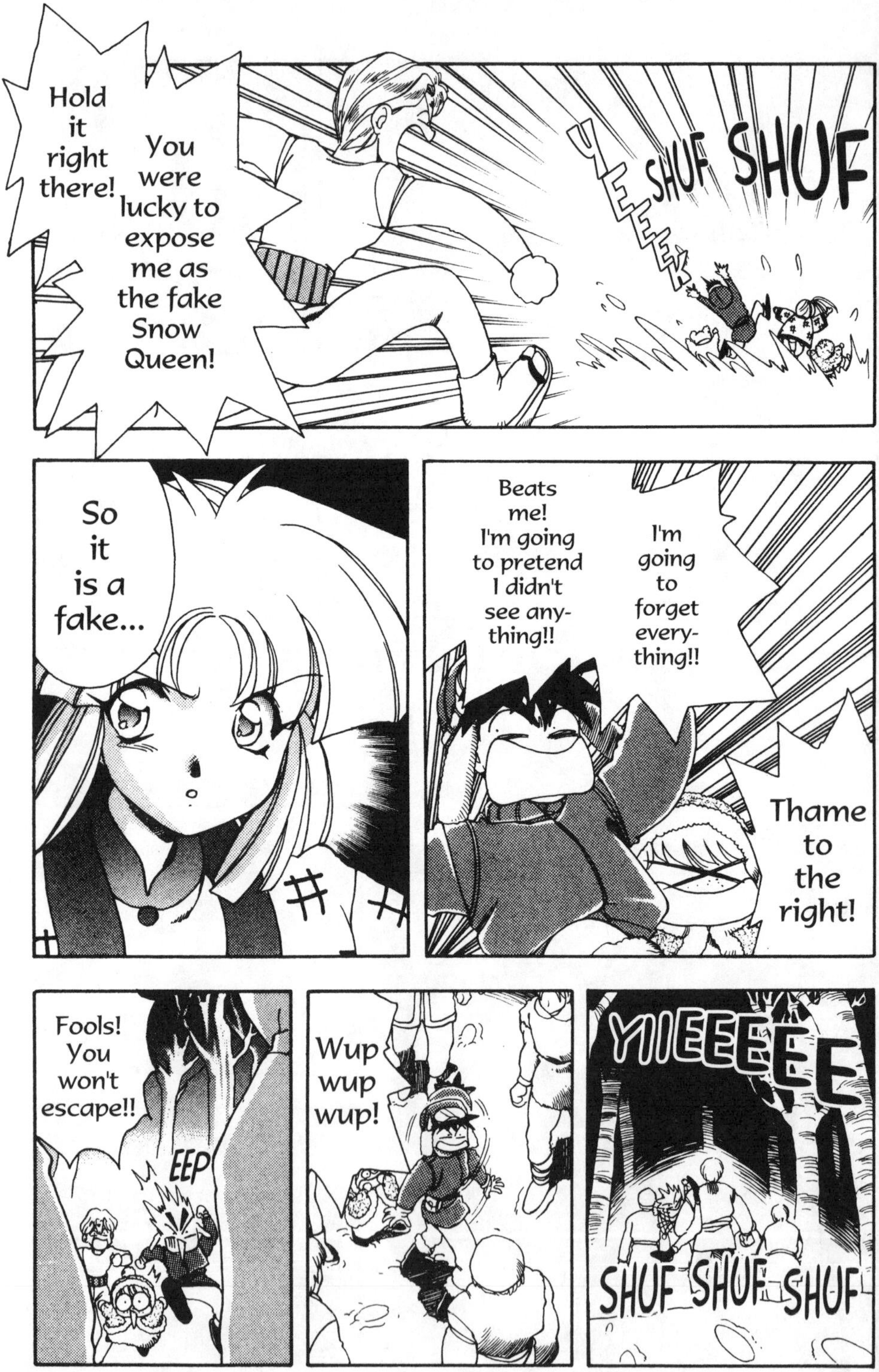
Hold it right there!
You were lucky to expose me as the fake Snow Queen!
YIEEEEK
SHUF SHUF
So it is a fake...
Beats me! I'm going to pretend I didn't see any-thing!!
I'm going to forget every-thing!!
Thame to the right!
Fools! You won't escape!!
EEP
Wup wup wup!
YIIEEEEEE
SHUF SHUF SHUF

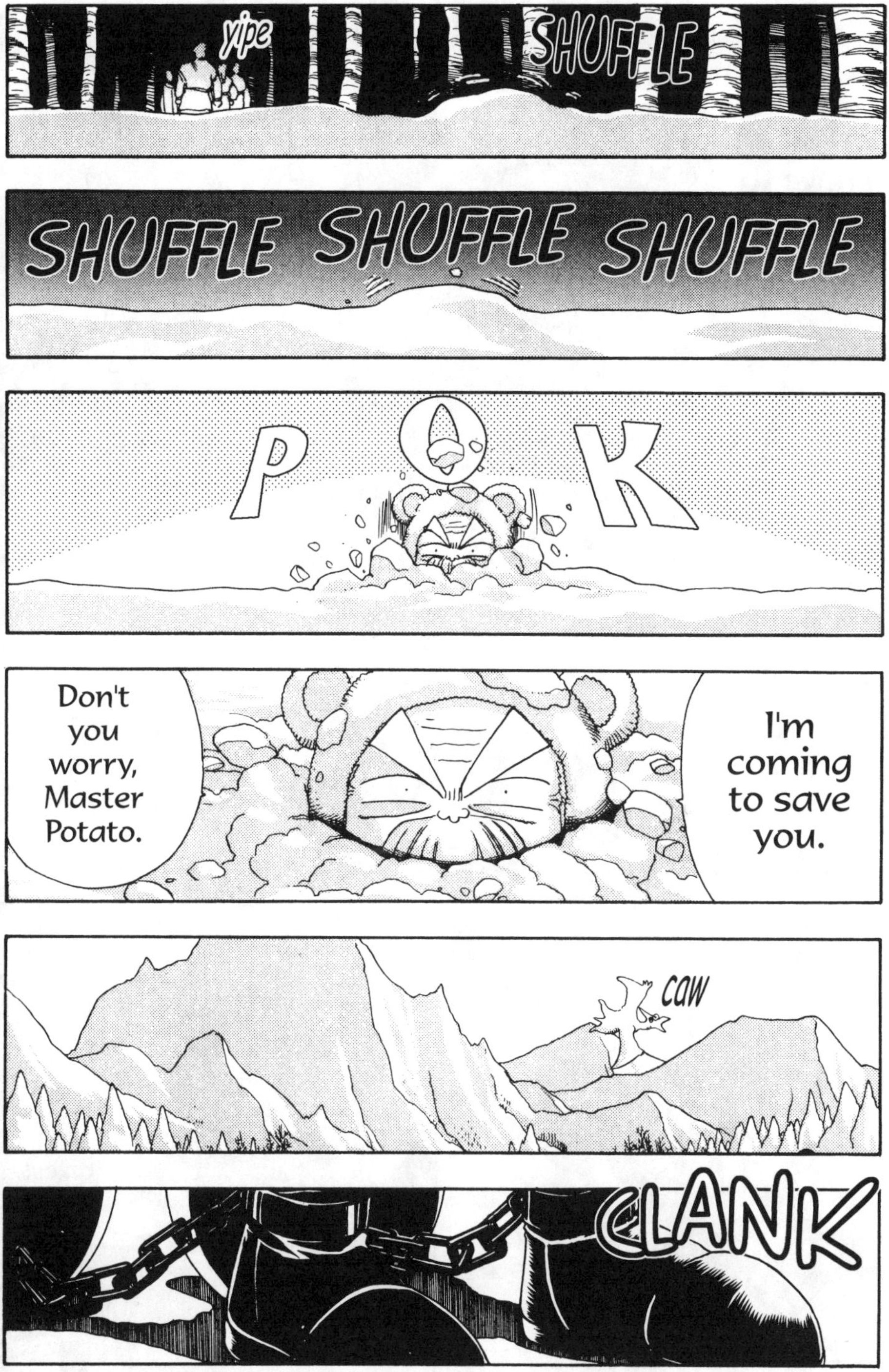
yipe
SHUFFLE
SHUFFLE SHUFFLE SHUFFLE
POK
Don't you worry, Master Potato.
I'm coming to save you.
caw
CLANK

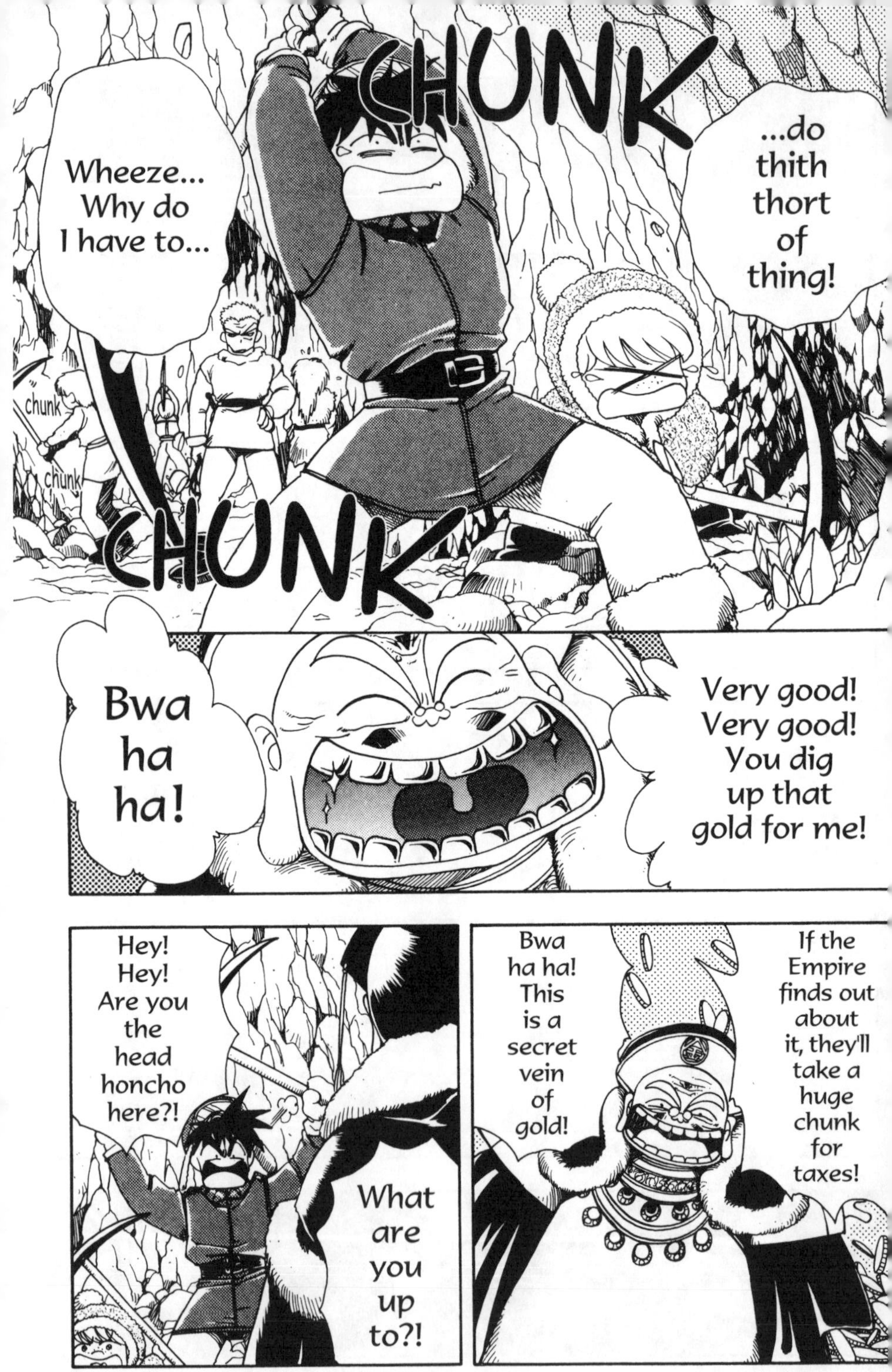
Wheeze... Why do I have to...
CHUNK
...do thith thort of thing!
chunk
chunk
CHUNK
Bwa ha ha!
Very good! Very good! You dig up that gold for me!
Hey! Hey! Are you the head honcho here?!
What are you up to?!
Bwa ha ha! This is a secret vein of gold!
If the Empire finds out about it, they'll take a huge chunk for taxes!

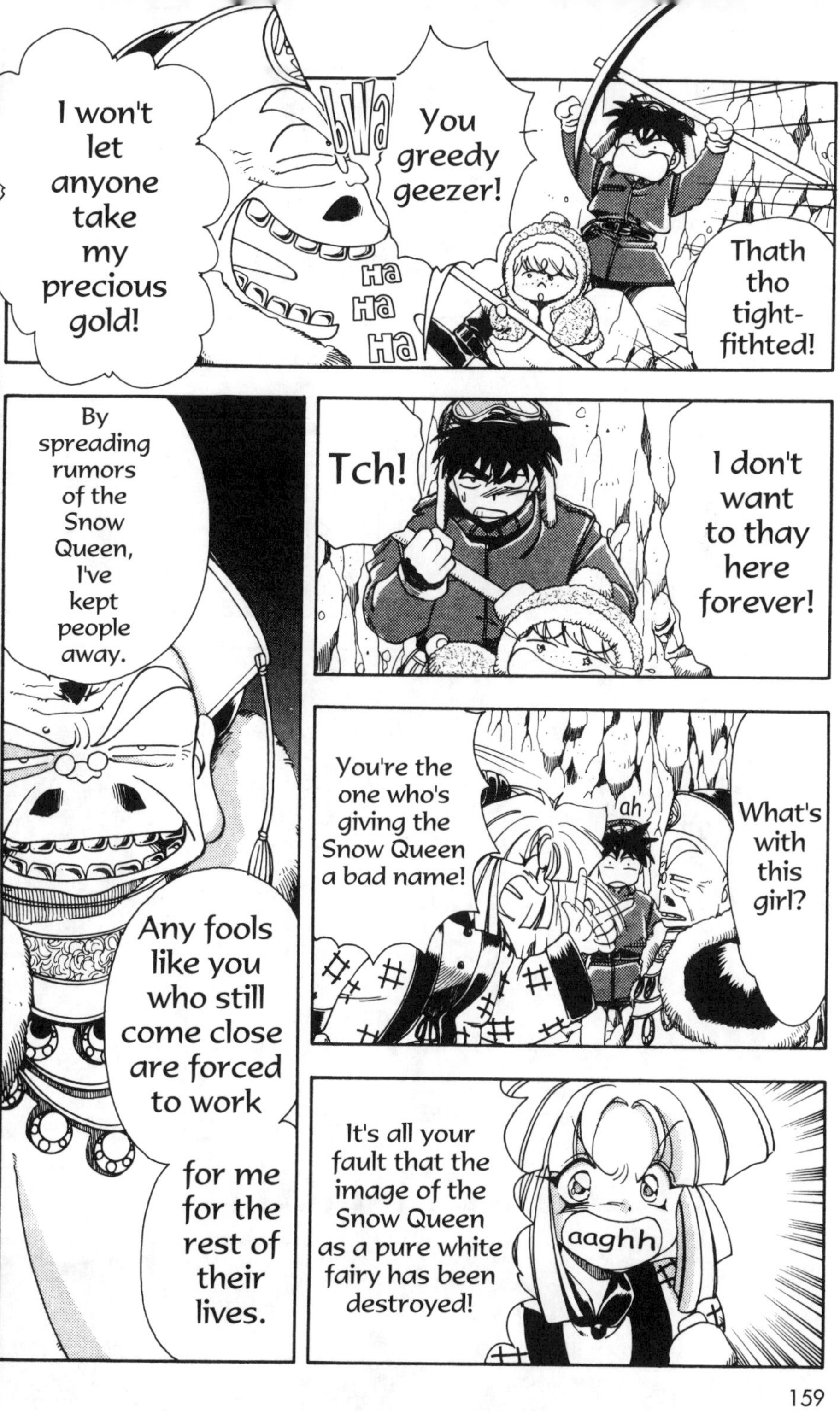
I won't let anyone take my precious gold!
bWa
Ha Ha Ha
You greedy geezer!
Thath tho tight-fithted!
By spreading rumors of the Snow Queen, I've kept people away.
Any fools like you who still come close are forced to work
for me for the rest of their lives.
Tch!
I don't want to thay here forever!
You're the one who's giving the Snow Queen a bad name!
ah
What's with this girl?
It's all your fault that the image of the Snow Queen as a pure white fairy has been destroyed!
aaghh

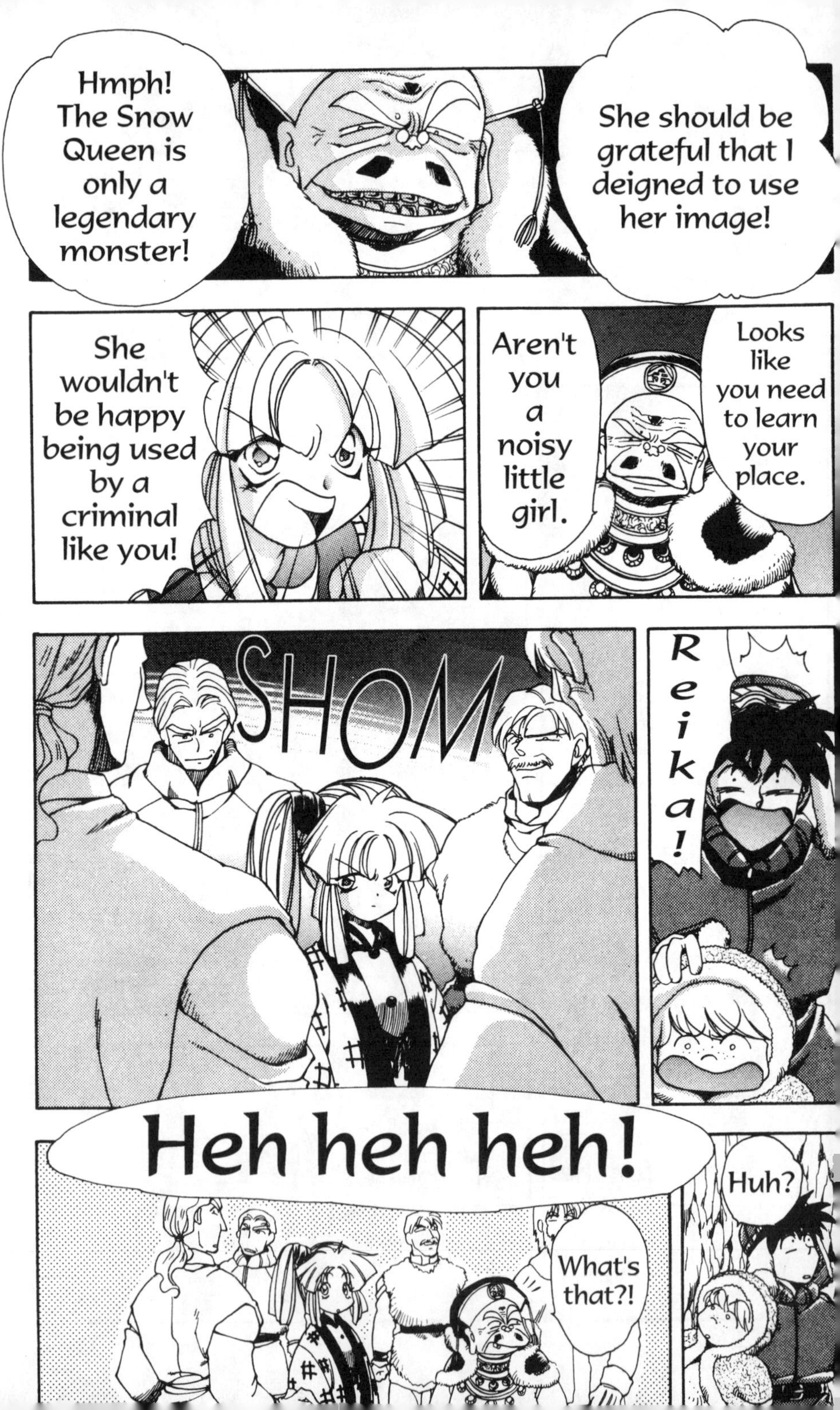
Hmph! The Snow Queen is only a legendary monster!
She should be grateful that I deigned to use her image!
She wouldn't be happy being used by a criminal like you!
Aren't you a noisy little girl.
Looks like you need to learn your place.
SHOM
Reika!
Heh heh heh!
What's that?!
Huh?

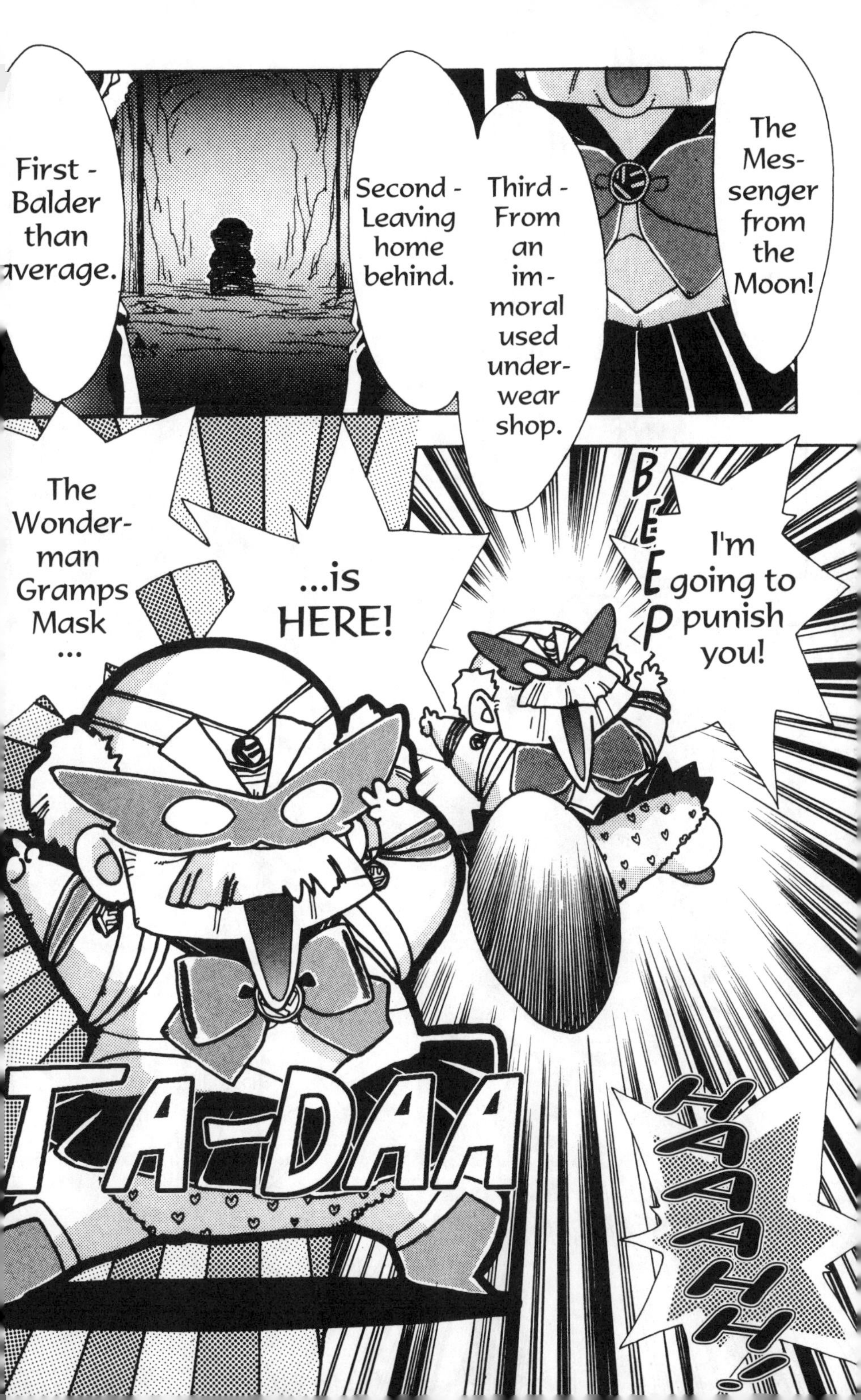
First - Balder than average.
Second - Leaving home behind.
Third - From an im-moral used under-wear shop.
The Mes-senger from the Moon!
The Wonder-man Gramps Mask ...
...is HERE!
BEEP
I'm going to punish you!
TA-DAA
HAAAH!!

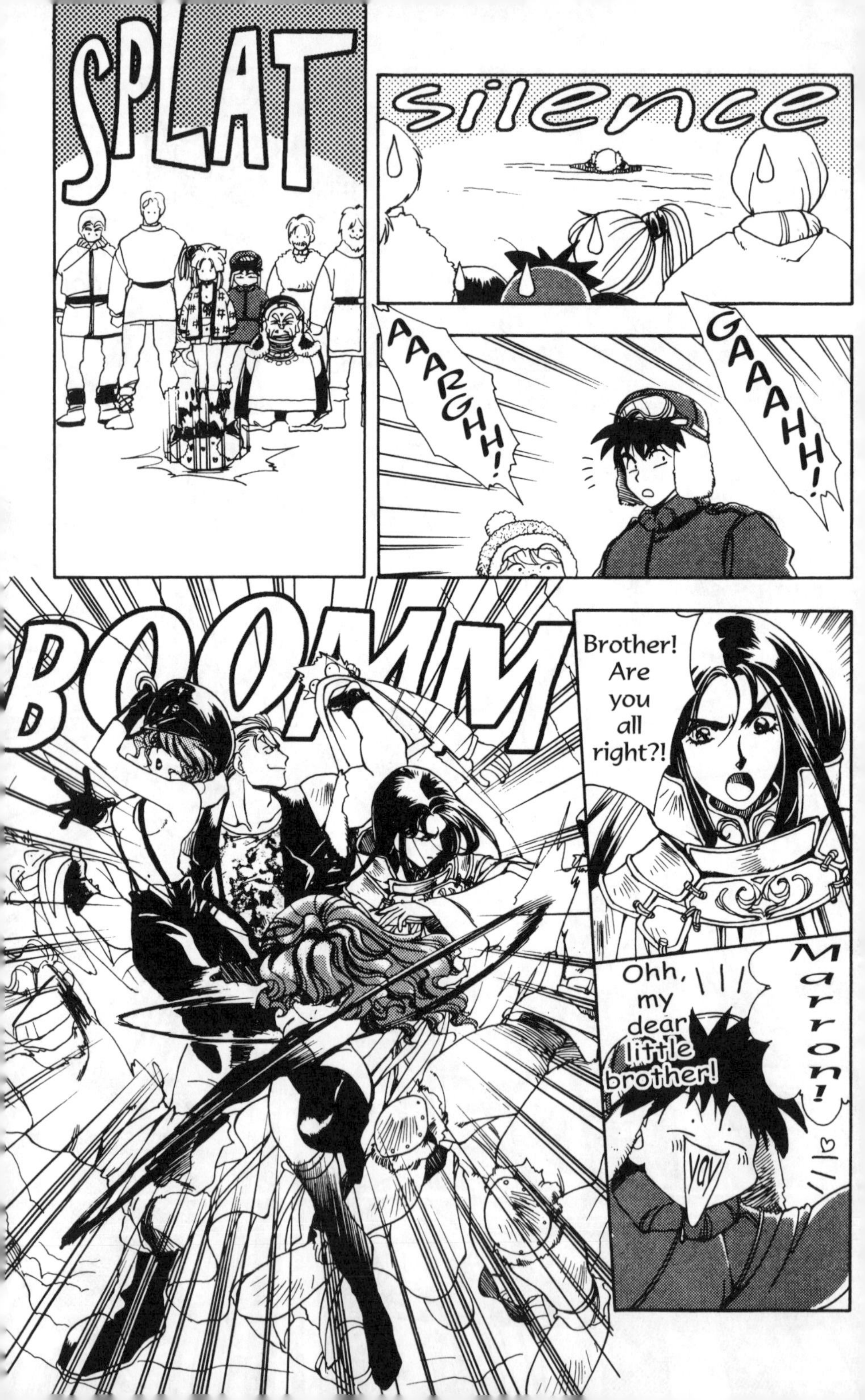
SPLAT
silence
AAARGHH!
GAAAHH!
BOOMM
Brother! Are you all right?!
Ohh, my dear little brother!
Marron!
yay

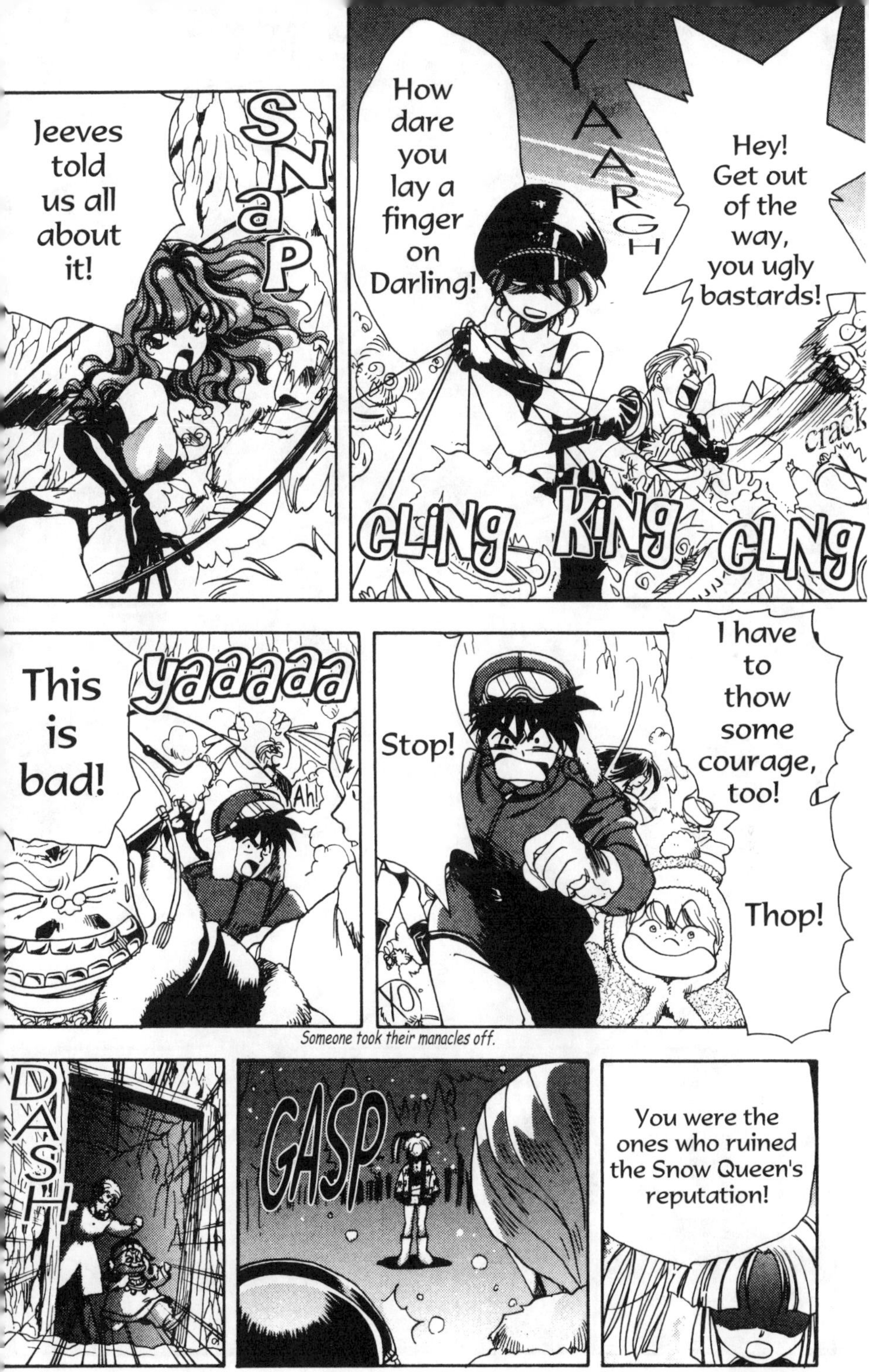
Jeeves told us all about it!
SNaP
How dare you lay a finger on Darling!
YAARGH
Hey! Get out of the way, you ugly bastards!
crack
CLiNG
KiNG
CLNG
This is bad!
yaaaaa
Ah!
Stop!
I have to thow some courage, too!
Thop!
Someone took their manacles off.
DASH
GASP
You were the ones who ruined the Snow Queen's reputation!

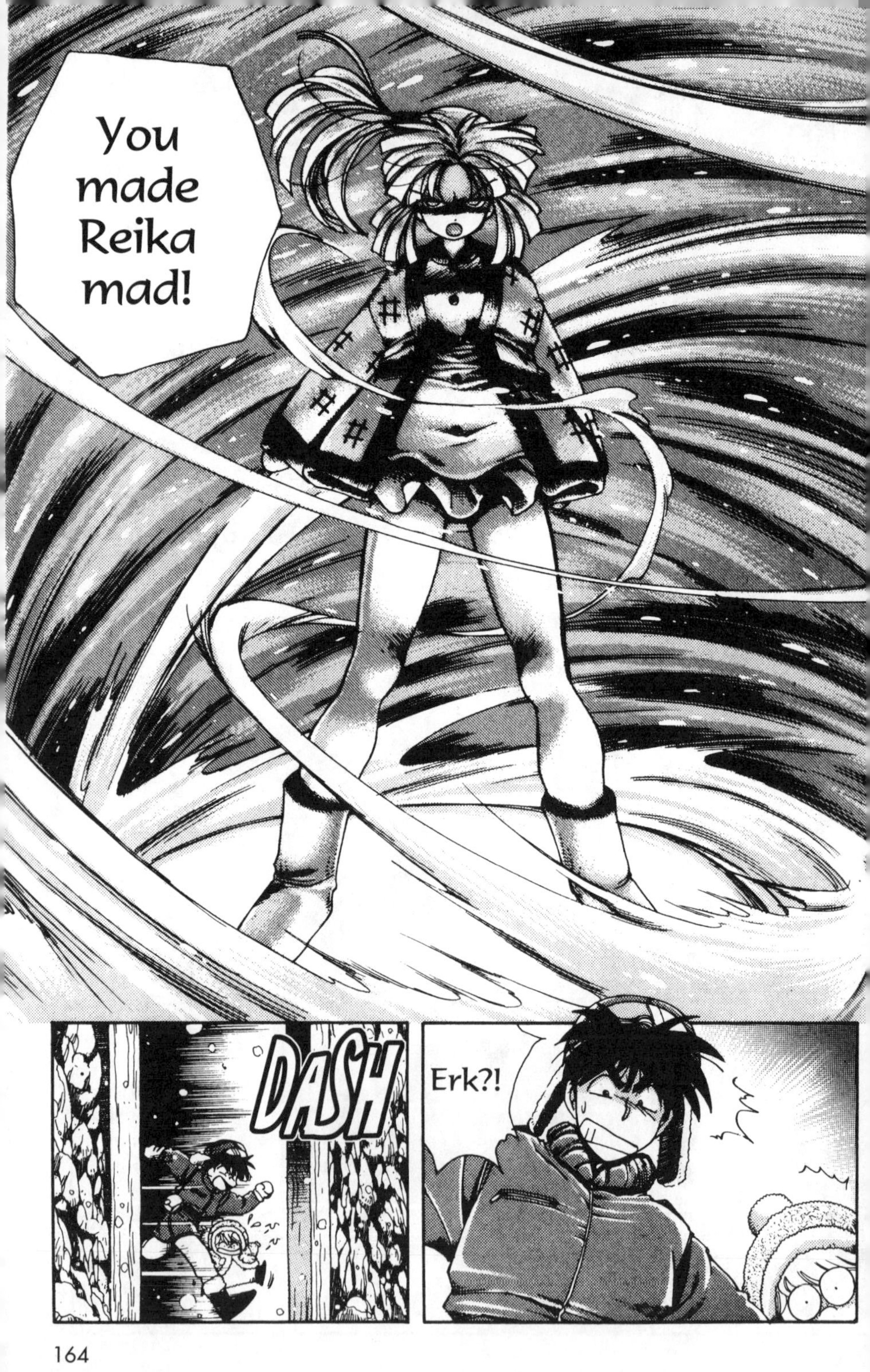
You made Reika mad!
DASH
Erk?!

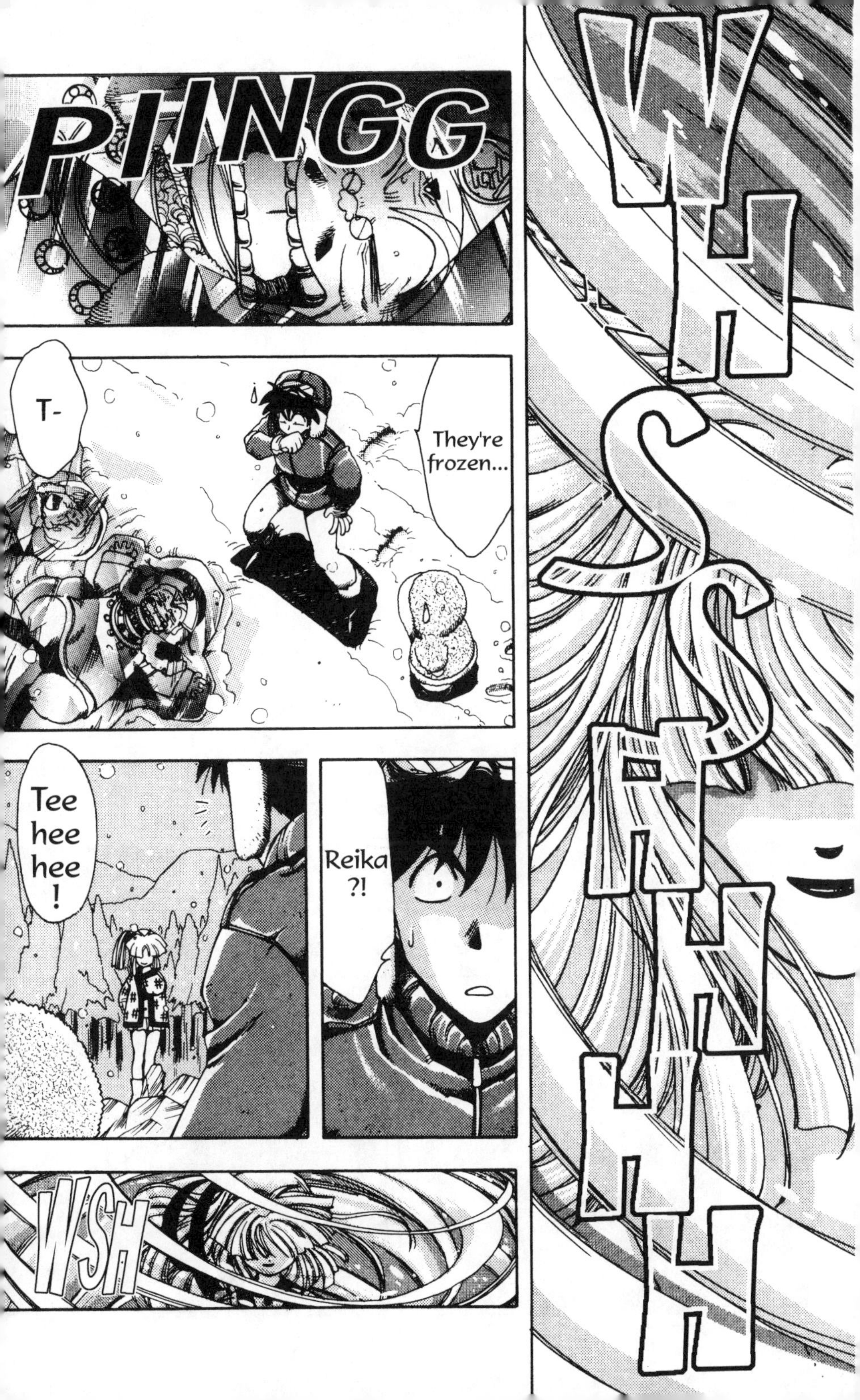
PIINGG
T-
They're frozen...
Tee hee hee!
Reika?!
WSH
WHSSAHHH

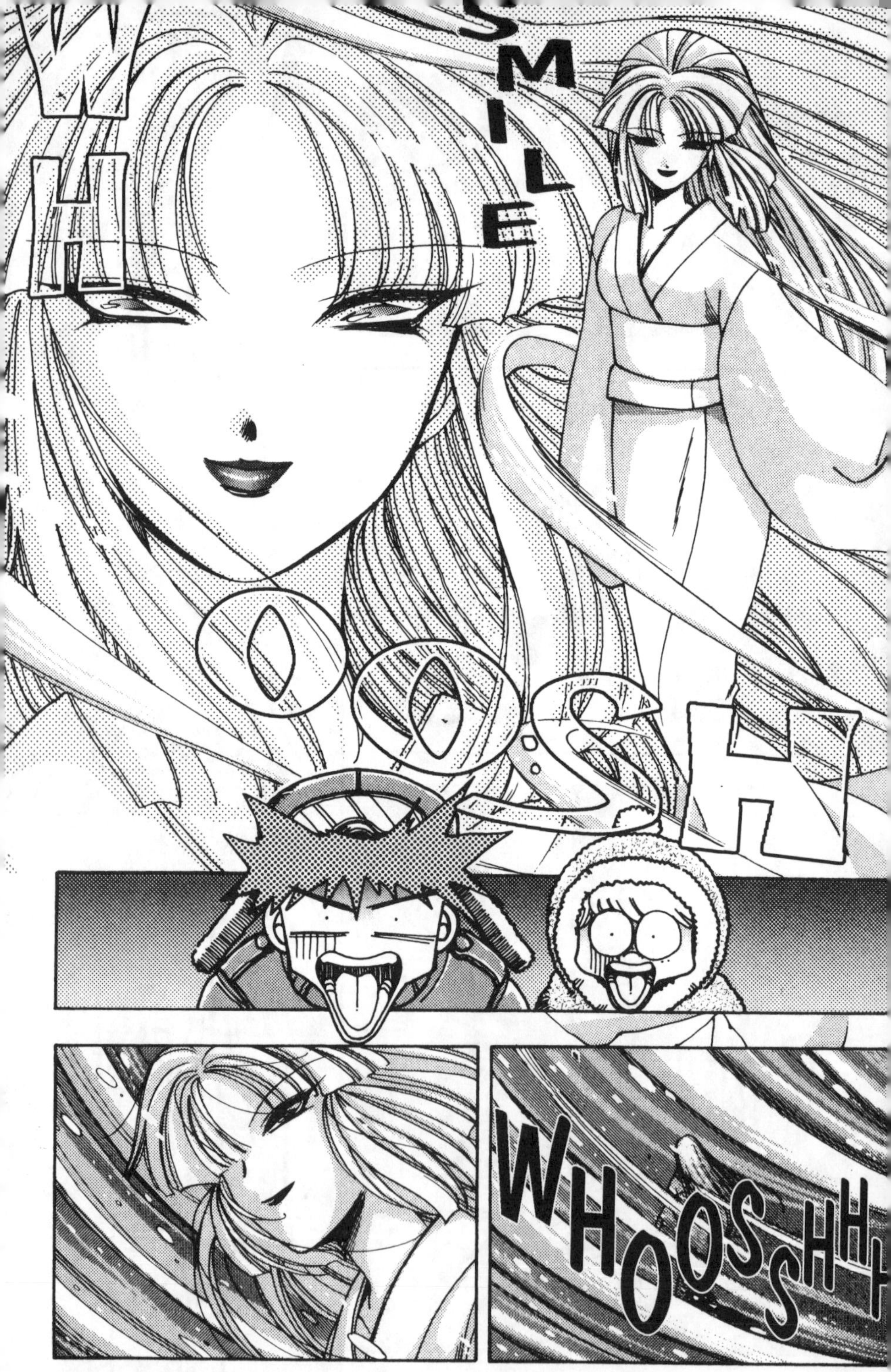
WHOOSH
SMILE
WHOOSHH

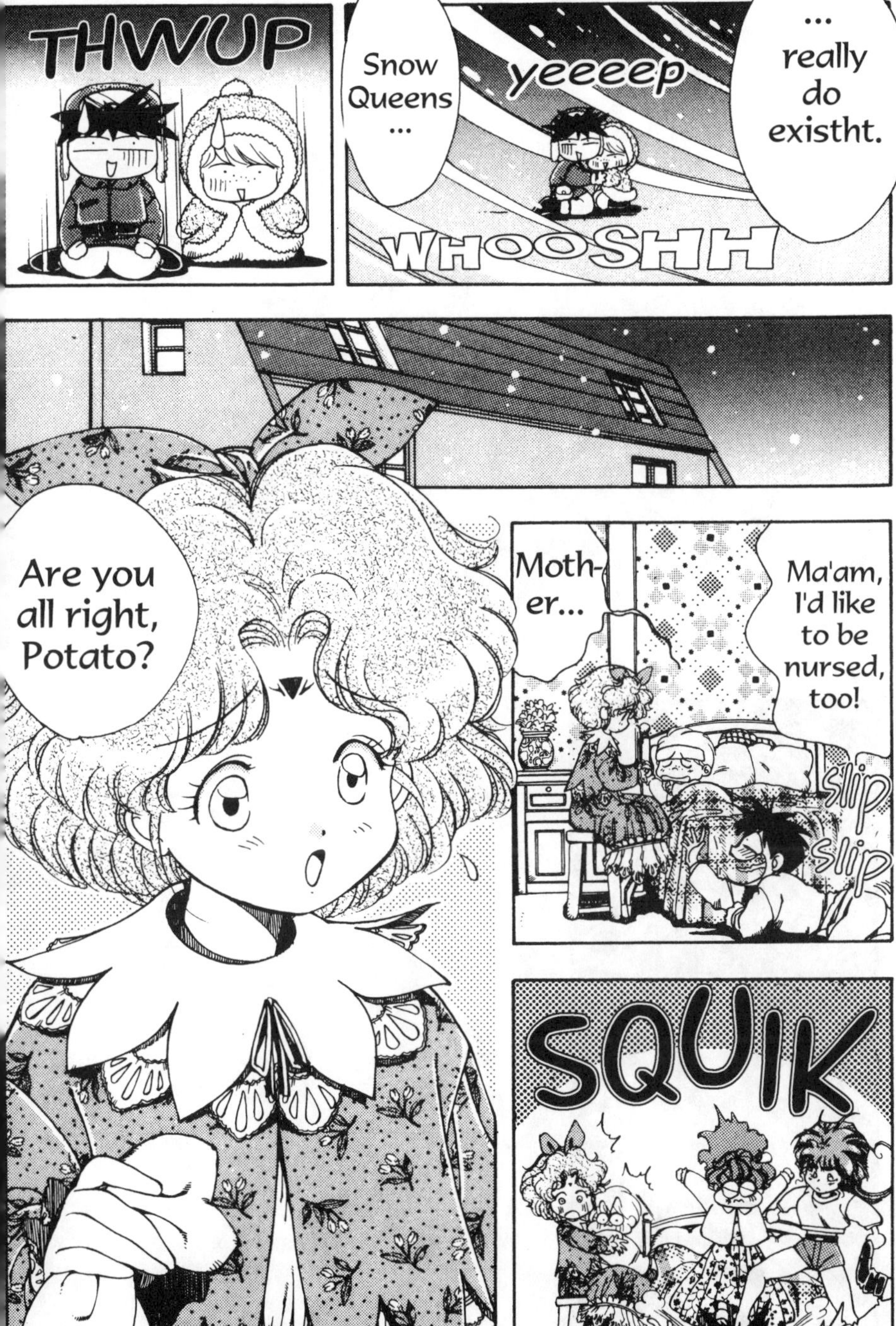
THWUP
Snow Queens ...
yeeeep
... really do existht.
WHOOSHH
Are you all right, Potato?
Moth-er...
Ma'am, I'd like to be nursed, too!
slip
slip
SQUIK

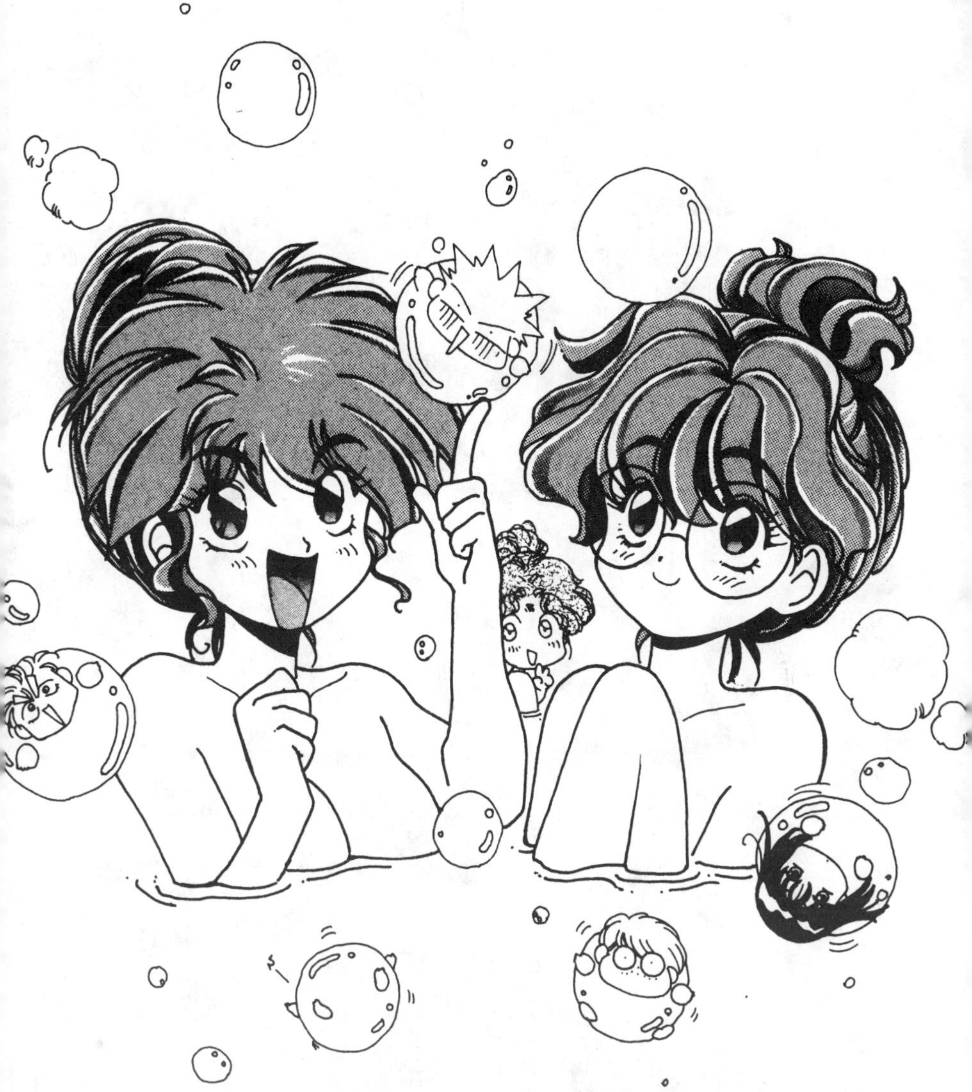

Seduction, Seduction, Whisper the Trees

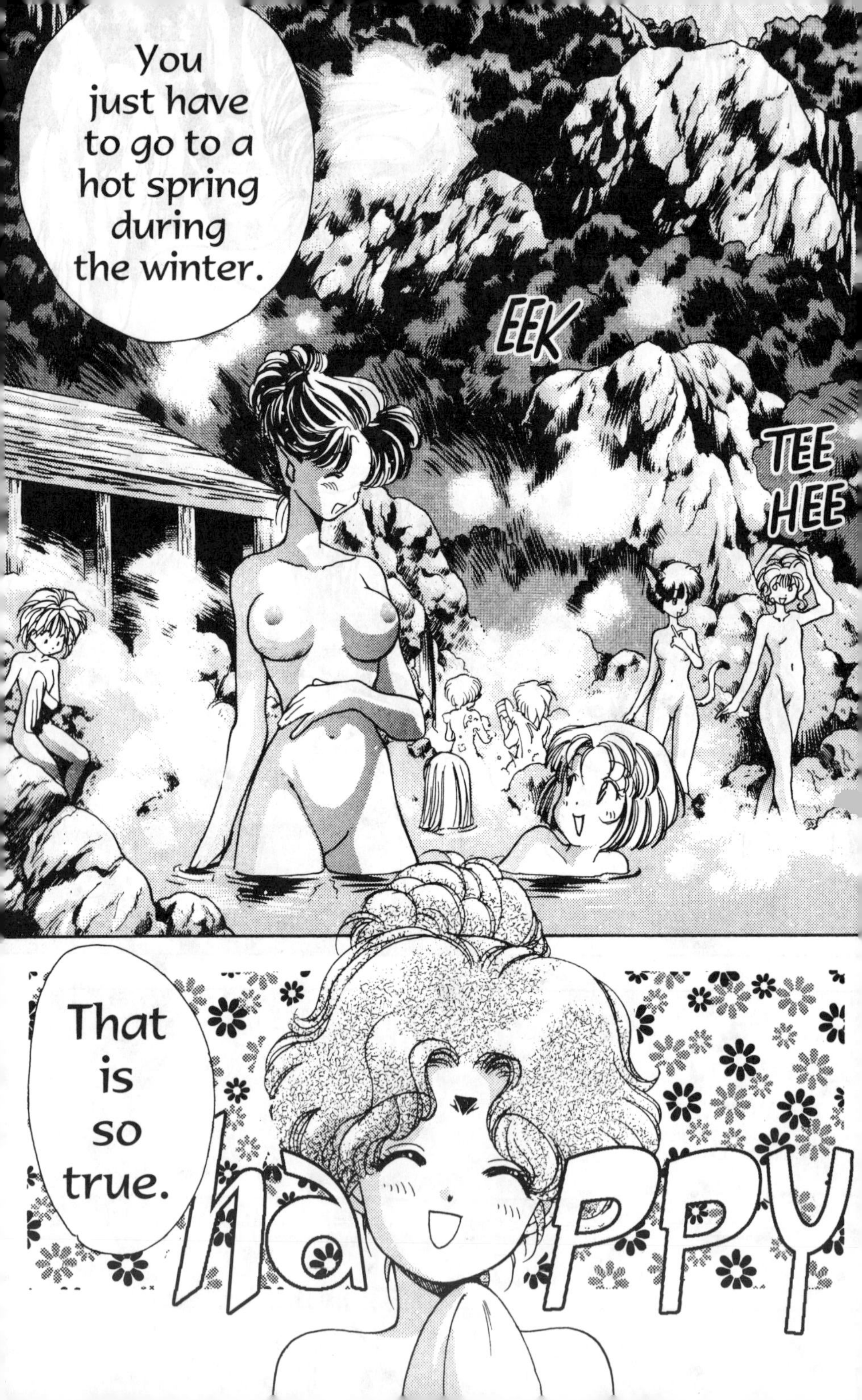
You just have to go to a hot spring during the winter.
EEK
TEE HEE
That is so true.
happy

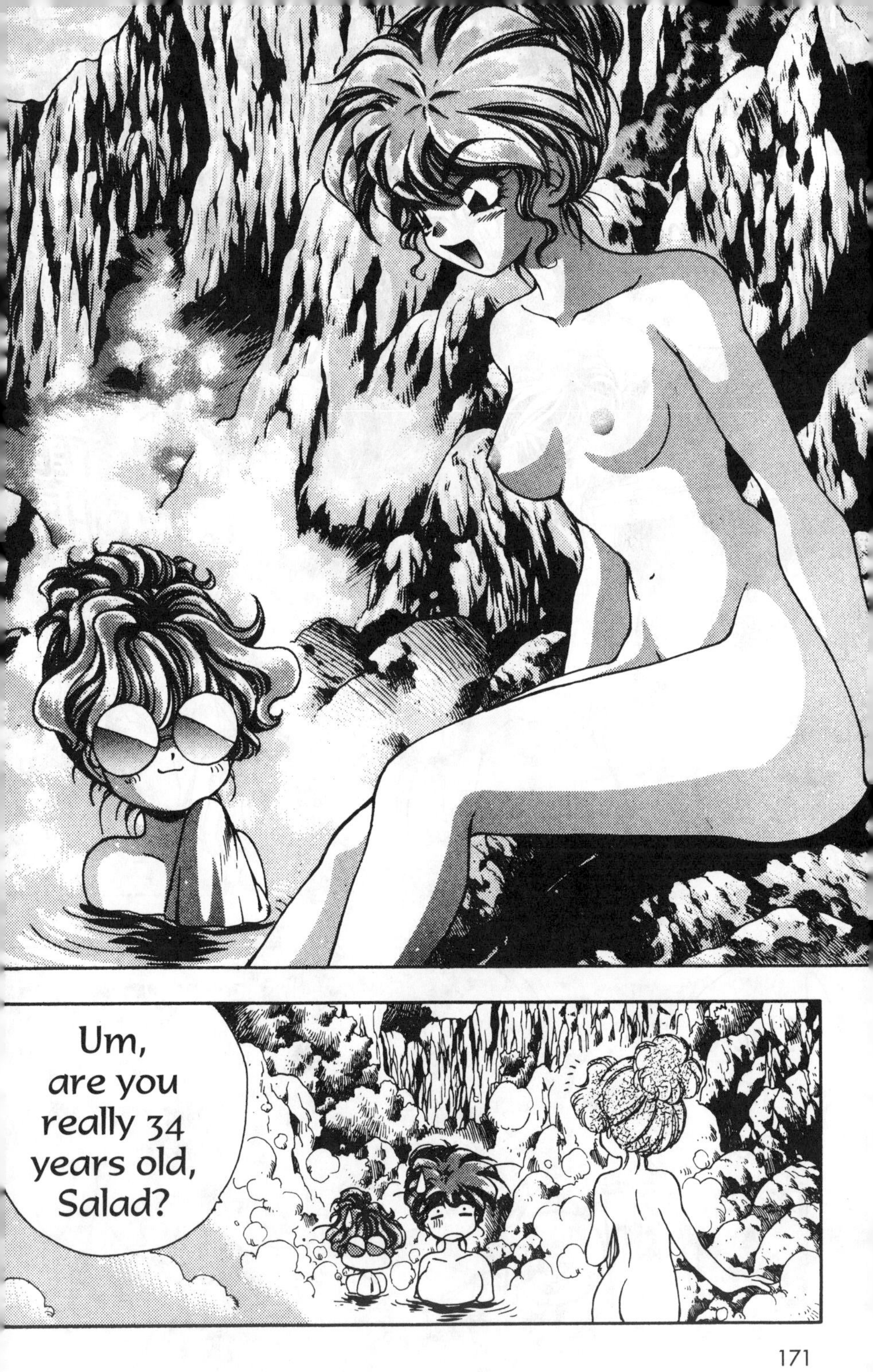
Um, are you really 34 years old, Salad?

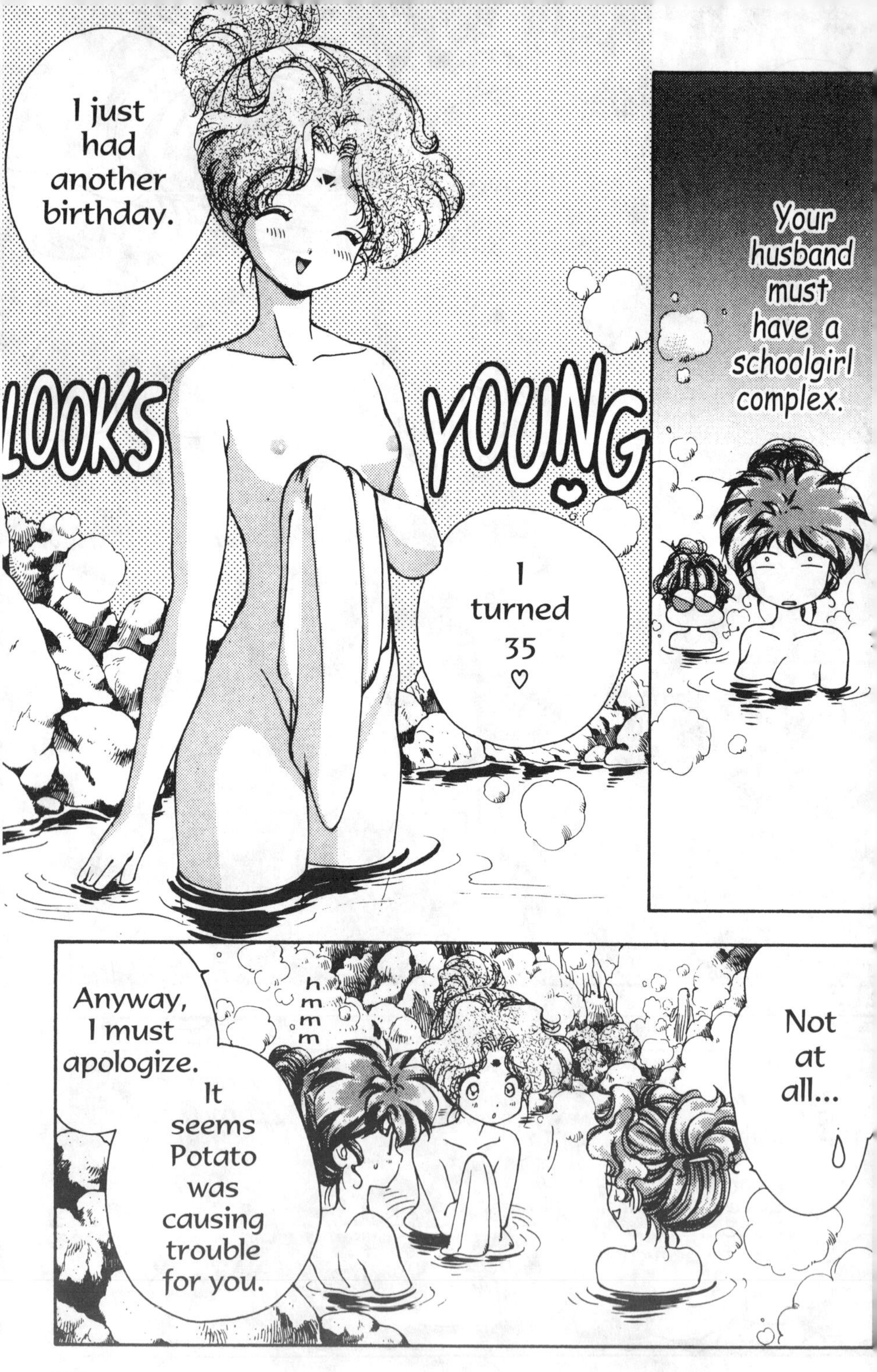
I just had another birthday.
LOOKS YOUNG
I turned 35 ♡
Your husband must have a schoolgirl complex.
Anyway, I must apologize.
hmmm
It seems Potato was causing trouble for you.
Not at all...

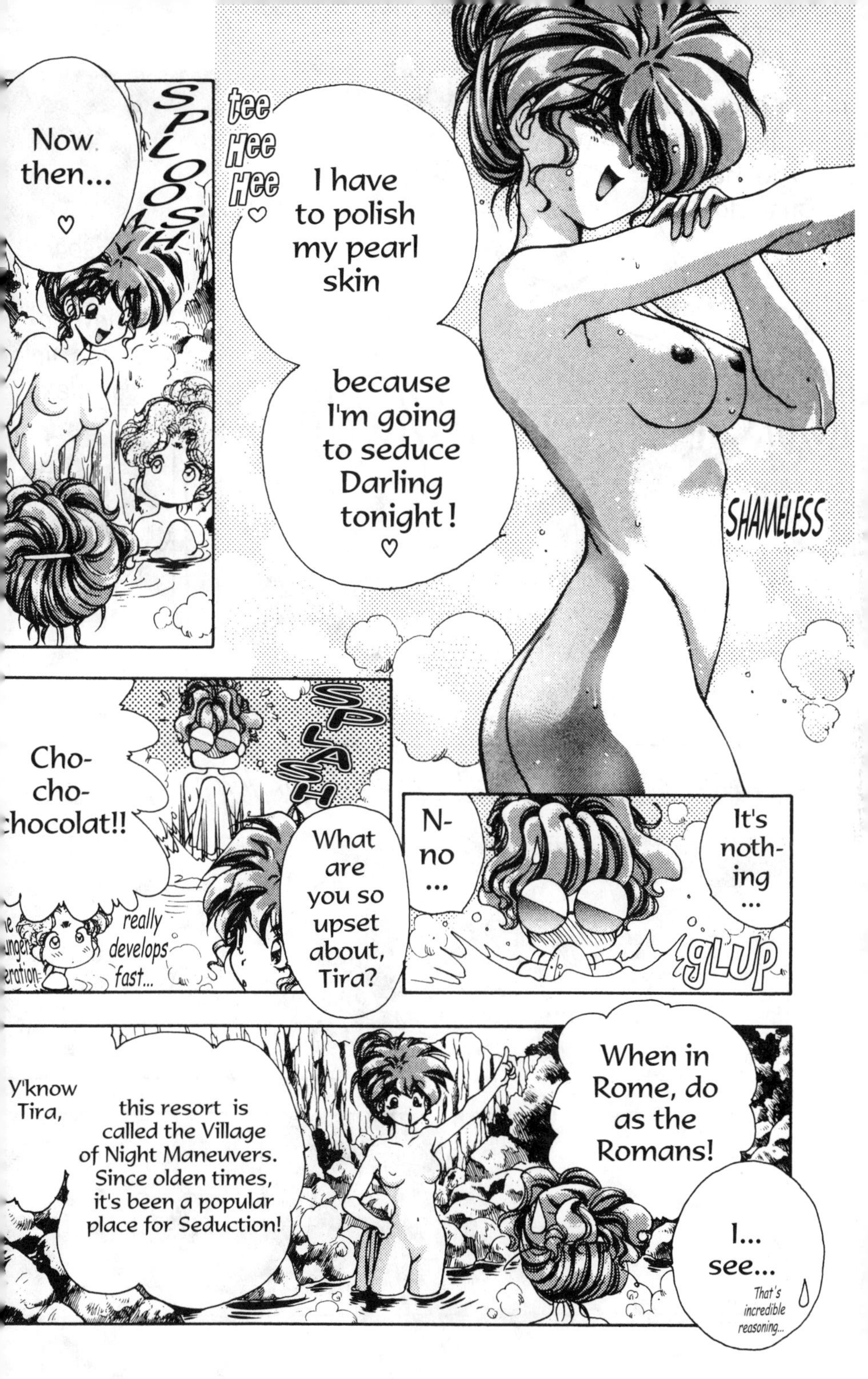

Now then... ♡
SPLOOSH
tee Hee Hee ♡
I have to polish my pearl skin
because I'm going to seduce Darling tonight! ♡
SHAMELESS
Cho-cho-chocolat!!
SPLASH
What are you so upset about, Tira?
really develops fast...
N-no...
It's nothing...
GLUP
Y'know Tira,
this resort is called the Village of Night Maneuvers. Since olden times, it's been a popular place for Seduction!
When in Rome, do as the Romans!
I... see...
That's incredible reasoning...

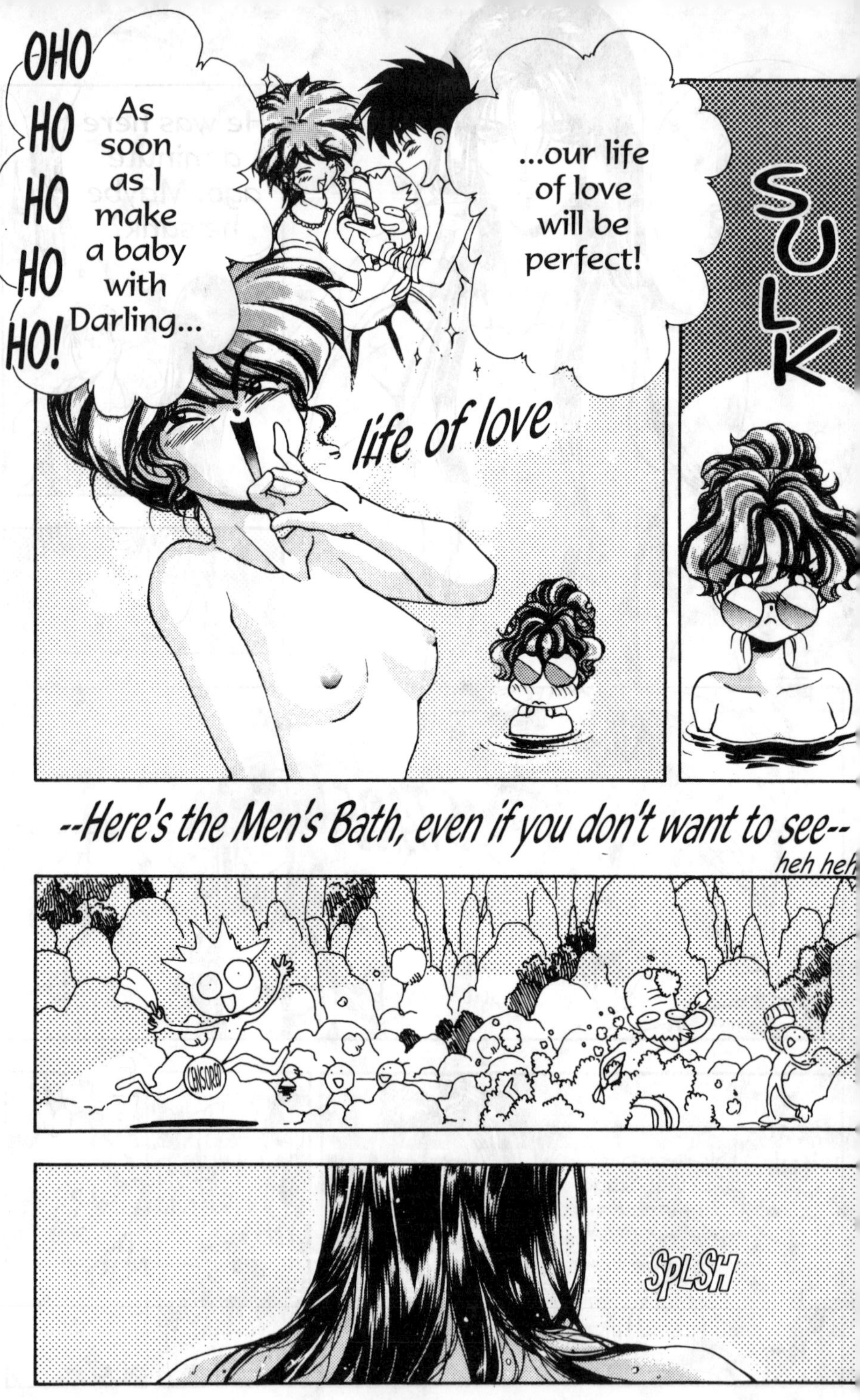

OHO HO HO HO HO!
As soon as I make a baby with Darling...
...our life of love will be perfect!
life of love
SULK
--Here's the Men's Bath, even if you don't want to see--
heh heh
CENSORED
SPLSH

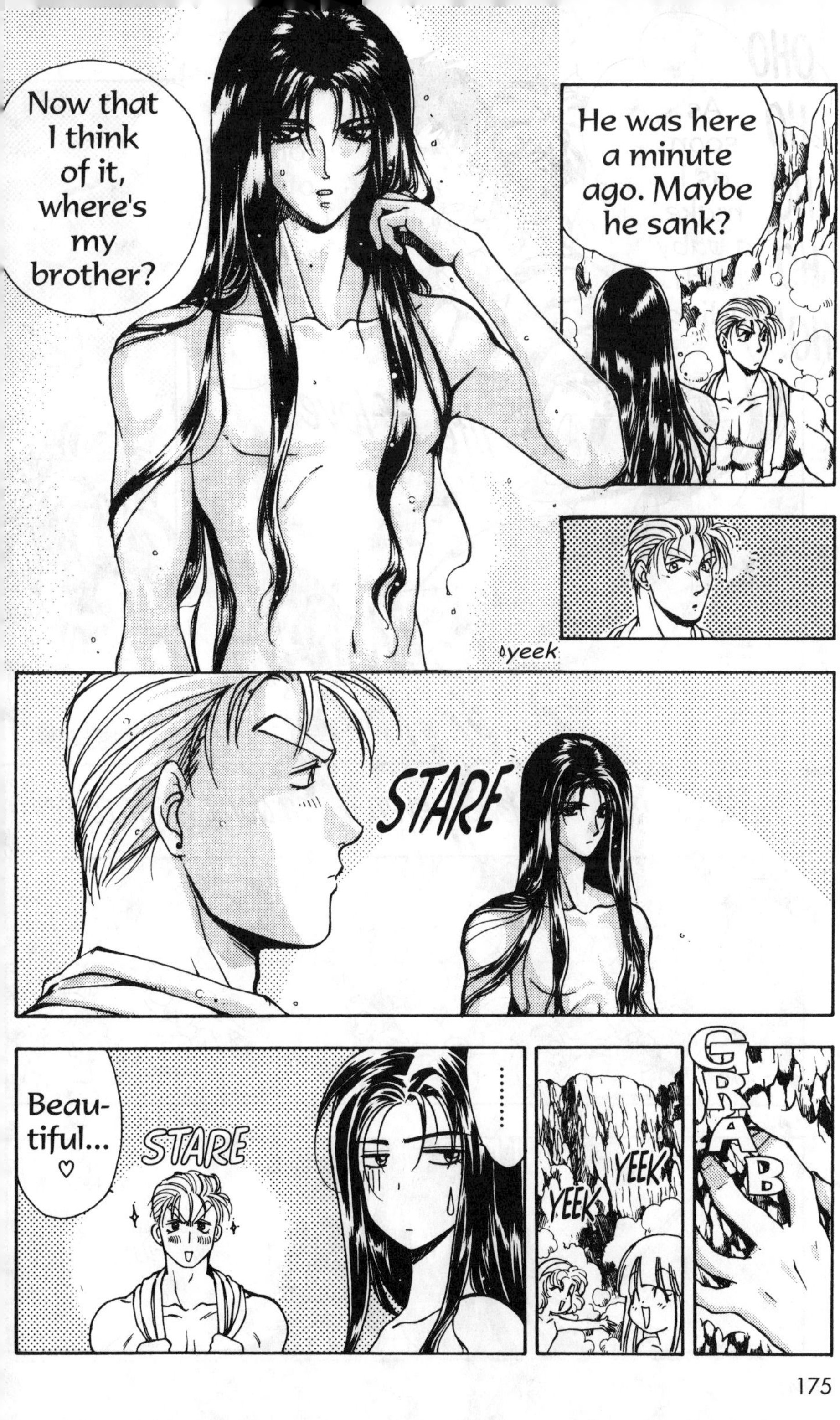

Now that I think of it, where's my brother?
He was here a minute ago. Maybe he sank?
yeek
STARE
Beau-tiful... ♡
STARE
......
YEEK
YEEK
GRAB

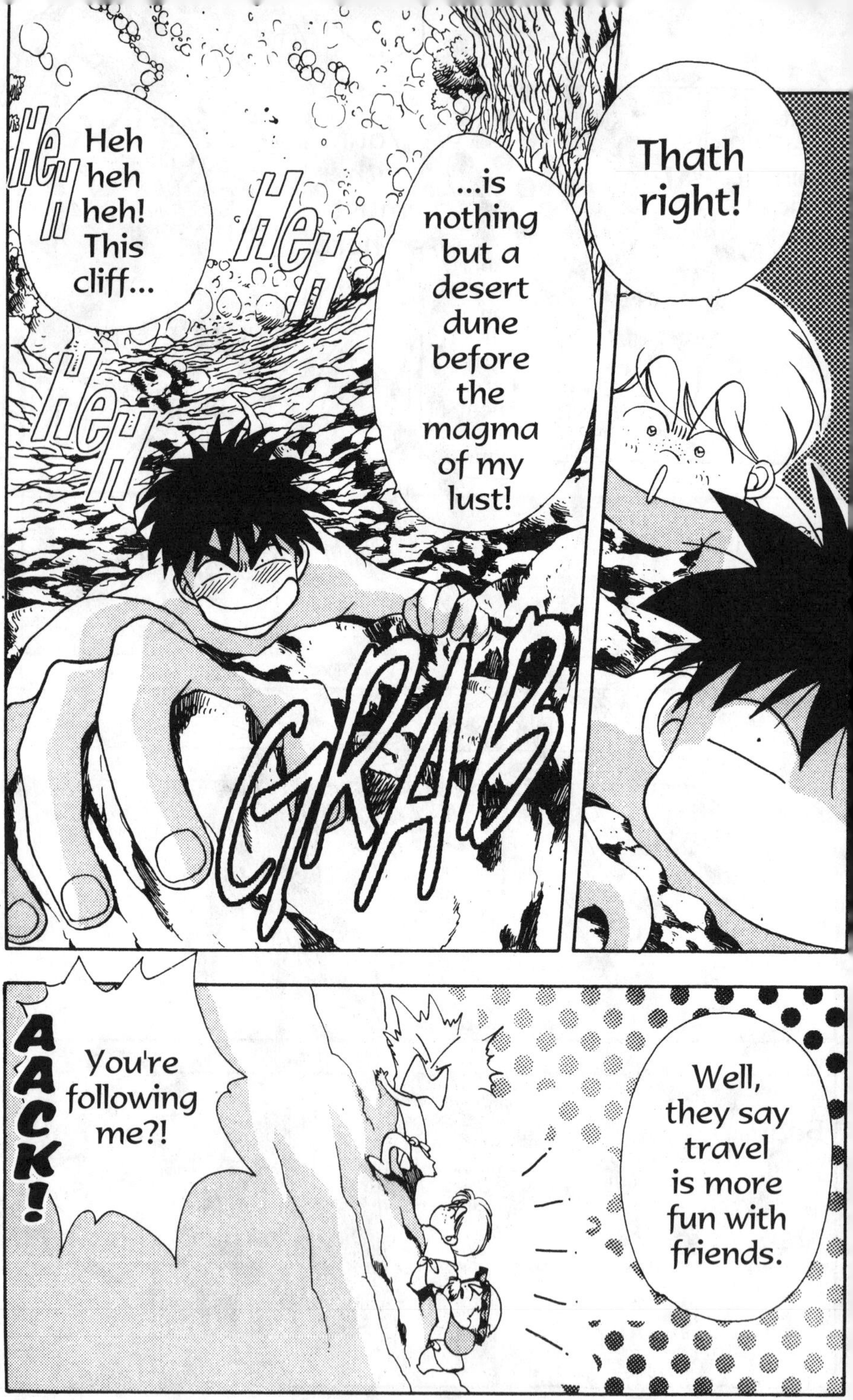
HEH
Heh heh heh! This cliff...
HEH
HEH
...is nothing but a desert dune before the magma of my lust!
GRAB
Thath right!
AACK!
You're following me?!
Well, they say travel is more fun with friends.

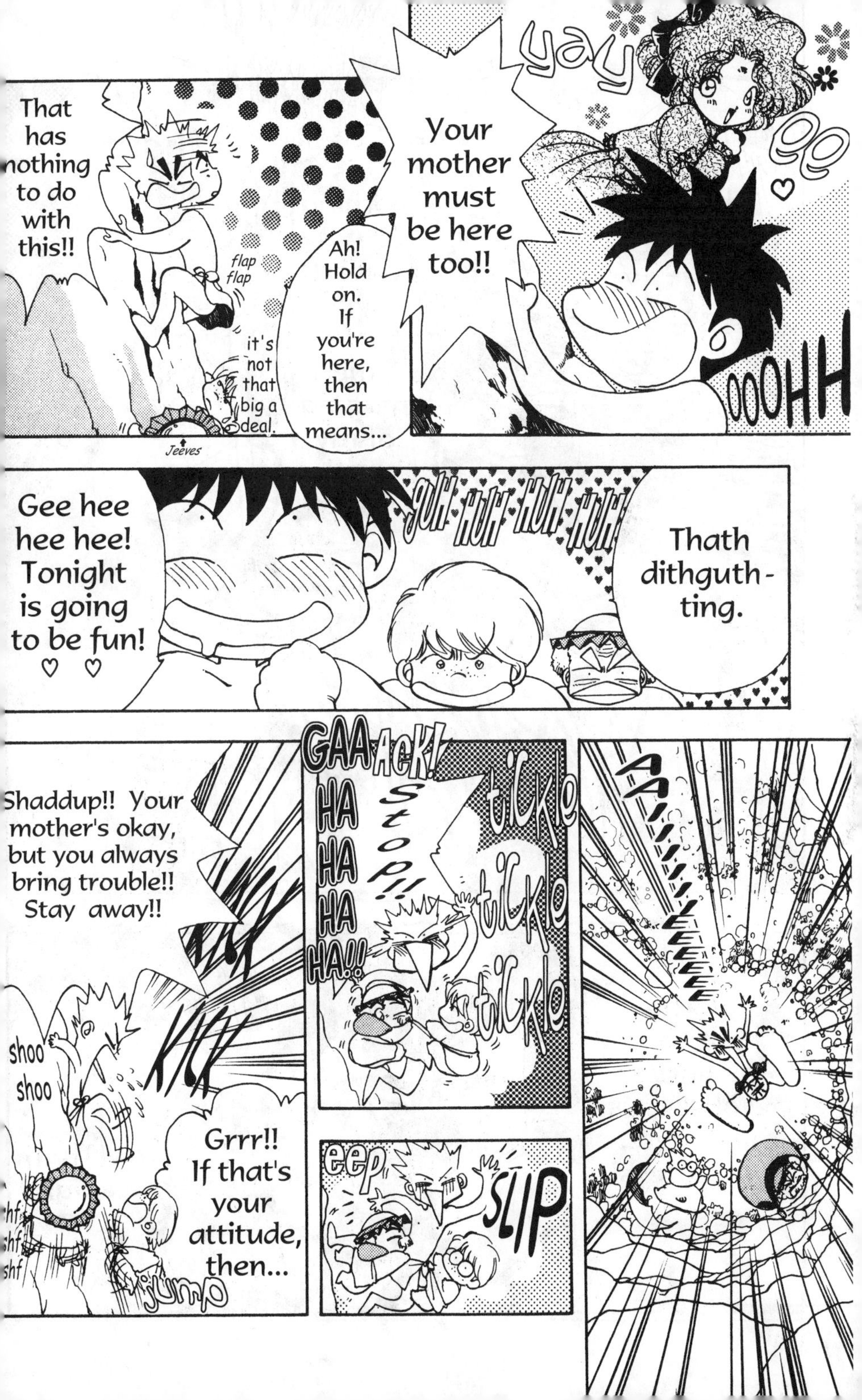
That has nothing to do with this!!
flap flap
it's not that big a deal.
Jeeves
Ah! Hold on. If you're here, then that means...
Your mother must be here too!!
yay
ee
OOOHH
Gee hee hee hee! Tonight is going to be fun! ♡ ♡
GUH HUH HUH HUH
Thath dithguth-ting.
Shaddup!! Your mother's okay, but you always bring trouble!! Stay away!!
KICK
shoo shoo
shf shf shf
jump
Grrr!! If that's your attitude, then...
GAAACK!
HA HA HA HA HA!!
Stop!!
tickle tickle tickle
eep
SLIP
AAIIIIIIEEEEE

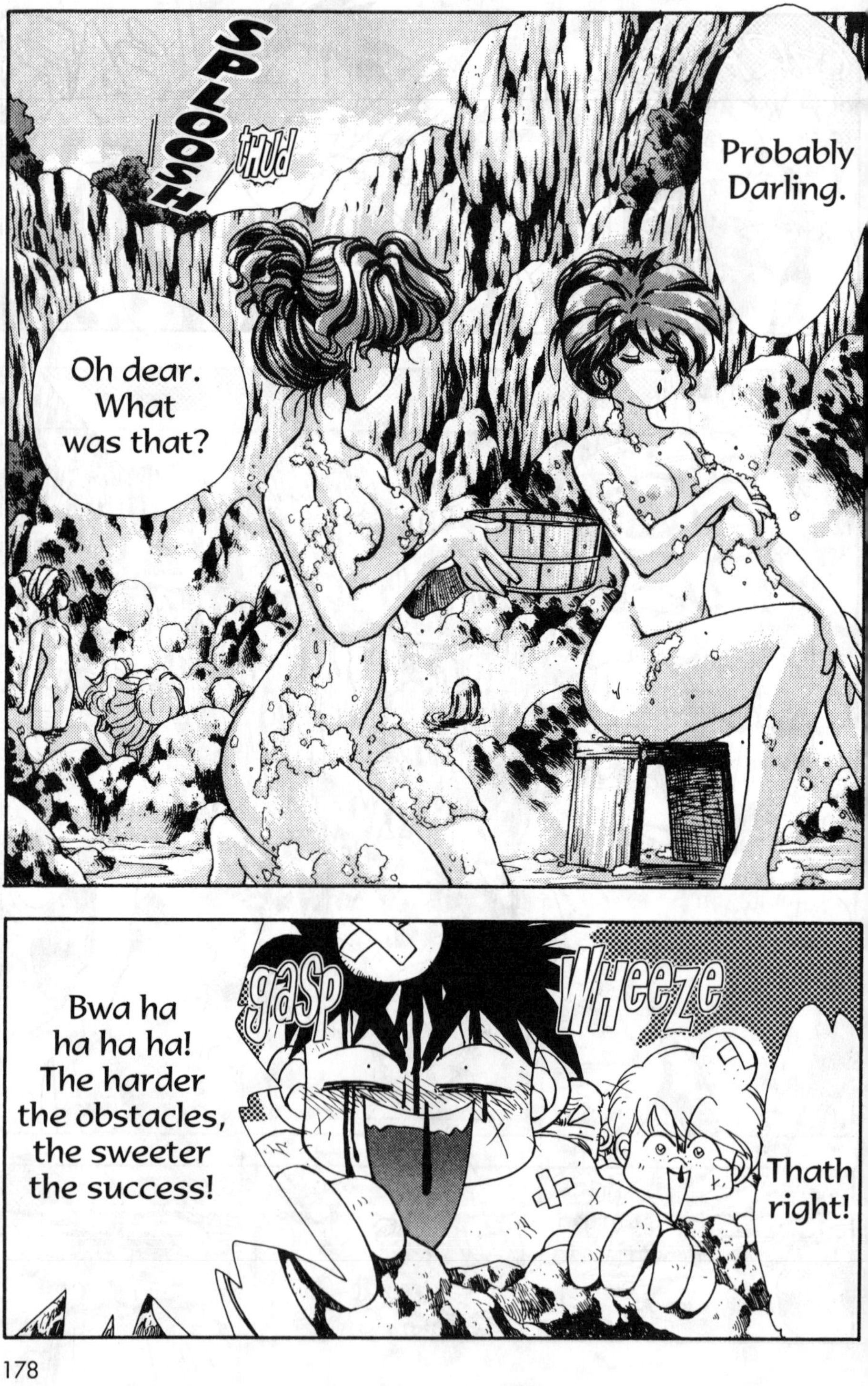
SPLOOSH
thud
Oh dear. What was that?
Probably Darling.
Bwa ha ha ha ha! The harder the obstacles, the sweeter the success!
gasp
WHeeze
Thath right!

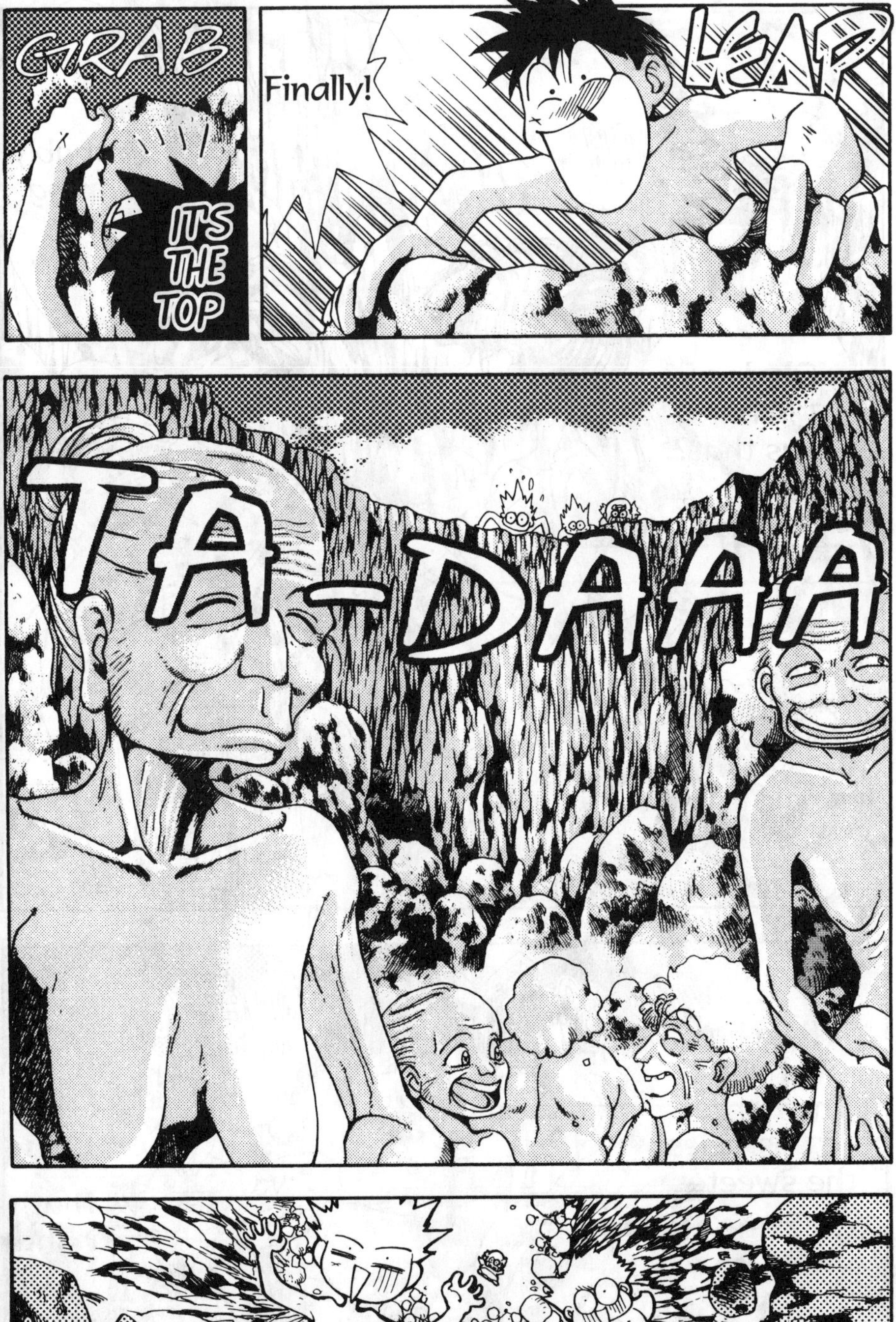
GRAB
IT'S THE TOP
Finally!
LEAP
TA-DAAA

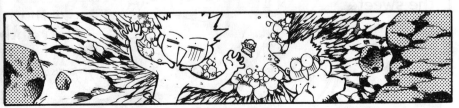

AAIIEEEE

SPLOOSH

THUD

crack

I thought I heard Carrot's scream.

There it goes again.

It's sad how easy you can picture what just happened.

CLINK

CLINK

The yukatas don't go with the background.

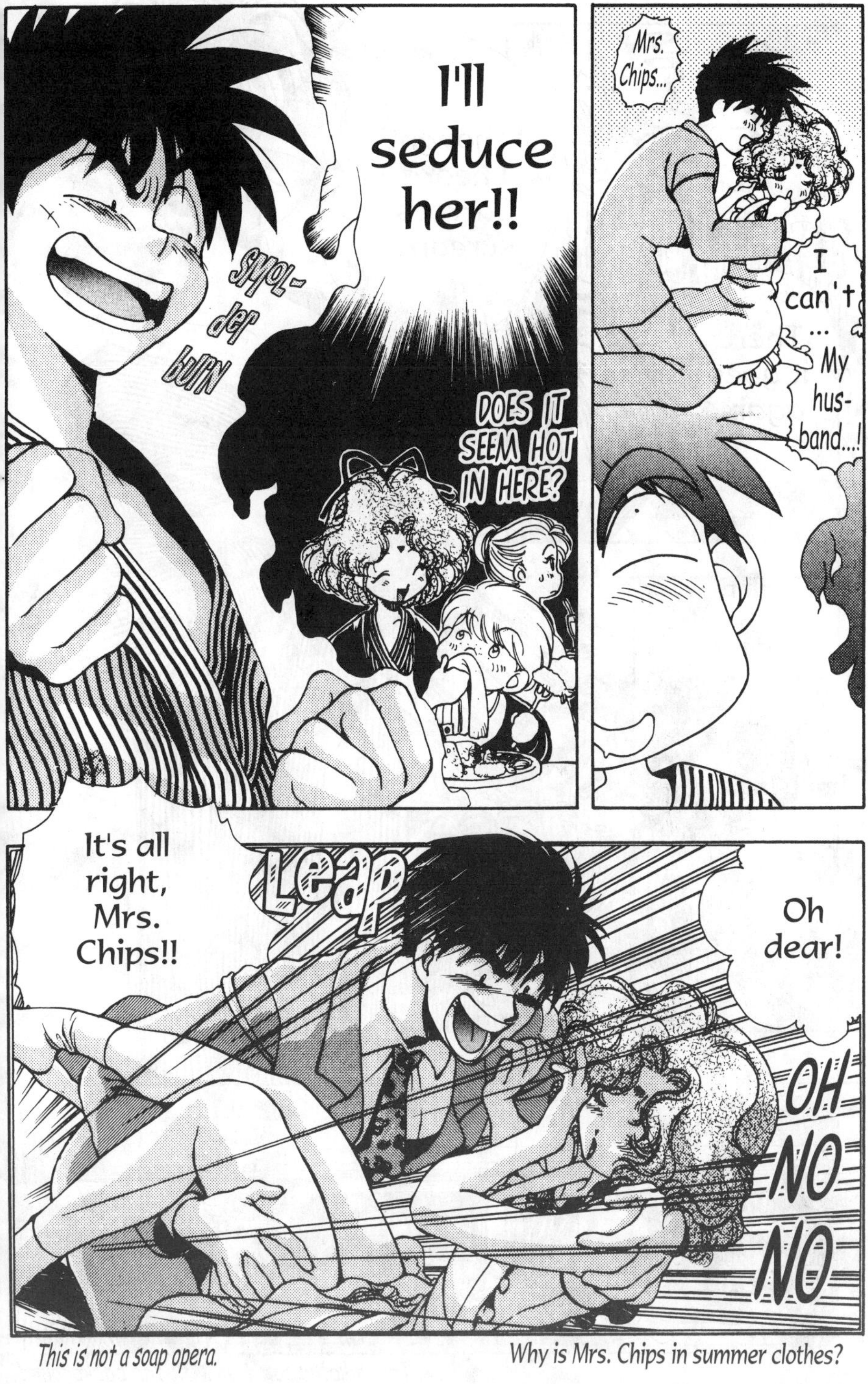
I'll seduce her!!
SMOL-der burn
DOES IT SEEM HOT IN HERE?
Mrs. Chips...
I can't ... My hus-band...!
It's all right, Mrs. Chips!!
Leap
Oh dear!
OH NO NO NO

This is not a soap opera.

Why is Mrs. Chips in summer clothes?

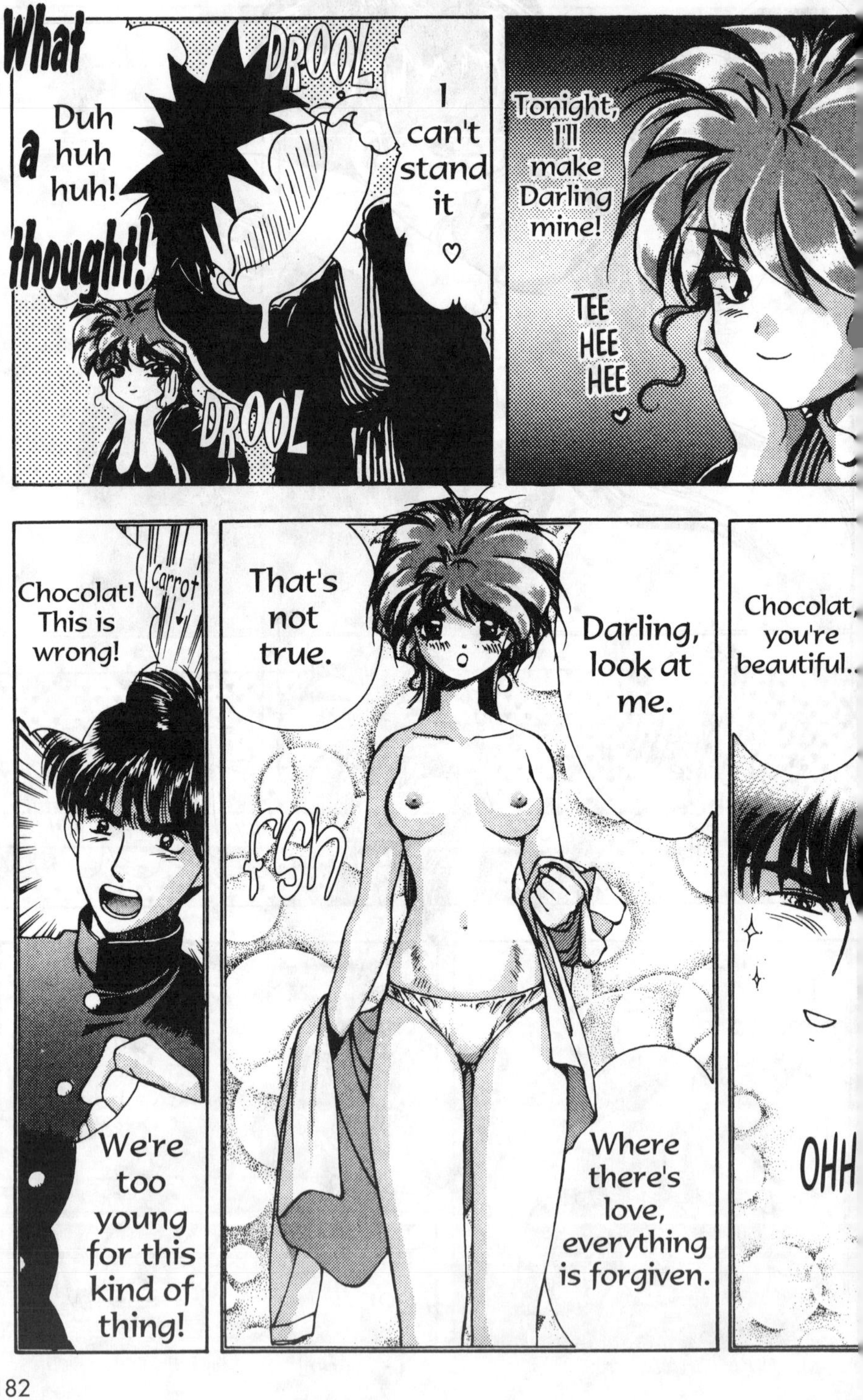
What a thought!
Duh huh huh!
DROOL
I can't stand it ♡
DROOL
Tonight, I'll make Darling mine!
TEE HEE HEE
Chocolat! This is wrong!
Carrot
We're too young for this kind of thing!
That's not true.
Darling, look at me.
fsh
Where there's love, everything is forgiven.
Chocolat, you're beautiful...
OHH

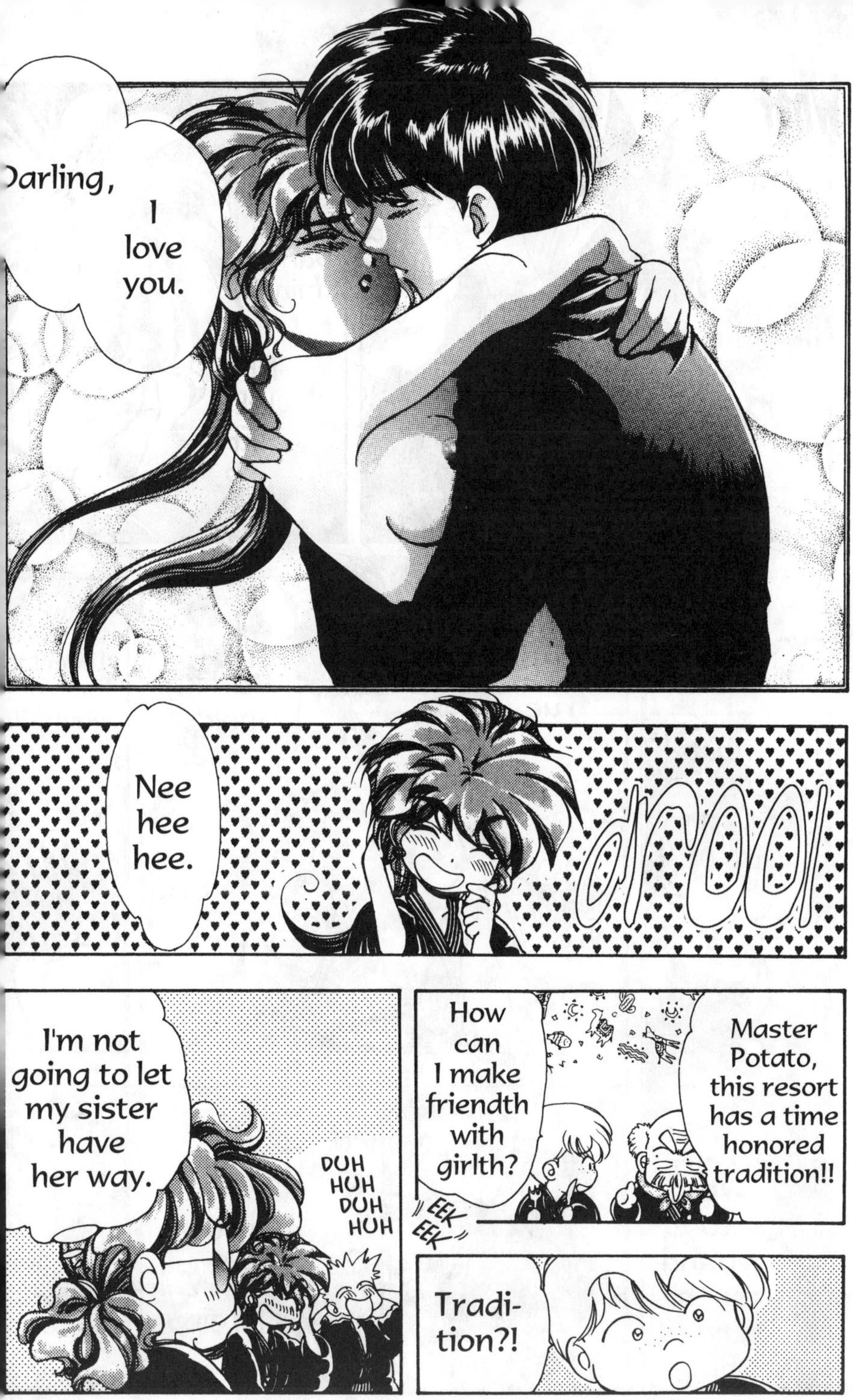
Darling, I love you.
Nee hee hee.
drool
I'm not going to let my sister have her way.
DUH HUH DUH HUH
How can I make friendth with girlth?
EEK EEK
Master Potato, this resort has a time honored tradition!!
Tradi-tion?!

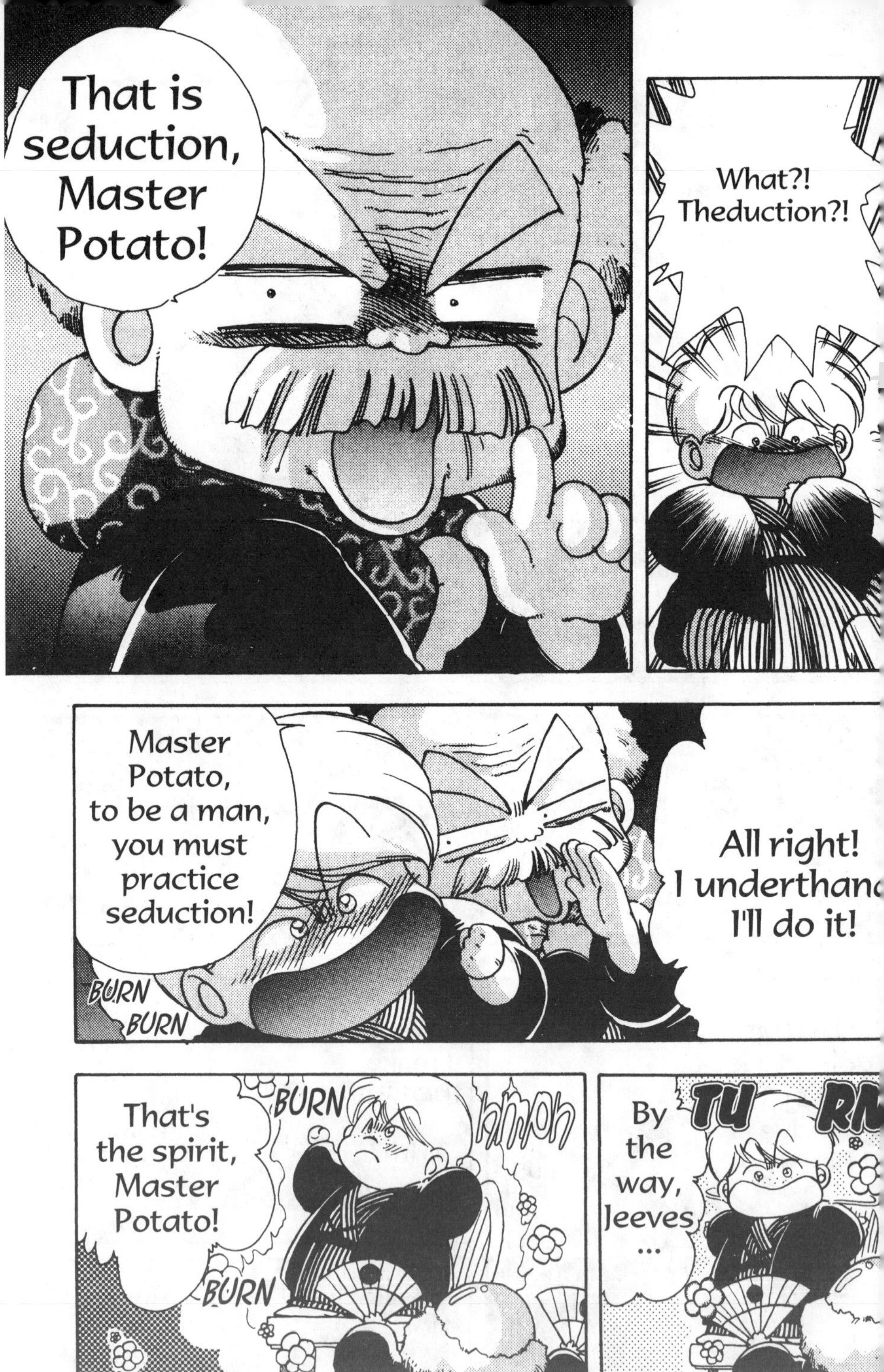
That is seduction, Master Potato!
What?! Theduction?!
Master Potato, to be a man, you must practice seduction!
All right! I underthand I'll do it!
BURN BURN
That's the spirit, Master Potato!
BURN
hmph
BURN
CHAIR
TU RN
By the way, Jeeves ...

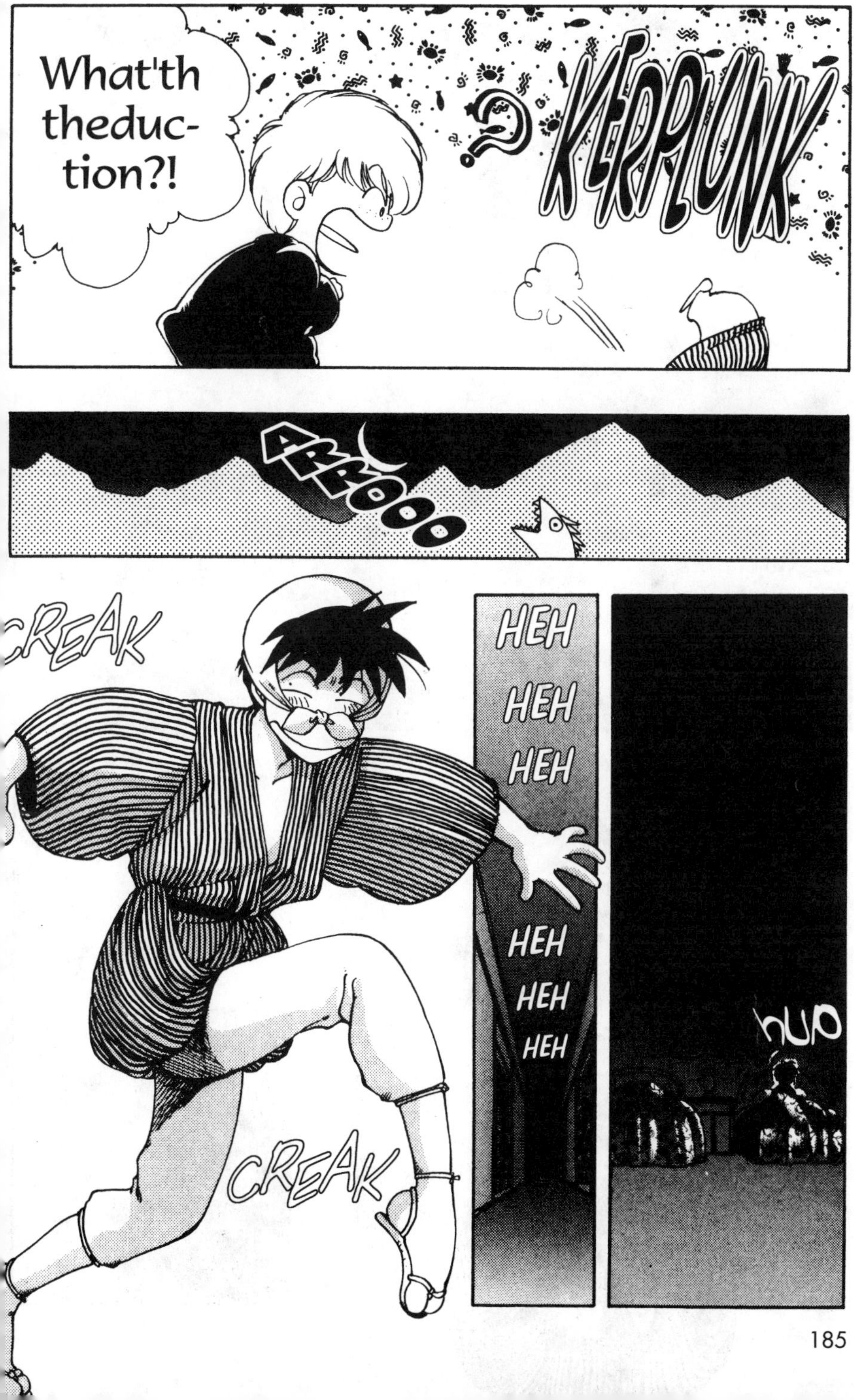
What'th theduction?!
?
KERPLUNK
ARROOO
CREAK
CREAK
HEH HEH HEH
HEH HEH HEH
hup

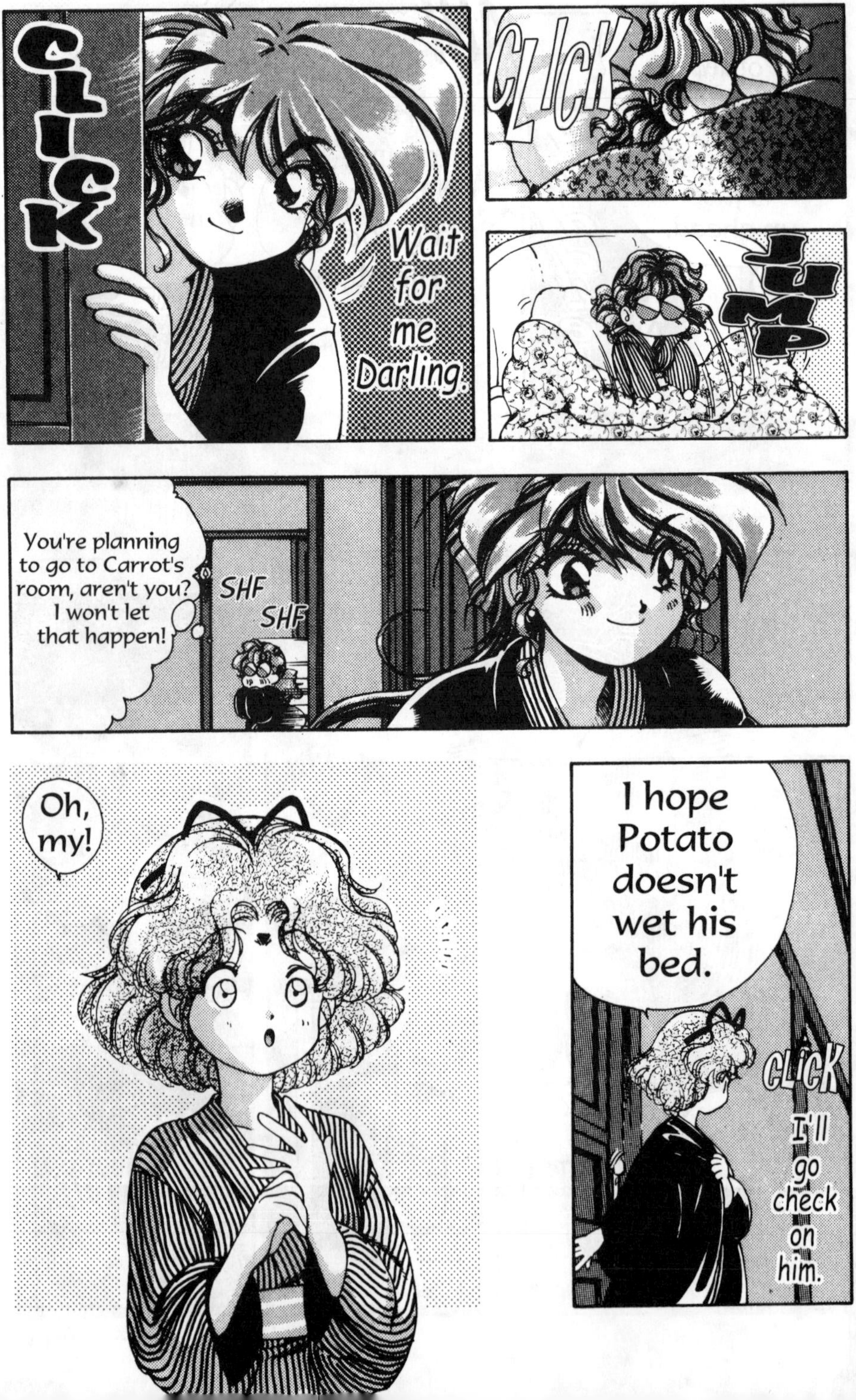
CLICK
Wait for me Darling.
CLICK
JUMP
You're planning to go to Carrot's room, aren't you? I won't let that happen!
SHF
SHF
Oh, my!
I hope Potato doesn't wet his bed.
CLICK
I'll go check on him.

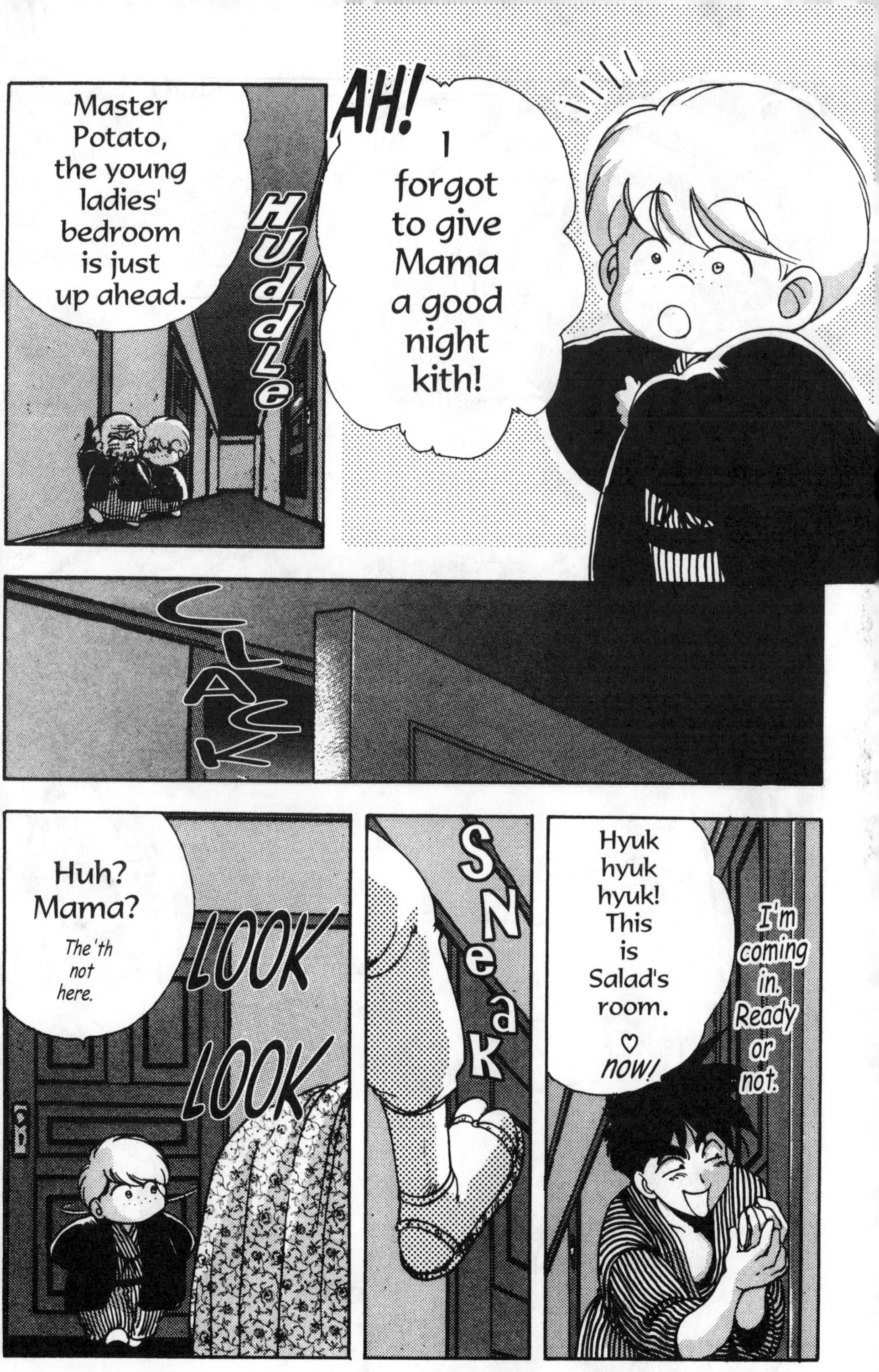
Master Potato, the young ladies' bedroom is just up ahead.
HUDDLE
AH!
I forgot to give Mama a good night kith!
CLACK
Huh? Mama?
The'th not here.
LOOK LOOK
SNeak
Hyuk hyuk hyuk! This is Salad's room. ♡
now!
I'm coming in. Ready or not.

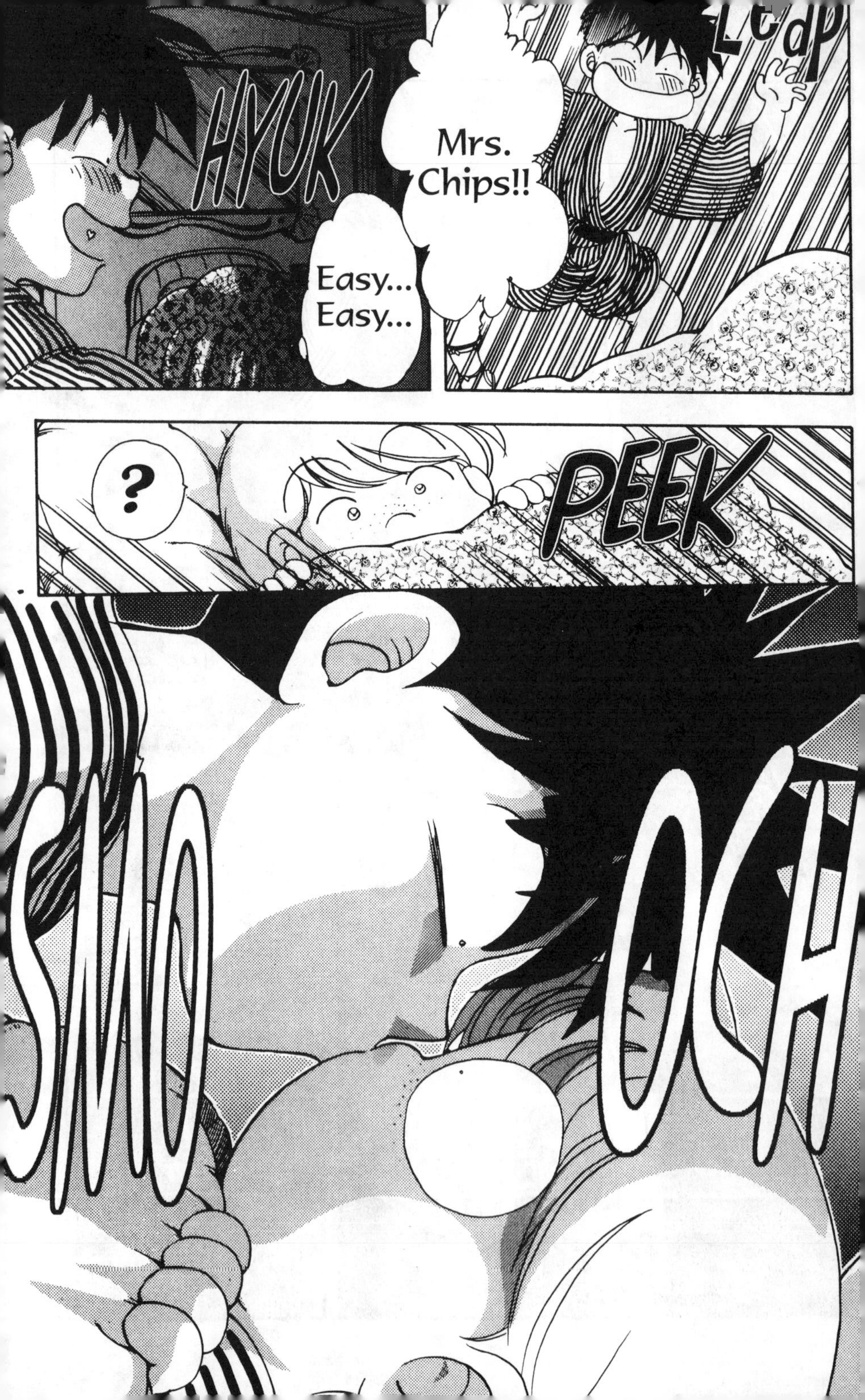
HYUK
Easy... Easy...
Mrs. Chips!!
Leap
?
PEEK
SMO
OCH

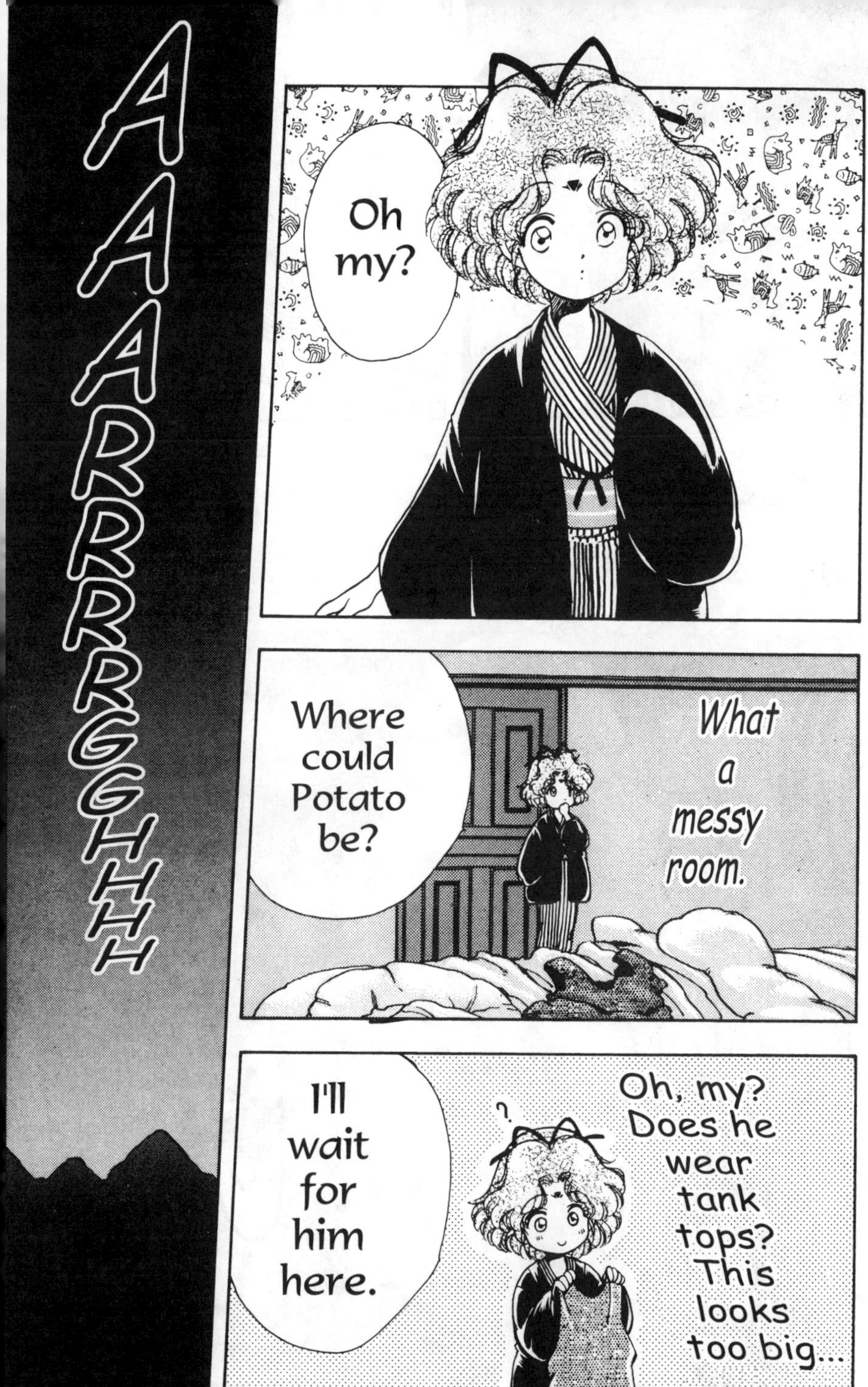
AAAARRRRGGHHH
Oh my?
Where could Potato be?
What a messy room.
I'll wait for him here.
?
Oh, my? Does he wear tank tops? This looks too big...

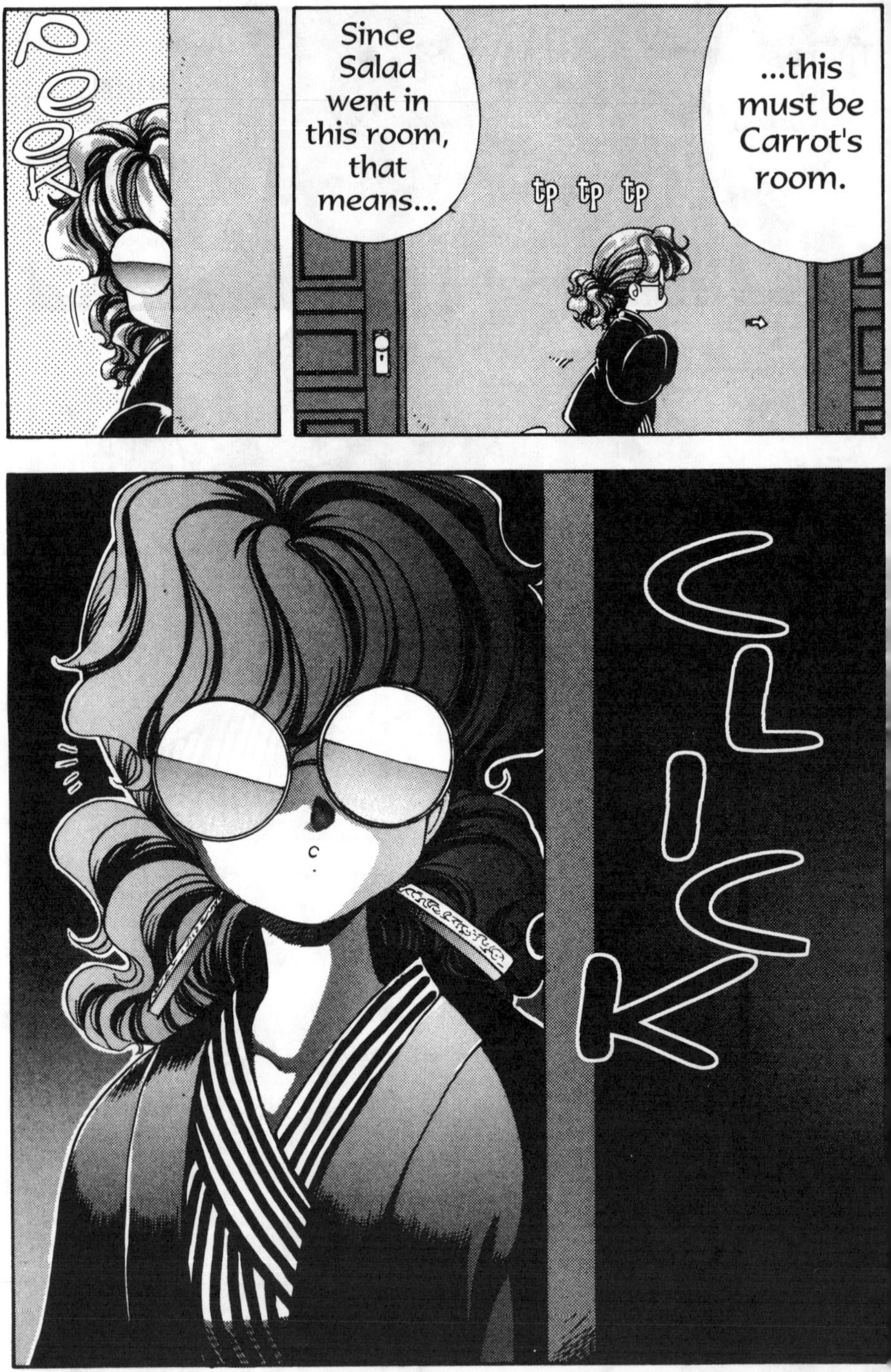
peek
Since Salad went in this room, that means...
tp tp tp
...this must be Carrot's room.
CLICK

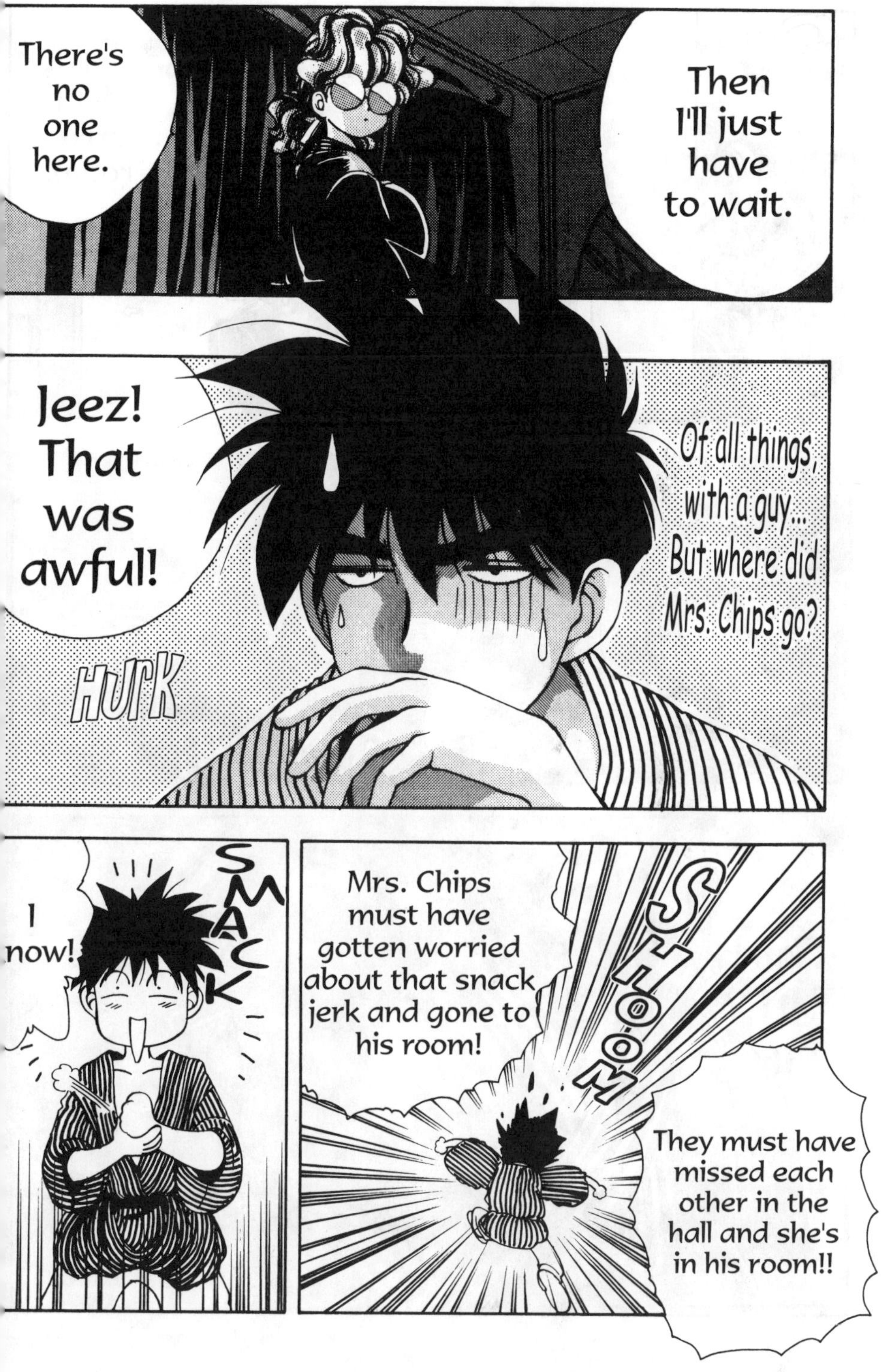
There's no one here.
Then I'll just have to wait.
Jeez! That was awful!
Of all things, with a guy... But where did Mrs. Chips go?
HURK
I now!
SMACK
Mrs. Chips must have gotten worried about that snack jerk and gone to his room!
SHOOM
They must have missed each other in the hall and she's in his room!!

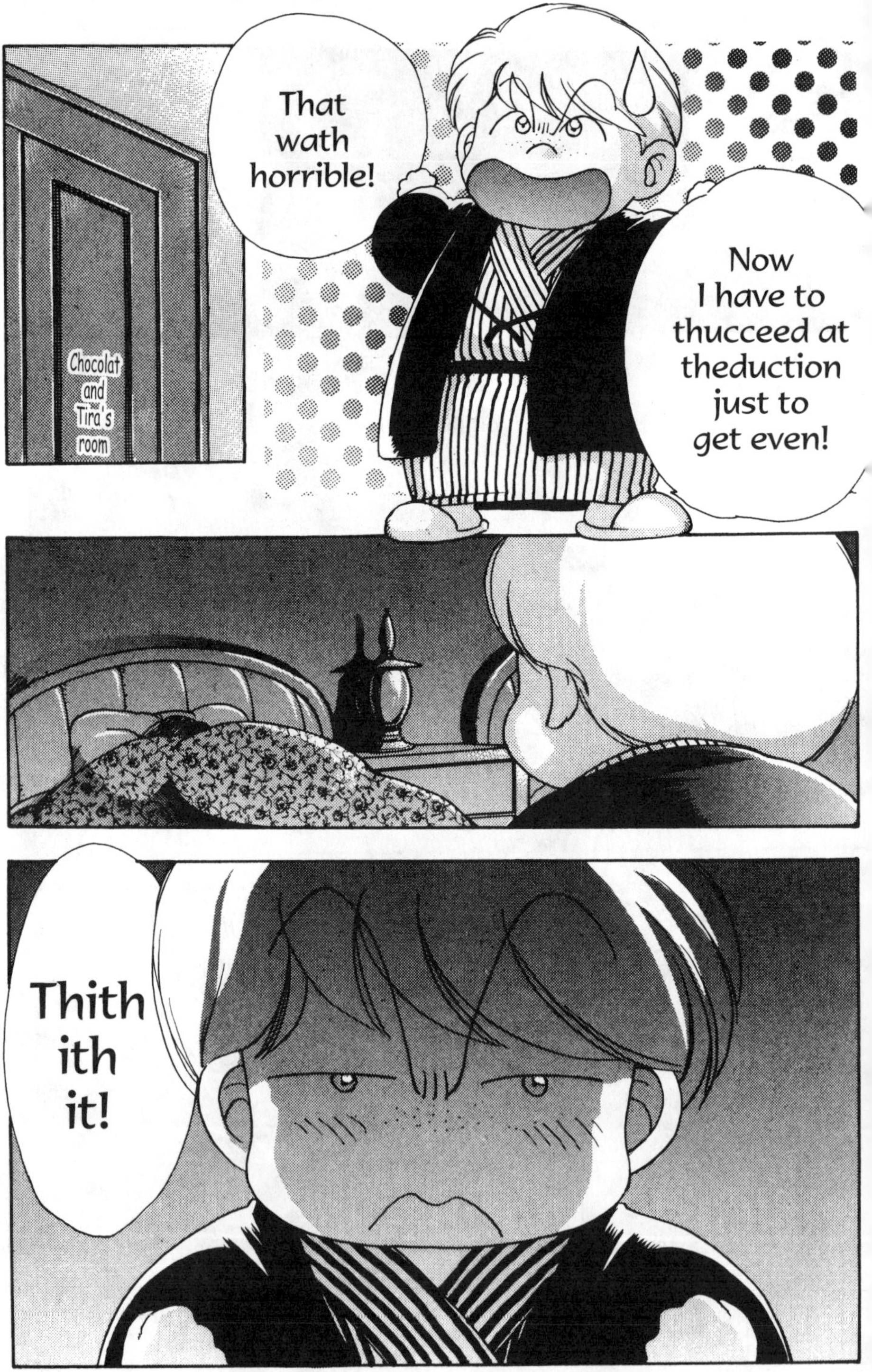
Chocolat and Tira's room
That wath horrible!
Now I have to thucceed at theduction just to get even!
Thith ith it!

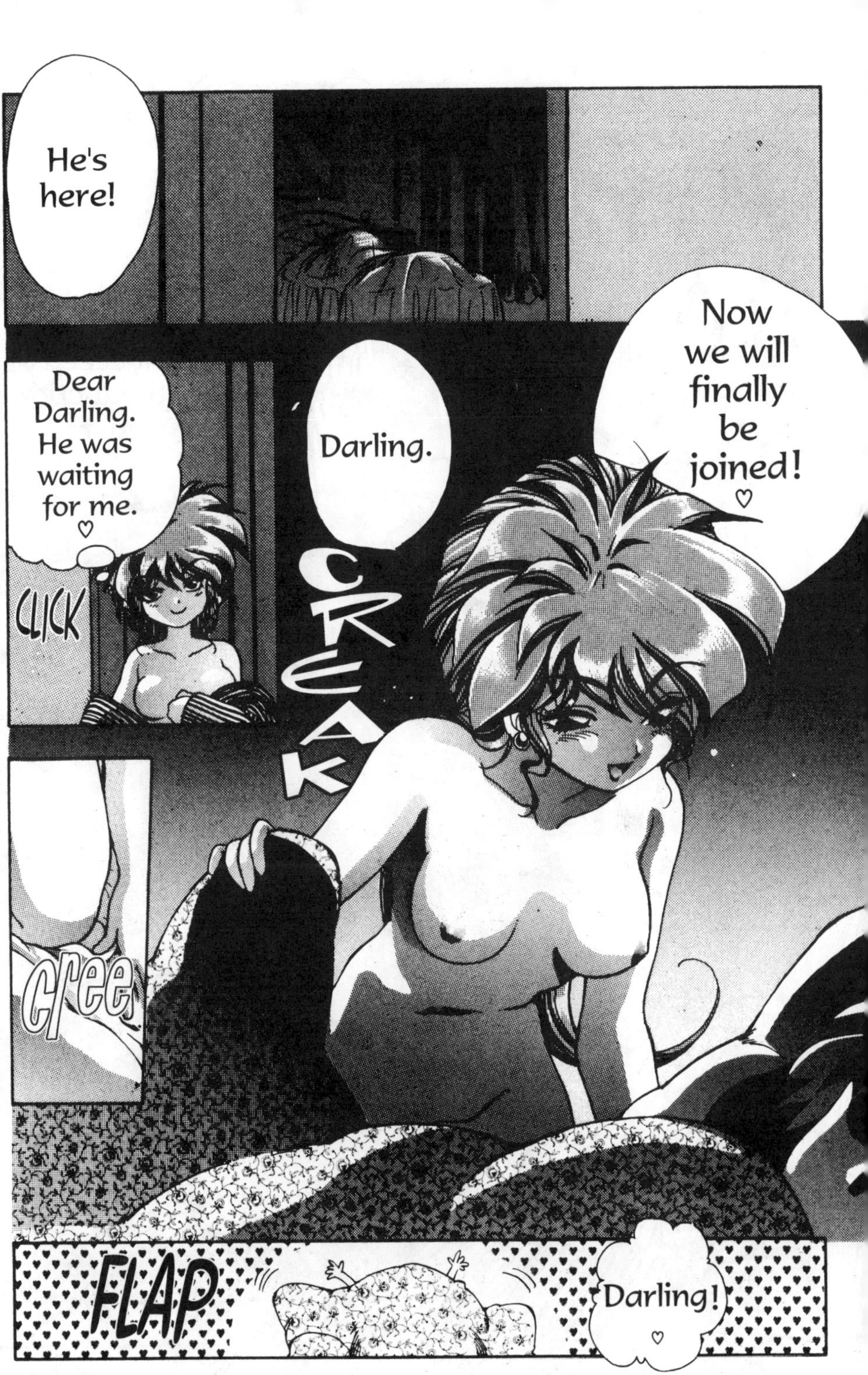

He's here!
Dear Darling. He was waiting for me. ♡
CLICK
cree
Darling.
CREAK
Now we will finally be joined! ♡
FLAP
Darling! ♡

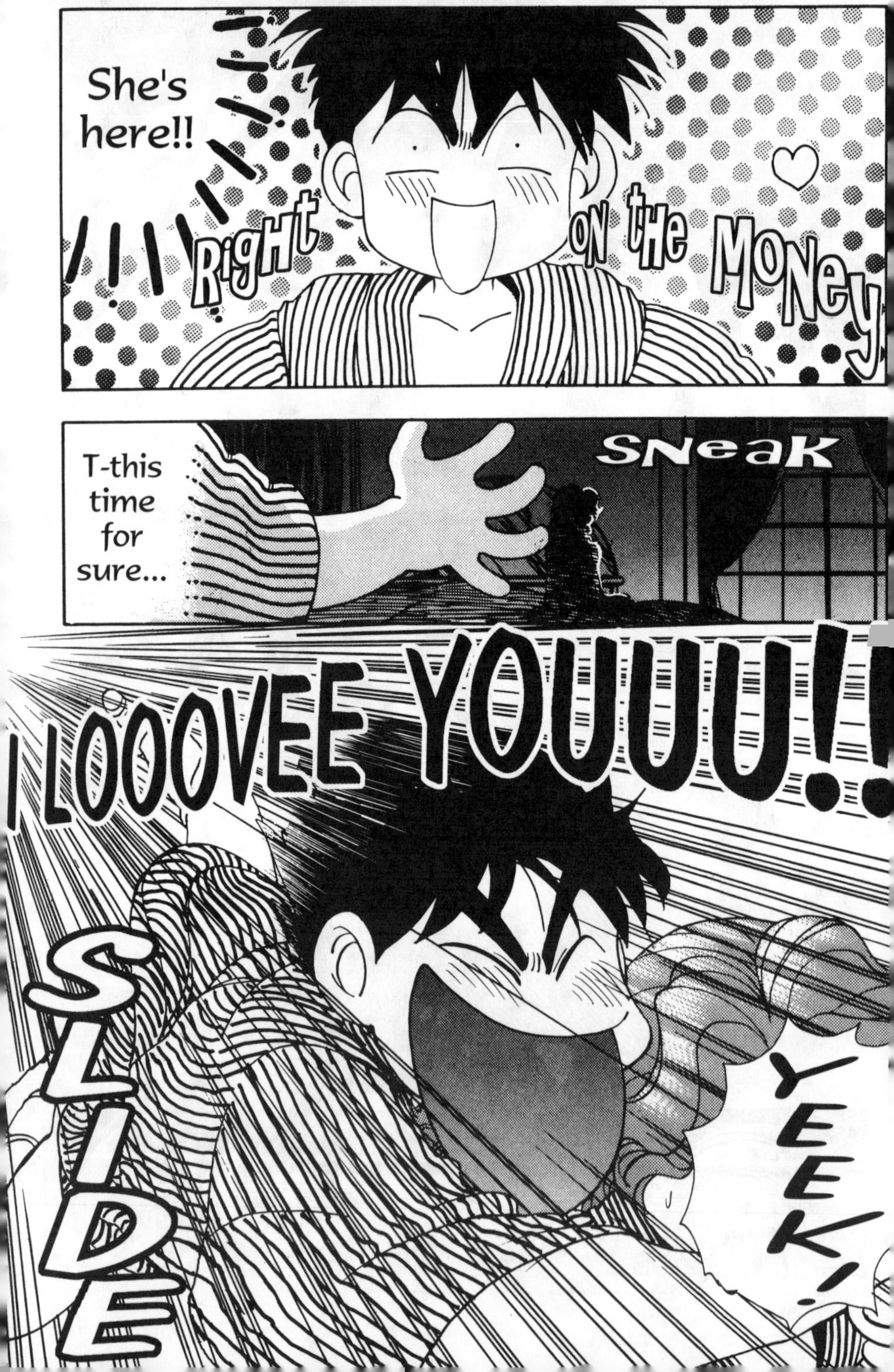
She's here!!
Right on the Money
T-this time for sure...
Sneak
I LOOOVEE YOUUUU!!
SLIDE
YEEK!

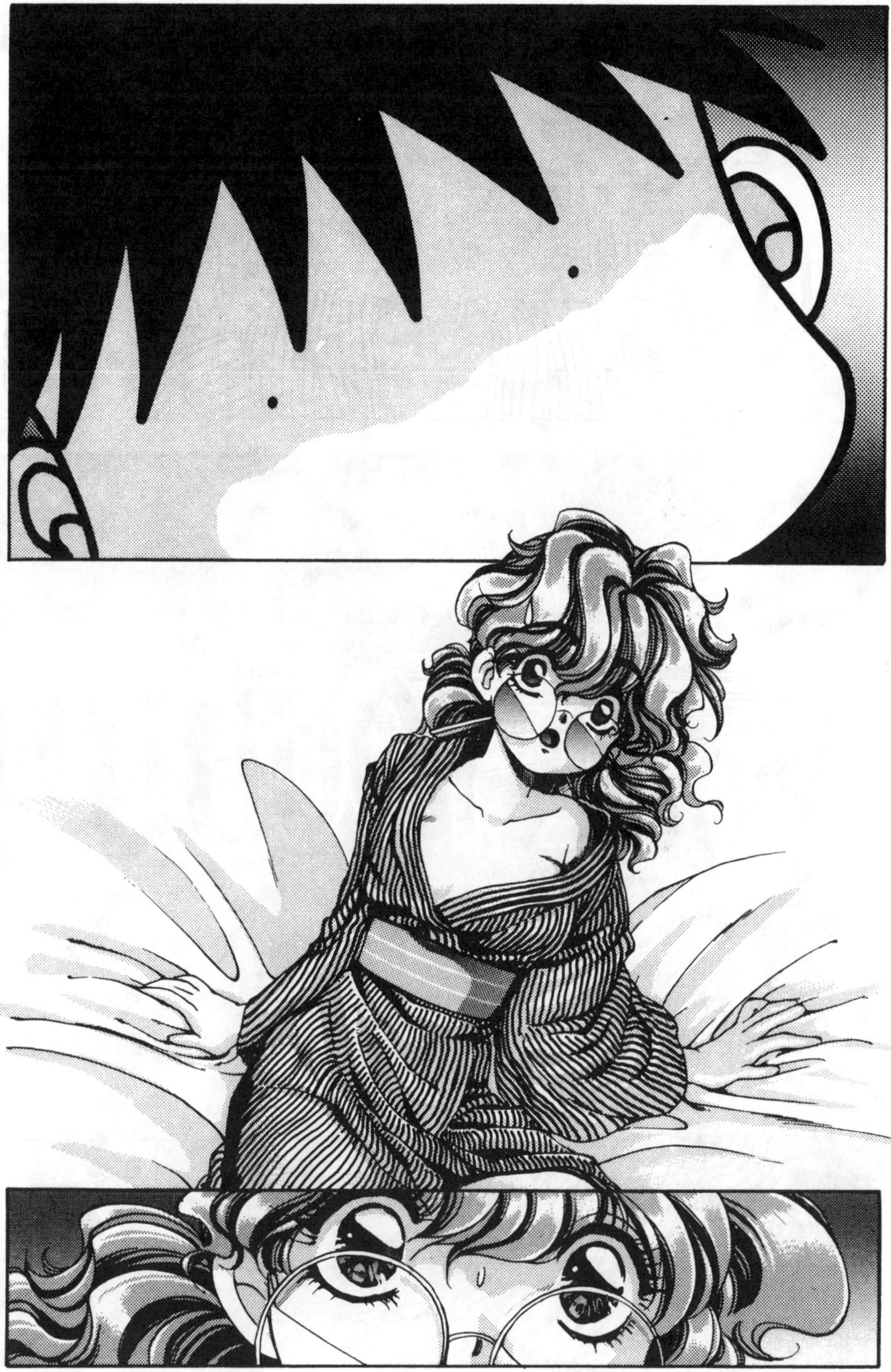

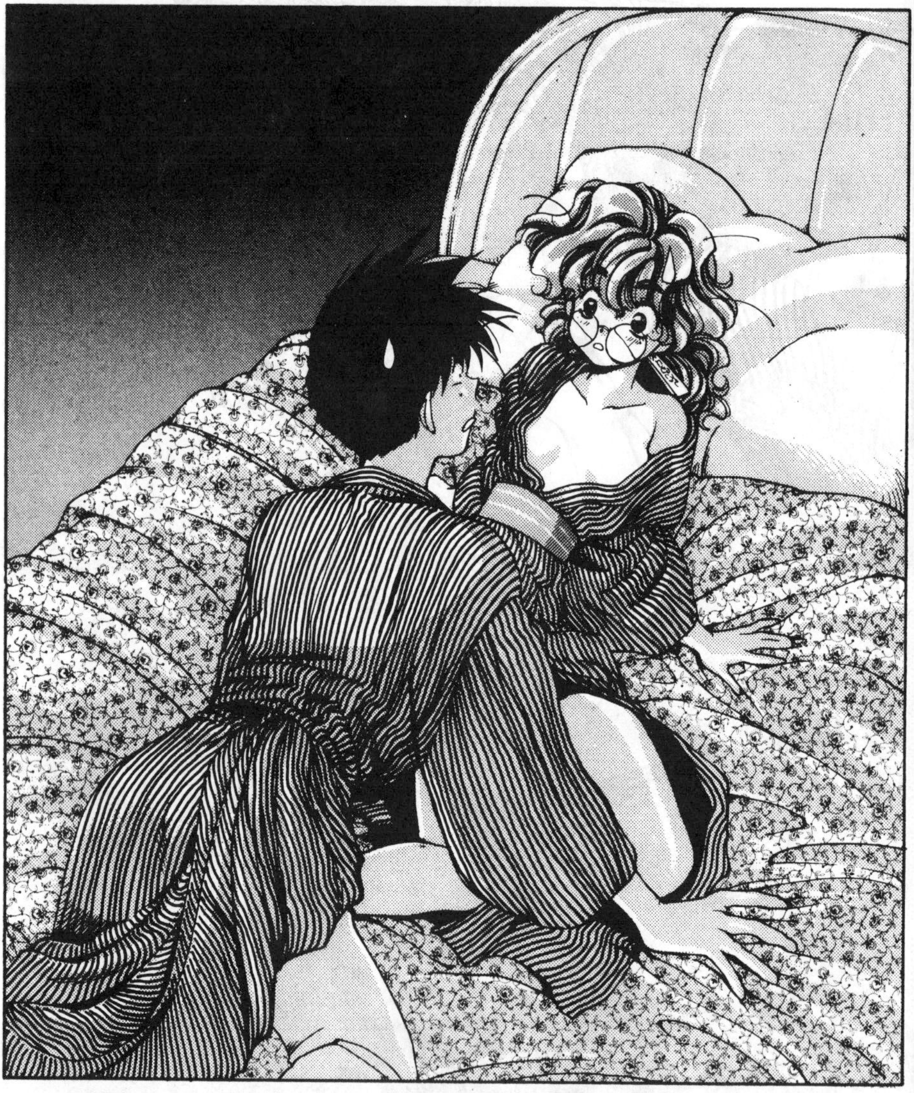

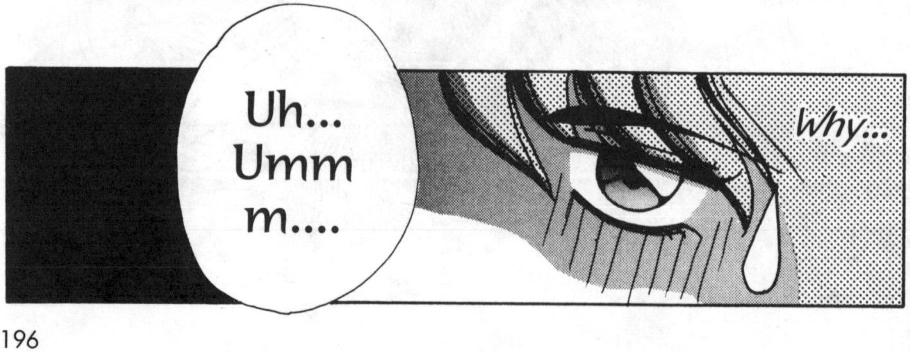

Uh... Umm m....
Why...

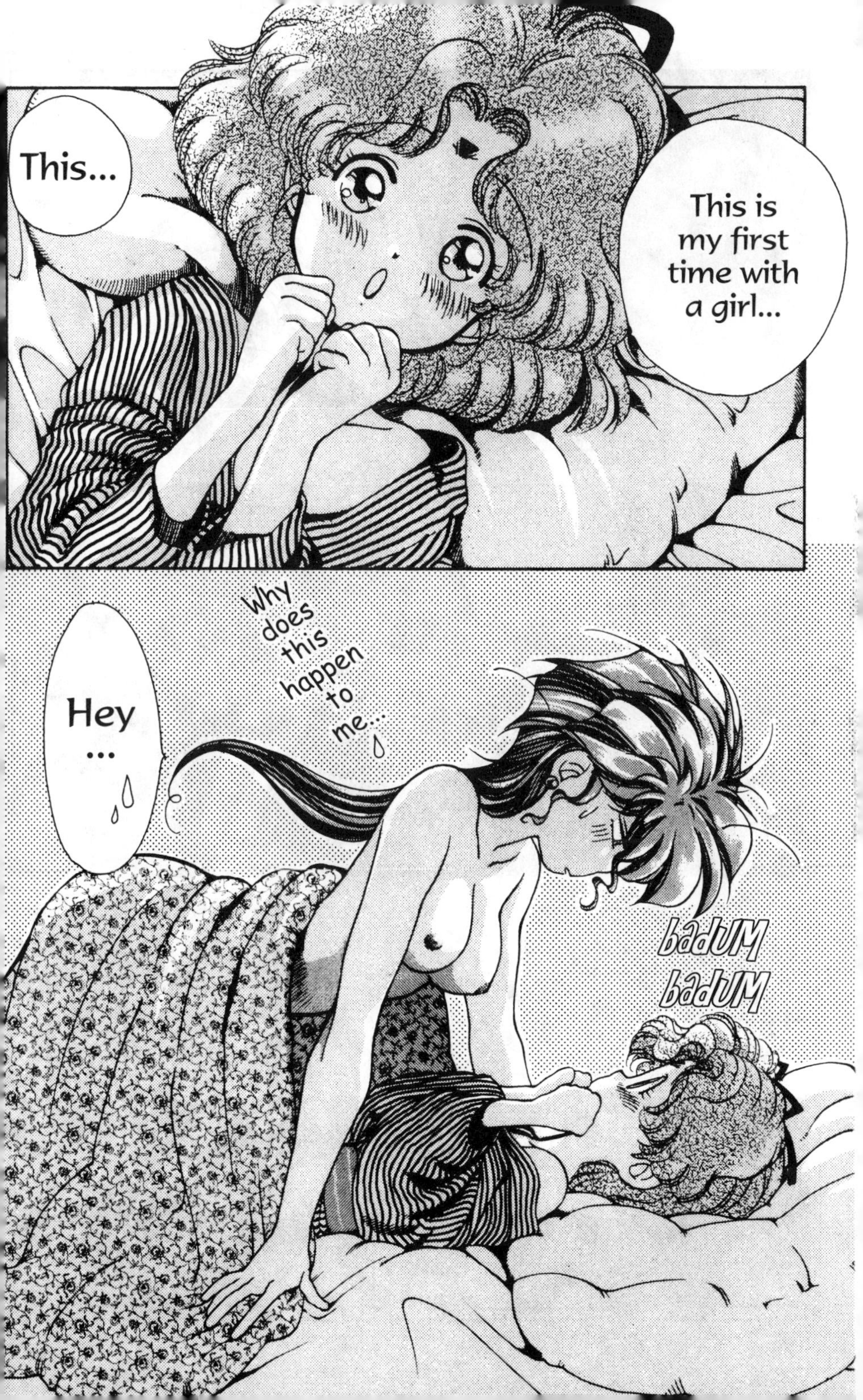

This...
This is my first time with a girl...
Hey ...
Why does this happen to me...
badUM badUM

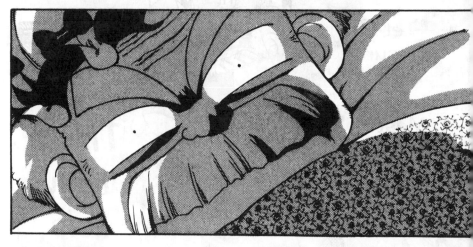

Master Potato, I never knew!

B·L·U·S·H

I never thought you would think of me that way!

No! There'th thome mithake!!

SCOOT SCOOT

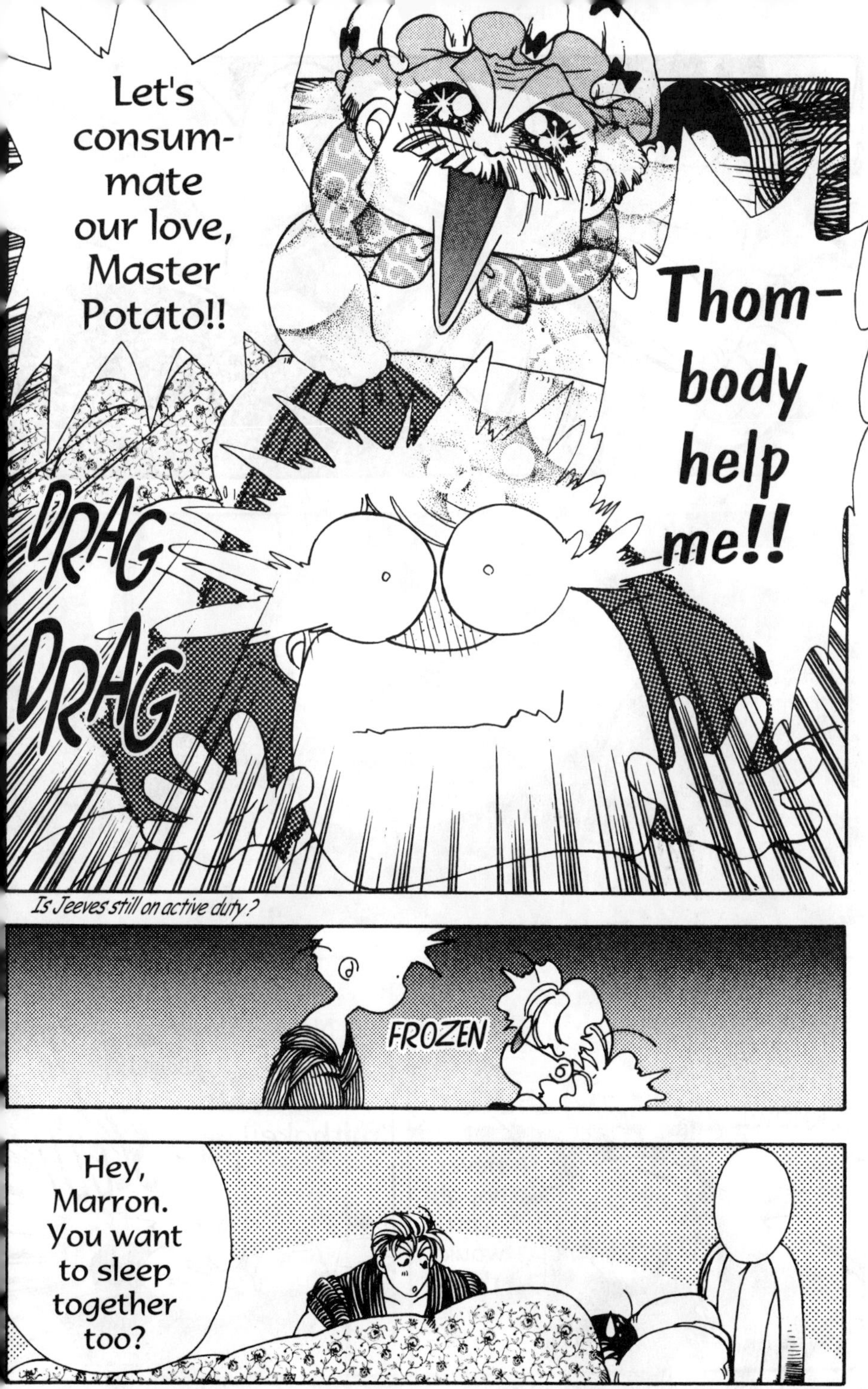
Let's consum-mate our love, Master Potato!!
Thom-body help me!!
DRAG DRAG
Is Jeeves still on active duty?
FROZEN
Hey, Marron. You want to sleep together too?

To be continued in Sorcerer Hunter #4!!!